The

BEST

of the

WEST

The BEST *of the* WEST

An Anthology of Classic Writing from the American West

Edited by

TONY HILLERMAN

HarperCollins*Publishers*

CONTENTS

Introduction xiii

Part 1: IN THE BEGINNING . . . 1

Part 5: **FRONTIER LIFE** 117

Part 6: **COWBOYS** 163

Part 13: **THE MILITARY** 443

Part 14: **THE WESTERN WAY WITH WORDS** 459

Part 15: **FICTION** 481

INTRODUCTION

The first time I attended a meeting of The Westerners, an elderly attorney told me of how his long-deceased uncle had satisfied his yearning to own a racehorse at the cost of only one dollar, wasted time and some careful thought.

The uncle had heard that Chingadero, winner of the Territorial Fair Derby that year, was for sale. Letters were exchanged, a $500 price was set, Uncle took his buggy to the owner's ranch, paid, and went to the stable to collect his horse. He found Chingadero newly deceased.

"My uncle said he told me this to illustrate how thought prevented a severe financial loss. He took Chingadero home, hid him in his barn and printed handbills, 510 for the cost of $10.

Chingadero For Sale
Only 510 Dollar Chances

Uncle said he sold the tickets, paid the printer his ten dollars and came out even.

"And I said: 'But Uncle, weren't the ticket buyers furious when they found out you'd sold them chances on a dead horse?' and my uncle said: 'Nobody cared but the winner, and I gave him his dollar back.'"

I should explain that The Westerners is an organization that has chapters (corrals) in most places west of the 100th meridian. People who love the West come to meetings and exchange such stories. I retell this one now to alert readers that this collection is not be taken too seriously and to illustrate our intentions. We intended to offer some social history—mostly about people and much less about the events in which they figured. This book is a collection of the odds and ends which seem to me, and to Jack Rittenhouse, to illuminate the way the West was, and still is.

This collection could be called "A Sampler of the Jack Rittenhouse Personal Library." Most of it came from the nine thousand or so volumes of Western Americana Rittenhouse has accumulated in a long career as a book lover, author, reviewer, publisher of the Stagecoach Press, editor of the Museum of New Mexico Press, Western Editor of the University of New Mexico Press and, for the past four decades, operator of his own antiquarian book dealership. Happily for this volume, Rittenhouse has read and remembered the contents of his library.

The Best of the West developed something like this:

Me: Maybe we should have a bit on Donner Pass.

Jack: A little girl survived that tragedy. When she reached California she wrote a letter to a cousin describing it.

Me: Wow! How about stagecoach travel?

Jack: There's a piece about how you could never find a place to put your feet. And I have another one by a fellow who had his feet frozen on a stagecoach ride. What about using Custer's last letter to his wife?

Me: Can you find it?

Jack: Sure. And we might add what she said when she got the news.

Why, then, isn't Jack Rittenhouse's name on the dust jacket? Because, odd as it seems, he didn't want it there. He explained his decision in terms of our purpose. He and I, being lovers of the West, want to use this book to spread some knowledge of this part of America. The people who recognize the Rittenhouse name are the professionals—historians, book people, scholars, collectors, those already familiar with much of the material. Those who recognize the Hillerman name are readers of mysteries, of novels, of fiction. They're the ones we're trying to reach.

"A two-line mention would please me most," Rittenhouse said. But I can't do it in two lines.

Typical of our rootless breed, Rittenhouse wasn't born in the West.

He was born in Kalamazoo, Michigan, in 1912, a descendant of folks who built the first (appropriately) paper mill in America in 1690. He was four before he reached the West, living at Rittenhouse Siding, Arizona, so named because his family were the only inhabitants. Driven east by hard times, Rittenhouse got most of his education in Indiana. He survived as a free-lance truant officer for the Fort Wayne library (recovering overdue books from offenders through a deal in which he kept the two-cents-a-day fine when the miscreants were willing to pay it) and as the unpaid book reviewer for a local daily, peddling the slightly used editions to augment his income. He hoboed back to Arizona, but then his love of books led him to New York to try for a job in the publishing industry. He worked as a vaudeville barker on 42nd Street, as a mail boy for Alfred A. Knopf, wrote advertising copy, and moved westward again in 1941. In 1946, his mile-by-mile guide to old U.S. Highway 66 was published. In 1949, he began his antiquarian book business, and in 1971, his definitive bibliography of the Santa Fe Trail was published. Aside from that, and his regular paid jobs as editor and publisher, he was twice president of the Historical Society of New Mexico, the first Sheriff of the Santa Fe Westerners Corral, and an avid traveler—having visited 81 percent of the places herein mentioned, including Salome, Ozona, Vinegarroon, Scotty's Castle, Fort Clatsop, Kemmerer, Medicine Bow and both Virginia Citys.

Most of the selections reproduced here are from letters, memoirs, government reports and diaries. Be reminded, however, that an authentic memory may not represent the authentic truth. We used original spelling and sentence structure, but condensed when brevity required by cutting out extraneous portions of paragraphs. The few bits of fiction were included because they reflected the reality of time or place in some artful way. Our idea here is to introduce a topic that those who are interested can pursue at greater length elsewhere. We originally managed to represent all of the contiguous states west of the 100th meridian—although some may have fallen away in the process of getting this book down to a reasonable size.

The volume contains a bit more of the macabre—fierce death sentences, lynching, cannibalism, etc.—than esthetics or balance justify. That's because of my personal taste for such things as hanging windmills and lunchrooms named for cannibals.

Finally, I confess that the Navajo Nation has received disproportionate space in relation to other tribes. I justify that partly because the Navajos, with almost a quarter million members, are by far the nation's largest tribe. But the principal reason lies in my admiration for their culture, their kindness to me and their never-failing wit. If the material included sparks an interest in these remarkable people, I recommend reading Raymond Friday Locke's excellent *Book of the Navajo,* and Paul G. Zolbrod's *Dine'bahane',* a highly readable version of the Navajo creation story. Literally scores of other books are available on ritualism, taboos, witchcraft, beliefs and other aspects of the tribe's culture. Other excellent sources of information about Western tribes include *The Book of the Hopi,* by Frank Waters, and *American Indian Myths and Legends,* by Richard Erdos and Alfonso Ortiz.

The list could go on and on. Which brings me to the only unpleasant aspect of putting together a book such as this—the omissions. We should have included some of Ivan Doig's beautiful fiction, an essay from Larry McMurtry's *In a Narrow Grave,* a fragment of the description of the Carrizozo Basin from one of Norman Zollinger's novels, Ross Calvin's chapter on a waterhole in the Chihuahuan Desert from *Sky Determines,* some of Joy Harjo's lyrical poetry, a piece from *Slouching Toward Bethlehem* by Joan Didion, who is my personal nominee as America's premier artist in prose.

Alas, either they didn't comfortably fit our theme or, more likely, we ran out of pages.

—*Tony Hillerman*

Part One

•

IN THE BEGINNING...

One starts a collection such as this at the earliest possible moment. But when was that? We haven't learned to translate the statements that artists of the Anasazi, Mimbres, and other preliterate cultures left in the pictures cut into the stone of Western cliffs. That should bring us to the sixteenth-century Spanish explorers, who wrote copious reports. But there may have been a literate visitor who predated the Spanish by almost two thousand years and chipped out the first "written language" message found in the West. It was left, appropriately for this part of the country, for no one in particular and for nothing more than to satisfy a need humans seem to feel when in empty places to communicate with somebody. So many travelers have carved such "Kilroy Was Here" messages in a cliff above a spring east of Zuni, New Mexico, that it has been named Inscription Rock and made a National Monument. Even today a rancher whose house is many dusty miles from the highway puts a wornout boot on the gatepost pointed in or out to tell passersby whether or not he's at home.

   And since we begin with a message, we will present several—including my favorite "message in a bottle" tale. But that was later—in 1540. And that will bring us, logically or not, to the explorers.

1

NEW MEXICO'S MYSTERY STONE

Dixie L. Perkins

The discovery of rune stones bearing inscriptions in early Scandinavian languages has long since cast doubt on the notion that Christopher Columbus was America's first tourist from Europe. Another inscribed stone, discovered in 1850 in the Rio Puerco Valley eighteen miles west of Los Lunas, New Mexico, makes the Norsemen, too, seem like latecomers. Long ago an inscription was chipped in a basalt outcrop in strange characters. Dixie L. Perkins, quoted here from her The Meaning of the New Mexico Mystery Stone, *believes the inscription was the work of a Greek sailor about 500 B.C. who wrote: "I have come up to this point . . . to stay. The other one met with an untimely death a year ago . . . I remain a hair of rabbit. I, Zakyneros . . . out of reach of mortal man, am fleeing and am very much afraid . . . I become hollow or gaunt from hunger."*

[A] significant communication was carved upon the Los Lunas, New Mexico, "inscription rock" or "mystery stone."

People were aware of the inscription when New Mexico became a territory in 1850, but no one could read it. However, one century later, Robert H. Pfeiffer of Harvard University, made the first known translation of the strange writing. He was considered to be an authority on the Old Testament; he concluded that the inscription was a copy of the Ten Commandments. He decided it was written in the Phoenician, the Moabite, and the Greek languages.

To my knowledge, Professor Pfeiffer did not state, at the time, who he thought carved the message. However, his translation seemed to satisfy the curiosity of the people of that era. Indeed, it stood for many years as the final word. The stone is still referred to, occasionally, as the "Ten Commandments rock."

Further speculation involved the origin or the author of the inscription. Some viewers conjectured a member of one of the lost tribes of Israel, spoken of in the Bible, wrote it. In 1936, an anthropologist from the University of New Mexico, Dr. Frank C. Hibben, saw the rock. He expressed the view the writing could have been carved by the Mormons when they migrated westward. . . .

In 1964, Robert H. LaFollette wrote an interesting translation of the inscription. As did Robert Pfeiffer in 1949, Mr. LaFollette determined some of the letters in the inscription were Phoenician. In addition, he concluded that other letters were in Hebrew, Cyrillic, and Etruscan. Thus, Robert LaFollette made the first attempt at a translation which would, in any way, challenge the established one of Robert Pfeiffer. . . .

Zakyneros, the Greek, left the metropolitan Mediterranean area with its empires, armies and navies. Behind him were the seething cities and towns with attendant manufacturing, marketing, and trading industries.

He arrived in the vast, relatively empty region of central New Mex-

A drawing of the inscription.

ico in 500 B.C. Blue, spruce-covered mountains stood apart in green grasslands. Lean red and purple mesas stretched themselves for many miles. From the north the great Rio Grande twisted to receive a watery contribution from the lesser Rio Puerco. Except for scattered ancient Indian tribes engaged in hunting, farming, and food-gathering pursuits, Zakyneros existed alone. . . .

At any rate, he carved his story into pink-gray basalt. Geologists identify basalt as an igneous or lava-type rock. It varies in texture and in color, also, but the one Zakyneros wrote upon is very fine.

The denseness of this particular rock made Zakyneros' self-assigned task more difficult. Possibly, he possessed bronze or iron tools. Archaeologists found several such European tools and weapons, too, in some of their digs in the United States.

In whatever manner he did it, Zakyneros cut letters about .25 in. or .635 cm. deep into the basalt. The letters average 1.75 in. or 4.45 cm. high, and 1.50 in. or 3.81 cm. wide. The great depth of his letters indicates an ancient inscription. Despite some weathering, it has been preserved in excellent condition. . . .

The size of the rock's writing surface measures 4.50 ft. or 1.37 m. wide, by 3.33 ft. or 1.02 m. high.

The inscription rock is located on the lower right side of a large mound of lava. The lava mound lies in a little canyon. The canyon dents the base of a small, extinct volcanic mountain. Its altitude is 5,500 ft.

The mountain is, appropriately, named Hidden Mountain on a present-day geological survey map. Scientifically, the area is known as the Lucero Basin, on the western edge of the Rio Grande trough. Hidden Mountain and the adjacent basaltic rocks, including the one on which Zakyneros carved, were formed only 20,000 years ago. The Lucero Uplift and the Puerco Fault Zone come together nearby.

Located approximately in the middle of New Mexico, Hidden Mountain rises eighteen miles west of the city of Los Lunas. The mountain stand on privately owned ranch land in the desert, a mile south of New Mexico Highway 6.

2

THE MESSAGE IN
THE BOTTLE

George Winship

What incredible optimist left a message in a bottle near the coast of an almost empty continent expecting someone two thousand roadless miles away to find it? Hernando de Alarcon is the answer. The year was 1540, generations before the first Englishman would set foot on our Eastern seaboard. Young Coronado had marched his Spanish army north from the Valley of Mexico to explore New Mexico, Arizona and California. Alarcon had been sent with a fleet up the Pacific Coast with orders to sail as far as he could up the Colorado River and meet Coronado with supplies. But Coronado had been lured eastward into Kansas by one of those magnificent "golden treasures" hoaxes which are so much a part of Western history. Thus Alarcon didn't find Coronado and he left behind a message. What follows is Historian George Winship's account of the incident.

Coronado found no gold in the land of the Seven Cities . . . but his search added very much to the geographical knowledge of the country. . . . The most important subsidiary result of the expedition of 1540–1542 was the discovery of Colorado river. Hernando de Alarcon, who sailed from Acapulco May 9, 1540, continued his voyage northward along the coast . . . until . . . August 26, 1540 when white men for the first time floated on the waters of the Colorado. Indians appeared on the river banks . . . Alarcon continued to question the Indian[s], and learned

6

[that there had been] a black man who wore a beard, whom the people of Cibola killed. . . . He was told that two men had just come from that country, where they had seen white men having "things which shot fire, and swords." . . .

Alarcon determined to make a second trip up the river, hoping to obtain further information. . . . Starting September 14 . . . he ascended the river, as he judged, about 85 leagues, which may have taken him to the point where the canyons begin. A cross was erected to inform Coronado, in case an expedition from Cibola should reach this part of the river, that he had tried to fulfill his duty, but nothing more was accomplished.

In September, 1540, seventy or eighty of the weakest and least reliable men in Coronado's army remained at the town of San Hieronimo, in the valley of Corazones or Hearts [in New Mexico]. Melchior Diaz was placed in command of the settlement, with orders to maintain this post . . . and also to attempt to find some means of communicating with the fleet under Alarcon.

After he had established everything in the town as satisfactorily as possible, Diaz selected twenty-five of these men to accompany him on an exploring expedition to the seacoast. . . . He proceeded to the seacoast, and . . . traveled slowly up the coast until he reached the mouth of a river which was large enough for vessels to enter. . . . Near the mouth of the river was a tree on which was written, "A letter is at the foot of this."

Diaz dug down and found a jar wrapped so carefully that it was not even moist. The enclosed papers stated that "Francisco de Alarcon reached this place in the year '40 with three ships, having been sent in search of Francisco Vazquez Coronado by the viceroy, D. Antonio de Mendoza; and after crossing the bar at the mouth of the river and waiting many days without obtaining any news, he was obliged to depart, because the ships were being eaten by worms," the terrible *Teredo navalis*.

Diaz . . . decided to return to Corazones valley . . . and then one night while Diaz was watching the camp, a small dog began to bark and chase the flock of sheep which the men had taken with them for food. Unable to call the dog off, Diaz started after him on horseback and threw his lance while on the gallop. The weapon stuck up in the ground, and before Diaz could stop or turn his horse, which was running loose, the socket pierced his groin. The soldiers could do little to relieve his sufferings, and he died before they reached the settlement, where they arrived on January 18, 1541.

3

DRAKE'S BRASS PLAQUE

James D. Hart

Sir Francis Drake did indeed nail a brass plate to a California tree, staking England's claim. But whether the brass plate found in 1936 and now preserved in the Bancroft Library at the University of California is the real article is the sort of nit Western scholars love to pick at. The following is by James D. Hart, director of the Library.

During his circumnavigation of the globe Francis Drake in 1579 put into a "conuenient and fit harborough" in California where he remained about a month to refit his ship. As evidence of his discovery and conquest, he nailed a brass plate to a firm post declaring that the land had been surrendered by its king and people to Queen Elizabeth. Her portrait, depicted on a silver sixpence, was displayed through a hole cut into the Plate.

In the summer of 1936, a young man, Beryle Shinn, chanced upon a metal plate on a hill overlooking the shore of Point San Quentin and San Francisco Bay. In course of time this object was brought to Dr. Herbert E. Bolton, professor of history at the University of California, who decided that the object appeared to be Drake's original Plate and said: "One of the world's long-lost historical treasures apparently has been found!"

Questions about the Plate's authenticity were immediately raised by other scholars but many persons were satisfied that this was not a forgery since tests made by Dr. Colin G. Fink, Professor of Electrochemistry at Columbia University and Dr. E. P. Polushkin, a consulting metallurgical engineer of New York City, concluded that this was "the genuine Drake Plate referred to in the book, *The World Encompassed by Sir Francis Drake*, published in 1628."

Nevertheless, the contention that the Plate was the work of a modern forger continued to be expressed orally and in print. Some of the questions were addressed to the crude manner of inscribing the Plate, the relatively modern spelling, the curious forms of some letters, particularly B, P, R, M and N, and some ostensible oddities of the text, such as reference to Queen Elizabeth of England rather than something like "Elizabeth, by grace of God, Queen of England. . . ." To such charges Professor Bolton countered that "a person working with crude equipment might easily depart from all conventional forms."

In time such misgivings led to a determination to test the Plate's metal with techniques refined or developed in the forty years since its discovery and first metallurgical examination. In 1976 three very small holes were made in the Plate and the resultant drillings tested at the Research Laboratory for Archaeology and the History of Art at Oxford University and at the Lawrence Berkeley Laboratory. The Oxford laboratory compared the results of its analyses with 22 examples of English and Continental brasses created between 1540 and 1720. The Lawrence Berkeley Laboratory made comparisons with old brass ranging from the fourteenth to the eighteenth centuries. The findings of both laboratories were similar. At Oxford the Plate was found to contain 34.8 percent (plus or minus 0.4 percent) of zinc and at Berkeley the average amount of zinc found was 35.0 percent. These slight variations were of no significance since the tests in both laboratories determined that no examples of English or European brass known to have been created prior to 1600 had a content as high as either measurement of the Drake Plate. Only two of those scrutinized at Oxford had a content exceeding 30 percent. Similarly, the analyses of early brass at Oxford found the lead content to be much greater than the 0.05 percent of the Plate in every example except one from England of 1630, whose testing revealed equivocal results. The abundance of lead in the early brasses examined at the Lawrence Berkeley Laboratory also far exceeded that which was found in the Drake Plate. Oxford's analysis showed the Plate's copper content to be 65.2 percent but its comparative examples from 1520 to 1598 all measured higher, ranging from 67.5 percent to 85 percent. This was analogous to the Berkeley finding that the Plate contains 64.6 percent copper, whereas examples that were surveyed from the fourteenth to seventeenth century contained from 75 to 84 percent.

A detailed binocular microscopic examination of the Plate by Dr. Cyril Stanley Smith, Professor Emeritus of the Massachusetts Institute of Technology, led him to disagree with the deduction of Fink and Polushkin that the Plate had been made by hammering, the common sixteenth-century process, rather than by rolling, the process common in later times. Moreover, he found that the edge of the Plate had none of the qualities of chisel cutting that one would expect in the sixteenth century but rather looked like a straight-cut made by the modern device of a guillotine shear. Other tests also failed to support the contention that the brass is of the Elizabethan era.

The full texts of all the investigations made between 1975 and 1977 were incorporated in a formal report titled *The Plate of Brass Reexamined* and issued in the latter year by the Bancroft Library, from which it is available. The findings it assembled turned out to be essentially negative.

Although the weight of evidence is apparently against the Plate's authenticity, many questions about it remain unanswered, including who created it and when, and why it should be left at an isolated spot where it might never be found.

Doubtless at later dates other inquiries and further commentary will be forthcoming from different sources to probe again into the nature and origin of an artifact that has attracted so much attention since its discovery.

James D. Hart, Director
The Bancroft Library

TEXT OF THE PLATE OF BRASS

BEE IT KNOWNE VNTO ALL MEN BY THESE PRESENTS
IVNE. 17.1579
BY THE GRACE OF GOD AND IN THE NAME OF HERR MAIESTY
QVEEN ELIZABETH OF ENGLAND AND HERR SVCCESSORS FOREVER
I TAKE POSSESSION OF THIS KINGDOME WHOSE KING AND PEOPLE
FREELY RESIGNE THEIR RIGHT AND TITLE IN THE WHOLE LAND
VNTO HERR MAIESTIES KEEPEING NOW NAMED BY ME AN TO BEE
KNOWNE VNTO ALL MEN AS NOVA ALBION.

G FRANCIS DRAKE
hole for
sixpence

4

THE REAL MANILA GALLEON

The ultimate treasure ship of fantasy and fable, target of a million dime-novel thrillers and B-movies, was a ship which sailed routinely from Mexico to Manila, carrying silver and gold to exchange for silks, spices, and oriental treasures. It sounds much less romantic when dealt with by a historian.

The Manila galleon was a vessel which started from Acapulco on the Pacific coast of Mexico, sailed across the Pacific to the Philippine Islands loaded with silver and luxury products, exchanged the silver for the riches of the East including silks and spices, and then returned to New Spain. Several voyagers led by Magellan had sailed westward across the Pacific to the Philippines, but the eastward voyage was first attempted in an expedition led by Andrés de Urdaneta in 1565. Urdaneta's achievement led to a rich annual voyage, under rigid government control as was the Spanish custom, which often produced for its backers profits of one hundred to four hundred per cent.

The problems of the Manila galleon were many. The westward voyage was the easiest and could be accomplished in less than ninety days because of favorable winds and the direct route thus permitted, but the return voyage presented a problem. It was necessary for the galleon to sail far north along the Japanese islands until it could be aided by the Japan current; but this route brought it into the severe weather of the northern Pacific, through the typhoon belt along the east Asiatic Coast, and into the storms, fogs, and gales of the northwest coast of North America. Seven months was not unusual for a return voyage. An additional complication consisted of the fact that Spaniards were human beings and engaged in much graft and corruption in the loading of the galleon. Although certain parts of the hold were supposedly strictly reserved for food and water, bribery often filled these provision spaces with profit-making cargo. Because of the shortage of supplies and the lack of elementary scientific knowledge about diet, the return voyage was usually accompanied by many fatalities from scurvy and other nutritional diseases. Sanitation was poor on the galleon and vermin of all sorts afflicted the passengers, while tempers flared and human relations became difficult because of the long period in confined quarters.

There were two reasons why the Manila galleon helped to bring California to the attention of the world. One was that certain of the galleon commanders were urged to search for the western entrance to the Strait of Anián which Spaniards were still looking for under the delusion that it was possible to cross North America by a water passage. Another and more important reason was the fact that the galleon badly needed a port of call along the coast of California so that it could replenish its supplies and water and provide some fresh vegetables for those of its passenger list who were afflicted with scurvy.

Certain of the galleon commanders, Gali in 1584, Unamuno in 1587, Rodríguez Cermenho in 1595, and a passenger, Gemelli Careri, in 1597, left records of visits to California. Gali encountered currents which made him believe that the Strait of Anián did exist, and he described California as being "a very high and fair land with many trees, wholly without snow, and four leagues from the land you find thereabout many drifts of roots, leaves of trees, reeds, and other leaves like fig leaves, the like whereof we found in great abundance in the country of Japan, which they eat; . . . there likewise we found great store of seals; whereby it is to be presumed and certainly to be believed, that there are many rivers, bays, and havens along those coasts to the haven of Acapulco."

Gali's successor in California exploration was an interesting adventurer named Pedro de Unamuno. During the summer of 1587 in command of a small, single-decked, three-masted frigate named the *Nuestra Señora de Buena Esperanza*, Unamuno began the voyage across the Pacific to Acapulco. Sighting the California coast late in October, he entered El Morro Bay near San Luis Obispo, and marched a considerable distance into the interior. Unamuno made formal claim to the land in the name of Philip of Spain, set up a cross on the site, and performed other ceremonies duly prescribed in the act of possession. He then continued his voyage to Acapulco.

Foreign pirates also stimulated the search for a port of call. In 1587 Thomas Cavendish, an English privateer, captured the Manila galleon near Cape San Lucas, and Spain consequently became more interested than ever in occupying California. In 1595, therefore, Sebastian Rodríguez Cermenho, a Portuguese, was appointed commander of the Manila galleon to search the California coast for a likely port. He located Drake's Bay and named it the Bay of San Francisco, not to be confused with the present port of that name. His vessel, the *San Agustín*, was wrecked, and he constructed a makeshift launch in which he continued his explorations, landing at many of the spots previously discovered by Cabrillo. Finally, in January 1596, he came to anchor in Navidad. But any glory which Rodríguez Cermenho deserved because of his persistence in carrying out his commission under difficulties was largely neutralized by the fact that he had lost the galleon and its cargo.

The most successful of the galleon commanders, at least insofar as exploring the California coast was concerned, was Sebastian Vizcaíno. Vizcaíno had previously engaged in the Manila trade, lost a considerable fortune when Cavendish took the *Santa Ana*, and participated unsuccessfully in exploration and pearl fishing in the Gulf. From all accounts he was a man with the knack of obtaining position and recognition out of all proportion to his talents. . . .

Substantial progress had been made by the Spaniards in the development of the sea-otter trade before the close of the eighteenth century. Between 1786 and 1790 nearly ten thousand skins, valued at over three million dollars, were shipped to China in the Manila galleon. On the return voyage the galleon brought back quicksilver for use in the all-important mining industry of New Spain.

5

THE LONG
WAY HOME

Meriwether Lewis

The Fort Clatsop Memo is another variation of the message in the bottle. Meriwether Lewis and William Clark had reached the Pacific Ocean in 1805, concluding their epic exploration of the West. They wintered at the mouth of the Columbia, and prepared to head for home in March 1806. But if they didn't survive the trip, how would the nation know what they had discovered? Lewis wrote a single paragraph and gave copies of it to Indians, asking them to give it to any white men who might appear. Thus the document was delivered to the captain of the brig, Lydia, which had made a stop at the river en route to China. At Canton, the captain gave it to another American, who sent it to a friend in Philadelphia. All for naught. Lewis got safely home to make his famous report.

We also circulated among the natives several papers, one of which we also posted up in the fort, to the following effect:

> "The object of this list is, that through the medium of some civilized person, who may see the same, it may be made known to the world, that the party consisting of the persons whose names are hereunto annexed, and who were sent out by the Government of the United States to explore the interior of the continent of North America, did penetrate the same by the way of the Missouri and Columbia rivers,

14

to the discharge of the latter into the Pacific ocean, where they arrived on the 14th day of November, 1805, and departed the 23rd day of March, 1806, on their return to the United States by the same route by which they had come out."

On the back of some of these papers we sketched the connection of the upper branches of the Missouri and Columbia Rivers, with our route, and the track which we intended to follow on our return. This memorandum was all that we deemed necessary to make; for there seemed but little chance that any detailed report to our government, which we might leave in the hands of the savages, to be delivered to foreign traders, would ever reach the United States. To leave any of our men here, in hopes of their securing a passage home in some transient vessel, would too much weaken our party, which we must necessarily divide during our route; besides that, we shall most probably be there ourselves sooner than any trader, who, after spending the next summer here, might go on some circuitous voyage.

6

THE STONE THOEN FOUND

Frank Thompson

Scholars have confirmed the authenticity of this famous last message found in 1887. As described by Frank Thompson in The Thoen Stone, *this one causes one to ponder the ultimate value of finding "all the gold we could carry."*

Let us roll back time to the fourteenth of March, in the year 1887. On this day two men drove a wagon to the foot of Lookout Mountain, overlooking beautiful Spearfish Valley in the northern Black Hills of South Dakota. One of these men, Louis Thoen, was a farmer, miner, and stone cutter. The other, younger than himself, was his brother Ivan. The two were looking for sandstone to be used in the basement of a business house on the main street of Spearfish.

While at work digging out the sandstone, Louis came, unexpectedly, upon a slab on which it appeared that a message has been scratched. After rubbing off the damp sand, he was able to make out the words, "Indians hunting me." On the reverse side was another message. How had those messages gotten there?

Louis Thoen did not know, but he laid the slab aside. That night, by lamp light, after rubbing the two surfaces of the stone thoroughly, he was able to make out a very strange message. On one side of the slab were the words:

16

came to these hills
in 1833   seven of us
De Lacompt   all ded
Ezra Kind   but me
G W Wood   Ezra Kind
T. Brown   Killed by Ind
R Kent   beyond the
Wm King   high hill got
Indian Crow   our gold June
                            1834

And on the reverse side:

> *Got all of the*
> *gold we could*
> *carry our ponys*
> *all got by the Indians*
> *I hav lost my gun*
> *and nothing to*
> *eat and indians*
> *hunting me*

The slab itself was 8″ x 10″ x 3″ in size; less than a foot in length by only two-thirds of a foot in width. The message had been scratched deeply into the sandstone.

For nigh unto three-quarters of a century, this piece of sandstone, now known as the Thoen Stone, has puzzled the minds of men.

The intelligence conveyed is that the six white men and one Indian, who arrived in the Black Hills in 1833, were, with the exception of Ezra Kind, who made the inscription, slaughtered by Indians, and that the redskins also captured the gold possessed by the party. This bloody tragedy happened in June, 1834, and at the time the inscription was made all but Kind were dead. Very probably a night attack had been made on the party and their treasure, and in the confusion of the attack Kind had managed to make his escape. There not being room enough on one side of the stone to tell the whole of the terrible story, Kind turned it over and scratched the following on the reverse side:

From this it would appear that the miners had a large load of gold, all they could carry, and it was probably this fact that incited the redskins to the bloody deed. . . .

These seven men were trespassing upon Indian land. Their aggressive intrusion into this Indian land opens an unsolved problem that has troubled the conscience of men for over 300 years or ever since white men set foot upon this continent. The Indians, literally with their backs to the Rocky Mountains, were fighting for survival. White men were conquering the land for the white man's advanced civilization. Many will ponder the right and wrong of this struggle.

7

BOULDERS TALLER THAN THE GREAT TOWER OF SEVILLE

Garcia Lopez de Cardenas

No literate person can see the Grand Canyon without wanting to describe it. The first to do so in writing was Pedro de Castaneda de Najera in his account of the Coronado expedition. Castaneda was retelling the description provided by Garcia Lopez de Cardenas, who had found the canyon on a scouting trip in 1540.

Information was obtained of a large river and that several days down the river there were people with very large bodies.

As Don Pedro de Tovar had no other commission, he returned from Tusayán and gave his report to the general. The latter at once dispatched Don García López de Cárdenas there with about twelve men to explore this river. When he reached Tusayán he was well received and lodged by the natives. They provided him with guides to proceed on his journey. They set out from there laden with provisions, because they had to travel over some uninhabited land before coming to settlements, which the Indians said were more than twenty days away. Accordingly when they had marched for twenty days they came to the gorges of the river, from the edge of which it looked as if the opposite side must have been more than three or four leagues away by air. This region was high and covered with low and twisted pine trees; it was extremely cold, being open to the north, so that, although this was the warm season, no one could live in this canyon because of the cold.

The men spent three days looking for a way down to the river; from the top it looked as if the water were a fathom across. But, according to the information supplied by the Indians, it must have been half a league wide. The descent was almost impossible, but, after these three days, at a place which seemed less difficult, Captain Melgosa, a certain Juan Galeras, and another companion, being the most agile, began to go down. They continued descending within view of those on top until they lost sight of them, as they could not be seen from the top. They returned about four o'clock in the afternoon, as they could not reach the bottom because of the many obstacles they met, for what from the top seemed easy, was not so; on the contrary, it was rough and difficult. They said that they had gone down one-third of the distance and that, from the point they had reached, the river seemed very large, and that, from what they saw, the width given by the Indians was correct. From the top they could make out, apart from the canyon, some small boulders which seemed to be as high as a man. Those who went down and who reached them swore that they were taller than the great tower of Seville.

The party did not continue farther up the canyon of the river because of the lack of water. Up to that time they had gone one or two leagues inland in search of water every afternoon. When they had traveled four additional days the guides said that it was impossible to go on because no water would be found for three or four days, that when they themselves traveled through that land they took along women who brought water in gourds, that in those trips they buried the gourds of water for the return trip, and that they traveled in one day a distance that took us two days.

This was the Tizón river, much closer to its source than where Melchior Díaz and his men had crossed it. These Indians were of the same type, as it appeared later. From there Cárdenas and his men turned back, as that trip brought no other results.

8

"THE MOST SUBLIME SPECTACLE ON EARTH"

John Wesley Powell

John Wesley Powell, the one-armed government explorer, led a boat expedition through the Grand Canyon in 1869 and produced this description, both accurate and poetic, in his Canyons of the Colorado *in 1895.*

The Grand Canyon of the Colorado is a canyon composed of many canyons. It is a composite of thousands, of tens of thousands, of gorges. In like manner, each wall of the canyon is a composite structure, a wall composed of many walls, but never a repetition. Every one of these almost innumerable gorges is a world of beauty in itself. In the Grand Canyon there are thousands of gorges like that below Niagara Falls, and there are a thousand Yosemites. Yet all these canyons unite to form one grand canyon, the most sublime spectacle on the earth. Pluck up Mt. Washington by the roots to the level of the sea and drop it headfirst into the Grand Canyon, and the dam will not force its waters over the walls. Pluck up the Blue Ridge and hurl it into the Grand Canyon, and it will not fill it.

    The carving of the Grand Canyon is the work of rains and rivers. The vast labyrinth of canyon by which the plateau region drained by the Colorado is dissected is also the work of waters. Every river has excavated its own gorge and every creek has excavated its gorge. When a shower comes in this land, the rills carve canyons—but a little at each storm; and though storms are far apart and the heavens above are cloudless for most of the days of the year, still, years are plenty in the ages, and an intermittent rill called to life by a shower can do much work in centuries of centuries.

The erosion represented in the canyons, although vast, is but a small part of the great erosion of the region, for between the cliffs blocks have been carried away far superior in magnitude to those necessary to fill the canyons. Probably there is no portion of the whole region from which there have not been more than a thousand feet degraded, and there are districts from which more than 30,000 feet of rock have been carried away. Altogether, there is a district of country more than 200,000 square miles in extent from which on the average more than 6,000 feet have been eroded. Consider a rock 200,000 square miles in extent and a mile in thickness, against which the clouds have hurled their storms and beat it into sands and the rills have carried the sands into the creeks and the creeks have carried them into the rivers and the Colorado has carried them into the sea. We think of the mountains as forming clouds about their brows, but the clouds have formed the mountains. Great continental blocks are upheaved from beneath the sea by internal geologic forces that fashion the earth. Then the wandering clouds, the tempest-bearing clouds, the rainbow-decked clouds, with mighty power and with wonderful skill, carve out valleys and canyons and fashion hills and cliffs and mountains. The clouds are the artists sublime.

In winter some of the characteristics of the Grand Canyon are emphasized. The black gneiss below, the variegated quartzite, and the green or alcove sandstone form the foundation for the mighty red wall. The banded sandstone entablature is crowned by the tower limestone. In winter this is covered with snow. Seen from below, these changing elements seem to graduate into the heavens, and no plane of demarcation between wall and blue firmament can be seen. The heavens constitute a portion of the facade and mount into a vast dome from wall to wall, spanning the Grand Canyon with empyrean blue. So the earth and the heavens are blended in one vast structure.

When the clouds play in the canyon, as they often do in the rainy season, another set of effects is produced. Clouds creep out of canyons and wind into other canyons. The heavens seem to be alive, not moving as move the heavens over a plain, in one direction with the wind, but following the multiplied courses of these gorges. In this manner the little clouds seem to be individualized, to have wills and souls of their own, and to be going on diverse errands—a vast assemblage of self-willed clouds, faring here and there, intent upon purposes hidden in their own breasts. In the imagination the clouds belong to the sky, and when they are in the canyon the skies come down into the gorges and cling to the cliffs and lift them up to immeasurable heights, for the sky must still be far away. Thus they lend infinity to the walls.

The wonders of the Grand Canyon cannot be adequately represented in symbols of speech, nor by speech itself. The resources of the graphic art are taxed beyond their powers in attempting to portray its features. Language and illustration combined must fail. The elements that unite to make the Grand Canyon the most sublime spectacle in nature are multifarious and exceedingly diverse. The Cyclopean forms which result from the sculpture of tempests through ages too long for man to compute, are wrought into endless details, to describe which would be a task equal in magnitude to that of describing the stars of the heavens or the multitudinous beauties of the forest with its traceries of foliage presented by oak and pine and poplar, by beech and linden and hawthorn, by tulip and lily and rose, by fern and moss and lichen. Besides the elements of form, there are elements of color, for here the colors of the heavens are rivaled by the colors of the rocks. The rainbow is not more replete with hues. But form and color do not exhaust all the divine qualities of the Grand Canyon. It is the land of music. The river thunders in perpetual roar, swelling in floors of music when the storm gods play upon the rocks and fading away in soft and low murmurs when the infinite blue of heaven is unveiled. With the melody of the great tide rising and falling, swelling and vanishing forever, other melodies are heard in the gorges of the lateral canyons, while the waters plunge in the rapids among the rocks or leap in great cataracts. Thus the Grand Canyon is a land of song. Mountains of music swell in the rivers, hills of music billow in the creeks, and meadows of music murmur in the rills that ripple over the rocks. Altogether it is a symphony of multitudinous melodies. All this is the music of waters. The adamant foundations of the earth have been wrought into a sublime harp, upon which the clouds of the heavens play with mighty tempests or with gentle showers.

The glories and the beauties of form, color, and sound unite in the Grand Canyon—forms unrivaled even by the mountains, colors that vie with sunsets, and sounds that span the diapason from tempest to tinkling raindrop, from cataract to bubbling fountain. But more: it is a vast district of country. Were it a valley plain it would make a state. It can be seen only in parts from hour to hour and from day to day and from week to week and from month to month. A year scarcely suffices to see it all. It has infinite variety, and no part is ever duplicated. Its colors, though many and complex at any instant, change with the ascending and declining sun; lights and shadows appear and vanish with the passing clouds, and the changing seasons mark their passage in changing colors. You cannot see the Grand Canyon in one view, as if it were a changeless spectacle from which a curtain might be lifted, but to see it you have to toil from month to month through its labyrinths. It is a region more difficult to traverse than the Alps or the Himalayas, but if strength and courage are sufficient for the task, by a year's toil a concept of sublimity can be obtained never again to be equaled on the hither side of Paradise.

9

FIFTY LEAGUES OF SILVER

Fray Alonso de Benevides

The report made by Fray Alonso de Benevides to the Spanish of discoveries on the Northern Frontier of New Spain was totally unreliable. But his story of fifty leagues of silver ore in the Socorro Mountains of Central New Mexico is one of the first of the fables of ore deposits, lost mines, and buried treasures that still inspire Western romantics and keep con men employed.

Of no less puissance is the temporal good which God our Lord hath been pleased to manifest in this Province, wherewith Your Majesty may recoup the great costs which like so Catholic a Monarch you are making to support, not only us, but also those churches. For all this [land] is full of very great treasures of mines, very rich and prosperous in silver and gold; a thing which as a regular duty [*bien de ordinário*], as so devoted chaplains and vassals, we besought of God; and, making special effort by means of an intelligent person, we came to discover; for which, in name of Your Majesty, we give Him infinite thanks. In particular, the hill of the pueblo of Socorro, chief [town] and head of this Province of the Piros. For all of it is of very prosperous minerals, which run from north to south more than fifty leagues; and for want of someone who might understand it and spend [money] on working it, the greatest riches in the world are not enjoyed, and Your Majesty loses your Royal fifths. The ease with which the silver

25

can be taken out from this hill is the greatest and best in all the Indies; and it will be worth more to get out a mark of silver here than many [marks] in the other mines; because in the rest all the materials and the food, and even to the water, have to be brought from very far, the cost of which eats up [*se lleva*: carries away] all the silver that is extracted. But in these mines of Socorro all is at the very foot of the work. And although it is true that at the beginnings of the conversions the Indians might be scared off by the labor of the mines, everything considered, I feel that if the [mines] were administered by persons of moderate greed, who would treat the Indians well and pay them for their work, conforming now at the beginning with their simple capacity, [which is] slack as to working, that not only would it not scare off the [Indians] but would win them by this path, and that they would submit themselves to treating and communication with us. And they themselves, seeing and knowing that they were not treated ill, and that they were paid for their work, would come to offer themselves for it. With this it would be easier for us ministers to reduce them to peace. Everything considered, I determined to take out a quantity of ores from different veins of those mines, and I gave them to sundry miners of New Spain. Having made assays of them, and [the assays] revealing so much riches, these [miners] were getting ready to enter New Mexico with workmen [*gente*] to work the [mines], and the Viceroy was making very extensive assays, with zeal for the service of Your Majesty, to augment in this quarter your Royal fifths. This province of the Piros extends along up the Rio del Norte, from the first pueblo of San Antonio de Senecu up to the last, San Luis de Sevilleta, fifteen leagues, where there are fourteen pueblos, on one and the other side of the river, in which must be [*aurá*] six thousand souls, all baptized; with three monasteries, as has been said, in which the Religious besides the teaching and indoctrination of our Holy Catholic Faith, teach [them] to sing, read and write, and all the trades, and to live in civilized fashion [*politicamente*] in their schools.

10

CAPTAIN JOSÉ
ZÚÑIGA'S REPORT

*The Mission at San Xavier del Bac, built just south of Tucson between 1774
and 1779, has been acclaimed as the finest example of mission architecture in
the United States. Captain Zúñiga, commandant of the Tucson Presidio, men-
tions it with approval in his 1804 report.*

August 4, 1804
SETTLEMENT AND POPULATION
The soldiers, settlers, and Indians of Tucson live in an area less than
two miles square. The total population of its civil jurisdiction comes to
1015. This jurisdiction includes the Indian village at San Xavier del Bac,
ten miles away, the Indian village at Tucson, and the presidio with its
settlers and retired troops.

WATER
The rivers of the region include the Santa Catalina (Rillito), five miles
from the presidio, which arises from a hot spring and in rainy seasons enjoys
a steady flow for ten miles in a northwesterly direction. It is thirty-three
feet wide near its headwaters.
Our major river, however, is the Santa María Suamca (Santa Cruz),
which arises ninety-five miles to the southeast from a spring near the
presidio of Santa Cruz. From its origin it flows past the Santa Cruz presidio,

27

the abandoned ranches of Divisaderos, Santa Barbara, San Luis, and Buenavista, then past the abandoned missions of Guevavi and Calabazas, the Pima mission at Tumacácori, the Tubac presidio. When rainfall is only average or below, it flows above ground to a point some five miles north of Tubac *and goes underground all the way to San Xavier del Bac.* Only during years of exceptionally heavy rainfall does it water the flat land between Tubac and San Xavier.

MINES

We have no full-time mining of gold, silver, iron, lead, tin, quicksilver, or copper. *Some twenty miles from this presidio is an outcropping of lime which supplies us with all we need and whenever we need it for construction.*

PUBLIC WORKS

The only public work here that is truly worthy of this report is the church at San Xavier del Bac, ten miles from this presidio. Other missions here in the north should really be called chapels, but San Xavier is truly a church. It is ninety-nine feet long. Its width is twenty-two feet in the nave and sixty feet at the transept which forms two side chapels.

The entire structure is of fired brick and lime mortar. The ceiling is a series of arches and domes. The interior is adorned with thirty-eight full-figure statues, three "frame-figures" dressed in cloth garments, and innumerable angels and seraphim.

The facade is quite ornate boasting two towers, one of which is unfinished. The atrium in front extends out twenty-seven and a half feet.

To the left of the atrium is a new cemetery surrounded by a fired brick and lime plastered wall measuring eighty-two and a half feet in circumference. At the far end of the cemetery is a domed chapel built of the same materials.

A conservative estimate of the building expense to date would be 40,000 pesos. This includes all of the construction mentioned above, plus the sacristy, the baptistry, and other rooms, all of arch and dome design.

The reason for this ornate church at this last outpost of the frontier is not only to congregate Christian Pimas of the San Xavier village, but also to attract by its sheer beauty the unconverted Papagos and Gila Pimas beyond the frontier. I have thought it worthwhile to describe it in such detail because of the wonder that such an elaborate building could be constructed at all on this farthest frontier against the Apache. *Because of hazard involved, the salaries of the artisans had to be doubled.*

11

ARE WE PRISONERS
OF WAR?

Zebulon Montgomery Pike

And then there was young Lieutenant Zebulon Montgomery Pike, sent with his little platoon through the Spanish frontier to explore California: Pike was found at his Colorado winter camp in 1807 by a detachment of Spanish dragoons and taken to Santa Fe to "visit" the Spanish authorities. Pike and his Spanish counterpart exchanged these letters to get such things as status and who is paying for what on the record, proving that military bureaucracy doesn't change.

The 1st lieutenant of the the Anglo American troops, named Z. Montgomery Pike, with the party of soldiers under his command, having been met with by the troops under my orders at four day's journey from the seat of government, in this province, which is under my charge; he was required personally to appear, which he voluntarily did, complying with the orders of the senior commanding general of these internal provinces. I bade the said lieutenant proceed on his march with his party, equipped with horses, provisions, and equipage, under charge of an officer and sixty men of our troops, with orders to introduce him to the said commanding general, in the town of Chihuahua. I permitted the said party to carry their arms and ammunition; actuated by proper considerations, and to comply with the petition of the said Anglo American. I certify the foregoing contents to be accurate.

> Joachim Real Allencaster.
> *Santa Fé 3d March* 1807.

Santa Fé, 3d March, 1807.

Sir,

On the arrival of your troops at my encampment last month, under the command of Lieut. Don Ignacio Saltelo and Mr. Bartholomew, they informed me, that your excellency had directed them to assure me that I should be escorted through your dominions to the source of Red river, as our being on the frontiers of your province gave cause to suspicion. I conceived it more proper to comply with the request, and repair to Santa Fé, in order to explain to your excellency any circumstance which might appear extraordinary, but on my arrival here, am informed by your excellency, that it is necessary that myself and troops pass by Chihuahua, in the province of Biscay, more than two hundred leagues out of my route. I have demanded of your excellency to know if we are to be considered as prisoners of war? you inform me you do not consider us in that light. Not to embarrass your excellency with many demands, I only request to receive it from under your hands, in what manner I am to consider myself, and the orders for my passing into the country; also whether the expence of the voyage is to be considered as defrayed by the government of Spain or the United States? Excuse my language, as I am not much accustomed to writing in French, but your excellency having no person who understands English, obliges me to attempt that language.

> I am, Sir, &c.
> Z. M. Pike.

12

THE RUSSIANS IN CALIFORNIA

William A. Slacum

Things were done less formally and more economically in 1835. When Secretary of State John Forsyth learned that William A. Slacum planned a visit to the Pacific coast he asked him to keep a journal and to ascertain "the sentiments entertained by all in respect to the United States, and to the two European powers having possessions in that region." Here's what Slacum wrote concerning his visit to Fort Ross, which the Russians had built in 1809 at the center of their sea-otter-fur collection business and which the Spanish were nervously tolerating.

We descended the Columbia in the Loriot on the 23d of January, and found the Hudson's Bay Company's ships Nereide and Llama still in "Baker's bay," having been detained since the 22d of December. On the 29th of January, a violent gale from the southeast commenced before daylight. On the morning of the 30th, the Loriot parted both cables, and was driven ashore. We received every assistance from the Nereide and Llama. In two or three days, the Loriot was got afloat. In the mean time, Captain Bancroft went up to Fort Vancouver, and succeeded in getting a good chain cable, stream, and anchor. On the 10th of February, the bar was smooth, and the wind from the eastward. We got under way with the Hudson's Bay Company's ships Nereide and Llama, and crossed the bar safely, and stood on our way towards "Bodega," the Russian settlement in California.

Nothing material occurred, from the day we left Columbia, until the morning of the 19th of February, when we made the land off the "Presidia Ross." The wind being light, I took the boat at eight miles' distant, and passed in for the fort. About three miles distant from the Loriot, I met three Bydackas coming off to us. An officer delivered a polite message from the Russian Governor, and immediately returned to the shore with me. About 2 o'clock I landed, and met a hospitable reception from Mr. Peter Kos-trometinoff, the Russian military and civil commandant of the Russian American Fur Company. The Presidia Ross lies in 38 deg. 40 min. north latitude, immediately on the ocean, on a hill sloping gradually towards the sea. The rear is crowned by a range of hills 1,500 feet in height, covered with pines, firs, cedar, and laurel, rendering the position of the fort highly picturesque. The fort is an enclosure 100 yards square, picketed with timber 8 inches thick by 18 feet high; mounts four 12-pound carronades on each angle, and four 6-pound brass howitzers fronting the principal gate; has two octangular block-houses, with loopholes for musketry, and 8 buildings within the enclosure, and 48 outside, beside a large boat-house at the landing place, blacksmith's shop, carpenter's and cooper's shop, and a large stable for 200 cows, the number usually milked. The Russians first settled at "Bodega," about 18 miles south of Ross, in 1813. It was thought to afford facilities for ship building, and a good point for seal fishing and "sea otter" hunting. Two vessels of upwards of two hundred tons have been built here, and several smaller vessels of 25 to 40 tons. The oak, however, of which these vessels have been built, is not good; although it is an evergreen, and resembles in grain the "post oak," it is of far inferior quality. This establishment of the Russians seems now to be kept up principally as a "point d'appui;" and hereafter it may be urged in furtherance of the claims of the "Imperial Autocrat" to this country, having now been in possession of Ross and "Bodega" for 24 years, without molestation. Two ships annually come down for wheat from Sitka. Their cargoes are pur-chased in California, likewise tallow and jerked beef, for bills on the Russian American Fur Company, St. Petersburg. These bills fall into the hands of the American traders from Boston and the Sandwich islands, who receive these bills from the Californians as money in payment of goods. Ross contains about 400 souls; 60 of whom are Russians and "Fins," 80 "Kodiacks," the remainder Indians of the neighborhood, who work well with the plough and sickle. All the Russians and Finlanders are artisans. Wages $35 to $40 per annum. They export butter and cheese to Sitka. But few skins (seals) are now taken; no sea otters. This year the farm is much increased; 240 fanegas, equal to 600 bushels of wheat, are sown. It generally yields 12 bushels for one. Stock—1,500 head of neat cattle, 800 horses and mules, 400 to 500 sheep, and 300 hogs. . . .

An agent of the Russian Government was here last year. He came through, via Siberia, from St. Petersburg, and visited all the posts in Kamschatka and on the northwest coast. He got permission from the late General Figaroa (then commandant general of California) to put up a large building on the bay of St. Francisco, ostensibly to be used as a granary to receive the wheat purchased in California; but, in effect, it was intended as a block-house, and was to have been made defensible. The timber was got out, and now lies ready to be used. General Figaroa died, and his successor, "Chico," prohibited the Russians from erecting their block-house.

Mr. Kostrometinoff readily granted me permission for the party that accompanied me from the Columbia to land at Bodega. He also furnished a house for their use until their cattle could be collected, and provided me with horses and guides to proceed by land to the bay of St. Francisco. Of my proceedings in California, I must beg to refer to the communication which I shall have the honor to lay before you in a few days, accompanied by a chart of the Columbia, &c.

In the mean time, I have the honor to remain your most obedient servant, William A. Slacum.

Part Two

◆

THE ORIGINAL
WESTERNERS

Europeans called them Indians and lumped dozens of rich and complex cultures as different from one another as Greeks are from Pakistanis into one stereotype. Varied as they were, these first Americans had several things in common. Unlike Europeans, their societies were (with rare exceptions) almost pure democracies, without repression, without a class system, and without hereditary rulers. They chose their leaders on the basis of wisdom or skill and replaced them at will. Unlike the Europeans, the Native Americans gave status to women. They did not abuse their children, killed neither animals nor each other for sport (with the exception of the grisly Aztecs), and did not practice slavery. Except for an area in the Northwest, they attached no social importance to possessions and believed no human could own any part of Mother Earth. Also unlike Europeans, who locked their insane in Bedlam or burned them as witches, the Native Americans protected the mentally ill. And unlike the Europeans, who had lived with it for generations, they were terribly vulnerable to smallpox.

So the Europeans slaughtered the Native Americans' game, cut their forests, pushed them off their land, called them savages when they resisted, and destroyed them. Lord Amherst wrote to King George III telling him that the savages died quickly from the pox and noting that pesthouse blankets that seemed to spread that plague might be used as gifts to cheaply eliminate them.

We honor Lord Amherst's memory by giving his name to a town and a college.

13

ISHI, THE LAST
ONE LEFT ALIVE

Theodora Kroeber

*White people who had settled around Oroville, California, believed the last of
the Yahi tribe had been hunted down and killed before the turn of the century.
But in August 1911, dogs were heard barking in a slaugterhouse corral and they
learned they had been mistaken. The following is from* Ishi, Last Stone Age
Indian, *by Theodora Kroeber, wife of Alfred Kroeber for whom the University
of California anthropology department is named. While she makes relatively little
of it, Ishi's story has seemed to me a summation of the Native American tragedy.*

Think, if you will, of all the Indians who have emerged from fact, fancy,
and fear to take their places in the pantheon of the American imagination:
in history Squanto, who fed the Pilgrims; Pocahontas, who loved an Englishman; Chief Logan the eloquent; Sacajawea, the girl-mother who
guided white men across the Continental Divide; Sequoia, who invented
an Indian alphabet; Crazy Horse, who outfought Custer; and in fiction
Hiawatha and the Last of the Mohicans. They are not many; and there
is not one of them whose story haunts the imagination more than Ishi's.

Ishi was, literally, a Stone Age man, the last of a "lost" tribe, when,
only half a century ago, he stumbled into twentieth-century California.
Undoubtedly Ishi anticipated death as a result of his arrival in an enemy
world, but almost miraculously he came to the hands of T. T. Waterman

and Alfred L. Kroeber, anthropologists who were among the few men in the country equipped to understand his dilemma and his personality. It is almost as miraculous that Ishi should today find a biographer able to tell his story with the scrupulous integrity, the poetic insight, and the sense of historic drama which give Theodora Kroeber's book its unique radiance.

For Ishi to adjust to what Mrs. Kroeber calls "the wilds of civilization" was as remarkable as for Mark Twain's Connecticut Yankee to settle down in King Arthur's England, or for a modern astronaut to survive in the worlds of outer space. It is far easier to romanticize such a story than to understand it.

The "discovery" of Ishi, "the last wild Indian," was well advertised in the newspapers of 1911, and in the next five years thousands of visitors watched him chip arrowheads, shape bows, and make fire by his age-old techniques in the halls of the modern museum where he so oddly made his home. And when Ishi died he had his "obits," some loosely journalistic, some semiscientific. But in 1916 the idea of a race dying out had for most Americans romantic rather than imminently realistic overtones, and Ishi was soon forgotten. Two world wars have since given new poignancy to the phrase "death of a race," as well as to the conception that patterns of life other than our own may have validity and significance. . . .

The story of Ishi begins for us early in the morning of the twenty-ninth day of August in the year 1911 and in the corral of a slaughter house. It begins with the sharp barking of dogs which roused the sleeping butchers. In the dawn light they saw a man at bay, crouching against the corral fence—Ishi.

They called off the dogs. Then, in some considerable excitement, they telephoned the sheriff in Oroville two or three miles away to say that they were holding a wild man and would he please come and take him off their hands. Sheriff and deputies arrived shortly, approaching the corral with guns at the ready. The wild man made no move to resist capture, quietly allowing himself to be handcuffed.

The sheriff, J. B. Webber, saw that the man was an Indian, and that he was at the limit of exhaustion and fear. He could learn nothing further, since his prisoner understood no English. Not knowing what to do with him, he motioned the Indian into the wagon with himself and his deputies, drove him to the county jail in Oroville, and locked him up in the cell for the insane. There, Sheriff Webber reasoned, while he tried to discover something more about his captive he could at least protect him from the excited curiosity of the townspeople and the outsiders who were already pouring in from miles around to see the wild man.

The wild man was emaciated to starvation, his hair was burned off close to his head, he was naked except for a ragged scrap of ancient covered-wagon canvas which he wore around his shoulders like a poncho. He was a man of middle height, the long bones, painfully apparent, were straight, strong, and not heavy, the skin color somewhat paler in tone than the full copper characteristic of most Indians. The black eyes were wary and guarded now, but were set wide in a broad face, the mouth was generous and agreeably molded. For the rest, the Indian's extreme fatigue and fright heightened a sensitiveness which was always there, while it masked the usual mobility and expressiveness of the features.

It should be said that the sheriff's action in locking Ishi up was neither stupid nor brutal given the circumstances. Until Sheriff Webber took the unwonted measure of keeping them out by force people filled the jail to gaze through the bars of his cell at the captive. Later, Ishi spoke with some diffidence of this, his first contact with white men. He said that he was put up in a fine house where he was kindly treated and well fed by a big chief. That he would eat nothing and drink nothing during his first days of captivity Ishi did not say. Such was the case; nor did he allow himself to sleep at first. Quite possibly it was a time of such strain and terror that he suppressed all memory of it. Or he may have felt that it was unkind to recall his suspicions which proved in the event groundless, for Ishi expected in those first days to be put to death. He knew of white men only that they were the murderers of his own people. It was natural that he should expect, once in their power, to be shot or hanged or killed by poisoning.

Meanwhile, local Indians and half-breeds as well as Mexicans and Spaniards tried to talk to the prisoner in Maidu, Wintu, and Spanish. Ishi listened patiently but uncomprehendingly, and when he spoke it was in a tongue which meant no more to the Indians there than to the whites. . . .

These accounts were read by Professors Kroeber and Waterman, anthropologists at the University of California, who were at once alerted to the human drama behind the event and to its possible importance. . . .

On August 31, 1911, Kroeber sent the following telegram: "Sheriff Butte County. Newspapers report capture wild Indian speaking language other tribes totally unable understand. Please confirm or deny by collect telegram and if story correct hold Indian till arrival Professor State University who will take charge and be responsible for him. Matter important account aboriginal history."

The sheriff's office must have confirmed the report promptly: Waterman took the train to Oroville the same day. That he and Kroeber correctly "guessed" Ishi's tribe and language was no *tour de force* of intuition. The guess was based on field work with Indians all up and down California; they knew that Oroville was adjacent to country which formerly belonged to the Yana Indians; presumably the strange Indian would be a Yana. He might even be from the southernmost tribe of Yana, believed to be extinct. If this were true, neither they nor anyone so far as they knew could speak his language. But if he were a Northern or Central Yana, there were files of expertly recorded vocabularies for those dialects from two old Yanas, Batwi, called Sam, and Chidaimiya, called Betty Brown.

With a copy of Batwi's and Chidaimiya's vocabularies in his pocket, Waterman arrived in Oroville where he identified himself to Sheriff Webber and was taken to visit the wild man. Waterman found a weary, badgered Indian sitting in his cell, wearing the butcher's apron he had been given at the slaughter house, courteously making what answer he could in his own language to a barrage of questions thrown at him in English, Spanish, and assorted Indian from a miscellaneous set of visitors.

Waterman sat down beside Ishi, and with his phonetically transcribed list of Northern and Central Yana words before him, began to read from it, repeating each word, pronouncing it as well as he knew how. Ishi was attentive but unresponding until, discouragingly far down the list, Waterman said *siwini* which means yellow pine, at the same time tapping the pine framework of the cot on which they sat. Recognition lighted up the Indian's face. Waterman said the magic word again; Ishi repeated it after him, correcting his pronunciation, and for the next moments the two of them banged at the wood of the cot, telling each other over and over, *siwini, siwini!*

With the difficult first sound recognition achieved, others followed. Ishi was indeed one of the lost tribe, a Yahi; in other words, he was from the southernmost Yana. Waterman was learning that the unknown Yahi dialect differed considerably but not to the point of unintelligibility from the two northern ones of his list. Together he and Ishi tried out more and more words and phrases: they were beginning to communicate. After a while Ishi ventured to ask Waterman, *I ne ma Yahi?* "Are you an Indian?" Waterman answered that he was. The hunted look left Ishi's eyes—here was a friend. He knew as well as did his friend that Waterman was not an Indian. The question was a tentative and subtle way of reassuring and being reassured, not an easy thing to do when the meaningful shared sounds are few. Between meetings with Ishi, Waterman wrote to Kroeber from Oroville:

> This man [Ishi] is undoubtedly wild. He has pieces of deer thong in place of ornaments in the lobes of his ears and a

wooden plug in the septum of his nose. He recognizes most of my Yana words and a fair proportion of his own seem to be identical [with mine]. Some of his, however, are either quite different or else my pronunciation of them is very bad, because he doesn't respond to them except by pointing to his ears and asking to have them repeated. "No!" *k'u'i*—it is not—is one. "Yes!" *ähä*, pleases him immensely. I think I get a few endings that don't occur in Northern Yana on nouns, for example. Phonetically, he has some of the prettiest cracked consonants I ever heard in my life. He will be a splendid informant, especially for phonetics, for he speaks very clearly. I have not communicated with him successfully enough to get his story, but what can I expect? He has a yarn to tell about his woman, who had a baby on her back and seems to have been drowned, except that he is so *cheerful* about it.

Waterman misunderstood. In the excitement and relief of having someone to talk to, Ishi poured out confidences and recollections which Waterman could by no means comprehend even with the aid of an elaborate pantomime. Ishi's seeming pleasure was not in the recollected event, but was rather a near hysteria induced by human interchange of speech and feelings too long denied.

Waterman's letters continue:

> We had a lot of conversation this morning about deer hunting and making acorn soup, but I got as far as my list of words would take me. If I am not mistaken, he's full of religion—bathing at sunrise, putting out pinches of tobacco where the lightning strikes, etc. I'll try rattlesnake on him when I go back after lunch. It was a picnic to see him open his eyes when he heard Yana from me. And he looked over my shoulder at the paper in a most mystified way. He knew at once where I got my inspiration. . . . We showed him some arrows last night, and we could hardly get them away from him. He showed us how he flaked the points, singed the edges of the feathering, and put on the sinew wrappings.

Even before Waterman had established a thin line of communication with Ishi, the sheriff had become convinced that his prisoner was neither insane nor dangerous. There were no charges against him; he did not properly belong in jail. The question was, what in place of the shelter of the jail was there for him? Waterman offered to take him to San Francisco.

Phones and telegraph wires were kept busy for the next forty-eight hours between Oroville and San Francisco, where the University's Museum of Anthropology then was, and between the museum and Washington, D.C.

While these negotiations were going forward, the sheriff, at Waterman's suggestion, sent a deputy to Redding to find and bring back with him the old man, Batwi, to act as interpreter-companion to Ishi. Batwi came, and although he patronized Ishi outrageously, he was for the present a help. He and Ishi could communicate in Yana, not without some difficulty, but quite fully. Meanwhile, the Indian Bureau in Washington telegraphed permission for Ishi to go to the University's museum whose staff was to be responsible for him at least until there was opportunity for fuller investigation. The sheriff of Butte County was greatly relieved; he at once made out a receipt of release from the jail to the University. This remarkable document seems not to have survived the years of moving and storing in odd corners which has been the fate of the museum files and specimens.

In any case, Waterman, Batwi, and Ishi, with the release and government permission, left Oroville on Labor Day, September 4, arriving in San Francisco somewhat before midnight. There remained to Ishi four years and seven months of life, years which were to pass within the shelter of the museum walls at the Affiliated Colleges, or in the hospital next door when he was sick.

14

THE MAN WHO KILLED THE DEER

Frank Waters

Frank Waters, born in 1902 in Colorado Springs, is best known for his Book
of the Hopi, *a study of the complex Hopi religion and culture written after long
association with elders of the tribe. In his novel,* The Man Who Killed the
Deer, *he looks into the mystique of Taos Pueblo, where he also had many close
friends.*

Let us move evenly together, brothers.

A young man went into the mountains. He killed a deer out of season.
He got arrested, and a knock on the head to boot. He will have to pay
a fine, doubtless, for disobeying those Government laws we have sworn to
uphold with our canes of office. A simple matter.

But wait. Was it so simple?

This young man was an Indian, born in our pueblo, belonging to our
tribe. Or was he, properly speaking? There was the definition of an Indian
by the Government—so much Indian blood, land ownership, all that. But
there was the definition of an Indian by the Council according to his
conformance to custom, tradition, his participation in ceremonials. Now
this young man has been lax, very lax; we have warned him. He has
disobeyed us; we have punished him. And now he has disobeyed the laws
of the Government outside, likewise. What have we to do with this, that
we should interfere?

Now there is this. There are good Indians among us, and there are those who look under their eyes. But we are all in one nest. No Indian is an individual. He is a piece of the pueblo, the tribe. Is it proper to consider that we have done wrong against the Government, our white father, betrayed our canes of office?

Yet there was this to consider. All this land was ours—the mountain, the valleys, the desert. Indian land. We have the papers to it from the Spanish King. The Mexicans came, the white people—the gringos. They built themselves a town on our land, Indian land. We got nothing for it. Now when the Spanish King opened his hand, Our Father at Washington closed his own hand upon the land. He told us, "You will be paid for it. The day will come with compensation." What did we want with money? We wanted land, our land, Indian land. But mostly we wanted the mountains. We wanted the mountains, our mother, between whose breasts lies the little blue eye of faith. The deep turquoise lake of life. Our lake, our church. Where we make our pilgrimages, hold our ceremonials . . . Now what is this? We have waited. The day of compensation has not come. The mountains are Government forests. Not ours. The Mexicans pasture their sheep and goats upon the slopes. Turistas scatter paper bags unseemly upon the ground. They throw old fish bait into our sacred lake. Government men, these rangers, ride through it at will.

Is any man safe? Look at this one's broken head. Will our ceremonials long be inviolate from foreign eyes? Now then, is it we who are injured and must seek reparation, demand our rights, our mountains? This is what I say. God knows, will help us, will give us strength.

The voices kept creeping around the room . . .

In the Government office two hundred miles away there is that Indian lawyer, our mouth in many matters. There is the judge in town, a short walk. Are we to turn this young man alone over to the judge? Or are we to call this Indian lawyer? And what are we to tell him? We must move evenly together. We must be one mind, one heart, one body.

Silence spoke, and it spoke the loudest of all.

There is no such thing as a simple thing. One drops a pebble into a pool, but the ripples travel far. One picks up a little stone in the mountains, one of the little stones called Lagrimas de Cristo—and look! It is shaped like a star; the sloping mountain is full of stars as the sloping sky. Or take a kernel of corn. Plant it in Our Mother Earth with the sweat of your body, with what you know of the times and seasons, with your proper prayers. And with your strength and manhood Our Father Sun multiplies and gives it back into your flesh. What then is this kernel of corn? It is not a simple thing.

Nothing is simple and alone. We are not separate and alone. The breathing mountains, the living stones, each blade of grass, the clouds, the rain, each star, the beasts, the birds and the invisible spirits of the air—we are all one, indivisible. Nothing that any of us does but affects us all.

So I would have you look upon this thing not as a separate simple thing, but as a stone which is a star in the firmament of earth, as a ripple in a pool, as a kernel of corn. I would have you consider how it fits into the pattern of the whole. How far its influence may spread. What it may grow into . . .

So there is something else to consider. The deer. It is dead. In the old days we all remember, we did not go out on a hunt lightly. We said to the deer we were going to kill, "We know your life is as precious as ours. We know that we are both children of the same Great True Ones. We know that we are all one life on the same Mother Earth, beneath the same plains of the sky. But we also know that one life must sometimes give way to another so that the one great life of all may continue unbroken. So we ask your permission, we obtain your consent to this killing."

Ceremonially we said this, and we sprinkled meal and corn pollen to Our Father Sun. And when we killed the deer we laid his head toward the East, and sprinkled him with meal and pollen. And we dropped drops of his blood and bits of his flesh on the ground for Our Mother Earth. It was proper so. For then when we too built its flesh into our flesh, when we walked in the moccasins of its skin, when we danced in its robe and antlers, we knew that the life of the deer was continued in our life, as it in turn was continued in the one life all around us, below us and above us.

We knew the deer knew this and was satisfied.

But this deer's permission was not obtained. What have we done to this deer, our brother? What have we done to ourselves? For we are all bound together, and our touch upon one travels through all to return to us again. Let us not forget the deer.

The old Cacique spoke. It was true that the young men nowadays did not observe such proper steps. And it was true that the game was becoming scarce because of it. Was it true that next the water would fail them, the air become dull and tasteless, the life go out of the land?

"So I would have you consider whether it is not time to be more strict with our young men so corrupted with evil modern ways, lest we ourselves dwindle and vanish entirely. This I say," he ended. "Dios knows, will help us, will give us medicine."

Here they were then, all these things and shadows of things ensnared like flies in the web of silence. They fluttered their wings. They shook and distorted the whole vast web. But they did not break free. For it was the web which binds us each to the other, and all to the life of which we are an inseparable part—binds us to the invisible shapes that have gone and those to come, in the solidarity of one flowing whole.

So the night grew thin as the thinnest gray blanket around the walls. The embers heaped upon growing gray ashes. The little wooden sand boxes filled with cigarette stubs. The two sentinels came in a last time for warmth. In with them stalked daylight.

And now the old men rose and stretched their stiff, bent limbs. They gathered their blankets about their dark faces and bent shoulders. They hobbled out across the plaza in the dawn-dusk.

The meeting of the Council was over. They were one body, one mind, one heart. They moved evenly together.

15

THE PACIFIST WARRIOR

Jack Schaefer

To his intense distaste the late Jack Schaefer was best known for Shane, *the classic old Western pitting the homesteader against ruthless cattle baron. Schaefer regretted putting the white hats on farmers, saying they did even more damage to the land than did the cattlemen, and he regretted seeing "the little wimp" Alan Ladd cast in the movie role of Shane. His favorites among his books were* Monte Walsh, *a much less romantic cowboy novel, and* The Canyon, *a novella-parable concerning a young Cheyenne brave who opposed the warfare culture of his people. Here's a taste of it.*

And Little Bear, the strange one, the different one, went forth into his canyon. He walked along his stream and saw his fish in the shallow pools. He saw his buffalo eating the good grasses. He saw the high protective rock walls of his canyon marching around him. "My mind has lived too long in the light of the moon of the night. Let it be in the light of the sun of the day."

—A man comes into a canyon and makes it his own. With the cunning of his mind and the courage of his heart he makes it his own. With one leg of bone and one leg of wood he kills the mighty buffalo and he has what he needs for food and clothing and shelter. He keeps the canyon his own when he kills the evil one that would despoil it, the blood-drinking one of the mountains. It is his and he has made it so. But he has not done this alone. . . . In his hand is a knife that was made far away by another man, a knife that was given to him by an old one, a great one. In his mind is the knowledge to make fire and weapons and clothing and to find food and to provide shelter, knowledge given to him by those who taught him when he was a boy and those who showed him by their own doing when he lived among them. By himself he is nothing. Only the courage is his alone. All of those others are with him, even in his canyon, and he cannot ever be free of them for what they have given is with him and is part of him and without them he could not have made the canyon his own—

—A man brings a woman into his canyon. That is good. That is what makes complete the goodness of the place for him. She misses the talking with other women, the gossip of the village, the dances of the younger people, the advice and storytelling of the older people, the companionship of the relatives who are close to her heart. For him she will miss those things. She will not talk about the missing and she will try not to let him know about the missing. But it is there. . . . She has a child. She has it alone with only a fumbling man to help her. The child is taken with a sickness. It does not have the care that old women of experience or an old man skilled in medicines could give. It dies. Perhaps that is as Heammawihio, the Wise One Above, meant it should be and no care could save the child. But how can one be certain of such a thing? . . .

There can be another child. It can live and be healthy and grow. It is a boy. Who is there to count a coup for it and pierce its ears? It has long legs and strong for fast running. Where are the other boys with whom it will play? Where are the old men to tell it tales of the old days of the tribe and the things it is needful to do? It grows and is troubled in its mind. Where is an old one, a great one, who can direct it in the test of a starving? It grows and the urging of a man begins in it. Where is a maiden who will look with favor on it when it waits in the dusk of the evening and plucks at her robe? . . . It is a girl. Where is the grandmother or other old woman to take the place of the grandmother and teach it the things a girl-child must be taught? Where are the other girls with whom it will play and make the endless girl-talk and practice the cutting of moccasins and the sewing of beads and of quills? Where is the young man on whom she will look with favor and for whom she will sit quiet and speak no objections while the father considers the presents the young man has sent and what is good for the daughter who is close to his heart?—

—What was it the old one meant with his words? A man must be certain that his heart speaks truth to him. . . . One man cannot change a tribe. But one man can live with a tribe and not let it change him too much—

And Little Bear, the strange one, the different one, the son of a laughing father and a soft-voiced mother, the small-fat-person with short legs whose ears were pierced by Standing All Night, went straight across his canyon to where the stones that had been piled into a slanting walkway lay heaved and thrown to both sides and the rock wall rose smooth with no niches up to the first ledge. He bent over and picked up a stone. He began to pile the stones one upon the other.

And Spotted Turtle, the great-granddaughter of Standing All Night, the sister of Yellow Moon and the wife of Little Bear, stood in the lodge entrance and saw him. She went to him.

"Why do you do that?"

"We are going back to our people."

The happiness of the words leaped in her and shone in her eyes and he saw and he was certain that his heart spoke the truth to him. Yet the sadness was a great sadness in him. It swelled until he thought his chest would burst. He turned away and went among the tall hiding berry bushes where the rocks thrust up from the ground and she remained and watched him go.

The badger was not there by the flat stone. There had been no meat for several days. It was off on its own secret ways hunting food. That was no matter now. He spoke to the rocks about him. "Oh badger, farewell. The blood of my breast runs downward with a new grief and I alone can see it."

But she was coming through the bushes to him. "Oh my husband. It is bad. But I am young. I am strong. I will have another child. And another. I will not let them die." She was very tired and her face was drawn from the pain of losing the little one and the pain of the cutting of the finger. But she was beautiful to him. "Oh my husband. I am not a silly woman who must have others clacking about her. It is enough that you are here. I would not take you from the place that is yours."

His voice was harsh and it grated in his throat. It was the voice of the man of the lodge speaking what was in his mind and what would not be changed. "You are not taking me out of this place. I am taking myself and my woman where we belong as a man must."

He left her. He returned to the stones by the near rock wall. He began to pile one stone upon another stone in the steep slanting walkway that would lead up to the ledge and the ladder of niches above. She came out of the bushes and stood still and watched him. On her face was a warm wisdom and an understanding. She moved forward to go to him and to help him.

16

THE WAY TO RAINY MOUNTAIN

N. Scott Momaday

N. Scott Momaday grew up at Jemez Pueblo where his parents—themselves both noted artists—were teachers. His House Made of Dawn *won him the Pulitzer Prize for fiction and a national reputation. It concerned the people of Jemez Pueblo, though Momaday is Kiowa by blood and spirit. He previously had published* The Way to Rainy Mountain, *a national classic which every literate American should read. The following is his introduction to that book.*

A single knoll rises out of the plain in Oklahoma, north and west of the Wichita Range. For my people, the Kiowas, it is an old landmark, and they gave it the name Rainy Mountain. The hardest weather in the world is there. Winter brings blizzards, hot tornadic winds arise in the spring, and in summer the prairie is an anvil's edge. The grass turns brittle and brown, and it cracks beneath your feet. There are green belts along the rivers and creeks, linear groves of hickory and pecan, willow and witch hazel. At a distance in July or August the steaming foliage seems almost to writhe in fire. Great green and yellow grasshoppers are everywhere in the tall grass, popping up like corn to sting the flesh, and tortoises crawl about on the red earth, going nowhere in the plenty of time. Loneliness is an aspect of the land. All things in the plain are isolate; there is no confusion of objects in the eye, but *one* hill or *one* tree or *one* man. To look upon that landscape in the early morning, with the sun at your back, is to lose the sense of proportion. Your imagination comes to life, and this, you think, is where Creation was begun.

I returned to Rainy Mountain in July. My grandmother had died in the spring, and I wanted to be at her grave. She had lived to be very old and at last infirm. Her only living daughter was with her when she died, and I was told that in death her face was that of a child.

I like to think of her as a child. When she was born, the Kiowas were living the last great moment of their history. For more than a hundred years they had controlled the open range from the Smoky Hill River to the Red, from the headwaters of the Canadian to the fork of the Arkansas and Cimarron. In alliance with the Comanches, they had ruled the whole of the southern Plains. War was their sacred business, and they were among the finest horsemen the world has ever known. But warfare for the Kiowas was preeminently a matter of disposition rather than of survival, and they never understood the grim, unrelenting advance of the U.S. Cavalry. When at last, divided and ill-provisioned, they were driven onto the Staked Plains in the cold rains of autumn, they fell into panic. In Palo Duro Canyon they abandoned their crucial stores to pillage and had nothing then but their lives. In order to save themselves, they surrendered to the soldiers at Fort Sill and were imprisoned in the old stone corral that now stands as a military museum. My grandmother was spared the humiliation of those high gray walls by eight or ten years, but she must have known from birth the affliction of defeat, the dark brooding of old warriors.

Her name was Aho, and she belonged to the last culture to evolve in North America. Her forebears came down from the high country in western Montana nearly three centuries ago. They were a mountain people, a mysterious tribe of hunters whose language has never been positively classified in any major group. In the late seventeenth century they began a long migration to the south and east. It was a journey toward the dawn, and it led to a golden age. Along the way the Kiowas were befriended by the Crows, who gave them the culture and religion of the Plains. They acquired horses, and their ancient nomadic spirit was suddenly free of the ground. They acquired Tai-me, the sacred Sun Dance doll, from that moment the object and symbol of their worship, and so shared in the divinity of the sun. Not least, they acquired the sense of destiny, therefore courage and pride. When they entered upon the southern Plains they had been transformed. No longer were they slaves to the simple necessity of survival; they were a lordly and dangerous society of fighters and thieves, hunters and priests of the sun. According to their origin myth, they entered the world through a hollow log. From one point of view, their migration was the fruit of an old prophecy, for indeed they emerged from a sunless world.

Although my grandmother lived out her long life in the shadow of Rainy Mountain, the immense landscape of the continental interior lay like memory in her blood. She could tell of the Crows, whom she had never seen, and of the Black Hills, where she had never been. I wanted to see in reality what she had seen more perfectly in the mind's eye, and traveled fifteen hundred miles to begin my pilgrimage.

Yellowstone, it seemed to me, was the top of the world, a region of deep lakes and dark timber, canyons and waterfalls. But, beautiful as it is, one might have the sense of confinement there. The skyline in all directions is close at hand, the high wall of the woods and deep cleavages of shade. There is a perfect freedom in the mountains, but it belongs to the eagle and the elk, the badger and the bear. The Kiowas reckoned their stature by the distance they could see, and they were bent and blind in the wilderness.

Descending eastward, the highland meadows are a stairway to the plain. In July the inland slope of the Rockies is luxuriant with flax and buckwheat, stonecrop and larkspur. The earth unfolds and the limit of the land recedes. Clusters of trees, and animals grazing far in the distance, cause the vision to reach away and wonder to build upon the mind. The sun follows a longer course in the day, and the sky is immense beyond all comparison. The great billowing clouds that sail upon it are shadows that move upon the grain like water, dividing light. Farther down, in the land of the Crows and Blackfeet, the plain is yellow. Sweet clover takes hold of the hills and bends upon itself to cover and seal the soil. There the Kiowas paused on their way; they had come to the place where they must change their lives. The sun is at home on the plains. Precisely there does it have the certain character of a god. When the Kiowas came to the land of the Crows, they could see the dark lees of the hills at dawn across the Bighorn River, the profusion of light on the grain shelves, the oldest deity ranging after the solstices. Not yet would they veer southward to the caldron of the land that lay below; they must wean their blood from the northern winter and hold the mountains a while longer in their view. They bore Tai-me in procession to the east.

A dark mist lay over the Black Hills, and the land was like iron. At the top of a ridge I caught sight of Devil's Tower upthrust against the gray sky as if in the birth of time the core of the earth had broken through its crust and the motion of the world was begun. There are things in nature that engender an awful quiet in the heart of man; Devil's Tower is one of them. Two centuries ago, because they could not do otherwise, the Kiowas made a legend at the base of the rock. My grandmother said:

> *Eight children were there at play, seven sisters and their brother. Suddenly the boy was struck dumb; he trembled and began to run upon his hands and feet. His fingers became claws, and his body was covered with fur. Directly there was a bear where the boy had been. The sisters were terrified; they ran, and the bear after them. They came to the stump of a great tree, and the tree spoke to them. It bade them climb upon it, and as they did so it began to rise into the air. The bear came to kill them, but they were just beyond its reach. It reared against the tree and scored the bark all around with its claws. The seven sisters were borne into the sky, and they became the stars of the Big Dipper.*

From that moment, and so long as the legend lives, the Kiowas have kinsmen in the night sky. Whatever they were in the mountains, they could be no more. However tenuous their well-being, however much they had suffered and would suffer again, they had found a way out of the wilderness.

My grandmother had a reverence for the sun, a holy regard that now is all but gone out of mankind. There was a wariness in her, and an ancient awe. She was a Christian in her later years, but she had come a long way about, and she never forgot her birthright. As a child she had been to the Sun Dances; she had taken part in those annual rites, and by them she had learned the restoration of her people in the presence of Tai-me. She was about seven when the last Kiowa Sun Dance was held in 1887 on the Washita River above Rainy Mountain Creek. The buffalo were gone. In order to consummate the ancient sacrifice—to impale the head of a buffalo bull upon the medicine tree—a delegation of old men journeyed into Texas, there to beg and barter for an animal from the Goodnight herd. She was ten when the Kiowas came together for the last time as a living Sun Dance culture. They could find no buffalo; they had to hang an old hide from the sacred tree. Before the dance could begin, a company of soldiers rode out from Fort Sill under orders to disperse the tribe. Forbidden without cause the essential act of their faith, having seen the wild herds slaughtered and left to rot upon the ground, the Kiowas backed away forever from the medicine tree. That was July 20, 1890, at the great bend of the Washita. My grandmother was there. Without bitterness, and for as long as she lived, she bore a vision of deicide.

Now that I can have her only in memory, I see my grandmother in the several postures that were peculiar to her: standing at the wood stove on a winter morning and turning meat in a great iron skillet; sitting at the south window, bent above her beadwork, and afterwards, when her vision failed, looking down for a long time into the fold of her hands; going out upon a cane, very slowly as she did when the weight of age came upon her; praying. I remember her most often at prayer. She made long, rambling prayers out of suffering and hope, having seen many things. I was never sure that I had the right to hear, so exclusive were they of all mere custom and company. The last time I saw her she prayed standing by the side of her bed at night, naked to the waist, the light of a kerosene lamp moving upon her dark skin. Her long, black hair, always drawn and braided in the day, lay upon her shoulders and against her breasts like a shawl. I do not speak Kiowa, and I never understood her prayers, but there was something inherently sad in the sound, some merest hesitation upon the syllables of sorrow. She began in a high and descending pitch, exhausting her breath to silence; then again and again—and always the same intensity of effort, of something that is, and is not, like urgency in the human voice. Transported so in the dancing light among the shadows of her room, she seemed beyond the reach of time. But that was illusion; I think I knew then that I should not see her again.

Houses are like sentinels in the plain, old keepers of the weather watch. There, in a very little while, wood takes on the appearance of great age. All colors wear soon away in the wind and rain, and then the wood is burned gray and the grain appears and the nails turn red with rust. The windowpanes are black and opaque; you imagine there is nothing within, and indeed there are many ghosts, bones given up to the land. They stand here and there against the sky, and you approach them for a longer time than you expect. They belong in the distance; it is their domain.

Once there was a lot of sound in my grandmother's house, a lot of coming and going, feasting and talk. The summers there were full of excitement and reunion. The Kiowas are a summer people; they abide the cold and keep to themselves, but when the season turns and the land becomes warm and vital they cannot hold still; an old love of going returns upon them. The aged visitors who came to my grandmother's house when I was a child were made of lean and leather, and they bore themselves upright. They wore great black hats and bright ample shirts that shook in the wind. They rubbed fat upon their hair and wound their braids with strips of colored cloth. Some of them painted their faces and carried the scars of old and cherished enmities. They were an old council of warlords, come to remind and be reminded of who they were. Their wives and daughters served them well. The women might indulge themselves; gossip was at once the mark and compensation of their servitude. They made loud and elaborate talk among themselves, full of jest and gesture, fright and false alarm. They went abroad in fringed and flowered shawls, bright beadwork and German silver. They were at home in the kitchen, and they prepared meals that were banquets.

There were frequent prayer meetings, and great nocturnal feasts. When I was a child I played with my cousins outside, where the lamplight fell upon the ground and the singing of the old people rose up around us and carried away into the darkness. There were a lot of good things to eat, a lot of laughter and surprise. And afterwards, when the quiet returned, I lay down with my grandmother and could hear the frogs away by the river and feel the motion of the air.

Now there is a funeral silence in the rooms, the endless wake of some final word. The walls have closed in upon my grandmother's house. When I returned to it in mourning, I saw for the first time in my life how small it was. It was late at night, and there was a white moon, nearly full. I sat for a long time on the stone steps by the kitchen door. From there I could see out across the land; I could see the long row of trees by the creek, the low light upon the rolling plains, and the stars of the Big Dipper. Once I looked at the moon and caught sight of a strange thing. A cricket had perched upon the handrail, only a few inches away from me. My line of vision was such that the creature filled the moon like a fossil. It had gone there, I thought, to live and die, for there, of all places, was its small definition made whole and eternal. A warm wind rose up and purled like the longing within me.

The next morning I awoke at dawn and went out on the dirt road to Rainy Mountain. It was already hot, and the grasshoppers began to fill the air. Still, it was early in the morning, and the birds sang out of the shadows. The long yellow grass on the mountain shone in the bright light, and a scissortail hied above the land. There, where it ought to be, at the end of a long and legendary way, was my grandmother's grave. Here and there on the dark stones were ancestral names. Looking back once, I saw the mountain and came away.

17

COLTER'S RUN

H. M. Chittenden

The Blackfeet warriors who captured John Colter in the Wyoming–Montana borderlands gave him a choice and a chance—outrun them or die. It happened in 1808. Colter lived to tell about it. Here's an account by H. M. Chittenden from his history of Yellowstone National Park.

The exact date of this adventure we are about to relate has seemed to be difficult to determine; but it has now been definitely settled on the authority of Thomas James that it was in the autumn of 1808. It was an incident of "one of Colter's many excursions from the post [Lisa's] to the Forks of the Missouri for beaver" (James). The adventure itself concerned only two white men—Colter and a companion named Potts, probably the same who had been a fellow-soldier in the Lewis and Clark expedition. Colter was in the prime of life, about thirty-five in years, nearly six feet tall, with an "open pleasing countenance of the Daniel Boone type." He was highly esteemed by his companions, among whom "his veracity was never questioned"—as it might well have been, considering the extraordinary character of the experiences which he related. Three reputable authorities have recorded these experiences as given to them by Colter himself. They agree more closely than such accounts generally do and undoubtedly represent with reasonable accuracy one of the most remarkable adventures in the whole range of American frontier history. The narrative which follows is made up from these three authorities, principally from James and Bradbury.

The scene of the adventure was on Jefferson Fork of the Missouri at a point not far above the junction with the Madison where the two streams were separated by about five miles of bottom land. Colter and Potts were moving up stream one morning, each in his own canoe in which were several beaver traps to be disposed of at suitable places. The high shores or the brushwood bordering the stream shut off their view beyond the immediate banks. Suddenly they heard a noise like the tramping of many buffalo. Colter was for instant flight, fearing it might be Indians, but Potts insisted that it was buffalo and so they kept on. A moment later their doubts were settled by the appearance of several hundred Indians upon the bank.

The chiefs motioned to Colter and Potts to come ashore, and as it was useless to attempt to escape, they pushed their canoes toward the bank, quietly dumping their traps into the shallow water. Evidently they did not fully realize their great danger and believed they could get away and could sometime recover their traps. They had been through too many dangers to feel that their end had yet come.

As the prow of Potts' canoe touched the bottom an Indian seized his gun. Colter leaped out, wrenched it away, and handed it back to Potts, who, strangely enough, pushed back into the stream. Colter protested and told him that any effort to escape simply meant suicide. In fact, the words were scarcely out of his mouth when an arrow struck Potts in the thigh and tumbled him into the bottom of the canoe. "Are you hurt?" asked Colter. "Yes, too much to escape. Save yourself, if you can. I'll get one of them at least before I go." Rising to a sitting position he leveled his gun at an Indian, killing him instantly. Scarcely had the sound of his shot died away when his own body was riddled with bullets from the shore and he fell dead in the bottom of the canoe. The Indians darted into the water, dragged the canoe ashore, and tore the poor trapper's body into shreds, flinging the flesh into Colter's face. Potts was perhaps wise to bring upon himself swift death instead of lingering torture by the savages, but he should have considered what he was bringing upon his companion, who now, helpless and alone, awaited his fate.

In the meantime the Indians had stripped Colter stark naked, and he stood there expecting every minute to feel the shot or blow which would be the beginning of a terrible end. But, Indian-like, simple killing was not enough for them; they must satisfy their savage cruelty by making death as prolonged and terrible as possible. They held a council as to what method to adopt, and here they made a capital mistake. They decided that

Colter should run for his life, never suspecting what a lively sprinter they had in their helpless captive. Colter was in fact noted among his white companions as being remarkably swift of foot. A chief led him out a hundred yards in front of the crowd, pointed across the plain in the direction of the Madison River, and made a gesture for him to go. Colter did not understand at first, but after more gestures, it dawned upon him that he was to run for his life. It looked like a forlorn hope, but it *was* a hope and he instantly acted upon it.

Away across the flat prairie, five miles wide between the Jefferson and Madison Rivers, sped Colter toward the latter stream—sped as never man sped before—as only the hope of life could make him. He said afterward that he was astonished at his own ability to run. Surely, a stranger sight the wild prairies never saw—this lone, naked man pursued by a pack of howling savages. But he was too much for them. The distance between him and them increased. By the time he had gotten halfway across the plain, however, he began to feel the effects of his terrible exertion. His breath was almost gone, his strength was failing, and splashes of blood blew out from his mouth and nostrils. He paused and looked around, and to his dismay he saw that one solitary Indian was close upon him. Compelled to pause for breath, he called to the Indian in Crow language (which the Blackfeet understood to some extent) and begged for his life. The Indian, intent only on his prize, replied by seizing in both hands the spear he was carrying and making a desperate lunge at Colter. Colter seized the spear shaft near the head, and the Indian, himself nearly exhausted, tripped and fell at the same instant. The iron spearhead broke off in Colter's hands and he instantly fell upon the prostrate Indian, who now in turn begged Colter in the Crow language to spare his life. Colter was no more accommodating than his foe had been. Stabbing the Indian to death, he took the spearhead and resumed his flight, feeling, as he said, "as if he had not run a mile."

The crowd behind were now furious at having lost another of their number, and on they came like a "legion of devils," as Colter put it, howling and gesticulating with rage. But Colter was again too much for them. The friendly fringe of willows on the bank of the Madison was growing nearer every moment. Reaching it at last, Colter darted through and his quick eye discovered near at hand an asylum of refuge in the form of a huge beaver house on the bank. As is well known, these houses are closed on the outside, the only entrance being under water. It was a risky venture, but Colter resolved to try it. He didn't have to wait to undress, as most swimmers do. Diving into the water, he made for the house and found an entrance large enough for his body. He climbed into the upper story and was soon sitting high and dry in a kind of shelter such as probably no man ever sought refuge in before. If he found any beaver there he didn't bother to kill them.

He escaped not a moment too soon. The tread of the Indians quickly told him that they had reached the river. For some time he could hear them all around, even clambering over the beaver house. It was a terrible moment. Would they suspect where he was? Would they smash the house in? Would they set it on fire? Fortunately they did none of these things. It evidently never occurred to the Indians that Colter had turned beaver, and so after a while they scattered for further search. Colter stuck snugly to his hiding place, and very wisely so, for in about two hours he heard the Indians again. Again they withdrew and Colter heard nothing more of them. He remained under cover until dark when, beaver-like, he ventured forth, and if any Indians had been about they might have thought that he *was* a beaver gliding noiselessly through the water. Swimming ashore, he paused to get his bearings, saw the low mountain pass far to the eastward where his only hope lay, and started off in that direction. He did not take the easy way through the pass for fear the Indians might be there, but scaled the almost perpendicular mountain wall on one side. There was snow on the mountains and this was another peril. Without food, without shelter, without weapons except the captured spear head, with his feet torn and bleeding from his long race over ground covered with sharp stones and the prickly pear, and now away up in the snow of the mountains, it certainly seemed as if no human being could survive such dangers. But physical endurance is a wonderful thing, and Colter found strength to keep on. Day and night for eleven days, with only a snatch of rest and a bite of food now and then, he held his way over the mountain, down into the valley of the Yellowstone and down that stream to Lisa's fort. The men at the fort did not recognize him at first and doubtless would not have believed his story if his terrible plight had not been proof of its truth.

18

"CAN YOU BLOT OUT THOSE STARS?"

Myron Angel

In 1860 the young Paiute leader Numaga made the following speech to the council of his tribe and representatives of the Shoshones and Bannocks at Pyramid Lake, Nevada. It is reproduced here by historian Myron Angel from interviews with Indians who were present. The incident that caused the council to be called was the kidnapping of an Indian girl by white prospectors. Just as Numaga finished his speech a messenger rode up and announced that Paiute braves had caught and killed the prospectors and rescued the girl. Hearing the news, Numaga declared there was no longer need for counsel because the white soldiers would now come to kill them. He was correct. The Army attacked in what became known as the Pyramid Valley War. As Numaga predicted, the Paiutes could not blot out the stars.

At the Pyramid Lake council [a] young Paiute chief named Numaga was pleading for peace. Historian Myron Angel, who interviewed Paiute Indians in later years, recorded his eloquent plea:

> You would make war upon the whites. I ask you to pause
> and reflect. The white men are like the stars over your heads.
> You have wrongs, great wrongs, that rise up like those moun-
> tains before you. But can you, from the mountaintops, reach

and blot out those stars? Your enemies are like the sands in the beds of your own rivers. When taken away they only give place for more to come and settle there. Could you defeat the whites of Nevada, from over the mountains in California would come to help them an army of white men that would cover your country like a blanket. What hope is there for the Pah-Ute? From where is to come your guns, your powder, your lead, your dried meats to live upon, and hay to feed your ponies with while you carry on this war? Your enemies have all of these things, more than they can use. They will come like the sand in a whirlwind and drive you from your homes. You will be forced among the barren rocks of the north, where your ponies will die; where you will see the women and old men starve, and listen to the cries of your children for food. I love my people; let them live; and when their spirits shall be called to the Great Camp in the southern sky, let their bones rest where their fathers were buried.

19

"I WILL FIGHT NO
MORE FOREVER"

The foredoomed and hopeless efforts of the Western tribes to protect their homes from Manifest Destiny and the United States Army produced several examples of military genius—notably among the Apaches and Kiowa-Comanches. But no one in the long years of the Indian wars led his people with more wisdom and bravery than Chief Joseph of the Nez Percé. Finally, on October 5, 1877, on Snake Creek in Montana, even genius could not cope with overwhelming odds. Here is a reporter from Harper's Weekly's *account of the end of freedom for the few Nez Percé still alive.*

On September 30 Colonel Miles made a sudden attack on the enemy, whose camp was situated on a bench or flat in the creek bottom. The Indians occupied the crests of the surrounding hills, and repulsed the charge made on the right by three companies of the Seventh Cavalry. A line of dead horses marked the course of the charge; and the loss, either killed or wounded, of every commissioned officer but one, of every first sergeant, and many non-commissioned officers, told how coolly it was received. . . . The men dismounted, tied their lariats round the left arm, and led their horses. Whenever a soldier stopped a moment, his horse would quietly graze—a strange sight on a battlefield! The Indians were finally forced to abandon their camp and to occupy the adjacent ravines, which were well protected from the fire, and which they honey-combed with pits and bombproofs. The Nez Percés occupied and held the crests on the north immediately overlooking their own position. Things remained in this condition until the surrender.

The same bugler who sounded "To the charge!" on the 30th, trumpeting the death-call of so many brave fellows, now blew the calming and welcome call of "Cease firing." The effect on the Indian camp was almost instantaneous. Where, a moment before, not a head was to be seen nor any sign of life, the ravines now swarmed with people, and little children capered in the sunshine and laughed in the face of death. They seemed to be the swarthy children of the earth, born in a moment, cast forth as if by magic.

General Howard arrived on October 4, bringing with him his two herders, "Captain John" and "George," friendly Nez Percés. Both these men had daughters in the hostile camp. Captain John is a friend of long standing to the whites. He fought by the side of Steptoe, and helped him during his retreat. One parley with Joseph, held on the 2d of October, had been unsuccessful; but after much discussion with the chief, old Captain John, with tears in his eyes, announced the surrender as concluded by Joseph's final reply.

Our artist was the only person present who committed the proceedings to writing, and took the reply as it fell from the lips of the speaker. Joseph's little girl was lost in the hills during the first day's fight, his brother was killed, his relatives dead or fugitives; he upheld now only a lost cause. His answer was: "Tell General Howard I know his heart. What he told me before, I have it in my heart. I am tired of fighting. Our chiefs are killed; Looking-Glass is dead, Ta-hool-hool-shute is dead. The old men are all dead. It is the young men who say 'Yes' or 'No.' He who led on the young men is dead. It is cold, and we have no blankets; the little children are freezing to death. My people, some of them, have run away to the hills, and have no blankets, no food. No one knows where they are—perhaps freezing to death. I want to have time to look for my children, and see how many of them I can find. Maybe I shall find them among the dead. Hear me, my chiefs! I am tired; my heart is sick and sad. From where the sun now stands I will fight no more forever."

Attended by five warriors, he on horseback, they on foot, Joseph rode slowly up the hill, where General Howard and Colonel Miles stood to receive him. His hands were crossed on the pommel of the saddle, and his head was bowed upon his breast. After receiving him, General Howard and Colonel Miles mounted their horses, and accompanied the chief to Miles's tent.

Part Three

◆

THE NAVAJOS

The Navajos had held their own fairly well against Spanish and Mexican pressure, defending the homeland they called Dine'tah in the northwest corner of New Mexico. But the United States took the territory from Mexico in 1847. In the Treaty of Guadalupe Hidalgo, Mexico required the United States to respect the land and water rights of its Pueblo Indians allies, but there was nothing to protect the Navajos from land-hungry whites. Shortly after the U.S. occupation, headmen of fifteen of the Navajo clans met with a representative of the new government and signed the Bear Springs treaty, promising an end to raiding by Navajos and protection of the tribe from Mexican slave and scalp hunters. (The territorial governor had been paying hunters $10 per Navajo or Apache scalp, including those of women and children.) The Navajos were to return any Mexican captives they might hold and satisfy Mexican claims for stolen cattle. The Mexicans (now American citizens) were to return the Navajo children they held as slaves. The Navajos returned herds of cattle but the whites made no effort to keep their promises. Slave raiding continued, retaliatory raids resumed, and battles ensued, each followed by a new treaty in which the Navajos were pushed westward and made to return stolen cattle. But there is no record that white authorities even tried to return captured Navajo children. Slave owners, perhaps fearing an unprecedented outbreak of honor among territorial authorities, baptized the young slaves as soon as they bought them, making them "Christians" and thus not subject to return to their "pagan" parents. In August 1849, Lieutenant Colonel John Washington, military commander of the territory, organized a full-scale invasion of the Navajo homeland, intending to crush tribal resistance and open its lands to white settlement.

20

THE MURDER OF NARBONA

Franc Johnson Newcomb

The following incident is from Hosteen Klah: Navajo Medicine Man and Sand Painter, *by Franc Johnson Newcomb. Narbona was Klah's great-grandfather. Like most tribes, the Navajos operated an almost pure democracy, selecting leaders for specific projects or problems. Narbona had been for many years one of those working for peace with the whites. He was eighty-three years old and crippled with arthritis when Colonel Washington's troops shot him in the back. Such treachery was not uncommon. For example, when gold was found up the Gila River, the Mangus Colorado and other leaders of the Gila Apaches were invited to a great Peace Banquet at Silver City. When the Indians were seated, a concealed cannon loaded with grapeshot was fired down the banquet table. Few Apaches escaped. (If you enjoy irony, note as you read the following that today when Navajos cross the Chuskas between their capitol at Window Rock and Sheep Springs, they drive over Washington Pass, named by white mapmakers for the murderous Colonel.)*

The Navahos of the eastern division were dismayed at the size of this army and the speed at which they were approaching. Families were then living

From Hosteen Klah: Navajo Medicine Man, Franc Johnson Newcomb (University of Oklahoma Press). Copyright 1946, University of Oklahoma Press.

in their fields, and the crops had not been harvested. Narbona collected fifteen horses, ten mules, and about fifty sheep to deliver to the soldiers with the request that the commander avoid the Naschiti cornfields where the hogans were located. Colonel Washington replied that he could not do so, as his horses and mules must feed on the cornfields. So the Navaho families gathered all the food they could carry, packed their possessions on their horses, and fled to the mountains.

The troops left the Río Chaco at the Big Bend and marched to the Tunicha Valley, destroying all the cornfields along their way, and always aware that hidden Navahos were keeping watch on their progress. Narbona had received reports from the army scouts informing him of the purpose and the destination of the troops. When he heard that the council meeting would be held on the western side of the mountains at the mouth of Canyon de Chelly, he decided he could not attend in person. He conferred with Chief José Largo, who was also quite old and infirm, and they decided to ask for a meeting with Colonel Washington, suggesting the names of two younger Navaho leaders to act as their proxies.

Wishing to appear before the white commander in the dignified role of a great Navaho chief, Narbona called together the majority of the Navaho men in his section, who may have numbered about eight hundred warriors. A smaller group was sent on ahead, driving one thousand sheep and a few head of cattle in obedience to the demand that all stolen livestock must be returned. Three of the younger chiefs asked to be given an interview with Colonel Washington and Mr. James Calhoun, superintendent of Indian affairs, to find out exactly what the government wished the Navahos to do. This delegation was informed that if they did not comply with the terms of the Nuby Treaty (Bear Springs) and give up all Mexican captives, all murderers of Mexicans who had found sanctuary among them, and all Mexican livestock, a body of troops would be sent to enforce their doing so. These two Navahos promised to send word to all other chiefs to be in camp tomorrow at noon and have these matters settled.

The next day, August 31, 1849, Narbona and his men rode to the guard lines of the army camp, where the main body halted and Narbona with his headmen were escorted to the tent of Colonel Washington. The Simpson report describes Narbona in these words: "Another man who was quite old and of very large frame, had a grave and contemplative countenance not unlike (as many of the officers remarked) that of General Washington. He wore a striped, hand-woven blanket over his shoulders." To this group, Calhoun proceeded to explain the terms of the treaty, with

Mr. Conkling as interpreter. Lieutenant Simpson gives us a detailed report of this conference, held between the government officials and the three elderly Navaho chieftains—Narbona, José Largo, and Archuletta.

Mr. Calhoun: Tell them they are lawfully in the jurisdiction of the United States, and they must respect that jurisdiction.

Interpreter: They say they understand it.

Mr. Calhoun: Tell them that after the treaty is made, their friends will be the friends of the United States, and their enemies the enemies of the United States.

Tell them when any difficulty occurs between them and any other nation, by appealing to the United States they may get redress.

Are they willing to be at peace with all the friends of the United States?

Interpreter: They say they are willing.

Mr. Calhoun: Tell them that by the treaty which it is proposed to make with them, all trade between themselves and other nations will be recognized as under regulations to be prescribed by the United States.

Colonel Washington: And the object of this is to prevent their being imposed upon by bad men.

Interpreter: They understand it, and are content.

Mr. Calhoun: Tell them if any wrong is done them by a citizen of the United States, or by a Mexican, he or they shall be punished by the United States, as if the wrong had been done by a citizen of the United States, and on a citizen of the United States.

Interpreter: They say they understand it, and it is all right.

Mr. Calhoun: That the people of the United States shall go in and out of their country without molestation, under such regulations as shall be prescribed by the United States.

Interpreter: They say they will.

Mr. Calhoun: Tell them that, by this treaty, the government of the United States are to be recognized as having the right to establish military posts in their country wherever they may think it necessary, in order to [assure] the protection of them and their rights.

That the government of the United States claim the right to have their boundaries fixed and marked, so as to prevent any misunderstanding on this point between them and their neighbors.

Interpreter: They say they are very glad.

Mr. Calhoun: For and in consideration of all this, and a faithful performance of the treaty, the government of the United States will, from time to time, make them presents, such as axes, hoes, and other farming utensils, blankets, etc.

Interpreter: They say it is all right.

After all nine points of the treaty had been explained to the chiefs and other headmen in attendance and they had indicated their approval, Narbona and José Largo expressed their wish to be excused from attending the council at De Chelly, stating that they would send delegates to take their places. Papers were signed giving powers of attorney to Armijo and Pedro José, both of whom spoke enough Spanish to make themselves understood. These two younger chiefs now had authority to act for them at the De Chelly council, in the same manner and to the same extent as if they were present.

The council having ended, the group of Navahos walked back to their tribesmen and mounted their horses. It was a colorful spectacle: all wore red, yellow, or blue striped blankets and some wore helmets topped by eagle feathers, while nearly all carried rifles erect in their right hands. Sandoval, the Navaho from Cebolleto, was riding back and forth in front of this group, pointing out the error of their ways and warning them of the consequences they might incur when suddenly someone espied a Navaho on a horse that had belonged to a Mexican trooper and had been missing for a couple of days. Word was sent to Colonel Washington, who immediately demanded its return. The Navaho youth riding the horse declared it was his own and immediately disappeared down a side gully. Then the Colonel ordered the Navahos to hand over one of their best horses to replace the one that had been stolen, but as the troopers came toward them, the Navahos became frightened and rode pell-mell down the slope in hasty retreat. The guards were ordered to fire a round of shots after them, and, as there were more than one hundred riflemen in the guard unit, the result was disastrous for the Navahos. They had halted at a little distance to collect their dead and wounded when the cannon sent its missiles among them, thus catching them off guard.

Narbona had been one of the last to retreat and, being in direct line of fire, was mortally wounded. Sixteen or seventeen Navahos were killed outright, and several others died later of the wounds they had received. Narbona lived to reach his hogan and to say farewell to his family. He knew he was about to die, and his last words were, "I am old and it is time for me to go, so do not be sorrowful at my passing, but grieve for the women and children whose men will not return." No other leader has been so long remembered.

Narbona's family prepared his body for burial. He was bathed and sprinkled with sacred corn pollen, then dressed in his finest buckskin garments with silver buttons and belt. Coral and silver beads and silver bracelets were included, and his feathered helmet was placed on his head. One of his long war bows with its quiver of arrows was placed by his side, and his body was wrapped, together with these items, in several layers of blankets, and then enclosed in a large buffalo pelt which was turned with the fur on the inside. The whole roll was then bound with strand after strand of horsehair rope, tied at intervals into the "death knot."

Toward evening, two of his sons saddled and bridled his two favorite horses, the palomino and the gray stallion, tied his body across the saddles, and proceeded slowly to Rock Mesa, where a deep crevice made a natural tomb. Lowering the bundled body into its final resting place, they covered it deeply with grass and small bushes, on top of which they shoveled a thick layer of earth. They then gathered rocks of every size and distributed them so as to completely hide the burial. When this was done, at sunset, they led the horses some distance to the north, as this was the direction his spirit would take on its journey to the "land of spirits." Since they did not wish to remain near the burial because some enemy might locate the spot and open the grave to obtain the wealth of jewelry it contained, they crossed the valley and stopped on a low hill.

Here they killed the horses and then proceeded to chop the saddles and bridles into small bits so that they could be of no possible use to anyone wandering that way. The ax and the shovel they had used were broken and hidden among the stones. As the darkness gathered, they found a sheltered spot where they could view Rock Mesa, found wood for a small fire, and prepared for a long vigil.

Four nights they remained, chanting prayers throughout the hours of darkness and going only short distances for water or wood during the day. They ate no morsel of food during this time and spoke only with signs or shakes of the head. After the fourth night of prayer they believed the Chief's spirit had traveled so far on the Rainbow Trail that their prayers could not reach him, and the next morning they started for home. When they reached the north bank of the Río Tunicha, they built a sweathouse near some rocks that had been recently piled in that spot and spent that day and night in and out of the sweat bath. The next morning they found the clean clothing their wives had left for them under the stones, and burying all the clothing they had worn during the burial, they went home to feast and sleep.

21

BARBONCITO'S
PLEA

For the Navajos things took a drastic turn for the worse in the 1860s. While
the federal army in the east was fighting the Civil War to abolish slavery it was
protecting slave raiders in New Mexico. By 1862 Navajo children were selling
for as much as $400 at auction in Santa Fe, and raid after raid was being made
by New Mexico militiamen under the pretext of recovering stolen sheep and
cattle. Louis Kennan, a Santa Fe physician, wrote in his memoirs that the raiders
admitted that their only motivation was that "the Navajos had a great many
sheep and horses and a great many children." He estimated that as many as six
thousand Navajos were held as slaves and said he knew of no family rich enough
to raise the price who didn't own at least one.

Into this situation rode one of the West's worst scoundrels, General James
H. Carleton, with his brigade of California volunteers. Arriving too late to fight
the Confederates, who had briefly invaded New Mexico territory, he remained
on as military commander.

Carleton had been been persuaded that the homelands of the Navajos and
Jicarilla Apaches were rich in gold. His plan was to hunt down and kill or capture
the Indians who (to use his language) "infested this territory." Survivors would
be penned in reservations, leaving their lands open to mineral exploration and
ranching by whites. For Navajo and Apache reservations Carleton picked almost
worthless land in eastern New Mexico, a treeless plain where a little grove of
cottonwoods gave it the name of Bosque Redondo. There these "wolves of the

mountains" would be held until the old ones died and the young ones became "Christian farmers."

General Carleton expressed his dream in a letter:

> As time elaspes and the race dies out, these islands [reservations] may become less and less, until finally the great sea of white men will engulf them one after another until they become known only in history, and at length are blotted out of even that, forever.

It was genocide refined. On July 1, Carleton called in Kit Carson to put it into effect. Carson added Ute war parties to his thousand-man army, exhorting them to reward themselves by taking Navajo slaves. He conducted a brilliant scorched-earth campaign, sweeping across Navajo country before harvest time, burning cornfields, homes, supplies, slaughtering cattle, keeping the Navajos from collecting food, and shooting down any they could catch. In December Carson rode into Canyon de Chelly, the home of an important Navajo spirit named Talking God, killed or captured the people living there and destroyed homes and food caches. That seems to have broken the tribe's spirit. Some fled west into the Grand Canyon and Utah. But thousands, freezing and famished, came in and surrendered. They were herded away on "The Long Walk" to Bosque Redondo. In his excellent Book of the Navajo, historian Raymond Friday Locke reported that the army shot those too weak to keep up. About 120 died or were killed on the walk and, even under army guard, slave dealers managed to steal three children. Five hard years and nearly 2,000 deaths later, President Andrew Johnson sent General William Tecumseh Sherman to Bosque Redondo to negotiate a treaty. What follows is from the transcript of the Proceedings of the Peace Commission.

General Sherman said: The Commissioners are here now for the purpose of learning and knowing all about your condition and we wish to hear from you the truth and nothing but the truth. We have read in our books and learned from our officers that for many years whether right or wrong the Navajos have been at war with us and that General Carleton had removed you here for the purpose of making you agriculturists—with that view the Government of the United States gave you money and built this fort to protect you until you were able to protect yourselves. We find you have done a good deal of work here in making Acequias, but we find you have no farms, no herds and are now as poor as you were four years ago when the Government brought you here. That before we discuss what we are to do with you, we want to know what you have done in the past and what you think about your reservation here.

Barboncito said: The bringing of us here has caused a great decrease of our numbers, many of us have died, also a great number of our animals. Our Grand-fathers had no idea of living in any other country except our own and I do not think it right for us to do so as we were never taught to. When the Navajos were first created four mountains and four rivers were pointed out to us, inside of which we should live, that was to be our country and was given to us by the first woman of the Navajo tribe. It was told to us by our forefathers, that we were never to move east of the Rio Grande or west of the San Juan rivers and I think that our coming here has been the cause of so much death among us and our animals. Our God when he created (the woman I spoke of) gave us this piece of land and created it specially for us and gave us the whitest of corn and the best of horses and sheep. . . . This ground we were brought on, it is not productive, we plant but it does not yield, all the stock we brought here have nearly all died. Because we were brought here we have done all we could possibly do, but found it to be labor in vain, and have therefore quit it, for that reason we have not planted or tried to do anything this year. It is true we put seed in the ground but it would not grow two feet high, the reason I cannot tell, only I think this ground was never intended for us, we know how to irrigate and farm, still we cannot raise a crop here, we know how to plant all kinds of seed, also how to raise stock and take care of it. The Commissioners can see themselves that we have hardly any sheep or horses, nearly all that we brought here have died and that has left us so poor that we have no means where-with to buy others—There are a great many among us who were once well off now they have nothing in their houses to sleep on except gunny sacks, true some of us have a little stock left yet, but not near what we had some years ago, in our old country, for that reason my mouth is dry and my head hangs in sorrow to see those around me who were at one time well off so poor now. . . . Outside my own country we cannot raise a crop, but in it we can raise a crop almost anywhere, our families and stock there increase, here they decrease, we know this land does not like us neither does the water. . . . It seems that whatever we do here causes death, some work at the Acequias take sick and die, others die with the hoe in their hands, they go to the river to their waists and suddenly disappear, others have been struck and torn to pieces by lightning. A Rattlesnake bite here kills us, in our own country a Rattle-snake before he bites gives warning which enables us to keep out of its way and if bitten we readily find a cure—here we can find no cure. When one of our big men die, the cries of the women causes the tears to roll down on to my moustache. I then think of my own country. . . . Now I am just like a woman, sorry like a woman in trouble. I want to go and see my own country. If we are taken back to our own country, we will call you our father and mother, if you should only tie a goat there we would all live off it, all of the same opinion. I am speaking for the whole tribe, for their animals from the horse to the dog, also the unborn, all that you have heard now is the truth and is the opinion of the whole tribe. It appears to me that the General commands the whole thing as a god. I hope therefore he will do all he can for the Indian, this hope goes in at my feet and out at my mouth. I am speaking to you (General Sherman) now as if I was speaking to a spirit and I wish you to tell me when you are going to take us to our own country.

General Sherman said: I have listened to all you have said of your people and believe you have told us the truth. . . . For many years we have been collecting Indians on the Indian Territory south of the Arkansas and they are now doing well and have been doing so for many years. We have heard you were not satisfied with this reservation and we have come here to invite some of your leading men to go and see the Cherokee country and if they liked it we would give you a reservation there. There we will give you cattle to commence with and corn, it being much cheaper there than here; give you schools to educate your children in English or Spanish and take care of you until such time as you will be able to protect yourselves. We do not want you to take our word for it but send some of your wisest men to see for themselves. If you do not want that we will discuss the other proposition of going back to your own country and if we agree we will make a boundary line outside of which you must not go except for the purpose of trading—we must have a clearly defined boundary line and know exactly where you belong to, you must live at peace and must not fight with other Indians. If people trouble you, you must go to the nearest military post and report to the Commanding Officer who will punish those who trouble you. The Army will do the fighting, you must live at peace, if you go to your own country the Utes will be the nearest Indians to you, you must not trouble the Utes and the Utes must not trouble you. If however the Utes or Apaches come into your country with bows and arrows and guns you of course can drive them out but must not follow beyond the boundary line. You must not permit any of your young men to go to the Ute or Apache country to steal—neither must they steal from Mexicans. You can come to the Mexican towns to trade. Any Navajo can now settle in this Territory and he will get a piece of land not occupied, but he will be subject to the laws of the country. Our proposition now is to send some of you at the Government expense to the Indian Territory south of Kansas or if you want to go to your own country you will be sent but not to the whole of it, only a portion which must be well defined.

Barboncito said: I hope to God you will not ask me to go to any other country except my own. It might turn out another Bosque Redondo. They told us this was a good place when we came but it is not.

General Sherman said: We merely made the proposition to send you to the Lower Arkansas country for you to think seriously over it. Tomorrow at 10 o'clock I want the whole tribe to assemble at the back of the Hospital and for you then to delegate ten of your men to come forward and settle about the boundary line of your own country which will be reduced to writing and signed by those ten men.

Barboncito said: I am very well pleased with what you have said, and if we go back to our own country, we are willing to abide by whatever orders are issued to us, we do not want to go to the right or left, but straight back to our own country.

General Sherman said: This is all we have to say to-day to-morrow we will meet again.

May 29th, 1868
FORT SUMNER, NEW MEXICO

The Council met according to adjournment. Present the Commissioners on the part of the United States Government. On the part of the Indians the Navajo nation or tribe.

General Sherman said: We have come from our Capital, Washington, where our Government consists of a President and a great Council. We are empowered to do now what is necessary for your good, but what we do must be submitted to our Great Father in Washington. We heard that you were not satisfied with this Reservation, that your crops failed for three years and that you wanted to go somewhere else. We know that during the time you have been here the Government has fed and done for you what was considered necessary to make you a thriving people; Yesterday we had a long talk with your principal chiefs and then told them, that any Navajo could go wherever he pleased in this territory and settle with his family but if he did he would be subject to the laws of the Territory as a citizen, or we would remove you as a nation or tribe to the lower Canadian and Arkansas if you were pleased to go there—but if neither of these

propositions suited you, we would discuss the other proposition of sending
you to your own country west of the Rio Grande. Barboncito yesterday
insisted strongly on going back to his own country in preference to the
other two propositions. We then asked him and all the Navajos to assemble
here today and for them to select (10) ten of their number as delegates
with whom we would conclude terms of treaty. We want to know if these
ten men have been chosen; the ten men then stood up, viz:

> Delgadito
> Barboncito
> Manuelito
> Largo
> Herrero
> Chiqueto
> Murerto de Hombre
> Hombro
> Narbono
> Armijo

and the Navajos upon being asked if satisfied with these ten men, unanimously responded—Yes—We will now consider these ten men your principal men and we want them to select a chief the remaining to compose his
Council for we cannot talk to all the Navajos. Barboncito was unanimously
elected Chief—now from this time out you must do as Barboncito tells you,
with him we will deal and do all for your good. When we leave here and
go to your own country you must do as he tells you and when you get to
your country you must obey him or he will punish you, if he has not the
power to do so he will call on the soldiers and they will do it. You must
all keep together on the march. Must not scatter for fear some of your
young men might do wrong and get you all into trouble. All these things
will be put down on paper and tomorrow these ten men will sign that paper
and now we want to know about the country you want to go to. We heard
Barboncito yesterday, if there are any others who differ from him, we would
like to hear them, we want also to hear if you want schools in your
country—

Blacksmiths or Carpenters Shops. We want to put everything on
paper so that hereafter there may be no misunderstanding between us, we
want to know if the whole Navajo nation is represented by those present
and if they will be bound by the acts of these ten men—unanimous
response of yes.

Barboncito said: What you have said to me now I never will forget. It is true I never liked this place, and feel sorry for being here, from here I would like to go back the same road we came by way of Tecalote, Bernal, Tijeras and Taralto. All the people on the road are my friends. After I cross the Rio Grande river I want to visit the Pueblo villages, I want to see the Pueblo Indians to make friends with them. I want to go to Cañon de Chelly leaving Pueblo village Laguna to the left. I will take all the Navajos to Cañon de Chelly leave my own family there—taking the rest and scattering them between San Mateo mountain and San Juan river. I said yesterday this was the heart of the Navajo country. In this place there is a mountain called the Sierra Chusque or mountain of agriculture from which (when it rains) the water flows in abundance creating large sand bars on which the Navajos plant their corn; it is a fine country for stock or agriculture—there is another mountain called the Mesa Calabasa where these beads which we wear on our necks have been handed down from generation to generation and where we were told by our forefathers never to leave our own country. For that reason I want to go back there as quick as possible and not remain here another day. . . . After we get back to our country it will brighten up again and the Navajos will be as happy as the land, black clouds will rise and there will be plenty of rain. Corn will grow in abundance and everything look happy. Today is a day that anything black or red does not look right everything should be white or yellow representing the flower and the corn. I want to drop this conversation now and talk about Navajo children held as prisoners by Mexicans. Some of those present have lost a brother or a sister and I know that they are in the hands of the Mexicans. I have seen some myself.

General Sherman said: About their children being held as Peons by Mexicans—you ought to know that there is an Act of Congress against it. About four years ago we had slaves and there was a great war about it, now there are none. Congress our great council passed a law prohibiting peonage in New Mexico. So that if any Mexican holds a Navajo in peonage he (the Mexican) is liable to be put in the penitentiary. We do not know that there are any Navajos held by Mexicans as Peons but if there are, you can apply to the judges of the Civil Courts and the Land Commissioners. They are the proper persons and they will decide whether the Navajo is to go back to his own people or remain with the Mexican. That is a matter with which we have nothing to do. What do you say about schools, Blacksmiths and Carpenter Shops for the purpose of teaching your children.

Barboncito said: We would like to have a blacksmith Shop as a great number of us can work at the trade, we would like a carpenter's Shop and if a school was established among us I am satisfied a great number would attend it. I like it very well. Whatever orders you leave here you may rely upon their being obeyed.

General Sherman said: Whatever we promise to do you can depend upon its being done.

Colonel Samuel F. Tappan asked: How many Navajos are among the Mexicans now?

Answer: Over half of the tribe.

Question: How many have returned within the five years?

Answer: Cannot tell.

Sherman said: We will do what we can to have your children returned to you. Our government is determined that enslavement of the Navajos shall cease and those who are guilty of holding them as peons shall be punished.

All are free now in this country to go and come as they please if children are held in peonage the courts will decide; you can go where any Navajos are and General Getty will give you an order or send a soldier and if the Navajo peons wishes to go back or remain he can please himself, we will not use force, the courts must decide. . . .

Then General Sherman said: We have marked off a reservation for you, including the Cañon de Chelly and part of the valley of the San Juan, it is about (100) one hundred miles square. It runs as far south as Canon Bonito and includes the Chusca mountain but not the Mesa Calabesa you spoke of; that is the reservation we suggest to you, it also includes the Ceresca mountain and the bend of the San Juan river, not the upper waters.

Barboncito said: We are very well pleased with what you have said and well satisfied with that reservation. It is the very heart of our country and is more than we ever expected to get. . . .

Ganado Mucho said: After what the Commissioners have said, I do not think anybody has anything to say. After we go back to our own country it will be the same as it used to be. We have never found any person heretofore who told us what you now have and when we return to our own country we will return you our best thanks. We understand the good news you have told us, to be right and we like it very much; we have been waiting for a long time to hear the good words you have now told us, about going back to our own country and I will not stop talking until I have told all the tribe the good news.

General Sherman said: Now we will adjourn until Monday the 1st day of June 1868 at 9 o'clock a.m. when we will meet and sign the treaty.

On June 1st the treaty was signed. That same day the Navajos began the return half of their Long Walk back to their homeland.

22

THE HOGAN

Gladys Reichard

Gladys Reichard (1893–1955) was one of the first women anthropologists to study the Navajo culture—living among the Dineh for thirty years. She wrote Dezba, Woman of the Desert in an effort to present the Dineh's way of life in fictional—more palatable to white readers—form. Most of the homesteads scattered across the Navajo reservation still have a hogan built as the Navajos were taught to build them by Changing Woman, one of their greatest spirits. Navajo curing ceremonials must be held in these structures.

The week after the dipping was a busy one for Dezba at home. Here it was cool, clean, and pleasant, for Dezba's dome-shaped *hogan* was set in the midst of her range on the high well-wooded mesa. Her house, which was one of the four in the cluster, was the largest, for it was used as the ceremonial *hogan* when necessary. Dezba's brother, Lassos-a-warrior, was an important leader of curing ceremonies, often called "sings," and there were many occasions when one of them was held at her home. The ceremonies required a special house, preferably a large one, and Dezba lived in this one. When, for five or nine days, it was needed for religious purposes, she moved out and lived in one of the other *hogans* for the time. She considered it no inconvenience to do so, for the fact of having a "sing" in the house brought blessings and good fortune to it.

The house was a large one, built of logs covered with adobe plaster. As usual it faced the east and in front of it, where most of the household activities were carried on in summer, there was a broad space which seemed to be paved. Anyone who used water threw it just outside the door. It dried almost instantly in the blazing sun. The impact of suddenly thrown water and the constant tread of feet made the sand hard and firm. Every day one of the women swept it like a floor, and daily a larger area became smooth and hardened.

There was a smokehole east of the center of the *hogan*, under which an open fire could be made, but Dezba used a fine ivory enamel cookstove which had a warming oven. In the summer it was set outside where she sometimes used it for baking. More generally, however, cooking was done over the open fire not far from the house door. The fireplace was large, near it were several grills on which meat was broiled; the coffeepots, stewpans, and skillets were all within reach of the fire. Under some trees there was a cupboard, and in it, out of reach of dogs, cats and goats, the flour, baking-powder, and coffee were kept. The trees furnished convenient spaces into which small objects were tucked and from which sacks, containing all manner of possessions, were hung. At a little distance a cedar tree formed one of the supports of a shade which served as a storage place for bulky objects. Wagon-wheels and other things which animals could not harm leaned against it at the bottom. Hay, corn and other food products dried on its roof safe from marauding goats. Horses were sometimes corraled under the shade. From one tree to another wires were strung on which surplus clothing, blankets and sheepskins were aired or stored. The *hogan* in summer was used chiefly for storage and sleeping.

About a quarter of a mile from the house in a hollow into which a wash led, there was a cornpatch of about an acre. The deep layer of sand here kept the precious water of melting snows and spring rains from rapid evaporation. In this seemingly unlikely spot the corn had been planted and, undiscouraged by the depth of the sand, the roots had pushed hopefully until they found moisture. As the plants grew, the season became drier and, instead of growing to large stalks and leaves, they had thrust roots ever deeper and deeper. Now in the harvest season they stood short, stocky, and full of ears, and so deeply rooted that a strong man could not pull one out.

2 3

LAUGHING BOY

Oliver La Farge

As an anthropology student at Harvard, Oliver La Farge spent time doing research on the Navajo Reservation. Later, while living in New Orleans he tried to write a short story about the impact a sophisticated woman of the streets would have on one of his Navajo friends. Laughing Boy grew into a novel. After eleven rejections, Houghton Mifflin published it in 1927 and it became the first Southwestern book to win the Pulitzer Prize for fiction. La Farge lived out his life at Santa Fe as a key figure in the American Association for Indian Affairs. I was proud to claim him as a friend. What follows is the opening chapter of an American classic.

I

He was riding the hundred miles from T'o Tlakai to Tsé Lani to attend a dance, or rather, for the horse-racing that would come afterwards. The sun was hot and his belly was empty, but life moved in rhythm with his pony loping steadily as an engine down the miles. He was lax in the saddle, leaning back, arm swinging the rope's end in time to the horse's lope. His new red headband was a bright colour among the embers of the sun-struck desert, undulating like a moving graph of the pony's lope, or the music of his song—

'*Nashdui bik'é dinni, eya-a, eyo-o* . . .
Wildcat's feet hurt, *eya-a, eyo-o* . . .'

Rope's end, shoulders, song, all moved together, and life flowed in one stream. He threw his head back to sing louder, and listened to the echo from the cliffs on his right. He was thinking about a bracelet he should make, with four smooth bars running together, and a turquoise in the middle—if he could get the silver. He wished he could work while riding; everything was so perfect then, like the prayers, *hozoji nashad,* travelling in beauty. His hands, his feet, his head, his insides all were *hozoji,* all were very much alive. He whooped and struck up the Magpie Song till the empty desert resounded—

'*A-a-a-iné, a-a-a-iné,
Ya-a-iné-ainé, ko-ya-ainé* . . .'

He was lean, slender, tall, and handsome, Laughing Boy, with a new cheap headband and a borrowed silver belt to make ragged clothes look fine.

At noon, having no money, he begged coffee from a trader at Chinlee and went on, treasuring his hunger because of the feasting to come. Now he began to meet Navajos of all ages, riding to the dance. The young men bunched together—a line of jingling bridles, dark, excited faces, flashing silver, turquoise, velveteen shirts, dirty, ragged overalls, a pair of plaid calico leggins, a pair of turkey-red ones. Some of them were heavy with jewelry; Horse Giver's Son wore over four hundred dollars in silver alone; most of them had more than Laughing Boy. They stopped to look at his bow-guard, which he himself had made.

'I am a good jeweller,' he said, elated; 'I make silver run like a song.'

'You should make a song about yourself,' they told him, 'and teach the burros to sing it.'

'Have you had any rain up by T'o Tlakai?'

'No, it is just like last year. It is the devil. The grass is all dried up and the sheep are dying.'

'They had a cloudburst over by T'isya Lani. It washed out the dam.'

'It washed out the missionary's house, they say. His wife ran out in something thin and got wet, they say.'

'*Ei-yei!*'

Tall Hunter and his wife drove past in a brand-new buckboard behind two fast-trotting, grey mules. He owned over five hundred head of horses, and his wife had thick strings of turquoise and coral around her neck.

'His brother is in jail for stealing cattle, they say.'

'What is jail?' asked Laughing Boy.

Slender Hair explained: 'It is something the American Chief does to you. He puts you in a room of stone, like a Moqui house, only it is dark and you can't get out. People die there, they say. They haven't any room; they can't see anything, they say. I do not like to talk about it.'

Laughing Boy thought, I should rather die. He wanted to ask more, but was ashamed to show his ignorance before these southern Navajos, many of whom wore hats like Americans, and who knew so much of Americans' ways.

They raced. His horse was tired, but it won by a nose, which was just as well, since he had bet his bow-guard. Now he had six dollars. He hoped there would be gambling.

Tsé Lani showed a distant bonfire in the dusk, with mounted Indians moving in on it like spokes of a wheel. About two hundred young men came together half a mile away, making their ponies prance, exchanging greetings. Crooked Ear carried the ceremonial wand. Now they all lined up, with the dull, red sunset behind their black figures. They started going like getting off to a race, right into a gallop, yelling. Over by the fire was shouting, and another line tearing towards them. The world was full of a roar of hooves and two walls of noise rushing together, the men leaning forward over their horses' necks, mouths wide. 'E-e-e-e!' They met in a great swirl of plunging, dodging horses, and swept on all together, whooping for dear life, with the staff in front of them, almost onto the fire, then dissolved with jingling of bits, laughter, and casual jokes as they unsaddled by the pool.

The steady motion of excitement was slowed then, in the last of the day, by the rocks and the piñons, by the reflection of the sky in the pool where flat, vague silhouettes of horses stooped to drink. The voices of many people, the twinkling of fires continued the motif, joining the time of quiet with elation past and to come; a little feeling of expectation in Laughing Boy's chest, a joyful emptiness, part hunger and part excitement.

He tended his pony minutely. The little mare had had two days of loping; shortly he wanted to race her; three days of rest would not be too much. She was his only horse; he had traded two others for her. She was tough, as a horse had to be to live at all in the North country. He ran his hands down her withers, feeling the lean, decisive muscles. In all that section, from Dennihuitso to Biltabito, from T'o Tlikahn to T'o Baka, where he knew every horse by sight, she was the best, but she would meet some competition here. He felt as if she were his own creation, like the bowguard; at least he had selected her, as he had chosen the soft blue turquoise in the ornament. Little, compact, all black save for the tiny white spot on her forehead, she had the ugly Roman nose of character. She was like an arrow notched to a taut bowstring—a movement of the hand would release level flight swiftly to a mark.

He was thinking some of these things, half hearing the noises of the people. Just like the prayer, 'travelling in beauty.' It would be good to be a singer as well, to express all these things through the prayers. He would like to know many of them, to learn to conduct the Mountain Chant, and know all the beautiful stories behind the songs and ceremonies inside the Dark Circle of Branches. That would be really on the trail of beauty; to work in silver and turquoise, own soft-moving ponies, and lead the Mountain Chant. Just thinking about it was good. It made him feel cool inside.

> '*Hozho hogahn ladin nasha woyen* . . .
> In the house of happiness there I wander . . .'

All the time he was passing his hand along the pony's neck, along her back, feeling the lines of tough muscles.

'*E-ya*, Grandfather, are you going to dance with the horse?' Jesting Squaw's Son called over to him, 'food is ready.'

'*Hakone!*' He returned abruptly to the quick-moving life of the dance. 'I can eat it. I did not know you were coming.'

'I came when I heard you were to race your mare. I think there is money to be made, then, and I want to see her race.'

They went up arm in arm into the crowd, pushing their way into the circle around one of the fires. Busy housewives gave them coffee, the big pot of meat was passed over, and a flat, round loaf of rubbery, filling bread. The meat was the backbone of a yearling calf, boiled with corn. It was good. He munched joyfully, feeling his empty stomach fill, wadding himself with bread, washing it down with bitter coffee. A couple of Americans carrying their own plates dipped in gingerly. A Hopi, having collected everything he could possibly eat, sat down officiously beside them to air his school English and his bourgeois superiority.

I I

A small drum beating rapidly concentrated the mixed noises into a staccato unison. Young men gathered about the drummer. Laughing Boy might have eaten more, but he left the fire immediately with Jesting Squaw's Son. Some one led off high-pitched at full voice,

'*Yo-o galeana, yo-o galeana, yo-o galeana . . .*'

By the end of the second word the crowd was with him; more young men hurried up to join the diapason,

'*Galeana ena, galeana eno, yo-o ay-e hena ena . . .*'

They put their arms over each other's shoulders, swaying in time to the one drum that ran like a dull, glowing thread through the singing, four hundred young men turning loose everything they had.

24

THE DEATH OF OLD MAN HAT

Walter Dyk

The following is from Son of Old Man Hat, a Navajo Autobiography, *in which anthropologist Walter Dyk recorded the memories of an old man called Left Handed. Here Left Handed (then known as Son of Old Man Hat) recalls the death and funeral of his father. Compare this with the funeral of Narbona. While some Navajos today follow standard American funeral practices, and only a few still kill the deceased's favorite horse, many of the traditional people still follow funeral customs much like this one. Note that Left Handed's wife believes a witch has caused her husband's sickness and wants the singer to do a sucking ceremony, in which "bean" or "bone" blown by the witch into the victim's breast is sucked out. And note the singer's traditional attitude about death. The complex Navajo shaman religion is focused on curing by restoring harmony with life and has nothing to do with life after death.*

The old man was about to die. The singer started singing and waving his eagle feathers over him, and my mother said, "Don't just wave those feathers. I didn't send for you for that. Get out that bad thing that's in him. Try to suck it out. Save him for me." But he said, "No, I don't like to do that. He's pretty far gone. If I cut him it'll be the end. I don't want to do him any harm. I don't want to hurt him. He's hurt enough now." My mother kept begging him to take out the "bean" that was in him, but he kept on saying, no. So he didn't, and nothing was done for him; everybody was just crying all night, and this man, Plucked Whiskers, was crying too.

He said to my father, Choclays Kinsman, "It's all right, my uncle, everybody's dying off. Every creature on this earth is dying. Even the mountains are caving down. He was like Blanca Peak, or like Mount Taylor, or like Carriso Mountain, or the La Plata Range, like Gobernador Knob or San Francisco Peak. He was like one of the mountains. He had everything and knew everything, and everyone knew him, and everybody named him. So don't be worrying about him. We'll all be gone. We want to take care of and look after ourselves. While we're still alive we should help and take care of each other. When we die that's the end of it. Nothing can be done about death. We've all got to die. When we die we're gone forever. No one will bring us back. So there's no use worrying so much about it."

He was lying still, just breathing a little all that night, and just as morning came, just as you saw a little white and blue sky coming over the mountain, he passed away. He died that morning and all his relatives and friends began to cry. As soon as he died they told me to go and round up the horses, and while his relatives and friends were holding him and crying I started out, and while I was running I was crying too. I caught my father's racehorse and rounded up the others and drove them back. Everybody had left him and come outside.

We used to have a blue horse. It was the best horse in the bunch. I put a rope around that horse's neck and led him over to the hogan where my father was and put the saddle and bridle on him. Some of his relatives were still inside, fixing him up. They put new moccasins on his feet and cut a great big buckskin of his in half and put it around him for leggings. They dressed him in all his clothes and put on two bunches of beads that he had.

When he was dressed one of his nephews and I went in and got him. Our hair was untied, and we were covered with ashes. We put him on the horse and all his things beside him. There were two big bundles of stuff, and then we started off. The other fellow was leading the horse, and I was by my father, holding him, so he wouldn't fall off. We went to a little cliff and put him in a hole under the rocks and built a wall around him and covered him with rocks and all the poles we could find, and over that we put some dirt. We fixed him so nothing would bother him. After that we destroyed all his things and faced the horse to the north and killed it.

Then we started back, running and jumping over the bushes, so no evil spirit would catch up with us. When we got home we set fire to the hogan in which he died, and after that his brother, Choclays Kinsman, came up with a rifle and shot the racehorse. We were standing by him, and he said to us, "Face the horse to the north." We went over and faced it north, and then he shot another. We went over and faced that one to the north again, and he turned around and shot another one, and we faced that one to the north. As he was turning to shoot again a fellow came up and grabbed his rifle and begged him not to kill any more.

A little way from home they had a pail of water ready for us to wash in. It was mixed with the leaves of a tree struck by lightning. We washed the ashes off ourselves over there and then went back in the other hogan. There was a place for us two, right beside each other, on the north side. Everybody else was on the south side. When we got inside we put our clothes back on, and while we were dressing the others started cooking. It was almost noon. All this time we hadn't eaten anything. They'd said, "Nobody should eat until everything has been fixed up."

When the food was cooked we started eating. We had ours apart from the other people. They said to us, "You two have to eat separately, not with the others, and you shouldn't leave anything in the dish. You must eat up everything. If you want more they'll put some in your dish, just enough for you to eat. And you mustn't touch anything, nor bother anything. You mustn't bother the fire. And nobody should walk in front of you, or go near you. You two mustn't separate. Whenever one wants to go out to take a leak, you should both go. Even though the other doesn't need to, you both should go. You have to stay right by each other, so nothing will go between you. None of you should go between them," they said. "When any of you go out you shouldn't go towards the north, nor look towards the north. As soon as you go out turn around towards the south. You should only be on the south side of the hogan, and none of you should look around. You might see something. If you look around you might see evil spirits, and that'll be bad for you. You'll get sick from it and die. You mustn't say, 'evil spirits,' and you mustn't say, 'grave,' and you shouldn't face toward where the hogan was burned. You have to do these things and not say things like that for four days. During the four days you must all be quiet. Don't do anything, or say anything out loud. You must all go easy on everything."

Three days after he was buried they got some soap-weed and hauled some water. That was for us and the others too, but ours was separate. Early the next morning we all got up and washed ourselves all over. When we were through the two of us washed our clothes and hung them up to dry. It was before the sun was up. Then the other fellow and I took our corn pollen and went out towards where we'd buried the body. Quite a way from the hogan we stopped and put some pollen in our mouths and some on top of our heads, and some we sprinkled about, naming the body and saying, "You've gone away from us now by yourself." Those were the only words we said, and then we turned around and started home.

Inside the hogan we gave the corn pollen to the fellow sitting by the doorway, and then all the people began taking some and saying their prayers, saying, "We'll live long, and we'll live good lives. We'll be on the good path, on the happy path all the rest of our lives." After that they talked to us, telling us how to take care of ourselves, and how to take care of the others. "In that way," they said, "you'll live a long and good life. And some day the same thing will happen to you. When you die you'll be fixed just the same way."

Part Four

◆

THE HISPANOS

Some say the West, too, has been homogenized in the great American melting pot and that only the names remain as reminders of lost cultures. The names are there of course: on the rivers, the Rio Grande, Las Animas Perdida, Gila, Colorado, Tecolote; on mountain ranges named Sangre de Cristo, Chuska, and Lukachukai; on terrain features called Kaibab, Coconino, Kletha, Dzilidushzhinih; and in places that sound like a litany—San Antonio, San Francisco, San Juan, Santa Barbara—or a chant—Moenkopi, Tesuque, Leupp, Nazhoni, Nakabito, Toadlena, Moqui, Tusayani, Shongopovi, Mishongovei, Sichomovi. But in much of the West, most notably in the Spanish Southwest, the overlay of races and cultures produced more of a mosaic than a meltdown.

In the mountain valleys of Northern New Mexico and Southern Colorado, the Penitente Brotherhoods still operate more than a hundred of their little "morada" chapels, maintaining a devotion to the Passion of Christ rooted in fifteenth-century Spain. In a score of dusty plazas costumed dancers perform rituals that originated across the Bering Straits. In Santa Fe, both the privileged class and the poor build adobe houses, just as the Moors built them, and paint their window sills with the blue that bars North African witches.

25

THE MULETEERS

Max Morehead

New Mexico, the northernmost appendage of the Spanish empire, was connected to its source of supplies, military aid, authority, and everything else by a network of terrible cart roads. Mules pulled the carts, sometimes as many as fifty in a team, and the men with the skill to handle them developed a culture of their own. In this passage from New Mexico's Royal Road, *historian Max Morehead describes one of their practices.*

[Below El Paso] was the Puerta de la Piedra, so called for a large stone weighing some two hundred pounds which had found its way there in a most peculiar manner. According to legend, the stone had been found near the Ojo de Samalayuca many years before by Mexican *arrieros*, who, to demonstrate their strength, took turns raising and heaving it over their heads. Each successive muleteer felt called upon in passing to duplicate the feat, and although only a few were equal to the task, the stone was supposedly advanced in this manner from the desert spring all of the way across the dunes, a distance of from 12 to 14 miles! . . .

The *atajo* [pack train] was a model of efficiency when managed by experienced Mexican labor. Six *arrieros*, or muleteers, could handle up to fifty mules at a time, and the cheapness of the *atajo* was due in large part to the low wages for which they worked. They expected only from two to five dollars a month, plus the simplest food and shelter. Their skill in roping, riding, loading, and caring for the mules impressed even the most veteran foreign traders and travelers and was therefore attentively described in their diaries and memoirs. From these and from the specifications in American military pack manuals of later date, it is clear that the transport division of the United States Army adopted not only the Mexican mule but also the *arriero's* techniques and even his Spanish terminology for the elaborate equipment of the *atajo*.

In preparation for a *jornada*, or day's journey, the *atajo* was first assembled by the *arrieros*, who either drove the grazing mules to their line of packs or, more often, enticed them there by leading the *mulera*, or bell mare, the others devotedly following. Well-broken mules instinctively found their own packs and patiently stood by them. Others were secured with a deftly thrown *riata*, or noose; blindfolded with the *tapajos*, a piece of embroidered leather, so as not to become frightened. All were then saddled with a succession of paraphernalia: the *salea*, a soft piece of raw sheepskin, the *xerga*, a woolen blanket, the *aparejo*, or packsaddle, which was a large leather pouch stuffed with straw to prevent chafing, the *carga*, or load itself, and finally the *petate*, or mat, to protect the latter from the rain. The *aparejo* was fastened around the mule's waist with a broad hempen belt drawn corset-tight and around its rump with a wide crupper to keep it from slipping forward. The *carga*, although weighing more than the *arriero* himself, was pitched on the mule's back with a single heave and adjusted so as to balance evenly. Usually two cases or crates coupled together and straddling the *aparejo* constituted the load, and these were bound to the packsaddle with an intricate network of knotted ropes. Then the blindfold was removed, and the mule was ready to travel. Although painfully tight at the outset, the girths and ropes gradually loosened during the jostling march as the weight of the load settled the *aparejo*, and from time to time the skillful *arrieros* cinched them up again one after another without slowing the progress of the train as a whole. The mules did not have to be driven along the road but merely led by the *mulera*, which they followed in perfect alignment.

26

BROTHERS OF THE LIGHT

Marta Weigle

When the deeply religious settlers of the northern frontier of New Spain were cut off from the Catholic Church by isolation, a shortage of clergy, and then by the anti-clerical Mexican Revolution, the faith was kept alive in many of the villages of Northern New Mexico and Southern Colorado by a religious order of laymen called "Penitentes," or "Hermanos de la Luz" (Brothers of the Light). After the U.S. occupation the brotherhoods gained considerable political influence, and with it the hostility of mostly Protestant Anglo-Americans. The Brothers' lenten practices of cross-carrying and flagellation were the subject of much lurid literature. Marta Weigle's Brothers of Light, Brothers of Blood *is considered the best account.*

The Brothers of Our Father Jesus, commonly known as the Penitentes, are men of Hispanic descent who belong to a lay religious society of the Roman Catholic Church. Membership requires sincere faith and unstinting commitment to Christian charity through mutual aid and unobtrusive good deeds for all neighbors and fellow citizens. The Brotherhood's headquarters are in Santa Fe, and the organization's greatest strength is in northern New Mexico and southern Colorado. Local chapters or moradas are governed by elected officials headed by an *Hermano Mayor*, or Elder Brother. Most moradas belong to larger councils which are organized into districts under the Archbishop's Supreme Council, headed by the *Hermano Supremo Arzo-bispal*, or Archbishop's Supreme Brother.

The pious observances of these Brothers are centered around the Passion of Jesus and the spirit of penance. During Lent and Holy Week they worship in retreat as well as in certain public rituals which devout members of the community may join. They also sponsor wakes for the dead and wakes for the saints. Both the Brotherhood's ritual practices and its social commitments have spiritually and substantively benefitted long-isolated communities. These benefits have too often been overlooked by superficial observers and apprehensive newcomers.

Penitente rites formerly involved closely supervised expressions of the penitential spirit through self-flagellation, cross-bearing, and other forms of discipline. Sometimes, in the past, a Brother was tied to a large cross in a short simulation of the Crucifixion on Good Friday. These more "spectacular" aspects of Penitente worship unfortunately attracted a disproportionate amount of attention from the media and from casual, uncomprehending observers. Their unwelcome scrutiny did and still does violate the religious freedom of the Brotherhood and desecrate a genuine devotional expression which has a long tradition in Spanish Catholicism. . . .

In a letter to Mary Austin dated March 7, 1920, Father Barrat described a group of some three hundred seemingly "ideal" Penitentes at Pina, Cerro, Questa, and Costilla:

> The people belonging to the "moradas" . . . are here all practical Catholics. Nobody is allowed to join that is not a practical Catholic. The members pledge themselves to go to church every Sunday, when possible; no man divorced or married outside the church can belong to them. Every Lent every member has to go to his Easter duties. They are the best men in the community. During Lent they have special private practices of penance, consisting mostly of hymns in the honor of the passion of Christ, a most proper exercise for Lent, and some other "private exercises" in their own "meeting halls" directed by a serious sense of sincere faith and, by a long shot, less ridiculous than anything practiced in secret by our American "Masons" and other secret societies forbidden by the church. . . .

Father Barrat also publicly defended his parishioner Brothers in an article for *The Southwestern Catholic*. Here, he is quite candid about the "few antiquated customs":

The "moradas" are now under the benign influence of the Church and are on their way to more perfection. Modern crucifixes, banners and statues are replacing the old, ugly, antiquated, wooden scarecrows. The singing still is to be "brought down" to the modern rules of music.

The only abuse that still exists is that in the missions: the Penitentes take charge of all the funerals and bury the dead according to their own ritual, even in the presence of the pastor, who sits "boiling mad" in the sacristy. But why get mad? "Argue, insist, scold in all science and doctrine," until the custom disappears little by little. . . . These men are serious, profoundly religious, sincere in their humble faith. Indeed, if anybody would try to touch the faith of their families, I believe they would eat him up. In the missions, in spite of a few abuses and antiquated customs, they are the defenders of our faith, and for that reason alone a good deal should be tolerated and we can afford to close our eyes on a few things that look queer to Christians of the East. . . .

The Penitentes observed *La Cuaresma* (Lent) as a time of preparation for Holy Week. The season was one of general moderation and sobriety for all, and the Brothers were no exception. Each morada had its traditional Lenten customs. In Cordova, New Mexico, Brothers appeared in procession on *Miércoles de Ceniza* (Ash Wednesday) to take the statue of *Nuestro Padre Jesús* from the church to the morada, where it remained throughout Lent, and to receive the church keys from the *mayordomo* (sexton). They met in the morada every Wednesday and Friday evening of Lent until Holy Week "for the purpose of prayer and adoration, with acts of penance performed in accordance with vows made . . . [and to] prepare for Holy Week and decide on the extent and scope of their activities during those days which are customarily observed: Holy Wednesday, Holy Thursday, and Good Friday." Some years, Brothers from Cuba, New Mexico, would undertake a long pilgrimage as far as St. John's, Arizona. This practice, called *La Procesión del Estandarte* (Procession of the Standard) was discontinued around 1912. Such a tradition was unusual, public recitations of the Stations of the Cross on Fridays, with private meetings and/or flagellant processions on Friday nights being customary Lenten practice.

The first Lenten observances rarely involved physical penances. However, "as the season progresses, the penitential passion rising with it, one is likely to meet anywhere in the deep lands between the fields, or in the foot-trails of the wild-sharp gorges, the solitary penitent, dragging his bloody cross, or two or three making their way from morada to morada on their knees, accompanied by the resador reciting the prayers that make the office effective." These were the exercises that inculcated spiritual discipline and expressed religious devotion.

Ejercicios ("exercises") were supervised by the Hermano Mayor, who granted permission to petitioners, assigned roles to participants, and governed the nature and duration of the penances. Some exercises were necessarily public; most were conducted inside the morada. Eventually, most public penitential processions came to be held at night or in remote places to preserve their sanctity.

Brothers doing active penance wore only white trousers, sometimes called *en paños menores* ("in undergarments"). If they emerged in procession, they wore black *vendas* ("hoods") over their heads to insure humility. At the end of the exercise, the *Coadjutores* "wash their lacerated back with *romerillo* [silver sage] tea which acts as an astringent." Whips were also dipped in this tea during the discipline, making them heavier and slightly antiseptic. Alcoholic or herbal stimulants may also have been used.

Modes of physical penance varied. Self-flagellation with whips called *disciplinas* was the most common form.

> These were loosely plaited yucca fibre whips which served as substitutes in New Mexico for the barbed link, iron whips of Spain and the iron-rich colonies. There was another form of small whip of finely knotted wool called *la cuerda,* the cord. Anciently used for personal discipline in Medieval Europe, the cuerda in New Mexico was reserved for lashes given by one member to another upon request, as an added form of devotion.

The other common form of penance was to drag the heavy wooden *maderos,* or crosses, which were taller than a man.

> Some idea of the weight of the maderos . . . may be gained by the fact that processions had to be halted at short intervals, to allow for the acompanadores to lift the maderos from the shoulders of the penitentes, to allow them to recuperate their strength. . . . And not all penitentes would be allowed to pull the maderos, as only those of sturdy physical development would be equal to the task.

Other penitents might wrap themselves in ropes, cacti, or chains, or bind their arms to small crosses. Tradition and imagination apparently influenced the choice. "The use of obsidian knives and spiny cactus, of yucca scourges, for drawing blood and causing pain, the penance of kneeling on *arroz* (rice) composed of tiny sharp stones from our Southwest anthills, all these were features and modifications suggested and provided by the local landscape."

Some penances were performed to fulfill personal vows, others traditional to the morada might be done by volunteers or appointed representatives. The upper morada at Arroyo Hondo had a special madero called *El Doncello:*

> This madero was much heavier than the rest. . . . [It] was seldom used, but on some rare occasions a strapping young penitente would ask to be permitted to carry it. The distance from the morada to the church is at least two hundred yards, altho it is down hill all the way, the road is rough, and the bumping of the rear end of the madero along the ground would cause severe injury to the bare shoulder of the penitente who dragged it. And then the return trip . . . would be uphill, requiring much more exertion . . . the scars resulting on the shoulder of the penitente, would bear mute evidence, throughout his life, of the sacrifice entailed.

A morada near Las Trampas, New Mexico, each year required a lone man, scourging himself at intervals, to cover the distance between that morada and a church some seven miles distant—a feat which took three or four hours. Groups of Brothers from neighboring moradas would also make *visitas* to worship and do penance together.

Whatever their form, the most important aspect of these penitential exercises is their "embeddedness." They were not random or uncontrolled. Brothers of Light who permitted and supervised them attempted to balance what could be expected of a man physically, what the season traditionally demanded, and what the man personally wished to do and why. Penitents were almost always accompanied, not only by helpers but also by persons singing, praying, playing the pito, and carrying sacred images as guides. Their exercises were thus a strict discipline within a total worship complex, *not* masochistic self-indulgences or sadistic tortures. These guarded and guided practices were considered appropriate devotional expressions beneficial for the individual and the community.

Brothers spend most of *Semana Santa* (Holy Week) in retreat at their morada. As a rule, they do not return home until officers for the coming year have been elected. In some communities, the men were absent from *Domingo de Ramos* (Palm Sunday) through *Sábado de Gloria* (Holy Saturday). A retreat from the evening of *Mártes Santo* through *Viernes Santo* (Good Friday) night is more usual, however. In keeping with Hispanic tradition, both the Brothers and their nonmember Catholic neighbors emphasize "not the resurrection message of Easter Sunday [*Pascua*] . . . but rather the mournful imagery of Good Friday: the crucifixion and the sorrowing Virgin."

During the retreat, Brothers slept little, maintaining constant vigils, welcoming and worshipping with many groups of visitors, and undertaking various public processions and services. Their meatless meals were brought in by mayordomos or auxiliadoras. The most popular and nutritious dish was *panocha*, a sweet, porridge-like substance made from the meal of sprouted wheat flour with boiling water and baked in an outdoor oven. This exchange of *charolitas* (Lenten dishes) was part of a community-wide network during Holy Week. The Brothers reciprocated by opening their chapel to visitors and by conducting public religious services.

27

BLESSING THE ANIMALS

John A. Lomax

In many parts of rural Mexico and the Spanish-colonial Southwest there was a practice of bringing animals to the church to be blessed, which still flourishes. John A. Lomax, a collector of Southwestern folklore, described the event in Southwesterners Write.

Father Silva, after helping me record "Los Pastores," urged me to be in the back courtyard of the Church of the Lady of Guadalupe in San Antonio by three o'clock the following Sunday. He thought I'd like to see him bless the animals. Father Silva was a sub-junior pastor of this church, an exile from Guadalajara, where he had been professor in a Catholic college. Father Transchese, his superior, did not favor this survival of what he considered Indian paganism. "Superstition, superstition," he whispered. But I was curious, and drove a hundred miles to join the gathering that filled the courtyard back of the church.

A few well-dressed San Antonians mingled with the motley crowd, many of whom were children. The greater number belonged to the Mexican poorer classes, most of the women and children carrying household pets in their arms or leading them by strings or ropes. Some of the animals were necessarily in cages. Here and there families of guinea pigs nosed and frittered their time away. From the cages of shivering, subdued-looking canaries come no sound. Pigeons abounded, various in breed and color. One dear old lady, very small and lonely-looking, toothless, with shiny black eyes, had stuffed her pigeon, tail downward, into a brown paper bag. Now and then she would glance down at her charge. Once I saw her lean over and whisper to it. The pigeon nodded its head and its eyes blinked solemnly.

Chickens of every variety, color and size were present. Tiny little girls bore the tiny little biddies that run about many homes. One happy girl held two brown twin chickens, a bit larger than quail, decorated with pink tissue paper neckbands with fluted edges. There were hens galore but only a single stately rooster, the lone barnyard male of his stripe in need of priestly meditation. Two tawny ducks—mates—frightened into solemnity, stretched and flopped their wings as if they would like to fly from the confusion.

The hundreds of dogs and cats could not be persuaded, even by religious pageantry, to bury their hereditary enmity. Some of the cats while the strife was fiercest, broke away and scaled the high board enclosure, outward bound for freedom. Little Mexican boys dangled puppies, one in each hand. Most of the smaller girls carried kittens, all adorned with blue or pink paper necklaces—I saw not one scrap of silk. A handsome, huge wolf-hound dashed about and barked loudly, to the terror of the cat tribe and smaller dogs. Poodles were abundant, some tiny and hairless. One Boston pug, hugged closely by his boy owner, wore a face so ugly and evil no amount of holy water could possibly mend it.

The goats came usually in pairs, twisting and winding and butting through the closely massed people. Two goats drew carts, a driver for each goat riding proudly behind. A venerable Billy stood in dignified quiet, solemnly chewing his undigested breakfast. Running around freely in the crowd, following closely the master of ceremonies, was a lovely half-grown ewe lamb, its neck banded with a broad green ribbon; her master called her Pacolita.

All day the crowd milled about the bleak courtyard. Although a chill wind blew from the North, the people kept coming, bringing more and more animals, until the sun hung low and the wintry day neared its end. At last, through this surging mass of men, women, children, dogs, cats, burros, goats, sheep, chickens, ducks, pigeons, guinea pigs, canaries, and other animals, strode tall, lank Father Silva in his long flowing black robe, followed by two white-robed lads, one carrying a glass bowl of precious holy water. In his hand Father Silva held a silver wand, at its end a porous sphere perforated with fine holes. When dipped into the bowl this sphere would fill with water, which would fly out in fine spray. Father Silva and his attendants stopped near the head of the long straggling procession, which at once began to move forward. I stood very close by Father Silva.

First came the marshal of ceremonies with his beautiful lamb. As it passed, Father Silva snapped his wand and dashed some of the holy water into its face, at the same moment chanting his blessing. The lamb dodged and flirted its long tail. Then followed the little old woman with her pink-necked pigeon imprisoned in a paper sack. It took the water without batting either of its starry eyes, while the old woman was muttering prayers through her wrinkled lips. She seemed to hold the pigeon dearer as she moved away. Next came miscellaneous groups as ordered by the busy master of ceremonies and busier lamb. The cats didn't like the holy water: one dog barked as it hit his nose. The sedate billy goat appeared oblivious of ablution. I think Father Silva missed a shot as the big wolfhound dashed by; and the face of the ugly Boston, wrinkling his ugly nose at the cold shower, took on an even more sinister expression. But the chickens, the ducks, the guinea pigs and the canaries behaved beautifully. They were attentive, quiet, respectful. I thought one of the guinea pigs twisted his face into a smile, but perhaps I was mistaken. As for the two gold fish in a big glass bowl, I fear for them. They were already deep under when Father Silva sprinkled the bowl. One brown, wrinkled old lady near the end of the procession suddenly drew an egg from her bosom and held it out for baptism. Father Silva looked a bit surprised, though he quickly recovered and blessed it, adding due quota of holy water.

When the last animal was sprinkled, the ceremony ended abruptly. No prayer, benediction or song followed. The crowd drifted away.

"I could not catch the Spanish words of your blessing," I said to Father Silva. "I saw you glance at your ritual. Does the Church officially recognize the custom?"

"Oh, yes," he answered. "And the words I repeated are a prayer to the Lord to bless each animal to the end that it may fulfill the purpose for which it was created."

"I understand," said I. "The hens should lay more eggs; the canaries sing more sweetly; the goats be more tractable to their drivers; the concerts of the tomcats on the back fence not so long drawn out; the roosters—." But Father Silva raised his hand, smiled a friendly protest and walked away.

28

RAMONA

Helen Hunt Jackson

The Zamorano Club of book collectors in Los Angeles named Helen Hunt Jackson's Ramona among the books which influenced California most. It is credited with spreading "Ramona-style" architecture—the white plastered arches and red tile roofs now called "California-style." Here is Jackson's description of Señora Moreno's house—and of the all-too-typical way Mexicans lost their lands when the Southwest and West became part of the United States.

The Señora Moreno's house was one of the best specimens to be found in California of the representative house of the half barbaric, half elegant, wholly generous and free-handed life led there by Mexican men and women of degree in the early part of this century, under the rule of the Spanish and Mexican viceroys, when the laws of the Indies were still the law of the land, and its old name, "New Spain," was an ever-present link and stimulus to the warmest memories and deepest patriotisms of its people.

It was a picturesque life, with more of sentiment and gayety in it, more also that was truly dramatic, more romance, than will ever be seen again on those sunny shores. The aroma of it all lingers there still; industries and inventions have not yet slain it; it will last out its century,—in fact, it can never be quite lost, so long as there is left standing one such house as the Señora Moreno's.

When the house was built, General Moreno owned all the land within a radius of forty miles,—forty miles westward, down the valley to the sea; forty miles eastward, into the San Fernando Mountains; and good forty miles more or less along the coast. The boundaries were not very strictly defined; there was no occasion, in those happy days, to reckon land by inches. It might be asked, perhaps, just how General Moreno owned all this land, and the question might not be easy to answer. It was not and could not be answered to the satisfaction of the United States Land Commission, which, after the surrender of California, undertook to sift and adjust Mexican land-titles; and that was the way it had come about that the Señora Moreno now called herself a poor woman. Tract after tract, her lands had been taken away from her; it looked for a time as if nothing would be left. Every one of the claims based on deeds of gift from Governor Pio Pico, her husband's most intimate friend, was disallowed. They all went by the board in one batch, and took away from the Señora in a day the greater part of her best pasturelands. They were lands which had belonged to the Bonaventura Mission, and lay along the coast at the mouth of the valley down which the little stream which ran past her house went to the sea; and it had been a great pride and delight to the Señora, when she was young, to ride that forty miles by her husband's side, all the way on their own lands, straight from their house to their own strip of shore. No wonder she believed the Americans thieves, and spoke of them always as hounds. The people of the United States have never in the least realized that the taking possession of California was not only a conquering of Mexico, but a conquering of California as well; that the real bitterness of the surrender was not so much to the empire which gave up the country, as to the country itself which was given up. Provinces passed back and forth in that way, helpless in the hands of great powers, have all the ignominy and humiliation of defeat, with none of the dignities or compensations of the transaction.

Mexico saved much by her treaty, in spite of having to acknowledge herself beaten; but California lost all. Words cannot tell the sting of such a transfer. It is a marvel that a Mexican remained in the country; probably none did, except those who were absolutely forced to it.

Luckily for the Señora Moreno, her title to the lands midway in the valley was better than to those lying to the east and the west, which had once belonged to the missions of San Fernando and Bonaventura; and after all the claims, counter-claims, petitions, appeals, and adjudications were ended, she still was left in undisputed possession of what would have been thought by any new-comer into the country to be a handsome estate, but which seemed to the despoiled and indignant Señora a pitiful fragment of one. Moreover, she declared that she should never feel secure of a foot of even this. Any day, she said, the United States Government might send out a new Land Commission to examine the decrees of the first, and revoke such as they saw fit. Once a thief, always a thief. Nobody need feel himself safe under American rule. There was no knowing what might happen any day; and year by year the lines of sadness, resentment, anxiety, and antagonism deepened on the Señora's fast aging face.

It gave her unspeakable satisfaction, when the Commissioners, laying out a road down the valley, ran it at the back of her house instead of past the front. "It is well," she said. "Let their travel be where it belongs, behind our kitchens; and no one have sight of the front doors of our houses, except friends who have come to visit us." Her enjoyment of this never flagged. Whenever she saw, passing the place, wagons or carriages belonging to the hated Americans, it gave her a distinct thrill of pleasure to think that the house turned its back on them. She would like always to be able to do the same herself; but whatever she, by policy or in business, might be forced to do, the old house, at any rate, would always keep the attitude of contempt,—its face turned away.

One other pleasure she provided herself with, soon after this road was opened,—a pleasure in which religious devotion and race antagonism were so closely blended that it would have puzzled the subtlest of priests to decide whether her act were a sin or a virtue. She caused to be set up, upon every one of the soft rounded hills which made the beautiful rolling sides of that part of the valley, a large wooden cross; not a hill in sight of her house left without the sacred emblem of her faith. "That the heretics may know, when they go by, that they are on the estate of a good Catholic," she said, "and that the faithful may be reminded to pray. There have been miracles of conversion wrought on the most hardened by a sudden sight of the Blessed Cross."

There they stood, summer and winter, rain and shine, the silent, solemn, outstretched arms, and became landmarks to many a guideless traveller who had been told that his way would be by the first turn to the left or the right, after passing the last one of the Señora Moreno's crosses, which he couldn't miss seeing. And who shall say that it did not often happen that the crosses bore a sudden message to some idle heart journeying by, and thus justified the pious half of the Señora's impulse? Certain it is, that many a good Catholic halted and crossed himself when he first beheld them, in the lonely places, standing out in sudden relief against the blue sky; and if he said a swift short prayer at the sight, was he not so much better? The house was of adobe, low, with a wide veranda on the three sides of the inner court, and a still broader one across the entire front, which looked to the south. These verandas, especially those on the inner court, were supplementary rooms to the house. The greater part of the family life went on in them. Nobody stayed inside the walls, except when it was necessary. All the kitchen work, except the actual cooking, was done here, in front of the kitchen doors and windows. Babies slept, were washed, sat in the dirt, and played, on the veranda. The women said their prayers, took their naps, and wove their lace there. Old Juanita shelled her beans there, and threw the pods down on the tile floor, till towards night they were sometimes piled up high around her, like corn-husks at a husking. The herdsmen and shepherds smoked there, lounged there, trained their dogs there; there the young made love, and the old dozed; the benches, which ran the entire length of the walls, were worn into hollows, and shone like satin; the tiled floors also were broken and sunk in places, making little wells, which filled up in times of hard rains, and were then an invaluable addition to the children's resources for amusement, and also to the comfort of the dogs, cats, and fowls, who picked about among them, taking sips from each.

The arched veranda along the front was a delightsome place. It must have been eighty feet long, at least, for the doors of five large rooms opened on it. The two western-most rooms had been added on, and made four steps higher than the others; which gave to that end of the veranda the look of a balcony, or loggia. Here the Señora kept her flowers; great red water-jars, hand-made by the Indians of San Luis Obispo Mission, stood in close rows against the walls, and in them were always growing fine geraniums, carnations, and yellow-flowered musk. The Señora's passion for musk she had inherited from her mother. It was so strong that she sometimes wondered at it; and one day, as she sat with Father Salvierderra in the veranda, she picked a handful of the blossoms, and giving them to him, said, "I do not know why it is, but it seems to me if I were dead I could be brought to life by the smell of musk."

"It is in your blood, Señora," the old monk replied. "When I was last in your father's house in Seville, your mother sent for me to her room, and under her window was a stone balcony full of growing musk, which so filled the room with its odor that I was like to faint. But she said it cured her of diseases, and without it she fell ill. You were a baby then."

"Yes," cried the Señora, "but I recollect that balcony. I recollect being lifted up to a window, and looking down into a bed of blooming yellow flowers; but I did not know what they were. How strange!"

"No. Not strange, daughter," replied Father Salvierderra. "It would have been stranger if you had not acquired the taste, thus drawing it in with the mother's milk. It would behoove mothers to remember this far more than they do."

Besides the geraniums and carnations and musk in the red jars, there were many sorts of climbing vines,—some coming from the ground, and twining around the pillars of the veranda; some growing in great bowls, swung by cords from the roof of the veranda, or set on shelves against the walls. These bowls were of gray stone, hollowed and polished, shining smooth inside and out. They also had been made by the Indians, nobody knew how many ages ago, scooped and polished by the patient creatures, with only stones for tools.

Among these vines, singing from morning till night, hung the Señora's canaries and finches, half a dozen of each, all of different generations, raised by the Señora. She was never without a young bird-family on hand; and all the way from Bonaventura to Monterey, it was thought a piece of good luck to come into possession of a canary or finch of Señora Moreno's raising.

Between the veranda and the river meadows, out on which it looked, all was garden, orange grove, and almond orchard; the orange grove always green, never without snowy bloom or golden fruit; the garden never without flowers, summer or winter; and the almond orchard, in early spring, a fluttering canopy of pink and white petals, which, seen from the hills on the opposite side of the river, looked as if rosy sunrise clouds had fallen, and become tangled in the tree-tops. On either hand stretched away other orchards,—peach, apricot, pear, apple, pomegranate; and beyond these, vineyards. Nothing was to be seen but verdure or bloom or fruit, at whatever time of year you sat on the Señora's south veranda.

A wide straight walk shaded by a trellis so knotted and twisted with grapevines that little was to be seen of the trellis wood-work, led straight down from the veranda steps, through the middle of the garden, to a little brook at the foot of it. Across this brook, in the shade of a dozen gnarled old willow-trees, were set the broad flat stone washboards on which was done all the family washing. No long dawdling, and no running away from work on the part of the maids, thus close to the eye of the Señora at the upper end of the garden; and if they had known how picturesque they looked there, kneeling on the grass, lifting the dripping linen out of the water, rubbing it back and forth on the stones, sousing it, wringing it, splashing the clear water in each other's faces, they would have been content to stay at the washing day in and day out, for there was always somebody to look on from above. Hardly a day passed that the Señora had not visitors. She was still a person of note; her house the natural resting-place for all who journeyed through the valley; and whoever came, spent all of his time, when not eating, sleeping, or walking over the place, sitting with the Señora on the sunny veranda. Few days in winter were cold enough, and in summer the day must be hot indeed to drive the Señora and her friends indoors. There stood on the veranda three carved oaken chairs, and a carved bench, also of oak, which had been brought to the Señora for safe keeping by the faithful old sacristan of San Luis Rey, at the time of the occupation of that Mission by the United States troops, soon after the conquest of California. . . . [Her] chapel was dearer to the Señora than her house. It had been built by the General in the second year of their married life. In it her four children had been christened, and from it all but one, her handsome Felipe, had been buried while they were yet infants. In the General's time, while the estate was at its best, and hundreds of Indians living within its borders, there was many a Sunday when the scene to be witnessed there was like the scenes at the Missions,—the chapel full of kneeling men and women; those who could not find room inside kneeling on the garden walks outside; Father Salvierderra, in gorgeous vestments, coming, at close of the services, slowly down the aisle, the close-packed rows of worshippers parting to right and left to let him through, all looking up eagerly for his blessing, women giving him offerings of fruit or flowers, and holding up their babies that he might lay his hands on their heads. No one but Father Salvierderra had ever officiated in the Moreno chapel, or heard the confession of a Moreno.

29

A SANTA FE
FANDANGO

George Frederick Ruxton

In 1846 George Frederick Ruxton, an Englishman who described the mountain men in articles for Blackwood's Edinburgh *magazine and tried to capture the sound of their language, looked in on fur trapper festivities in Santa Fe, then a Mexican village.*

The trappers followed the Yuta trail over a plain, skirting a pine-covered ridge, in which countless herds of antelope, tame as sheep, were pasturing. Numerous creeks intersect it, well timbered with oak, pine, and cedar, and well stocked with game of all kinds. On the eleventh day from leaving the Huerfano, they struck the Taos valley settlement on Arroyo Hondo, and pushed on at once to the village of Fernandez—sometimes, but improperly, called Taos. As the dashing band clattered through the village, the dark eyes of the reboso-wrapped muchachas peered from the doors of the adobe houses, each mouth armed with cigarito, which was at intervals removed to allow utterance to the salutation to each hunter as he trotted past of *Adios Americanos,*— "Welcome to Fernandez!" and then they hurried off to prepare for the fandango, which invariably followed the advent of the mountaineers. The men, however, seemed scarcely so well pleased; but leaned sulkily against the walls, their sarapes turned over the left shoulder, and concealing the lower part of the face, the hand appearing from its upper folds only to remove the eternal cigarro from their lips. They, from under their broad-brimmed sombreros, scowled with little affection upon the stalwart hunters, who clattered past them, scarcely deigning to glance at the sullen Peládos, but paying incomprehensible compliments to the buxom wenches who smiled at them from the doors. Thus exchanging salutations, they rode up to the house of an old mountaineer, who had long been settled here with a New Mexican wife, and who was the recognised entertainer of the hunters when they visited Taos valley, receiving in exchange such peltry as they brought with them.

No sooner was it known that Los Americanos had arrived, than nearly all the householders of Fernandez presented themselves to offer the use of their "salas" for the fandango which invariably celebrated their arrival. This was always a profitable event; for as the mountaineers were generally pretty well "flush" of cash when on their "spree," and as open-handed as an Indian could wish, the sale of whisky, with which they regaled all comers, produced a handsome return to the fortunate individual whose room was selected for the fandango. On this occasion the sala of the Alcalde Don Cornelio Vegil was selected and put in order; a general invitation was distributed; and all the dusky beauties of Fernandez were soon engaged in arraying themselves for the fête. Off came the coats of dirt and "alegnía" which had bedaubed their faces since the last "funcion," leaving their checks clear and clean. Water was profusely used, and their cuerpos were doubtless astonished by the unusual lavation. Their long black hair was washed and combed, plastered behind their ears, and plaited into a long queue, which hung down their backs. *Enaguas* of gaudy colour (red most affected) were donned, fastened round the waist with orna-mented belts, and above this a snow-white *camisita* of fine linen was the only covering, allowing a prodigal display of their charms. Gold and silver ornaments, of antiquated pattern, decorate their ears and necks; and massive crosses of the precious metals, wrought from the gold or silver of their own placeres, hang pendant on their breasts. The enagua or petticoat, reaching about halfway between the knee and ancle, displays their well-turned limbs, destitute of stockings, and their tiny feet, thrust into quaint little shoes (*zapatitos*) of Cinderellan dimensions. Thus equipped, with the reboso drawn over their heads and faces, out of the folds of which their brilliant eyes flash like lightning, and each pretty mouth armed with its cigarito, they coquettishly enter the fandango. Here, at one end of a long room, are seated the musicians, their instruments being generally a species of guitar, called heaca, a *bandolin,* and an Indian drum, called *tombé*—one of each. Round the room groups of New Mexicans lounge, wrapped in the eternal sarape, and smoking of course, scowling with jealous eyes at the more favoured mountaineers. These, divested of their hunting-coats of buckskins, appear in their bran-new shirts of gaudy calico, and close fitting buckskin pantaloons, with long fringes down the outside seam from the hip to the ancle; with moccasins, ornamented with bright beads and porcupine quills. Each, round his waist, wears his mountain-belt and scalp-knife, ominous of the company he is in, and some have pistols sticking in their belt.

The dances—save the mark!—are without form or figure, at least those in which the white hunters sport the "fantastic toe." Seizing his partner round the waist with the gripe of a grisly bear, each mountaineer whirls and twirls, jumps and stamps; introduces Indian steps used in the "scalp" or "buffalo" dances, whooping occasionally with unearthly cry, and then subsiding into the jerking step, raising each foot alternately from the ground, so much in vogue in Indian ballets. The hunters have the floor all to themselves. The Mexicans have no chance in such physical force dancing; and if a dancing Peládo steps into the ring, a lead-like thump from a galloping mountaineer quickly sends him sprawling, with the considerate remark—"Quit, you darned Spaniard! you can't 'shine' in this crowd."

During a lull, guagés filled with whisky go the rounds—offered to and seldom refused by the ladies—sturdily quaffed by the mountaineers, and freely swallowed by the Peládos, who drown their jealousy and envious hate of their entertainers in potent aguardiente. Now, as the guagés are oft refilled and as often drained, and as night advances, so do the spirits of the mountaineers become more boisterous, while their attentions to their partners become warmer—the jealousy of the natives waxes hotter thereat—and they begin to show symptoms of resenting the endearments which the mountaineers bestow upon their wives and sweethearts. And now, when the room is filled to crowding,—with two hundred people, swearing, drinking, dancing, and shouting—the half-dozen Americans monopolising the fair, to the evident disadvantage of at least threescore scowling Peládos, it happens that one of these, maddened by whisky and the green-eyed monster, suddenly seizes a fair one from the waist-encircling arm of a mountaineer, and pulls her from her partner. Wagh!—La Bonté—it is he—stands erect as a pillar for a moment, then raises his hand to his mouth, and gives a ringing war-whoop—jumps upon the rash Peládo, seizes him by the body as if he were a child, lifts him over his head, and dashes him with the force of a giant against the wall.

The war, long threatened, has commenced; twenty Mexicans draw their knives and rush upon La Bonté, who stands his ground, and sweeps them down with his ponderous fist, one after another, as they throng around him. "Howgh-owgh-owgh-owgh-h!" the well-known warwhoop, bursts from the throats of his companions, and on they rush to the rescue. The women scream, and block the door in their eagerness to escape; and thus the Mexicans are compelled to stand their ground and fight. Knives glitter in the light, and quick thrusts are given and parried. In the centre of the room the whites stand shoulder to shoulder—covering the floor with Mexicans by their stalwart blows; but the odds are fearful against them, and other assailants crowd up to supply the place of those who fall.

The alarm being given by the shrieking women, reinforcements of Peládos rushed to the scene of action, but could not enter the room, which was already full. The odds began to tell against the mountaineers, when Kit Carson's quick eye caught sight of a high stool or stone, supported by three long heavy legs. In a moment he had cleared his way to this, and in another the three legs were broken off and in the hands of himself, Dick Wooton, and La Bonté. Sweeping them round their heads, down came the heavy weapons amongst the Mexicans with wonderful effect—each blow, dealt by the nervous arms of Wooton and La Bonté, mowing down a good half-dozen of the assailants. At this the mountaineers gave a hearty whoop, and charged the wavering enemy with such resistless vigour, that they gave way and bolted through the door, leaving the floor strewed with wounded, many most dangerously; for, as may be imagined, a thrust from the keen scalp-knife by the nervous arm of a mountaineer was no baby blow, and seldom failed to strike home—up to the "Green River" on the blade.

The field being won, the whites, too, beat a quick retreat to the house where they were domiciled, and where they had left their rifles. Without their trusty weapons they felt, indeed, unarmed; and not knowing how the affair just over would be followed up, lost no time in making preparations for defence. However, after great blustering on the part of the prefecto, who, accompanied by a *posse comitatus* of "Greasers," proceeded to the house, and demanded the surrender of all concerned in the affair—which proposition was received with a yell of derision—the business was compounded by the mountaineers promising to give sundry dollars to the friends of two of the Mexicans, who died during the night of their wounds, and to pay for a certain amount of masses to be sung for the repose of their souls in purgatory. Thus the affair blew over; but for several days the mountaineers never showed themselves in the streets of Fernandez without their rifles on their shoulders, and refrained from attending fandangos for the present, and until the excitement had cooled down.

Part Five

◆

FRONTIER LIFE

Life is pretty much the same in every region—with nuances of difference. At Sacred Heart, Oklahoma, in boyhood one's value was determined by such things as being able to hit a frog floating in a cowpond with a .22 caliber bullet so that it was stunned and retrievable to become froglegs, but not punctured and sunk. I remember my father recalling how his first-day-of-school job as a one-room schoolteacher in the Texas panhandle was to prove to the older boys he could whip them in a fair fight. Tales told of frontier life concerned such matters as arriving home from a nocturnal tent revival to discover the babies sleeping in the back of the wagons were strangers—pranksters having switched kids around during the hymn singing—or the indescribable aroma of a sod dugout where the only fuel was dried buffalo chips.

30

THE BURNING
BUSH

A. W. Whipple

Here's a description by A. W. Whipple of the U.S. Topographical Engineers of how Christmas Eve was observed in a railroad route survey camp in the mountains near Flagstaff in 1853.

December 24—Camp 89.—Having a sheltered spot on the edge of a forest, with plenty of water and grass, it was deemed necessary for the welfare of the mules, upon which we are so dependent, to rest till Monday. The weather in the morning was very cold, the thermometer at sunrise reading 35° below zero. Later in the day the sun's rays were warm and powerful, melting the snow upon the southern slopes. Several of the party went out to hunt turkeys and other game, thinking to have a feast, but were quite unsuccessful. They found plenty of tracks in the snow. One young hunter got upon the trail of a bear; but the foot-prints were so enormous that he preferred to return to camp.

Christmas eve has been celebrated with considerable éclat. The fireworks were decidedly magnificent. Tall, isolated pines surrounding camp were set on fire. The flames leaped to the tree-tops, and then, dying away, sent up innumerable brilliant sparks. An Indian dance, by some *ci-devant* Navajo prisoners, was succeeded by songs from the teamsters, and a pastoral enacted by the Mexicans, after their usual custom at this festival.

Leroux's servant, a tamed Crow Indian, and a herder, then performed a duet improvisatore, in which they took the liberty of saying what they pleased of the company present—an amusement common in New Mexico and California, where this troubadour singing is much in vogue at fandangoes. These last entertainments are interesting to a stranger from their singularity. The plaintive tones of the singers, and the strange simplicity of the people, lead one's fancy back to the middle ages. In this state of society, so free from ambition for wealth or power, where the realities of life are in a great measure subject to the ideal, there is a tinge of romance that would well repay the researches of a literary explorer. Their impromptu ballads alone would make an interesting collection.

31

A TWENTY-DOLLAR CHRISTMAS BALL

Alexander Kelly McClure

Alexander Kelly McClure described the 1867 Christmas Ball thrown by the social elite in booming Virginia City in his Three Thousand Miles Through the Rocky Mountains.

Virginia City, Montana Terr., January 4, 1868. Holidays in the Rocky Mountains are the most festive of all our festive occasions. Dull care is thrown far in the background, and business is subordinated to social and general enjoyment. Christmas was one of the balmiest days I ever witnessed in any climate. I sat most of the day in an office with the windows and doors open; and fire would have been uncomfortable. The air was as soft as Eastern spring, and the sun shone out upon the hills and cliffs with such warmth as to start their winter crowns of snow in murmuring streamlets down their rugged sides. The city was gay throughout. The mines had poured forth their sturdy men to have a holiday frolic, and "The Pony" (the chief saloon) had crowded tables from early morn until the "wee sma' hours" told that another Christmas had departed. The street-auctions were unusually lively; the stores were swarming with customers of all classes, from the unshorn and unshaven mountaineer to the fashionable belle; the "sports" had their lively games, and billiards attracted nearly all the dignitaries of state to try their skill. Sumptuous dinners were spread

121

in various uninviting-looking shanties, and fair hands and fascinating faces inside made guests forget the rude architecture that encircled them. In the evening mine host, Chapin, of the Planters', gave a ball, and one hundred jolly people responded. Tickets were twenty dollars each; but the supply was unequal to the demand. A second floor over one of the large store-rooms was fitted up most tastefully for the occasion. Evergreens and flowers were festooned around the walls, and the Stars and Stripes hung in graceful folds over the orchestra. For the first time in the Far West I found nearly as many ladies as gentlemen at the ball; but they varied rather more in their ages than is usual in Eastern gatherings of the kind. Young misses of ten and twelve years not unfrequently aided to fill up the dance, and, as a rule, did their part very well; while my partner in the only active participation I had in the ball (the promenade to supper) was a grandmother who owned to nearly sixty winters. She was, like all Western ladies, fond of social parties, and looked with just pride upon her children and grandchildren as they "tripped the light fantastic toe" to the best of music. Supper came with midnight; and it would have done credit to any Eastern town of thrice our population. Oyster soup opened the course,—the oysters having been shipped three thousand miles. Elegant salads, delicious jellies, game of all kinds, candies manufactured here into temples and monuments, almost every variety of fruits, and sparkling wines, combined to tempt the appetite; and a jollier party I never saw sit down to a repast. While there was a freedom from the severe exactions of social rules in the East, there was the most scrupulous care on the part of all to restrain social freedom within the bounds of propriety. After an hour at the table, the middle-aged portion of the party returned to the ball-room, while the old folks and little ones retired to their homes. Altogether, it was one of the most agreeable gatherings I have ever witnessed; and it was enjoyed by most of the company as only Western people can enjoy social parties. With all the freedom of Western life, I have never seen a man intoxicated at a ball or other social meeting; and the sincere cordiality evinced by the ladies to each other would be an improvement on the more cultivated customs of the East.

32

CHRISTMAS IN ROUND VALLEY

John Wesley Clampitt

John Wesley Clampitt was off touring post offices in Utah in 1867, three-thousand miles from home when Christmas Eve came. This is from his Echoes from the Rocky Mountains.

It was pitch dark without, and a drizzling rain added to our misery as we thought of the morrow. Although we were obliged to sit up all night, at least we were sheltered from the cold rain, and a blazing fire of logs on the stone hearth imparted a somewhat cheerful glow to the surroundings. Our "kind" host informed us that if we were disposed to invest a part of our surplus currency, he could obtain for us some home-brewed beer. Being thus disposed, and only too happy of the opportunity, we gave him the greenbacks and he shortly returned with a good-sized bucket of the malt. To this we added some peppersauce to give it a taste, otherwise it would be as flat as the Dead Sea, this was the case with all beer brewed in the Territory, and inviting the "head of the house" to imbibe also, we sat around the fire and drank the beer until the last cupful was gone. The Mormon host performed his part of the undertaking, and never flinched at a single detail. In fact, he sat up with us all night long—whether it was from "gentlemanly politeness," love of the beer, or distrust of the Gentiles he had let within his gates, we were unable to fathom. But true it was, he sat with us by the fire, occasionally replenishing it, until the gray mists of the morning.

During the long night I could not help thinking that this was Christmas eve. That the morrow was the day celebrated all over the Christian world as the birthday of the Redeemer. My thoughts wandered to my home in the far East, where dwelt the loved ones of my heart. What a sun-burst of memory poured in upon me! . . . Three thousand miles separated us. I was away off, locked in the mountains in an inhospitable land, where even the luxury of a bed was denied on that night! But the gray dawn of the morning came at last, and with it a surprise. I heard the beating of a drum, the shrill notes of a fife, the firing of guns and the loud shouts of men and boys. What could it mean? Was it a call to arms? Had the wily savage chosen that dark morning for an attack upon the sleeping town? Were we to engage in battle in Round Valley with the white man's foe? Were they already at its gates? No! What, then, means this call to arms from fife and drum? Ah, my Gentile friend—it is the sound of the Mormon boys of Round Valley ushering in the dawn of Christmas! They are marching around the hollow square with drum and fife; they are firing a salute at each household; they are singing the songs that are now being sung by Christian millions all over the world; they are ringing the bells and shouting their loud huzzas, and their notes shall be borne over the distant mountain tops on the electric chords of sympathy to swell the anthems of praise and rejoicing—the chorus of the world song that the Redeemer liveth! Three thousand miles from home, and three hundred from a base line of civilization, in the very heart of the mountains, and in the midst of the wild haunts of Indian foes, these Mormon boys are celebrating the birth of Christ. No wonder that we bought a tub of beer, the bucket was too small, and when they came to "our" house singing their Christmas carols, drank with them the early morning toast of a "Merry Christmas to all the Mormon boys of Round Valley."

33

"A RATHER PRETENTIOUS SOD HOUSE"

Everett Dick

In his The Sod-House Frontier, *Everett Dick provided the details of how one builds his home where there are neither trees for timber nor knowledge of how to make adobe bricks. It's estimated that, on the western prairie, as many as 90 percent of the settlers built with sod.*

These structures were of various sizes but a rather pretentious sod house followed a common building plan of sixteen feet wide and twenty feet long. The sod bricks were made by turning over furrows on about half an acre of ground where the sod was thickest and strongest. Care was taken to make the furrows of even width and depth so that the walls of the cabin would rise with regularity and evenness.

A spade was used to cut the sod into bricks about three feet long. These bricks were then carried to the building site by wagon or by a float made of planks or the forks of a tree. J. Clarence Norton of La Harpe, Kansas, related that in building the house on the homestead, the line for the wall was drawn after dark so that it could be located by the north star. For the first layer of the wall the three foot bricks were placed side by side around the foundation except where the door was to be made. The cracks were then filled with dirt and two more layers were placed on these. The joints were broken as in brick laying. Every third course was laid crosswise of the others to bind them together. This process was continued until the wall was high enough to put a roof on the structure. A door frame and two window frames were set in the wall and the sod built around them at the proper time. Sometimes the builder drove hickory withes down into the wall as a sort of reinforcement. The gables were built up of sod or frame according to the means of the settler. The poorer settler built a roof in the crudest manner. A forked post set in each end of the cabin furnished a support for the ridge pole. The rafters were made of poles and the sheeting of brush; a layer of prairie grass covered this, and over all sod was placed. The settler who could afford it put a frame roof on his sod house. In that event sheeting was nailed on the rafters and tar paper spread over the sheeting boards. This was then covered with sods thinner than those used to cover the side walls, and laid with grass side down; the cracks were filled with fine clay. From time to time this dirt filling had to be renewed as the rains carried it away. In a short time great growths of sunflowers and grass appeared on the roofs. If the house were to be plastered, a mixture of clay and ashes was used. If it were to be a smooth finish, the builder took a spade and hewed the wall to a smooth finish and symmetrical proportions. The whole thing, as one pioneer said, was "made without mortar, square, plumb, or greenbacks." All that was needed was a pair of willing hands, and many homeseekers came to the plains with no assets other than a wagon cover. The little sod cabin was frequently divided into two rooms by a piece of rag carpet or quilt. The windows and door were closed with buffalo robes or other blankets. The house was crudely furnished. A nail keg and a soap box did duty as chairs. A dry goods box made a table and a rude bed of boards was fashioned in the corner. When the migration immediately following the Civil War broke in its fury, the demand for doors, sashes, and blinds was so great that even small towns ordered in carload lots. The dealer at the little town of Milford, Nebraska, advertised in March, 1871, that he had three carloads of this type of merchandise on the way.

The ordinary sod house had grave faults. Its few windows permitted little light and air for ventilation. The immaculate housekeeper abominated them because they were so hard to keep clean. The dirt and straw kept dropping on everything in the house. The most disagreeable feature of these houses was the leaky roof. Few of the sod-covered houses really turned water. A heavy rain came, soaked into the dirt roof, and soon little rivulets of muddy water were running through the sleepers' hair. The sod-house dweller had to learn to migrate when it rained. If the rain came from the north, the north side of the house leaked, and it was necessary to move everything to the south side; if from the south, a move had to be made again. When the roof was saturated it dripped for three days after the sky was bright without. Dishes, pots, pans, and kettles were placed about the house to catch the continual dripping. One pioneer woman remembered frying pancakes with someone holding an umbrella over her and the stove. A visitor at the home of a Dakota woman said that when great clouds rolled up in the afternoon the lady of the homestead began gathering up all the old dishes in the house and placing them here and there on the floor, on the stove, and on the bed. The visitor remarked that the prairie woman seemed to understand her business for when the rain came down in torrents a few minutes later every drop that came through the numerous holes in the roof of the shack went straight into those vessels. After a heavy rain it was necessary to hang all the bed clothing and wearing apparel on the line to dry. One old settler mentioned keeping the clothes in the covered wagon to keep them dry.

When the roof was well soaked its weight was immense. The heavy rafters sank deeper and deeper into the soggy walls until occasionally the roof caved in or the walls collapsed, burying people underneath the ruins. To prevent this kind of accident, heavy posts were placed in the house to support the roof; these were a great nuisance because they took up so much room. Frequently the cabin was covered with long coarse prairie grass. This type of roof also had the fault of dripping water after a heavy rain.

There were, however, some striking advantages of the sod house. It was cool in summer and warm in winter. There was no fear of the wind blowing it over and no danger of destruction by prairie fires. Neither was there danger of fire from a faulty fireplace. A fireplace was safely built of sod. The average life of a sod house was six or seven years.

34

"QUITE DISCOURAGED AND IMPATIENT FOR HIS DEATH..."

George Yount

Movies and popular fiction show us that the mountain men were tough hombres. How about reality? Here's an account from the memoirs of fur trapper George Yount of how a fellow trapper, named Hugh Glass, mangled by a grizzly bear and left to die, walked 300 miles to postpone that fate.

"Among the numerous veteran Trappers, with whom Yount became acquainted, & was from time to time associated, was one by the name of Glass—In point of adventures dangers & narrow escapes & capacity for endurance, & the sufferings which befel him, this man was preeminent— He was bold, daring, reckless & excentric to a high degree; but was nevertheless a man of great talents & intellectual as well as bodily power— But his bravery was conspicuous beyond all his other qualities for the perilous life he led. . . .

"With the Pawnees Glass roamed the wilderness in security many months, until they visited St. Louis; where he found means to escape from the Indians—Having resided in the City some eight or ten months, until Ashley sought him out & employed him to join a band of Thirty Trappers, which he had furnished & equipped to trap upon the Yellow Stone River under Maj. Henry—

"Glass with this party of Trappers, ascended the Missouri, till they reached the territory of the Pickarees [Arickara]. . . .

"Glass, as was usual, could not be kept, in obedience to orders, with the band, but perservered to thread his way alone through the bushes & chapparel—As the two hunters were wending their way, up the River, Allen discovered Glass dodging along in the forest alone; & said to his companion, 'there look at that fellow, Glass; see him foolishly exposing his life—I wish some Grizzly Bear would pounce upon him & teach him a lesson of obedience to orders, & to keep in his place—He is ever off, scouting in the bushes & exposing his life & himself to dangers'—

"Glass disappeared in the chapperel, & within half an hour his screams were heard—The two hunters hastened to his relief & discovered a huge Grizy Bear, with two Cubs—The monster had seized him, torn the flesh from the lower part of the body, & from the lower limbs—He also had his neck shockingly torn, even to the degree that an aperture appeared to have been made into the windpipe, & his breath to exude at the side of his neck—It is not probable however that any aperture was made into the windpipe—Blood flowed freely, but fortunately no bone was broken—& his hands & arms were not disabled—

"The whole party were soon there, the monster & her cubs were slain, & the victim cared for in the best degree possible, under existing circumstances—A convenient hand litter was prepared & the sufferer carried by his humane fellow-trappers from day to day—He retained all his faculties but those of speech & locomotion—Too feeble to walk, or help himself at all, his comrads every moment waited his death—Day by day they ministered to his wants, & no one counted it any hardship—

"Among those rude & rough trappers of the wilderness, fellow feeling & devotion to each others wants is a remarkable & universal feature or characteristic—It is admirable & worthy the imitation of even the highest grade of civilized men—We have remarked it at ever step in the investigation, which, in preparing this work, has devolved on us—

"After having thus carried Glass during six days, it became necessary for the party to croud their journey, as the season for trapping was fast transpiring—Maj. Henry therefore offered four hundred Dolls to any two of his men, who would volunteer to remain until he should die, decently bury him & then press on their way to overtake the main body—One man & boy volunteered to remain—They did so, & the party urged forward towards the Yellow Stone—

"The two waited several days, & he still lived—No change was apparent,—They dressed his wounds daily, & fed & nourished him with water from the spring & such light food as he could swallow—Still he was speechless but could use his hands—Both his lower limbs were quite disabled—As he lay by the spring, Buffalo berries hung in clusters & in great profusion over him & around his bed, which was made soft with dry leaves & two blankets—

"Quite discouraged & impatient for his death, as there remained no hope of his recovery, the two resolved to leave him there to die alone in the wilderness—They took from him his knife, camp kettle & Rifle, laid him smoothely on his blankets, & left him thus to die a lingering death, or be torn in pieces by the ferocious wild beasts & to be seen no more till they should meet him at the dread tribunal of eternal judgement—

"He could hear their every word, but could not speak nor move his body—His arms he could use—& he stretched them out imploringly, but in vain—They departed & silence reigned around him—Oppressed with grief & his hard fate, he soon became delirious—Visions of benevolent beings appeared, Around him were numerous friendly faces, smiling encouragement & exhorting him not to despond, & assuring him that all would be well at last—He declared to Yount that he was never alone, by day or by night—

"He could reach the water & take it to his mouth in the hollow of his hand, & could pluck the berries from the bushes to eat as he might need—One morning, after several weeks, he found by his side a huge Rattlesnake—With a small stone he slew the reptile, jambed off its head & cast it from him—Having laid the dead serpant by his side he jambed off small parts from time to time, & bruised it throughly & moistened it with water from the spring & made of it a grateful food on which he fed from day to day—

"At length the wolves came & took from under him his Blankets, & having dragged them some distance, tore them in pieces—, Thus he was left solely on his bed of leaves—In this condition he must have lain many weeks how many he could never tell—Meantime the two, the man & boy, false to their trust, came up with Maj. Henry & the party, & reported that Glass had died & they had decently buried his remains, & brot his effects with them, his gun, knife & Camp kettle, & received the promised reward for their fidelity, Four Hundred Dollars—

"After a long period, his strength began to revive, & he crawled a few rods, & laid himself down again during several days—Then again he resumed his journey, every day increasing his distance some rods—after many long & tedious days, & even weeks—he found himself upon his feet & began to walk—Soon he could travel nearly a mile in a day. This distance he even increased daily more & more—Thus covered with wounds, which would frequently bleed, & require much attention, he urged his journey through a howling wilderness, a distance of more than Two Hundred miles, to the nearest trading post—

"Often by the way he would find the decaying carcases of Buffalos, which, wounded by the hunter, or some more powerful animal, had died— From these he gained nourishing food, by pounding out the marrow from the bones, & eating it seasoned with Buffalo-berries & moistened with limped water from the brooks & springs—With sharp stones he would dig from the earth nourishing roots, which he had learned to discriminate while sojourning with the Paunees—

"At this trading post [Fort Kiowa] he passed the winter, as Autumn had worn away, & the cold season had overtaken him there—During the bracing season of winter, his strength was rapidly restored—As the following spring opened [actually in October], he found himself again a well man, & able to resume his journey to rejoin Maj Henry & his band of trappers— Fortunately as he was about to depart, an express party arrived, on its way to carry orders to Maj. Henry, at his post on the Yellow Stone, & Glass joined this party [under Antoine Langevin] to accompany them to Henry's Fort."

35

THE BASHFUL
TRAPPER

Jacob Fowler

*Jacob Fowler (1765–1850) was one of the first Indian traders and trappers on
the frontier. Fortunately he kept a detailed journal; unfortunately, he spelled
words the way they sounded to him. Here is his account of the embarrassment
of a young black friend named Paul (Pall) in the village of San Fernando de
Taos, New Mexico, in 1821.*

Sunday 10th Feby 1822. Remained In the village all day But Sent out two
parteys of trapes to Remain out till the first of may next—Hear it may be
Remembered that a Capten and and Sixty men of the Spanierds Came in
from the arkensaw With Conl glann and little party—and now the Same
Capten and party Has Crossed the mountaines again—but before He let
[left] Home Has Interdused Conl glann and Mr. Roy to His family Consisting a Wife and two daughters both young Woman the old lady Haveing
paid us a visid In the morning appered In a few minet quite formiler and
as Well aquainted With us as If She Head knone us for several years tho
She did not Stay more than about Half an Hour—But in the after noon
a boy Came With a mesege for Conl glann mr Roy and the negro. Who
after Some Ceremony acCompanyed the two gentlemen but With Some
Reluctance aledgeing that He Was not Settesfyed to go With out His
master aledgeing as the ladys appeerd more atached to Him than [to] the

White men—that there might be Some mischeef Intended and uder those doupts He Went as I before Stated and from the Statement of those two gentlemen I Will Indevour to State What followed—it Is a Custom With the Spanierds When Interdused to Imbrace With a Close Huge—this Ceremoney So Imbareshed Pall and maid Him So Shaimed that I[if] a Small Hole Cold Have been found He Wold Sartainly Crept Into it. but unfortnetly there Was no Such place to be found. and the trap door threw Which the desended Into the Room being Shut down [for the Went In at the top of the House] there Was no Poseble Way for Him to make His Escape—now the Haveing but one Beed in the House and that So large as to be Cappeble of Holding the three Copple of poson—there Ware all to lodge to geather and the mother of the daughters being oldest Had of Corse the ferst Chois of Bows. and took pall for Hir Chap takeing Hold of Him and drawing Him to the beed Side Sot Him down With Hir arms Round His Sholders. and gave Him a Kis from [?] Sliped Hir Hand down Into His Britches—but it Wold take amuch abeler Hand than mine to discribe palls feelings at this time being naturly a little Relegous modest and Bashfull He Sot as near the wall as Was Poseble and it may be Soposed He Indevoured to Creep Into it for Such Was His atachment to the old lady that he kept His [eyes] turned Constently up to the trap door—and to His great Joy Some person oppened it to Come In to the Same Room— But Pall no Sooner Saw the light [for their Rooms are dark] than He Sprang from the old lady and Was out In an Instent—and maid to our lodgeing as fast as Poseble Wheare the other two Soon followed and told What Head Happened to Pall

36

"AND THE SKIES
ARE NOT CLOUDY
ALL DAY"

Alan Bosworth

*Popular culture suggests the Colt revolver tamed the West. In fact it was barbed
wire and the windmill. The following is from Ozona County, by Alan Bos-
worth. Ironically, tiny Ozona became the richest, by per capita income, town in
America when the drillers went a little deeper and opened the Ozona oilfield.*

September rain means greened-up pastures, and juicy calf ribs in the spring.
But Ozona ranchmen were not long in discovering that many a September
is hot and dry, that the annual precipitation in Crockett County averages
just a fraction over sixteen inches, and that it is a long way to water in
any direction—especially down. The first comers were quick to acquire the
few dependable waterholes, such as Howard's Well and Escondido—both
historic overnight camping places on the old San Antonio-Chihuahua
Trail. The whole land is tilted southwestward, and water runs off it with
flash-flood speed. What stayed behind, in Gurley or Johnson Draws, was
soon "too thick to swallow and too thin to chew," and cowboys forced to
drink out of cowtracks in the mud quickly developed the habit of straining
the water through their teeth. They could have understood the wariness
of the late Gene Fowler, who all his life would never drink to the bottom
of any glass because, when he was a boy in the Rockies, "there was always
some sort of a bug surprise at the bottom."

Well drillers and windmills saved the day, and the nineties in the Ozona country might well be called the Windmill Era. It seems rather strange and a little sad that no literature has ever really given the well driller and the windmill man their due. I do not know of a man of either breed who ever got rich, although they helped others to riches. The drillers were a peripatetic sort, always moving westward with the frontier; they might be compared with Johnny Appleseed, on an earlier and more fruitful border. Some of the windmill men stayed, or grew up to practice their trade . . . usually one or two to an entire county. But the time came when a single large ranch had a half dozen or more windmills and could afford to hire its own full-time windmill man. Cowboys were sometimes forced to learn a new skill.

A ranch hand might curse the windmill for its rhythmic creaking and rattling at night, but it was not long before this became a sort of lullaby, and if the noise suddenly stopped due to a breakdown he would sit upright in his bed tarp, knowing that about sunup he would have to be up on the platform, perhaps in a freezing wind, trying to fix the dadblamed thing. Until later models came out with a self-oiling device, windmills had to be greased at appallingly short intervals, and you could always tell a windmill man from afar by the spatter of oil that inevitably dripped on his hat and jumper when he went back down the ladder after finishing a greasing job. Still, there was pride in being an all-around ranch hand. . . .

The well Joe Moore drilled in 1885, on land that later became Judge Charles E. Davidson's ranch, seems to have been the first; the E. M. Powell well on the Ozona townsite probably was the second, but from then on through the turn of the century and for long afterward well drillers were exceedingly active. Some used steam drills; others had rigs powered by horses walking in a circle, with water that had to be hauled a long way being poured into the hole at intervals to soften the earth and hasten the progress. Some wells struck "blue mud"—a sure sign, in those days, of a "dry hole"—and the rig would be moved to a new location. The depth might be a hundred feet, two hundred, or four hundred, before the long bailing bucket with a valve in its bottom brought up water. When this sloshed out on the trampled grass, the liquid sound was music, the sight was answer to a prayer.

Having struck water, the ranch owner would then either take his own wagons to the Findlater Hardware Company or another dealer in San Angelo, or would order his windmill and pipe brought down by a freighter. Almost invariably, the tail fans bore the brand names of Eclipse, Sampson, or Aermotor. The Eclipse had a huge, slatted wooden wheel and tail fin, and required a considerable breeze. It would, in the memory of ranchman

Ernest Dunlap, "bring up water with every turn of that big wheel—and then not run again until next March." But whatever brand it was, the new windmill worked its magic deep in the earth, day and night, to bring a thin stream of bright water fluting from the lead pipe and splashing into some sort of storage reservoir—a dirt tank scraped out of the ground, a circular stone and cement tank, or a taller one made of galvanized iron. The perhaps apocryphal cowboy who swore he could drink water faster than the new mill could pump it was talking through his Stetson: given time, with the incessant wind, and the tank would be brimming over.

There was no assurance of getting *good* water. Old-timers insisted that the Pecos River was so alkaline a kildee only had to fly across it to get the diarrhea, and the subterranean water was often even more strongly mineral—usually sulphurous. Ranchmen theorized that sulphur water most often came from wells drilled in the mesquite flats. Besides, a windmill on a divide or hillpoint got more breeze. But many of these pumped sulphur water too—some of it smelling uncomfortably like rotten eggs. Nobody ever bothered to bottle this for medicinal use, although not far away on the South Concho River near Christoval, a health resort was springing up around a series of sulphur springs, and small boys who swam in ranch tanks found that sulphur water very quickly healed skinned shins and stubbed toes.

The George Harrell ranch south of Ozona had only sulphur water for a long time. It made wretched coffee, shriveled the *frijole* beans, and formed black sediment in the pipes and troughs. Then Mr. Harrell's only son, R. A. (Alvin), went off to the University of Texas and came back with a degree.

Mr. Harrell, a progressive man, was eager for his son to take over and put his learning to work along scientific lines. There were advancements in livestock breeding, in range management, and in drenching sheep for stomach worms. He asked Alvin what was the first thing he intended to do.

After one is around sulphur water for a time one becomes accustomed to both the taste and the smell. But Alvin was newly home from Austin. He sniffed downwind from the well, and said, "I'm going to do something about this water!"

Mr. Harrell stepped back and waited for geological surveys and other scientific tests. There was none. Instead, Alvin went to Ozona and arranged for Tom Smith to "witch" for water with a pronged willow switch.

Tom Smith—an unlikely name for a necromancer—had been black-smith and constable in Ozona from the earliest days. A very powerful man physically, he never carried a gun, and he set something of a record by never making an arrest. (This, much later, got him featured in Robert L. Ripley's *Believe It or Not*.) He simply heaved troublemakers out of public places and sent them home.

Now he walked across the mesquite flat at the Harrell ranch with the willow fork held before him at chest level, something like a man walking in his sleep. George Harrell followed, shaking his head dubiously.

They went a long way through the tangled chaparral. About a mile from the ranch house, the willow dipped sharply in Tom's grasp. He scratched a mark on the hard ground with his boot heel, and said, "Drill right here."

They drilled, and struck abundant water, cold and sweet, which still supplies the ranch house and the stock in that pasture.

Mr. Harrell told the story for a long time. It plainly showed, he said, the advantages of a college education.

37

THE $175,000 SACK
OF FLOUR

Early westerners were noted innovators. In 1864 miners in the boomtown of Austin, Nevada, wanted to raise money for their Sanitary Fund, the Civil War forerunner of the American Red Cross. This is from Pioneer Nevada, *a publication of Harold's Club in Reno.*

Fifty pounds of flour is something of a prize package in these expensive days, but even so it couldn't hold a candle to the fabulous Gridley Sack of Flour which netted $175,000 for the Sanitary Fund in 1864. It started in the boom mining town of Austin over an election bet, but when the final take was counted cash and currency worth nearly a fifth of a million dollars had been accumulated for the Sanitary Fund and the sack of flour had travelled across the land, selling over the auction blocks of the nation's major cities.

R. C. Gridley was an Austin grocer, a native of Missouri with pronounced secessionist leanings. When the city elections of 1864 showed signs of a heated campaign between the Democratic and Republican contenders for the mayor's position, Gridley made a bet with H. S. Herrick, also of Austin, who supported the Republican candidate.

The loser was to carry a fifty-pound sack of flour from Clifton to Upper Austin. If Gridley lost the bet his march was to be accompanied by a brass band playing "John Brown's Body," while if Herrick lost, he was to do his chore to the tune of "Dixie."

On the day following election, Herrick appeared in front of Gridley's store, for the Republican candidate had won the election. The Austin brass band struck up the opening bars of "John Brown's Body," and Gridley, shouldering the sack of flour, started his march at the head of a parade which featured a crepe-draped broom (the insignia of democracy). The flour sack was completely decorated with red, white and blue ribbons and numerous Union flags.

The parade soon drew attention of the entire population of Austin and when the march was completed the flour was returned to Central Austin and placed upon the auction block with the announcement that proceeds would be turned over to the Sanitary Fund, a Charity which sought to relieve suffering created by the Civil War.

So spirited was the bidding that the day's sale netted more than six thousand dollars. Each time it was bid in over the auction block, cash was paid and the flour was returned to be auctioned again. Such was the success of the venture that Gridley took the sack of flour to the Comstock where twenty-five thousand dollars went into the coffers of the Sanitary Fund from the auction proceeds.

From Virginia City the flour travelled with Gridley to San Francisco and the principal Pacific Coast cities and then eastward across the nation. Nevada and California alone raised $175,000, and a great deal more was added to the fund in the eastward journey.

So great was the fame of the Sanitary Sack of Flour that Austin adopted its replica for the city seal and coat of arms, and Gridley, who had been a staunch secessionist, became an ardent Unionist.

38

HOW AMERICANS
GET AHEAD

William Shepherd

Britisher William Shepherd came to California in 1883, bought 5,000 head of sheep and herded them from there to Montana. As this passage from his Prairie Experiences Handling Cattle and Sheep *suggests, the experience impressed him with American ingenuity.*

For riding, driving, and the heavy work during a few weeks' harvesting, Americans cannot be beaten. Self-reliance is their prominent characteristic; every man will undertake any class of work without any previous training, and with the greatest self-assurance will proceed to lose your sheep, smash your machinery, or spoil your crop, for thirty dollars wages and all found. "You cannot teach him anything," is a common saying among the boys, which hits off very well the exaggeration of a great good point; for to this self-reliance is due a great deal of the wonderful advances in America. It induces the men to widen their experiences, to turn their hands to all trades, and to start off on the longest journeys, trusting in themselves to pull through. One result could hardly be avoided—that is, the number of indifferent workmen all over the West. A boy of eighteen attaches himself, say to a blacksmith, wheelwright, and wagon repairer; this trade would in most countries require at least a couple of years' apprenticeship. Not so with our intelligent citizen; after six months he will try to boss the shop, or start an independent concern in a neighboring town.

This would not answer in the East, but forasmuch as the numbers of people settling out West are continually demanding a proportionate increase of the trades, the young fellow will probably hire an industrious German or Swede who does know the business, and the chances are the trade thrives. If he is now steady he is nearly bound to get on. After a few years he marries, runs for the county constable, lends his surplus money out at 24 per cent, and will have in the mean time located a ranch and bought cattle. Before he is forty years old he has sold his business, has been for some time living on his farm, and is worth—well, it is hard to say—there is one sum on which he is assessed for taxes, another and considerably higher one which sounds better in conversation.

3 9

J.C. PENNEY'S
FIRST DAY

Norman Beasley

James Cash Penney was a newlywed twenty-six-year-old with $500 cash and a $1,500 debt when he opened his Golden Rule Store in Kemmerer, Wyoming, and began a revolution in retailing. Here's his first day described in Norman Beasley's Main Street Merchant.

The first Penney store consisted of one room on the street level and an attic, with the joists and rafters standing exposed. One small window served as a source of light, while an outside stairway led to the ground. There was no water on the premises. Water, Penney was told, could be obtained from a Chinese restaurant a few doors down the main street. As for the store itself, it was as bare as the attic. Nothing but four walls and a floor. No fixtures, no plumbing—but Penney imagined the store already crowded with customers and saw the attic as a home for his wife, himself, and for a baby one year old. The rent was forty-five dollars a month.

Within the week boxes of merchandise began coming in. Penney carefully drew out the nails, made counters and shelves out of the boxes, and put out the merchandise—dress goods, clothing, thread, needles, neckties, socks, shoes, overcoats, overalls, something of almost everything in dry goods. He left some of the merchandise inside the opened boxes because there wasn't room on the shelves.

From the empty crates he carefully selected three, one a dry goods box and the others, shoe boxes.

These he took upstairs, upending them—the dry goods box to serve as a table, the shoe boxes as chairs. He had already bought a small, pot-bellied stove to do the double duty of cooking and heating. The stove and one new bed were the extent of his purchases as furnishings for the attic, while to the small window he fastened a rope for pulling up a pail of water borrowed from the restaurant each morning.

Before opening day he had the names of the 500 miners, and as the day approached he mailed fliers to each name on the list, telling the recipients about the new store and the savings they could make by trading there. The day before the opening he distributed handbills all over town— handbills that confirmed the savings, at *cash* prices, he had promised the 500 miners.

At sunrise on Monday, April 14, 1902, in Kemmerer, Wyoming, Penney opened for business.

It was nearly midnight of the same day when the last customer departed. Penney locked the front door and helped his wife, who had been his only clerk, up the outside stairs; he unlocked the attic door, went inside, locked the door again behind him, and lighted a lamp. With his wife sitting on one upended shoe box while he sat on the other, he used the dry goods box for a counting table. Spilling out the pennies, nickels, dimes, quarters, half dollars, silver dollars, and a few paper bills from a paper bag, he sat counting while his wife checked the piles of coins and thumbed through the paper money.

The first day's sales amounted to $466.59.

40

WOLF WILLOW

Wallace Stegner

Like N. Scott Momaday, Wallace Stegner has the genius to turn prose into poetry. His recollections of his childhood at Wolf Willow on the Montana-Saskatchewan border provide an uncommonly true and beautiful look at life under the big sky.

In spite of my mother's flimsy pretense that we were farmers of the kind her Iowa parents were, drawing our full sustenance from the soil and tending the soil as good husbandmen should; in spite of her cow and her dasher churn and her cloths of cottage cheese dripping from the clothesline; in spite of her chickens and eggs and vegetable garden, she was not fooled. It was not a farm, and we were not farmers, but wheat miners, and trapped ones at that. We had flown in carelessly, looking for something, and got ourselves stuck. The only question now was how to get free.

She knew it was failure we were living; and if she did not realize, then or ever, that it was more than family failure, that it was the failure of a system and a dream, she knew the family failure better than any of us. Given her choice in the matter, she might have elected to go on farming— get some better land somewhere, maybe in the Cypress Hills, and become one of the stickers. She had the character and the skills for it as my father did not. But she likewise had impulses toward a richer and more rewarding life, and ambitions for her sons, and she must have understood that compared to what a Saskatchewan homesteader considered his opportunity, five years of Siberian exile would have been a relatively comfortable outing. She had gone to school only through the sixth grade. It would never have occurred to her to think that her family and thousands of others had been betrayed by homestead laws totally inapplicable on the arid Plains; or that she and hers had been victimized by the folklore of hope. She had not education enough to know that the mass impulse that had started her parents from Ulvik on the Hardanger Fjord, and started her and my father from Iowa into Dakota and on across the border, had lost its legitimacy beyond the hundredth meridian. She knew nothing about minimal annual rainfall, distribution of precipitation, isohyetal lines. All she knew was that we were trapped and licked, and it would not have helped her much to be told that this was where a mass human movement dwindled to its end.

For her sake I have regretted that miserable homestead, and blamed my father for the blind and ignorant lemming-impulse that brought us to it. But on my own account I would not have missed it—could not have missed it and be who I am, for better or worse. How better could a boy have known loneliness, which I must think a good thing to know? Who ever came more truly face to face with beauty than a boy who in a waste of characterless grass and burnouts came upon the first pale primrose on the coulee bank, or on some day of great coasting clouds looked across acres of flax in bloom? Why, short of exile, would anyone ever submit to the vast geometry of sky and earth, to the glare and heat, to the withering winds? But how else could he have met the mystery of nights when the stars were scoured clean and the prairie was full of breathings from a long way off, and the strange, friendly barking of night-hunting owls?

There may be as good ways to understand the shape and intensity of the dream that peopled the continent, but this seems to me one good one. How does one know in his bones what this continent has meant to Western man unless he has, though briefly and in the midst of failure, belatedly and in the wrong place, made trails and paths on an untouched country and built human living places, however transitory, at the edge of a field that he helped break from prairie sod? How does one know what wilderness has meant to Americans unless he has shared the guilt of wastefully and ignorantly tampering with it in the name of Progress?

One who has lived the dream, the temporary fulfillment, and the disappointment has had the full course. He may lack a thousand things that the rest of the world takes for granted, and because his experience is belated he may feel like an anachronism all his life. But he will know one thing about what it means to be an American, because he has known the raw continent, and not as tourist but as denizen. Some of the beauty, the innocence, and the callousness must stick to him, and some of the regret. The vein of melancholy in the North American mind may be owing to many causes, but it is surely not weakened by the perception that the fulfillment of the American Dream means inevitably the death of the noble savagery and freedom of the wild. Anyone who has lived on a frontier knows the inescapable ambivalence of the old-fashioned American conscience, for he has first renewed himself in Eden and then set about converting it into the lamentable modern world. And that is true even if the Eden is, as mine was, almost unmitigated discomfort and deprivation.

41

THE MELTING POT

Robert Laxalt

Robert Laxalt wrote the following essay about a copper mining town in Nevada for his bicentennial history of that state, but much of what he writes here could apply to any western boom town that attracted immigrant laborers.

"You would call it a real international settlement these days, but there were some other words, not so nice, for it then. It was a copper company town, and the whole population only amounted to a few thousand people. But, Jesus, was it divided! There was Greek Town, Hunky Town, Jap Town, Wop Town, and Mid Town. That meant the middle of town, and it was where all the 'white people' lived. The rest of us were cheap labor for the copper mines and the smelter. The 'foreigners' stuck together for the most part, but once in a while, you could get a scrap if you were a Hunky and you crossed the line into Greek Town. Our common enemy was Mid Town. Anytime you crossed that line, you were in for big trouble. I was a Serb, and my mother had a cow in Hunky Town. It was my job to sell milk to houses in Mid Town. The first couple of times, I went alone. And sure enough, there would be a gang of 'white' kids waiting for me. They would take the milk pail away from me and spill it on the ground, and then they would beat me up. So I went to my father and said 'I am tired of getting beat up because I'm a Hunky.' And he said, 'I don't care how many times you get beat up. You are a Serb and you got to be proud of it. If I ever hear of you running away from a fight, you will get a worse beating from me than them.' So I went back and I got beat up a thousand times, but I won a few, too, when I could get some of my Hunky friends to go with me.

"Then a funny thing happened. When we got into high school, we were all together—'whites' and 'foreigners' alike. When the 'foreigners' showed they were good at sports, the people in Mid Town began to look at us differently. And when we won a few state championships, it changed altogether. That was when all the barriers broke down. They finally accepted us as human.

"I guess it's the way life is, but now I go back there and some of my best friends are the guys from Mid Town. We can laugh about it now, but it was sure nothing to laugh about then."

"All of us together were of a generation born of old-country people who spoke English with an accent and prayed in another language, who drank red wine and cooked their food in the old-country way, and peeled apples and pears after dinner.

"We were among the last whose names would tell our blood and the kind of faces we had, to know another language in our homes, to suffer youthful shame because of that language and refuse to speak it, and a later shame because of what we had done, and hurt because we had caused a hurt so deep it could never find words.

"And the irony of it was that our mothers and fathers were truer Americans than we, because they had forsaken home and family, and gone into the unknown of a new land with only courage and the hands that God gave them, and had given us in our turn the right to be born American.

"And in a little while even our sons would forget, and the old-country people would be only a dimming memory, and names would mean nothing, and the melting would be done."

42

BASQUES IN
NEVADA

Robert Laxalt

Every spring, anyone who drives down backroads in the West will find his way blocked by thousands of sheep being moved into the mountains. They spend the summer grazing the high meadows guarded by a solitary shepherd and his dogs. It's probably the world's most solitary occupation and the Basques have a reputation for being the best at tolerating loneliness. This is from Robert Laxalt's Nevada, A Bicentennial History.

I had known this sheep ranch since I was a boy. My father had trailed sheep through here on their way to summer range in the forested Sierra that reared in the distance. And more than once I had stopped here to rest and water the horses that I was driving from winter range to the foothills of the Sierra. Then, the ranch had always been a bustle of activity, corrals filled with milling sheep, the plaintive wails of lambs and the bleating of mothers looking for their wayward offspring.

Now, the ranch was deserted and the corrals abandoned. As we wandered through the maze of weathered brown boards and trampled earth, Batista said in his soft, outside voice, "I had to sell out. The Basque boys don't want to come over from the old country anymore, because life is getting better over there. They don't want to spend their best years out in the desert or the mountains herding sheep. You could say they were

149

spoiled, but I can't blame them for not coming over. We didn't know it then, because there wasn't much choice for us, but I guess it was a hard life at that. . . ."

He was echoing a lament that can be heard throughout Nevada's range country today. Yet, it is only part of the reason for the decline of the sheep industry. The development of synthetic wools, uncertain world markets, importation of cheaper wool from foreign countries, and a lessening demand for mutton have all contributed to the decline. Dwindling from a peak of more than a million sheep in 1910, Nevada's sheep empires have vanished, and only a handful of outfits remain to tend less than two hundred thousand sheep on private land and on the diminishing public domain.

The story of sheep in Nevada was one that began almost by accident. The discovery that sheep could fare on the sagebrush deserts was made in the years of the California gold rush. Profits to be made by selling meat to the gold camps were realized by such as Kit Carson, who had been a scout for Frémont in his explorations of the Great Basin. In 1853, Kit Carson trailed some thirteen thousand sheep from New Mexico through Nevada to Sacramento, setting in motion a movement of half a million sheep across the Nevada deserts.

When the fortunes of the California gold camps waned and silver was discovered in 1859 near what was to become Virginia City, the sheep made a return journey over the Sierra to Nevada to feed the new boom camps. As mining strikes proliferated across the state's landscape, sheepmen followed. From then on, sheep were never again absent from Nevada.

The years immediately before and after the turn of the century were the years of biggest expansion in the sheep industry. They also saw the beginning of a period of violence between cattlemen and sheepmen over the scarce range forage and water of a desert state.

The range disputes were effectively settled in 1934 by the passage of the Taylor Grazing Act, which divided the open range between warring factions. From then on, cattlemen and sheepmen learned to live and prosper together. Contrary to the Hollywood-created myth of cowboy versus sheepherder forever, cattlemen often became sheepmen, sheepmen became cattlemen, and the most far-seeing ran cattle and sheep at the same time. It all depended upon the market, and both cattle and sheep used the same essentials of corrals and range and water. And sheep did not ruin a range, as the myth went. Instead, they were more delicate grazers than either cattle or horses.

I have known cowboys who herded sheep when buckarooing jobs were scarce, and sheepherders who became buckaroos when market prices for wool and mutton dropped and they in turn were left without jobs. My father and my uncles were typical. All of them came to America as young sheepherders. My father began with sheep, expanded to sheep and cattle together, and finally returned to sheep exclusively. Both of my uncles alternated between sheep and cattle until they died. All of them were good sheepherders and top buckaroos. And along the trail, they had all been riders enough to have tried their hand at the most demanding horseman's endeavor of all, running down and roping mustangs on the open range.

Though English, Scots, Irish, Mexican, and Chinese were predominant as herders in the beginning, the Basques emerged as the backbone of the range sheep industry. I once asked an English-born sheepman why this was so. He told me that of all the nationalities he had hired as sheepherders, he considered the Scots the most skillful. "But they and the Irish had a breaking point when it came to too much time spent alone," he said. "When they got fed up, they would walk away from their sheep and go to town for a tear. Not the Basques. They would stay with those sheep until they dropped in their tracks, or went nuts from being alone, or got rich. Usually, it was the latter."

The Basques have lived to see themselves regarded as a group unique to the Far West. But plagued by a lack of young herders and a public domain slowly being withdrawn for recreational uses, the tradition of the Basque sheepman on the open range will soon be a closed chapter in history. And the aspect of a sheepherder guarding his flocks through winter deserts and summer mountain meadows will have vanished forever from the Nevada scene.

"In them days, we no sooner got off the train from New York after the boat from the old country than we found ourselves out in the desert. We had our provisions, a bedroll, a carbine, strong walking shoes, an American hat, a burro, and a dog. And oh, yes, three thousand head of sheep. The boss would take a stick, and looking at that miserable desert stretching out there forever, he would scratch a map on the ground. To show where the water was, where the good feed was, and where the poisoned feed was. Then you just moved out. You got up with the stars so that the sheep could feed before the sun made the buds on the sagebrush and the little patches of grass too hot. That would change the taste, you know, and the sheep didn't like that. You took coffee then and came back in the middle of the morning and took bacon and eggs, which you had put in the burro's barley can so they wouldn't break. That was when the sheep was resting. Then they would get up and go again until nighttime. In a year we would walk thousands of miles. But that wasn't the hard part. The hard part was the loneliness. You would almost die from the loneliness, just to hear a human voice. Then a funny thing happened. You turned a corner in your mind, and you wouldn't walk over the next hill to see someone, even if they was someone there. They paid you thirty dollars a month and board. The room you didn't have to worry about. There was a lot of that around. Anyway, you made up your mind to suffer for that money, because you was poor. But poorer makes tougher, you know."

43

NAILS AND WHISKEY

Alexander Toponce

The Yankees are famous for ingenuity, but the West had its share also. In his Memoirs of Alexander Toponce, Toponce recalls how, as an independent wagon freighter between Denver and Montana in the 1860s, he offset the lack of travel money.

When I was loading at Denver the last day there was still a little balance coming to me at the store and the storekeeper says, "Alex, what else will you take to balance the account?"

"Give me nails," I told him. He gave me a package of eight pounds of ten-penny nails. I could not have chosen more wisely. In Montana I found fellows ready to trade their eye-teeth for a handful of nails.

In my wagon I also placed ten gallons of whiskey and five gallons of brandy. It sounds like a lot of liquor in these prohibition days, but we did not have very much left when we got to Bannock, Montana.

I traded liquor for lumber, with which I made the first sluice box ever set up on Alder Gulch. It was owned and operated by Henry Carman, Enos A. Wall and myself.

When we were coming across Wyoming we had trouble in buying feed for our stock. When we asked the keepers of the stage stations to sell they would say "Against orders—can't sell anything. We are saving it for teams on the stage line."

After everybody had gone to bed I would go over to the stage station, sit down and have a talk with the keepers. I had a supply of "Nigger Twist" tobacco, good for smoking and chewing. They would ask for a chew and I would cut off about six inches of twist for each of the two men.

Then I would say, "Maybe you would like a drink." Always they would and I would get out a quart flask and put it on the table and for an hour we would smoke and touch up the bottle.

About the time I was ready to go I would say, "By the ways, boys, how are you off for grain for feed?"

"Got plenty," they would say. "Which is your wagon?"

"The lead wagon in the right-hand row," I would tell them, and when I left I would set out another bottle on the table.

In a few minutes after I would get to bed in my wagon I would hear a noise and look out and see my two friends coming, each with a sack on his shoulder. They would set the sack against the wheel and back for more sacks. At one place I got six sacks that way.

The next day some fellow would set up a "holler" that he would give so much a pound for feed and I would sell him a supply. I picked up over $600 that way coming from Denver to Montana. I left Denver with hardly a cent for traveling expenses.

44

DEATH VALLEY
SCOTTY'S STORY

Eleanor Jordan Houston

From Death Valley, borax was hauled to market in massive twenty-mule wag-
ons. Walter Scott first saw one of these when he was thirteen. Soon he became
"Death Valley Scotty." In Death Valley Scotty Told Me, *Eleanor Jordan*
Houston recalls his story.

Scotty transferred his attention to me. "Sit down, Lady," he said pointing
to the kitchen chair he usually occupied when he ate at the Castle. "I'm
going to tell you about how I first happened to come to Death Valley and
about swamping on the 20-Mule Teams.

"It was like this. When I left Tombstone, I went back to Wells,
Nevada, and got a job with a man named John Clark. He sent me to Los
Angeles as wrangler helping take a herd of eleven hundred horses. It was
a long trip through Star Valley and Railroad Canyon to Belmont, then
through Fish Lake, Owens River Valley, Mojave and Elizabeth Lake. From
Los Angeles we drove the horses on to Downey, where we put them to
pasture in filaree grass.

"After that, I came into Death Valley in the fall of 1884 with a party
of surveyors under Mr. St. Clair. I was water boy and roustabout for the
outfit at a dollar a day. I helped run the line for the state boundary between
California and Nevada. Remember I told you that was when St. Clair spoke

of building a castle up here on the mesa. I was only twelve then, but the
words stuck in my mind wherever I'd go.

"After the survey was finished in the fall of 1885—I was thirteen that
year—I went to Mojave and worked as call boy for a while. I made a
dollar-forty a day getting the train crews out of the sporting houses and
cafes when it was time for them to go to work.

"Mojave was a hundred and sixty-five miles from the Death Valley
borax mines. Every day, I'd see the big 20-Mule Team outfits coming in,
and I'd talk to some of the swampers. William T. Coleman, a rich San
Francisco man, headed it. No, he wasn't the one discovered borax in Death
Valley. I thought you knew that story about old Aaron Winters. He was
an old hairy lollapalooza living with his Indian wife Rosie down the valley
at Ash meadows, you know where they got that dude ranch now. He'd
heard a lot about borax and found out how to test for it.

"One day in 1880, he picked out a salt crust near Furnace Creek in
Death Valley, poured on a mixture of alcohol and sulphuric acid. He and
Rosie held their breath as he lighted it. Then they saw a green flame.
'Rosie, she burns green!' he yelled. 'We're rich!'

"They were rich for those days for Coleman paid Winters twenty
thousand dollars for his claim. Lot of money for folks that had been living
the way they did—in a one-room dugout with a dirt floor.

"That was just the start for Coleman. Ever been by the Old Harmony
Borax Works, not far from Furnace Creek Ranch? The old boilers are still
there. The Chinks would fill the carts with the cotton ball borax from the
floor of the valley nearby. You know that white stuff that some ringtails
ask the rangers is it snow? They dumped it in the vats with water and
chemicals and fired up the boilers with mesquite wood from the flat where
the Indian village is now. At just the right temperature, the borax would
stick to iron rods that they put down in the vats. Then they drained the
water off and let the borax dry. Then it was loaded into the wagons for
the long haul to Mojave.

"I decided I wanted to work with those teams. I applied to Mr.
Delameter for a job. He thought I was too light, but he was short of
swampers and took me. Let's see, if he was living now, he'd be way over
ninety, for his son was about my age. I was assigned to the mule team
Walter Smith drove. Smith was about thirty-five at that time. I thought
a lot of him. Most of the teams had twenty large mules, but Smith had
twenty-six small ones.

"The paymaster's name was Valentine. My pay was sixty dollars a
month. That was good then because things didn't cost so much. My pants
cost forty cents. I saw some the other day for ten times the price, and no

better. Pioneer flour was four dollars a hundred, bacon, six cents a pound.

"As I said, it was a hundred and sixty-five miles from Death Valley to Mojave, and there was just three wells along the way. Teams could go only sixteen or eighteen miles a day to make the trip. Chinese laborers had made a road over the salt flat. Gosh, it was rough! They had to beat down the big chunks of borax crystals with sledge hammers. They call that section The Devil's Golf Course.

"From the floor of the valley we'd go up through Wingate Pass on a rutty dirt road. It was twenty-two miles from the bottom of the grade to the top. There were springs only at Bennett Wells, Lone Willow and Black Mountain. Between these places they had what they called dry camps. They would haul water from springs to these dry camps in twelve-hundred-gallon tanks. In summer the temperature got around 138 degrees, but even in spring and fall it was hot—115 to 120 degrees.

"We usually made it to Mojave about two or three o'clock of the tenth day. We would stop at the Wilson Company store where the wagons would be checked for repairs. We had to make camp four miles out, because they didn't want the outfits drinking in town.

"The old wagon down at Furnace Creek Ranch gives you an idea of what our wagons were like. They were about sixteen feet long, four feet wide, and six feet deep. The hind wheels were seven feet across and had steel tires an inch thick and eight inches across. A wagon weighed ten or twelve tons before it was loaded and would carry a load up to twenty-three tons. We had to carry hay and that big water tank too. Brake rods on the wagons were steel three inches wide and almost an inch thick.

"The driver's whip had a six-foot handle and a lash more than twenty feet long. For animals out of reach of his whip, the driver would use pebbles. It was my job to keep the rock box full. Guiding those teams was a job. The driver and mules had a kind of telegraph system, a quarter-inch rope that ran to the heads of the lead animals. When the driver pulled on the rope, that meant to turn right; when he jerked it or slapped it on the neck, that meant turn to the left.

"They couldn't use just any dumb mule on jobs like that. Sometimes a good span of mules would cost a thousand dollars. I had to feed and water the mules when we stopped, and of course Smith had to know what to do for one that was sick or had lost a shoe. And he had to get that string of animals around all the twists and turns of the road, up and down hills, over steep grades. It was a tough job to pass when we would meet another outfit. The lead mules could make the others step over the traces to give room for passing on a curve or a grade. The empty wagons had the right of way. The drivers hated each other's guts, and most of them looked down on swampers. But Smith always treated me fair and square. The skinners would cuss each other and the mules. You wouldn't hear that much goddamning anywhere else in ten years. It was a tight squeak on that old road and it would have been easy to get the wheels locked or to crowd a wagon over the edge. But we always got through, hot as it was and dust so thick you could slice it and serve it for bread. . . .

"After they stopped hauling borax off the floor of the valley in 1886, borax was found by company prospectors and others up Furnace Creek. The company would offer to buy out private claims and when they wouldn't sell, something would usually happen to their camp—always some Destroying Angel around to take care of 'em.

45

BURIAL CUSTOMS AT FORT PIERRE

Thaddeus Culbertson

Thaddeus Culbertson, a Princeton graduate, came west in 1850 to improve his health and left a detailed description of Fort Pierre, which the American Fur Company had built across the Missouri from what is now Pierre, South Dakota. Culbertson then went home and died of a "prevalent disease."

I have for some time intended giving a description of Fort Pierre Chouteau and its environs, but have postponed it from day to day for no good reason. A person coming up the country on the other side of the river has his first view of it about half a mile below, and it then presents a most beautiful sight.

The main object in the picture is the fort itself, having a white appearance, lying four-square, surrounded by a square palisade wall fifteen feet high and three-hundred feet on each side, with bastions at the North, West and South East corners; then the Indian lodges are seen around the fort; by their irregularity of position, their conical shape and varied colors, giving life and a picturesque air to the scene; and for a couple of miles below the fort and between it and the bluffs, the whole plain is dotted with horses grazing and moving leisurely about, while the bold bluffs a mile west of the fort affords a fine back-ground for the picture. The shores immediately opposite the fort are high bluffs almost from the water's edge, and with their steep barren sandy sides, look as if determined to wrap themselves up forever in the dignity of their own sterility. The main channel runs along this shore, although at present there is a probability that the boat will be able to land at the fort.

The fort is situated on a beautiful piece of bottom land which extends for some miles along the bank of the river, and is skirted by a range of bluff hills on the West, by which you rise to the rolling prairie beyond. The bottom land affords fine pasture and has a beautiful appearance when the grass and flowers are out on it; but the company pasture their horses on the Bad River about eight miles from the fort, as the Indians always have so many horses here.

On entering the fort two large gates are seen, over each of which there is a large picture intending to represent scenes of interest to the Indian; we shall enter by the one to the left, as the other leads to the stable-yard, and we shall choose a dry day for our visit, as on any other our shoes will suffer very much from the mud. A number of Indians, men and women, with their blankets wrapped around them, with their bare legs, painted faces and curiously ornamented heads, will probably be lounging in perfect listlessness about the gate. The main building stands opposite the gate and occupying nearly the whole length of that side, with a porch along its entire front, windows in the roof and a bell on the top, and above it the old weather cock, looking for all the world, like a Dutch tavern. The main building contains the mess hall, kitchen and rooms for the traders; to the right of it you see a neat log house with a pleasant little portico in front, and oil painted window blinds—that is the boujier or boss' house, and the long one storied building painted red, and occupying almost the whole of the North side of the fort, is the store and warehouse where the goods and robes are kept. To your immediate right as you enter the gate are the blacksmith's shop and several rooms for the men, and to your left is a small building containing the carpenter shop and further accommodations for the men; nearly the whole south side is occupied by a low building divided into seven rooms, occupied by the laborers and traders. These low houses are covered with dirt roofs; none of the houses are built against the fort walls, but behind them is a space of about twenty-five feet, and this is occupied in various ways. The north side has a house for the deposit of harness and implements of labor—the powder-house, milk-house for quite a good dairy—the stable and stable-yard; the south side has two large buildings for corn, meat, skins, &c., while the south west corner is occupied by the office, a one-story building ranging with the main building, and having behind it a house occupied by one of the clerks, and a yard in which the feathered tribe live and lay eggs. This arrangement of the buildings leaves quite a large square in the centre, from the middle of which generally rises a tall flag staff, but at present there is none—the last was blown down by the wind.

The Fort Pierre grave yard lies about a quarter of a mile south of the fort; it is a square piece of ground which has been well fenced in but not ornamented in any way; it contains the bodies of a number of dead, both Indians and Whites: the latter are in the ground and their graves are marked with wooden crosses, or with tombstones recording their names and dates of their death. The Indians however have followed their own customs in disposing of their dead, which is to place them on a scaffold about eight or ten feet from the ground. As you approach the yard coming from the fort, you see elevated on a scaffold supported by rough willow poles and now half broken down, a confused pile of old boxes of various lengths—old trunks and pieces of blankets hanging out. These may seem strange things for a grave yard, but these old boxes contain the bodies of dead Indians: they were originally placed on a good scaffold and had piles of blankets wrapped around them, but the scaffold has broken down from exposure to weather and weight of the bodies, which appear to have been heaped on without order of any kind. If you look over the fence to the left of this scaffold, you will see on the ground one of these boxes which has probably fallen down and broken open: and there the bones lay exposed, except the skull which perhaps has been buried by some friend of the deceased; if you look a little more closely you will see lying with the bones, a dark looking object about three inches broad and perhaps fifteen long, tied around with a string: this is some tobacco given to the dead to smoke in the other world; they always place with their dead almost every article of common use, for their benefit in the other world: blankets, sometimes as many as twenty, the best the parties can afford—tobacco, sugar, coffee, molasses, kettles of mush and other things of use. These remain undisturbed until they decay, or are destroyed by the weather or wolves. On the east side is a scaffold put up a few months since; the box is a rough one, daubed with black paint, and is surrounded by several old trunks, that were the property of the old squaw who rests within. On the opposite side is another scaffold, on which is placed the body of a man who died not many months since; you can see the scarlet blanket through the large cracks in this rude coffin. It appears to me, that this method of burial originated in a desire to protect the bodies from the wolves, more than in any of their religious opinions: they frequently bury the bones, after the flesh has decayed entirely. On a large tree, a little above the fort, is a body which must have a great pile of blankets on it, from the size.

Part Six

◆

COWBOYS

Some years ago, while fishing in northern New Mexico, I encountered a cowboy, dirty and tired, who had ridden in to tell his boss that a veterinarian was needed to save a pregnant heifer. We introduced ourselves. His name was the same as one of the state's most prominent families, and of one of its wealthiest men—recently deceased.

"Any relation?" I asked.

"He was my father," said the young man.

"So you could be running a bank holding company instead of cows," I said.

"I guess I could be," he said. "If I was crazy."

Any intellectual will tell you that nothing is proved by such anecdotal evidence, but it does illustrate the mystique of the cowboy that has captured the imagination of Americans (and Europeans, and Japanese) generation after generation. It's a hard, dangerous, and poorly paid life. But it represents freedom better than any other job.

46

THE HARVARD COWBOY

Richard Trimble

Richard Trimble, twenty-five, and not long out of Harvard College, stopped off at Cheyenne in 1882 to visit a classmate. He recounted the results for those at home in a long letter, which was published in Gene M. Gressley's Cowboys and Cattlemen.

Cheyenne Club, August 27th, 1882.
Dear Family,

. . . I left last Saturday morning to go to see Teschy who was on the "roundup" cutting out his beef cattle for market. After an all day's ride in a stage we reached Hunton's ranch (64 miles) where I stayed all night sleeping on the floor of a new barn for fear of the boys in the house. Sunday morning I got on one of Teschy's horses that had been left there and rode thirty-five miles to Red's where they told me that the round-up was then at Fish Creek about eight miles off and as my horse was "busted" (he was a miserable little Mustang foundered and tender footed) I slept there bunking with one of the cow boys and rode over to the round up in the morning. (Monday). I wandered about for some time before I found Teschemacher who was "holding" his beef at some distance from the camp. At first

165

he didn't know me on account of my whiskers. At noon he
drove his cattle down to the creek for water and then we
went to camp for dinner where for the first time I saw them
branding in the pens. The calves they "wrestle" and throw
by main force but to brand a grown animal is quite a skillful
piece of business. First one man on horseback "ropes"
(throws his lariat round) the horns, another round one of
the hind feet; then the horses strain away from each other,
the lariats being made fast to the horns of the saddles.
When the hind leg is straight out in the air the poor beast
is perfectly helpless and if it doesn't fall at once in its
struggles some men on foot run in to topple it over. As
soon as it falls one man grabs its tail, passes it between the
hind legs and over the upper flank. He then kneels on the
back and tugs with all his might. This is called "tailing" and
now with the two horsemen straining away from each other
in a straight line and the man with the tail pulling at right
angles to them the wretched creature can't move a muscle.
Then a man comes up with the branding irons and applies
them till the hair is burnt off and the skin scorched. And
now comes the funny part. If the beast "puts on the fight"
as they say, the men whose business it is to loosen the
lariats from the horns and leg have to be very nimble in
scaling the sides of the corral or they are liable to get help
from behind. After dinner, a somewhat "impromptu" meal,
Teschy put me on a beautiful little horse "Bay Billy" and we
rode off about eight miles to his ranch. Thus far I had seen
nothing but plains but as we neared the ranch we got into
the foot hills under Laramie Peak and the scenery became
very beautiful. The ranch lies in a little valley with
surroundings as pretty as anything can be. The Cottonwood
Creek which they control from its source to the Laramie
river runs within a few yards of them. Here I remained till
Friday afternoon spending most of the time in helping cook
and wash as the cook was laid up with a sore hand. We had
a few games of tennis and one afternoon Billy deBillier, a
brother of Fred deBillier took me for a ride in the hills. We
saw one deer but didn't get him. On Wednesday Teschy
went back to the round up and on Friday Billy deBillier, a
fellow by the name of Wister, several cow boys and I
followed. We found them on the Laramie river taking a tally

of their beeves. They were all ready for the drive to the railroad. That night I shall never forget. The camp was on a little point of about ten acres ground by a bend in the river. Just across the river was the bunch of beef with two men riding slowly round them all night. Round the mess wagon were the beds of the men and within a few steps of each a saddled horse picketed in case of a stampede. At a few rods distance was the herd of about 125 horses with their night herder riding round them and down on all fell the light of an almost full moon. A few hundred yards from camp the coyotes formed a circle and from time to time burst out in their agonizing wail. Altogether, it was a night to be remembered—. Long before sunrise Teschy and I were on our way (20 miles) to Huntons where we got something to eat and took the stage at eight o'clock. Last night I was pretty tired and a *little* sore but this morning am in fighting trim. Teschemacher and deBillier is now a stock Co. with $205,000 capital. The first 5% after paying expenses goes to stock holders, the next 5% to the two Teschemachers and deBillier for management and all additional profits to stockholders. The stock is almost entirely owned by classmates of Teschemacher and deBillier, Jim Parker, H. Leeds, etc. This year they will clear at least 25% that is 20% for stockholders of which 10% to 15% will be paid in cash and rest in increase of herd. They have almost decided to increase the capital (their year begins Nov. 1) and put the limit at $500,000. If they do, and the chances are 10 to 1 in favor of it, they will gladly take whatever money I have to put in and pay me cow boys wages until I can either command more or prove myself unable to earn that. I am inclined to think that this is my chance. There is not so much money in it as if I could run a ranch myself on a larger scale in Montana say but I am unfitted for that (now at any rate) . . . The Teschemacher and deBillier ranches are beautifully situated, hunting fine, and companionship agreeable and atmosphere intellectual if the term doesn't strike you as incongruous with surroundings. Teschemacher tells me that he has gone over nearly all his college courses on the ranch and has studied more than when he was in Cambridge and as Grind knows he is mentally all alive. They have followed a very good plan I think in buying the herds about them instead of driving in new cattle. This gives them a firmer hold on the range according to the honor of cattle men and puts them on a more friendly footing with their neighbors. I am going to think this all over for a day or two but if I decide to go in I think I shall ask father to lend me fifteen thousand ($15,000) at nine per cent (9%). Of course I could give no security but the twenty five thousand ($25,000) stock. If any of the rest of the family want to go in of course they can but simply as investment independently of me, for fifteen thousand would be the outside limit that I would borrow on my ten thousand. Nine per cent I find is what Teschemacher pays his father for some money he borrowed of him. Lovingly, Dick.

47

THE SPREE AT THE
END OF THE
TRAIL

*As the mythic Camelot had its knights, the mythic Old West had its cowboys.
In neither case did the descriptions provided by romantic literature have much
relationship with truth. But where there's smoke, there's fire. Stereotypes, no
matter how grotesque they may become, tend to originate in a grain of reality.
Here, from the Dodge City Times of July 10, 1880, is the sort of incident from
which a thousand scenes in a thousand B-movies have grown. Note that the
unruly ones were Texans (Tejanos in New Mexico); note also that the names
of the dead men were not even mentioned; and note that the incident must have
been unusual for the story ran successively in papers in Trinidad, Colorado,
Denver, and Dodge City.*

Henry Sturgis, editor of the *Trinidad News,* informs the *Denver Tribune* of
a lively encounter between a Sheriff's posse and a party of four cow boys
from the Texas Pan Handle, which took place in Cimarron, N. M., last
Saturday. The Texans were en route to Morrison's ranch, somewhere in
the San Juan country, and had camped near Cimarron for the night. Friday
evening they all went into town, and soon began a carouse such as only
a Pan Handle cow-boy knows how to inaugurate. After a few glasses of
Taos lightning were had the inevitable pistol was pulled from belt and a
firing at lamps, mirror, etc. begun. When fully satisfied with firing at

bar-room ornaments the gang betook themselves to a disreputable house, where the desperadoes continued their orgies until a late hour, when they mounted their ponies and rode off to their camp.

The next morning Sheriff Burleson and a posse, on complaint of some citizens, went out to arrest the gang. Before reaching the camp the Sheriff detached Deputy Bowman and a man named Bragg to go below the camp and follow up the arroyo to it, while the sheriff and major posse would close in from the above, the object being to capture the men and disarm them without a conflict.

Deputy Sheriff Bowman suddenly saw one of the men lying on the bank with a Winchester sighted toward himself and his companion, and before he could speak a word of warning the man fired, the ball striking Bragg, killing him instantly. Bowman then brought down his shot gun and killed the man who had shot Bragg.

The Sheriff's party here hastened on to the scene and opened on the desperadoes in camp, and so effectual was their aim that all were slain. Sheriff Burleson received a serious but not dangerous wound in the arm.

The names of the Texans killed are not known.

48

CHARLIE
SIRINGO'S
FLIRTATION

Charlie Siringo

Charlie Siringo (1855–1928) became a cowboy in Texas when he was twelve. At thirty he wrote A Texas Cowboy, *the first cowboy autobiography. Here he describes an incident at Las Cruces, New Mexico.*

I found El Paso, to be a red-hot town of about three thousand inhabitants. There were also about that number of people in Paso Del Norte, across the river in Old Mexico. I spent several days in each place.

I finally, after leaving my ponies in good hands, boarded one of the Atchison, Topeka and Santa Fe trains for Las Cruces, two and a half miles from Mesilla, the county seat.

There being better accommodations, in the way of Hotels, in "Cruces," nearly every one who was attending court would stop there and ride to the county seat in one of the "hacks" which made hourly trips between the two places. Consequently I put up at the Montezuma House, in Las Cruces.

There were several Lincoln County boys there when I arrived. Poe and Garrett came down next day. Mr. and Mrs. Nesbeth also came as witnesses against Cohglin. Mrs. Nesbeth had heard Mr. Cohglin make the contract with, "Billy the Kid," to buy all the stolen cattle he would bring to his ranch. But the good lady didn't live long afterwards, for she, her husband, a stranger, who was going from "Cruces" to Tulerosa with them, and a little girl whom they had adopted were all murdered by unknown parties. Cohglin was accused of having the crime committed, but after fighting the case through the courts, he finally came clear.

A few days after my arrival in Las Cruces I went back to El Paso after my ponies. I ate dinner there and rode into Las Cruces about sundown. A pretty quick fifty-five mile ride, considering part of it being over a rough mountain road. The cause of my hurry was, we couldn't tell what minute the Cohglin case would be called up for trial.

I had a little love scrape while loafing in Las Cruces. I don't mention it because my love scrapes were so scarce, but because it was with a Mexican girl, and under curious circumstances, that is, the circumstances were curious from the fact that we became personally acquainted and never spoke to one another, except by signs, and through letters.

Her name was Magdalena Ochoa, niece to the rich Bankers Ochoa's in El Paso, Tucson, Arizona, and Chihuahua, Old Mexico, and she was sweet sixteen. She lived with her grandmother, whose residence was right straight across the street from the Montezuma Hotel, and who wouldn't let a young man, unless he was a Peon, come inside of her house. And she wouldn't let Magdalena go out of her sight, for fear she would let some of the young "Gringoes" make love to her.

I first saw her one Sunday morning when she and her grandmother were going to church. I was standing out in front of the Hotel hugging an awning post, and wishing that I had something more human-like to hug, when they passed within a few feet of me. The girl looked up, our eyes met, and such a pair of eyes I had never seen. They sparkled like diamonds, and were imbedded in as pretty a face as was ever moulded. Her form was perfection itself; she had only one drawback that I didn't like and that was her grandmother. I immediately unwound my arms from around the post and started to church too.

The church house was a very large building, and the altar was in one end. The couple I was following walked up near the altar and took a seat on the right hand side—on the dirt floor, there being no such thing as seats in the building—which was reserved for ladies, while the left hand side, of the narrow passage way, was for the men. I squatted myself down opposite the two, and every now and then the pretty little miss would cast sparks from her coal black eyes over towards me which would chill my very soul with delight.

When church was over I followed, to find out where she lived. I was exceedingly happy when I found she was a near neighbor to me, being only a few steps across the street.

I spent the rest of that day setting out under the awning in front of the Hotel, straining my eyes in hopes of getting a glimpse of her beautiful form through the large bay window which opened out from the nicely furnished parlor onto the street. But not a glimpse did I get. I retired that night with the vision of a lovely sunburnt angel floating before my eyes.

The next morning I went to Mesilla and answered to my name when it was called, by the Judge, and then told Poe that I had some very important business to attend to in "Cruces" and for him, in case the Cohglin case was called, to hire a man at my expense and send him after me.

On arriving back to the Hotel I took a seat in an old armchair under the awning. I was all alone, nearly every one being in Mesilla.

Finally Magdalena brought her sewing and sat down among the flowers in the bay window. It was indeed a lovely picture, and would have been a case of "love among the roses" if it hadn't been for her old grandparent, who every now and then appeared in the parlor.

At last I, having a good chance, no one being in sight but her and I, threw a kiss, to see how I stood in her estimation. She immediately darted out of sight, but soon reappeared and peeping around a cluster of roses, returned the compliment. She then left the room and I never seen her again till after dinner.

I then started into the Hotel, but was detained by a voice calling, through the closed blinds of a window near by: "Me ketch you! Me ketch you!" Come to find out it was the proprietor's wife, Mrs. Duper, an old Mexican lady, who had been watching our maneuvers. She then opened the blinds and asked me in broken English, what I was trying to do?

"Oh, nothing, much, just trying to catch on, is all;" was my answer.

The old lady then broke out in one of her jovial fits and said: "You ketch on? Me bet you ten thousand dollars you no ketch him!" She then went on and told me how closely the old lady "Grandma Ochoa" watched her young niece. In fact, she gave me the girl's history from the time of her birth: Her father and mother were both dead and she, being the only child, was worth over a million dollars, all in her own name. This of course was good news to me, as it gave my love a solid foundation, and spread a kind of gold-like lining over the young lady's beauty.

Finally, after court had been in session two weeks the Cohglin case was called up. His lawyers were Col. Rynerson and Thornton, while the Territory was represented by Newcomb, District Attorney, and A. J. Fountain whose services Poe had secured.

Mr. Cohglin began to grow restless, for the "Pen" stared him in the face. There were eight indictments against him, but the worst one was where he had butchered the cattle after being notified by me not to.

His only hopes now was to "sugar" the prosecuting Attorney, and that no doubt was easily done, or at least it would have looked easy to a man up a tree. You see Cohglin was worth at least a hundred thousand dollars, and therefore could well afford to do a little sugaring, especially to keep out of the Penitentiary. At any rate whether the Attorney was bought off or not, the trial was put off, on account of illness on said Attorney's part, until the last days of court.

When the case came up again Mr. Prosecuting Attorney was confined to his room on account of a severe attack of cramp-colic. Judge Bristol was mad, and so was Poe. They could see through the whole thing now.

That night Cohglin made a proposition that he would plead guilty to buying stolen cattle knowing they were stolen, if the one case in which he had killed cattle after being notified not to, would be dismissed, or thrown entirely out of court.

It was finally decided to do that, as then he could be sued for damages, so the next day he plead guilty to the above charge, and was fined one hundred and fifty dollars besides costs.

Fountain, our lawyer then entered suit against him for ten thousand dollars damage.

I was then relieved. My mileage and witness fees amounted to something over a hundred dollars, this time. Of course that was appreciated as it was my own, over and above my wages. It came handy too as I was almost broke and needed it to take me home. I had spent all of my own money, besides nearly one hundred and fifty dollars borrowed from Poe.

It was the first day of May, I think, when I mounted Croppy in front of the Hotel, threw a farewell kiss at Miss Magdalena, who was standing in the bay-window, and started east, in company with Chas. Wall—the young man I mentioned as being a prisoner in Lincoln at the time of "Kid's" escape. I hated to part with the pleasant smiles of my little Mexican sweetheart, but then it had to be done. I still hold a rose and a bundle of beautifully written letters to remember her by.

We stopped at San Augustine the first night out from "Cruces," and from there we struck south-east across the white sands for the mouth of Dog canyon—the noted rendezvous of old Victoria and his hand of blood-thirsty Apache's.

I had heard so much about this beautiful Dog canyon that I concluded to see it before going home, so that if it proved to be as represented I could secure it for a cattle ranch.

It was a ticklish job going there by ourselves, as a telegram was received in Las Cruces, the morning we left, that a band of Apache's had crossed the Rio Grande at Colorow, killing three men there, and were headed toward Dog canyon. But I had faith in Croppy and Buckshot, they being well rested and hog fat, carrying us out of danger should we come in contact with them.

We arrived at the noted canyon after being away from water nearly two days. It was a lovely place, at the foot of Gandalupe mountains.

After leaving there we went through the following towns: La Luz, Tulerosa, South Fork and Ft. Stanton.

At the last named place Charlie Wall left me, and I continued on alone.

I remained in White Oaks a few days, looking over my town property, I having bought some lots and built cabins thereon, and examining the "Old Panhandle Tiger" gold mine, the one Stone, Chambers and I owned. I had some of the rock assayed and it run twelve dollars in gold to the ton, besides a few ounces in silver and about two million dollars worth of hopes.

From White Oaks I went through Anton Chico, San Lorenzo, Liberty and Tascosa, and arrived at the "L. X." ranch after an absence of nearly eight months, and about a three thousand mile ride.

49

"I THREW MY TIMID FRIEND A BISQUIT"

Theodore Baughman

The second cowboy autobiography, Baughman, the Oklahoma Scout, *appeared in 1886, written by Theodore Baughman. Baughman had been a Union soldier and marched with Sherman through Georgia. He became a Kansas cattleman and an Army scout in the Indian wars. Here he describes a trip to Tucson in 1875.*

In the spring of 1875 I went to Prescott, Arizona. I went there in the employment of Jim Kennedy to locate a cattle ranch. I found too many rustlers in that country to render it safe to let cattle run loose, and I concluded it wouldn't do to make the venture, although it was a good cattle country.

From Prescott I went to Camp Grant, and then started for Las Vegas, N. M. There I met an Illinois boy who was buying wool for an eastern company. He wanted to travel with me and bought a saddle horse for that purpose. We rode together some time and I found him good company.

One day after heavy rains we came to a creek which was high. I told him we had to cross. When I got my horse in I found it was swimming. I had the pack-mule fastened to the horn of my saddle with a rope. With the young man's assistance I got him in, but the baggage proved top heavy, and it turned the mule over with his head under the water. My Sucker friend yelled out, "You'll drown the mule!" But I kept on and dragged the mule to the other shore. I unpacked the mule and called to him to come over, but he said, "Not by a large majority," and went up and down the stream hunting for a ford. I made a fire and cooked dinner and threw my timid friend a bisquit across the river. He finally found a ford away up the creek and joined me. My chance-made friend has since written to me, but his name has escaped my memory. He made himself very agreeable, and I remember our acquaintance with pleasure.

On our journey we had to travel through a sterile country, barren of water and food for our horses. We provided ourselves with three gallons of water each, which had to answer for ourselves and stock. We watered them out of the crowns of our hats. We commenced our journey at 3 o'clock in the afternoon and rode all night and reached water and food the next day about 6 o'clock in the afternoon. The sun was extremely hot, and my friend, more dead than alive, begged to be forgiven for being so fool-hardy as to take this journey. Wool, he said, was no object.

About the year 1876 Dorsey and Campbell were cattle dealers, and have since become the most extensive horse trading firm in the southwestern country. Dorsey was born in Bellaire, Ohio, and deserves more than a cursory notice. Raised on a farm, in his early youth he became thoroughly conversant with the handling and breeding of stock. Having saved some money, at the age of twenty-one he started out for himself, went to Texas, where he purchased a herd of cattle and started them north over the trail. I first met him on the nine mile ridge, near Dodge City, grazing a large drove of cattle, in the summer of 1876. I was very much struck with his appearance at the first meeting, and we have continued warm friends ever since. He was a little above the medium height, thick set and sinewy, with blue eyes, a handsome, open countenance, always smiling, and possessing a good-natured, genial disposition, which now, as then, made him liked by all his associates. His word was as good as "gilt-edged" paper, and he has always been an unswerving and helping friend to the stockmen. Although he is now but thirty-two years old his name is familiar from King's ranch to St. Louis. At present he is settled in Wichita, where he owns large stables—handling from 1,500 to 2,000 head of horses and mules annually. His partner, Mr. James Campbell, is a native of Illinois, and has been in the cattle business for a number of years and in his disposition and general demeanor is a good counterpart of his partner. He resides at Caldwell, where he manages the range for cattle and horses. No two better men ever struck a trail, and they have the entire confidence of every dealer in the Southwest.

In January, 1877, Edward Finlan telegraphed to me at Dodge City to come to Wichita and join a party to lay out a trail from Wichita to Barrel Springs. On reaching Wichita I found the party all ready for service and awaiting my arrival.

50

THE COWBOY
STRIKE

David Dary

*Not only was this the earliest-known strike organized by cowboys, it may well
have been the only such strike. Historian David Dary tells of it in his* Cowboy
Culture.

Early in the spring of 1883 the outfits of three large ranches—the LX, the
LIT, and the LS, all in the Canadian River country of the Texas panhandle—happened to come together near the mouth of Frio Creek east of
modern Hereford, Texas. The outfits had been rounding up cattle that had
drifted south during the winter. All of the men enjoyed a meal together
and then began talking about their wages and the *new* rules being imposed
on all cowhands. Everyone voiced dissatisfaction. Since their employers
had organized an association, it was only natural that the cowboys began
to talk about having their own organization. Before the three outfits broke
camp they had formed a loose organization and issued a proclamation, the
original of which ended up in the Panhandle-Plains Historical Museum at
Canyon, Texas.

The proclamation, announcing what was the first cowboy strike in the
American West, reads:

We, the undersigned cowboys of Canadian River, do by these
presents agree to bind ourselves into the following obligations,

viz—First, that we will not work for less than $50 per month, and we furthermore agree no one shall work for less than $50 per month, after 31st of March.

Second, good cooks shall also receive $50 per month.

Third, anyone running an outfit shall not work for less than $75 per month. Anyone violating the above obligations shall suffer the consequences. Those not having funds to pay board after March 31st will be provided for 30 days at Tascosa.

The ultimatum was signed by twenty-four men, including the wagon bosses for the LX, the LIT, and the LS ranches—Roy Griffin, Waddy Peacock, and Tom Harris. The cowboys set April 1, 1883, as the date for their strike.

Exactly what happened next is a bit clouded, but individual negotiations occurred between cattlemen and some of the cowboys involved. A few hands were fired and found themselves afoot, something no self-respecting cowboy could fathom. Many of the striking cowboys gathered at Tascosa, where they drank and talked and drank some more. A few near-violent acts occurred, but no one is believed to have been killed as a direct result of the strike. The cattlemen did not suffer from the cowboys' absence because of the influx of many young men looking for work. Within a week or two the striking cowboys seem to have sensed failure, and the strike ended less than a month after it started. Some of the striking cowboys returned to work, but others left the country. . . .

51

THE FIRST RODEOS

Charles Nordhoff

It is said that the five most popular sports on the Navajo reservation are rodeo, rodeo, rodeo, rodeo, and basketball. The same could be said of much of the West. Here Charles Nordhoff describes how the sport began in his California; For Health, Pleasure, and Residence.

Every spring, in the cattle country, rodeos are held. *Rodeo* comes from *rodeár*, the Spanish verb to gather or surround. A rodeo is, in fact, a collection of cattle or horses, made to enable the different owners to pick out their own, count them, and, if they wish, drive them off to their own pastures. It is held in the spring, because then the calves still follow the cows, and the great object of the gathering is to brand the calves.

Rodeos are held in the San Joaquin Valley at stated places and preordained times; and one succeeds the other, going from south northward, until at last all the cattle have been seen, and all the calves branded. In San Diego County, where the Santa Margarita rancho lies, they begin in the same way, far south near the Mexican border, and work northward.

Sometimes 20,000 head of cattle are gathered on a plain, and the work of "parting out," as it is called, and branding, lasts for several days. A carefully defined set of laws regulates this work, and law officers, called "Judges of the Plains," attend to settle disputes as to ownership, and regulate the procedure. These officers appoint the times and places of rodeos, and attend at each.

In the old times, I have been told, a rodeo was a formal and stately affair. It was held in turns upon the estates of the owners; and each entertained the assembled company. When I tell you that such a gathering commonly included from twelve to twenty proprietors, each attended by from six to fifteen vacqueros, and with six or eight horses for each person, you will see that there was a little army to keep.

But the old Californians were not only hospitable; they receive visitors with less inconvenience to themselves than any people I have ever known. I staid this winter for some days, with my wife, at an old Spanish rancho, where the "housekeeping" was so quietly arranged that it seemed as though the house was empty; yet I learned, on inquiring, that from forty to forty-five persons, exclusive of servants, ate in the house every day while we were there.

Partly this is accounted for by the very simple habits of the people. They eat very moderately, and of few dishes, beef being, of course, the chief article of diet; and they sleep anywhere. Moreover, they drink only tea or coffee, and very little wine; they are very quiet and decorous in their manners, and they rise early.

In the old times, when the cattle had been gathered, and all was ready, the mayor-domo—an important person on all these estates—came to the proprietor with hat in hand, and formally announced that all was ready. Then the company, dressed in holiday attire, got to horse and rode out to the plain, and at the word the work began.

Then were seen some really magnificent feats of horsemanship; each vacquero vied with the other in this display; and as the day grew, fresh horses were saddled, and no bull was so wild that he did not find his master.

The state and ceremony have gone out; but the skillful riding still remains, as well as the feats with the lasso, which are really like jugglery or witchcraft. I have a hundred times watched the fling of the riata, and yet have never in a single instance been able to detect the precise moment of the capture. But I am certain that a part of the trick is in the vacquero's intimate knowledge of the animal's motions; for I have seen a riata carelessly thrown down at a bull's heels, and, as the next instant he was fast, he must have stepped into the noose, and he who flung it must have known by experience what would be the animal's next motion.

At the Santa Margarita we attended a rodeo where the horsemen displayed in our honor some of their finest skill; and it was marvelous to see not only the certainty with which the lasso or riata is flung, and the admirable training of the horses, which co-operate with their riders and turn like a flash when a mad bull flies at his pursuer, but the jokes of the field. One of these is to single out a bull or cow, chase it out of the herd, dash after it at full speed, and lean out of the saddle until the rider catches the tail of the flying beast. This he winds quickly about his hand, and at the same time he tucks it under his leg, holding it between the leg and the saddle. At the same instant the horse, feeling the tail on his flank, and perfect in his own part, increases his speed, and both running in nearly parallel lines close together, if the horse's speed is greater than the bull's, the latter is flung heels over head. I saw this practical joke played a dozen times; it is one of the favorite diversions of the rodeo.

The rodeo grounds are usually permanent; and it was to me an odd fact that when the vacqueros went out to gather in the cattle from the hills and valleys for some miles on every side, they had only to begin driving, when all within sight turned at once to the big tree in the centre of the plain, where they were accustomed to be collected.

52

THE CHUCK WAGON

Eugene Manlove Rhodes

Eugene Manlove Rhodes was a working cowboy at the turn of the century. He speaks with the authority of personal knowledge in the following description from The Rhodes Reader, *a compilation of his stories, of the veritable Rolls Royce of chuck wagons.*

"Water," said Emil James, slowly and seriously, counting his fingers by way of tally—"matches, coffee, coffee-pot, sugar, tincow, tin cups and spoons—that's coffee." As he spoke he carefully packed the objects named on the shelves of the chuck-box, misses' and children's size, of "the slickest little spring wagon."

That spring wagon was the especial pride and comfort of Emil's heart. When you learn that he kept it painted and sheltered you will know—if you are a frontiersman—just where that little wagon stood in Emil's affections.

It was wrought by the best skill under Emil's jealous supervision: built to be both light and strong. Six woods went to the making of it—hickory, oak, tough hornbeam, black birch, whitewood—clear stock, straight grained—with gnarled Bois d'Arc for the hubs; all seasoned for seven years, and kiln dried to stand up in the dry air of the desert. The highest quality of iron and steel went to the fittings, the toughest and easiest of springs.

The wagon bed, framed and panelled for lightness, had no nail or screw in it; cunningly joined by mortise, tenon, dowel and dovetail and housed joints; all locked to place by long and slender bolts at the four corners. A touch on the strong footbrake locked the wheels and there was a step in front of the front wheel.

Where the tail-gate might have been, the chuck box was "built in" to avoid superfluous weight, floor and sides of the wagon box being also floor and sides of the chuckbox. Between chuckbox and the only seat, the wagon box flared over the wheels, after the fashion of a hay rigging, just long enough and wide enough to accommodate a light set of bed springs. The deep space beneath it was for promiscuous cargo. Under the lazyback spring seat was a low oaken water-tank, also "built in"; doing away with the customary water-kegs, usually slung at the sides of such a wagon by iron straps.

The whole was surmounted by a ribbed top, braced and firm, leather covered. There were light racks and straps at the top for clothing or small effects; there were leather side curtains, with pockets in them, marvelous because they would go up and stay up, or come down and stay down; there was also that rarest of luxuries, a lantern that would give light.

"Bacon, frying-pan, knives, forks and plates—that's bacon. Flour, water, salt, baking powder, lard, dutchoven—that's bread. Beans, canned truck, spuds, pepper,—that's extrys."

"Don't forget the water for potatoes. Or are you doing that little ditty to exercise your lungs?"

"Son, if this is delayin' you any," said Emil benignly, "try to put up with it, will you? I'm considerable old maidish and set in my ways. And I can tell you something useful."

"Go as far as you like."

"All right! John Sayles Watterson, Junior; I have twice heard you strongly voice opinion that most men in this country do things well. It is true. We admit it. And now I am to tell you why. It is because a man in this country is always trying for two things; to be his own foreman, who says what now and next to do, and to be his own inspector, to see that before he quits he makes a good job of it. I'm inspecting; and I don't want my attention distracted. You keep still! . . . Shot gun and shells—that's quail and rabbits. Rifle and cartridges—that's venison. Blankets—that's bed. Your saddle and truck—that's under the bedsprings. Canteens, water-buckets, hobbles, ropes, nosebags—that's sundries. Corn for horses—that's good. Water—that's life. That's all. Let's go!—There! I near forgot the axle-grease!"

53

WHEN YOU CALL ME THAT, SMILE!

Owen Wister

It is sometimes said that Jack Schaefer's Shane *ended the genre of the Western novel because it told the myth so perfectly. Whether or not Schaefer perfected the form, Owen Wister started it with* The Virginian, *published in 1902. It invented the "Code of the West" and influenced tens of thousands other writers of Westerns, including Schaefer. Here is the most famous incident from Wister's book.*

Already I had forgotten my trunk; care had left me; I was aware of the sunset, and had no desire but for more of this conversation. For it resembled none that I had heard in my life so far. I stepped to the door and looked out upon the station platform.

Lounging there at ease against the wall was a slim young giant, more beautiful than pictures. His broad, soft hat was pushed back; a loose-knotted, dull-scarlet handkerchief sagged from his throat, and one casual thumb was hooked in the cartridge-belt that slanted across his hips. He had plainly come many miles from somewhere across the vast horizon, as the dust upon him showed. His boots were white with it. His overalls were gray with it. The weather-beaten bloom of his face shone through it duskily, as the ripe peaches look upon their trees in a dry season. But no dinginess of travel or shabbiness of attire could tarnish the splendor that radiated from his youth and strength. The old man upon whose temper his remarks were doing such deadly work was combed and curried to a finish, a bridegroom swept and garnished; but alas for age! Had I been the bride, I should have taken the giant, dust and all. . . .

I left that company growing confidential over their leering stories, and I sought the saloon. It was very quiet and orderly. Beer in quart bottles at a dollar I had never met before; but saving its price, I found no complaint to make of it. Through folding doors I passed from the bar proper with its bottles and elk head back to the hall with its various tables. I saw a man sliding cards from a case, and across the table from him another man laying counters down. Near by was a second dealer pulling cards from the bottom of a pack, and opposite him a solemn old rustic piling and changing coins upon the cards which lay already exposed.

But now I heard a voice that drew my eyes to the far corner of the room.

"Why didn't you stay in Arizona?"

Harmless looking words as I write them down here. Yet at the sound of them I noticed the eyes of the others directed to that corner. What answer was given to them I did not hear, nor did I see who spoke. Then came another remark.

"Well, Arizona's no place for amatures."

This time the two card dealers that I stood near began to give a part of their attention to the group that sat in the corner. There was in me a desire to leave this room. So far my hours at Medicine Bow had seemed to glide beneath a sunshine of merriment, of easy-going jocularity. This was suddenly gone, like the wind changing to north in the middle of a warm day. But I stayed, being ashamed to go.

Five or six players sat over in the corner at a round table where counters were piled. Their eyes were close upon their cards, and one seemed to be dealing a card at a time to each, with pauses and betting between. Steve was there and the Virginian; the others were new faces.

"No place for amatures," repeated the voice; and now I saw that it was the dealer's. There was in his countenance the same ugliness that his words conveyed.

"Who's that talkin'?" said one of the men near me, in a low voice.

"Trampas."

"What's he?"

"Cow-puncher, bronco-buster, tin-horn, most anything."

"Who's he talkin' at?"

"Think it's the black-headed guy he's talking at."

"That ain't supposed to be safe, is it?"

"Guess we're all goin' to find out in a few minutes."

"Been trouble between 'em?"

"They've not met before. Trampas don't enjoy losin' to a stranger."

"Fello's from Arizona, yu' say?"

"No. Virginia. He's recently back from havin' a look at Arizona. Went down there last year for a change. Works for the Sunk Creek outfit." And then the dealer lowered his voice still further and said something in the other man's ear, causing him to grin. After which both of them looked at me.

There had been silence over in the corner; but now the man Trampas spoke again.

"*And* ten," said he, sliding out some chips from before him. Very strange it was to hear him, how he contrived to make those words a personal taunt. The Virginian was looking at his cards. He might have been deaf.

"*And* twenty," said the next player, easily.

The next threw his cards down.

It was now the Virginian's turn to bet, or leave the game, and he did not speak at once.

Therefore Trampas spoke. "Your bet, you son-of-a——."

The Virginian's pistol came out, and his hand lay on the table, holding it unaimed. And with a voice as gentle as ever, the voice that sounded almost like a caress, but drawling a very little more than usual, so that there was almost a space between each word, he issued his orders to the man Trampas:—

"When you call me that, *smile!*" And he looked at Trampas across the table.

Yes, the voice was gentle. But in my ears it seemed as if somewhere the bell of death was ringing; and silence, like a stroke, fell on the large room. All men present, as if by some magnetic current, had become aware of this crisis. In my ignorance, and the total stoppage of my thoughts, I stood stock-still, and noticed various people crouching, or shifting their positions.

"Sit quiet," said the dealer, scornfully to the man near me. "Can't you see he don't want to push trouble? He has handed Trampas the choice to back down or draw his steel."

Then, with equal suddenness and ease, the room came out of its strangeness. Voices and cards, the click of chips, the puff of tobacco, glasses lifted to drink,—this level of smooth relaxation hinted no more plainly of what lay beneath than does the surface tell the depth of the sea.

For Trampas had made his choice. And that choice was not to "draw his steel." If it was knowledge that he sought, he had found it, and no mistake! We heard no further reference to what he had been pleased to style "amatures." In no company would the black-headed man who had visited Arizona be rated a novice at the cool art of self-preservation.

One doubt remained: what kind of a man was Trampas? A public back-down is an unfinished thing,—for some natures at least. I looked at his face, and thought it sullen, but tricky rather than courageous.

Something had been added to my knowledge also. Once again I had heard applied to the Virginian that epithet which Steve so freely used. The same words, identical to the letter. But this time they had produced a pistol. "When you call me that, *smile!*" So I perceived a new example of the old truth, that the letter means nothing until the spirit gives it life.

Part Seven

◆

TALL TALES
AND
PRACTICAL
JOKES

In 1990, the Albuquerque Journal *reported with high excitement and documentary photographs an odd pattern laid out on the mesa west of town, quoting local experts on the occult as identifying it as a site for devil worship. (It was actually laid as a court for playing fuzzball.) Earlier, Albuquerqueans were startled to see black smoke pouring from the cone of one of the old volcanoes that line the same mesa. (University of New Mexico students had produced the simulated volcanic eruption through the immense effort of hauling old tires to the cone and igniting them.) More recently, a fellow fishing in a New Mexico stream found a dead hammerhead shark, presumably deposited by a prankster. Periodically, the Department of Defense is besieged by demands for access to its New Mexico missile testing range's Victorio Peak by folks convinced that wagonloads of Spanish gold were hidden in a cave there. This tendency of Westerners loving to fool others, and be fooled themselves, is rooted deep.*

54

THE TRAVELLING STONES, AND OTHER SUCH AFFAIRS

Duncan Emrich

Duncan Emrich, then chief of the folklore section of The Library of Congress, went to the trouble of collecting a variety of hoaxes in his It's an Old Wild West Custom.

The early newspapers of the West were essentially personal in character. The owners and reporters were lords of all they surveyed and gave not one tinker's damn for the opinions of the outside world or of their rivals. They potshot at each other editorially and, in literal fact, often resorted to guns to settle their disputes. They had more fun than a barrel of monkeys and kept themselves and their subscribers wide awake. So awake, in fact, that the editor of the *Central Utah Press* reported in 1879: "This thing is becoming awful. Nearly every newspaperman in the Territory during the past year has received a terrible thrashing." There were no such things as wire service, syndicated and synthetic columns, or boiler plate. . . .

The editors and reporters for the Western papers, however, had a besetting problem which did not exist in the big cities. There were, of course, vivid items of shootings and knifings, murder trials, inquests, and big stories of mine accidents or political scandals, but there were also blank periods and lulls which could prove fatal to the paper and to the reporter who was not resourceful. Out of very necessity, then, the editors concocted the hoaxes which were so characteristic of Western journalism. To fill space, to entertain their readers, and to amuse themselves, they created stories which traveled around the world, stories often believed completely by the literal-minded and, for others, sources of high amusement.

Not only did editors create stories, but they created whole communities in which to set their stories, as well as purely fictitious newspapers with which to fight. The *Carson Appeal* fought tooth and nail with the nonexistent *Wabuska Mangler* over a period of several years, and there are perhaps Westerners alive today who will swear that the *Mangler* was one of the liveliest sheets ever published—simply on the basis of the *Appeal's* attacks. The *Appeal* reprinted savage editorials credited to the *Mangler* and called its editor a "disgrace to journalism." When it grew tired of keeping the *Mangler* alive, the *Appeal* killed off the editor by announcing that he had skipped the country one jump ahead of the sheriff. . . .

Chief of all hoaxsters was Dan de Quille, the greatest of the reporters for *The Territorial Enterprise*. His daily work was a model of accuracy, and his news accounts were implicitly believed. His reputation for dependability was such that all his readers who were unacquainted with his joking proclivity accepted as truth every word he wrote. This made De Quille's hoaxes all the more dangerous, particularly since he prepared them with scientific minuteness and presented them in a straightforward, reportorial style.

Best known were his two hoaxes about the traveling stones of Pahranagat Valley and the death of Jonathan Newhouse, inventor of the solar armor. De Quille claimed that a prospector roaming through the wild Pahranagat Mountains of southeastern Nevada had discovered a large number of round, heavy stones about the size of walnuts. "When scattered about on the floor, within two or three feet of each other, they immediately began traveling toward a common center, and then huddled up in a bunch like a lot of eggs in a nest." The full story traveled around the world, and De Quille was plagued and bedeviled for the next fifteen years answering letters about these stones. Scientists in Germany accused him of a lack of professional ethics when he refused further information about them. Barnum offered him $10,000 if he could make them perform. A gentleman named Haines wanted a carload to sell, offering to split the profit with Dan. At last, weary of the jest, he retracted in the *Enterprise* on November 11, 1879: "We have stood this thing about fifteen years, and it is becoming a little monotonous. We are now growing old, and we want peace. We desire to throw up the sponge and acknowledge the corn; therefore, we solemnly affirm that we never saw or heard of any such diabolical cobbles as the traveling stones of Pahranagat. If this candid confession shall carry a pang to the heart of any true believer, we shall be glad of it, as the true believers have panged it to us, right and left, quite long enough."

Jonathan Newhouse, "a man of considerable inventive genius," constructed an apparatus to protect men from desert heat, the chief characteristic of which was an evaporating agent which saturated a special, tightly laced hood and jacket, thus producing any degree of cold desired as the sun drew off the moisture. Unfortunately for Newhouse, the mechanism went haywire and the inventor was found in Death Valley by an excited Indian, frozen to death with an icicle a foot long dangling from his nose. This tale likewise reached Europe and was published somewhat cautiously by the London *Daily Telegraph:* "We confess that, although the fate of Mr. Newhouse is related *au grand serieux,* we should require some additional confirmation before we unhesitatingly accept it. But everyone who has iced a bottle of wine by wrapping a wet cloth round it and putting it in a draught, must have noticed how great is the cold that evaporation of moisture produces."

Dan recounted the story of a wonderful hot spring located one mile out from Elko on the White Pine road, "the water of which, when properly seasoned with pepper and salt, cannot be distinguished from the best chicken soup." He placed "sugar-cured, fat, Salt Lake grasshoppers" on sale at the store of E. Feusier and Company, comparing them favorably in succulence to crab and shrimp. He located a hill of peculiar "ringing rocks and singing stones" near Pyramid Lake in the old Truckee Mining District. "These stones gave out a constant tinkling sound, and their myriads of tinklings blending together produced a musical murmur of considerable volume. The stones emitting these sounds were described as containing much iron, and some supposed that the musical tinklings were produced by magnetic action, while others thought that the whole drift of stones might be slowly working downhill, and that the sounds were caused by the attraction of the fragments composing the mass."

He discovered the rare Shoo Fly, a "monster insect inhabiting a shallow, slimy lake, situated fourteen miles northeast of Mud Lake. These flies are seen in large flocks about the lake and dive into the water, where they can remain on the bottom for an indefinite length of time, being supplied with air from a large bubble which forms about and incloses the head. The grub or larva from which the fly is hatched is of a deep green color and is some six inches in length by four inches in circumference. It is much esteemed by the Indians, who roast it in the ashes, when it looks not unlike a sweet potato. It also has a vegetable taste, perhaps from feeding upon the rushes, whereas the flies found at Mono Lake and greedily devoured by the Paiutes living in the neighborhood have a strong fishy taste, as also have the ducks which fatten on them." There was much more, and a learned entomologist in San Francisco wrote Dan, giving him elaborate packing instructions and saying, "I presume them to be rather a hymenopteron (wasp or bee) than a depteron (two-winged insect). Corresponding with the Smithsonian and other Societies, I shall communicate your contribution without delay, and you shall have all the merit and acknowledgement." Dan published the entomologist's request in the columns of the paper and commented, "What the professor says may be true, but when we view the insect and consider its cuspidated tentacles and the scarabaeus formation of the thoracic pellicle, we are inclined to think it a genuine bug of the genus 'hum.'"

5 5

THE FIRST
JUMPING FROG

Ever wonder where Mark Twain came up with the idea for his famous "The Celebrated Jumping Frog of Calaveras County"? Here's an article that appeared in the Sonora, California, Herald on June 11, 1853—fourteen years before Twain wrote his short story.

A toad story.— A long stupid-looking fellow used to frequent a [California] gambling saloon, some time since, and was in the habit of promenading up and down, but never speaking. The boys began to play with him, at last, and in down-east drawl he gave them Rolands for their Olivers till they left him alone. At night he spread out his blankets on an empty monte table and lived like a gambler, except that he talked to no one nor gambled a cent. He became, at length, an acknowledged character, slunk in and out, and the boys tittered as they saw him pass. One day he came in with an important air, and said:

"I have got a toad that'll leap further than any toad you can scare up."

They soon surrounded him, and roared and laughed.

"Yes," says he, "I'll bet money on it. Barkeeper, give me a cigar box to hold my toad in."

The fun was great, and the oddity was the talk of all hands. A gambler, in the evening, happened to come across a big frog, fetched him to the gambling house, and offered to jump him against the Yankee's toad.

"Well," says Yank, "I'll bet liquors on it." A chalk line was made and the toad put down. They struck the boards behind the toad and he leaped six feet, then the frog jumped seven. Yank paid the liquors; but, next morning, he says aloud:

"My toad waren't beat. No man's toad can leap with my toad. I have two ounces and two double eagles, and all of them I bet on my toad." The boys bet with him again, and his toad leaped six feet, but the frog leaped only two feet.

"The best two out of three," said the gamblers.

"Very well," says Yank. But still the frog could not go over two feet. Yank pocketed the bets.

"My frog is darn heavy this morning, says the gambler.

"I reckoned it would be, stranger," says the Yankee, "for I rolled a pound of shot into him last night."

5 6

HOW TROUT
SURVIVE
MOUNTAIN
WINTERS

One of the more common Colorado tall tales concerns fur-bearing trout. Here's a version from the November 15, 1938, Pueblo Chieftain.

Old-timers living along the Arkansas river near Salida [Colorado] have told tales for many years of the fur-bearing trout indigenous to the waters of the Arkansas near there.

Tourists and other tenderfeet in particular have been regaled with accounts of the unusual fish, and Salidans of good reputation have been wont to relate that the authenticity of their stories has never been questioned—in fact, they're willing to bet it's never even been suspected.

Then, last week, out of Pratt, Kansas, where water in any quantity large enough to hold a trout—fur-bearing or otherwise—is a rarity, came an urgent request for proof of the existence of the furry fin flappers.

Directed at the Salida Chamber of Commerce, the message read:

"Answer collect by Western Union if you have fur-bearing trout in Arkansas river there."

Upon the sturdy shoulders of Wilbur B. Foshay, secretary of the Chamber of Commerce, fell the delicate task of informing the credulous Kansan, without detracting from the obvious tourist-attracting qualities of the pelted piscatorial prizes.

With admirable diplomacy, and considerable aplomb, Foshay despatched posthaste a photograph of the fish, obtained from a Salida photographer, and told the Kansan to use his own judgment as to the authenticity of the species. The photograph sent has been available in Salida for some time.

Foshay's cautious letter accompanying the photograph left nothing to be desired, except maybe a little more evidence of the authenticity of the trout.

So a survey of real old-timers of the area was conducted, and the following corroborative evidence uncovered:

From Narrow-Gauge Ned of Poncha Pass came this report:

"Fur-bearing trout? We used to have 'em around here, but I haven't seen any lately. My pappy had some over at the hot springs, but the stream ruined all their fur in the course of several generations, and they finally left. We were mighty sorry to see them go, but it was a shame to see such valuable furs being spoiled, so we finally agreed. Last I heard, they'd settled up at Iceberg lake."

Texas Creek Tess, one-time impresario of the naughty can-can dance at the Owl-Ear Bar, recalled:

"The boys tell me that them pesky trout got to carrying on over around the silver fox farms on moonlight nights, and the fox growers had to shoot 'em to protect their valuable fox strains."

Willy Axletree, the Hermit of Wet Mountain valley, had another explanation:

"Tess told you only one side of the story. The trout got to running about with the foxes, all right, but they weren't silver foxes until *afterwards*. It was that trout strain that accounted for the silver coloration to begin with, and as the silver foxes came in, the fur-bearing trout just naturally moved out, rather than play second-fiddle to their own descendants."

Agate Creek Andy, however, insisted:

"You ain't heard the real tale of them fur-bearing trout yet. They left after they lost their race to the Spiral Mango-bats around Tenderfoot Mountain. The trout claimed a victory in the first two laps, but they got bested on the home stretch when the Mango-bats really got their sidehill leg-action going. There was just no beatin' 'em. That's where that big 'S' up thar come from," he declared, lapsing into the vernacular. "Hit don't stand for Salida at all, like they tell ya."

But to Harrison Hickoryhead, the Gorgemore graybeard, went the official award for the most logical explanation:

"Wa-a-al, it's just like y'said, pardner. Them leetle trouts was fur-bearin', shore enuff. In fact, that wuz whut brought on their downfall, as y'mought say. They wuz just *too* fur-bearin', and folks got to imposin' on them t'beat anything, knowing the leetle trouts wouldn't retaliate. Things wuz bad fur a long time, but 'twant till them eastern cappytalists got to settin' beaver traps for them that they got real discouraged. Then it just seemed like their leetle hearts bursted wide open.

"And after that they wasn't near so fur-bearin' as they had been.

"There's still some of 'em around, if you know where to look, which I do, but I ain't tellin', but their fur is pretty few and fur between compared to what it was. And they ain't near as fur-bearin' as they wuz, not near."

57

"I AM NOT AWARE THAT ANYONE HAS BEEN BORN LATELY"

J . R o s s B r o w n e

J. Ross Browne was a popular newspaper humorist of the mid-nineteenth century. This, from his Letters, Journals and Writings, *seems to have been written to his wife in February 1860.*

To Lucy, San Francisco, Feb. 17, 1860. I am going to be very pleasant and gossipy to-night and tell you all the news. To begin with there is no news at all, but I will try and remember something and if I can't succeed it will be easy to make some. Let me see—Deaths, Births and Marriages. To be sure! In that category comes my friend Frank Miller. He is not dead; neither has he been born for some time; but he is married.

Having thus disposed of marriages and deaths, I come to the births. I am not aware that anybody has been born lately, but have no doubt some little has been done in that line. The fact is, since you and Mrs. Coffee and Mrs. Hays left Oakland, there has been a great scarcity of births. The Doctors shake their heads and say the obstetric branch of their professions has been greatly injured by the removal of this prolific trio. While on the subject of babies, I am happy to inform you that Mrs. Hays' baby has recovered and is now as fat as a little butter-ball. She thinks it is beautiful of course. For my part I never saw a pretty baby except my own; but I am free to admit Mrs. Hays' young one has an open and rather pleasing countenance. Mrs. Johnny Brown is as amiable and lady-like as ever, but she has not yet been successful in the family way. I think she ought to take pills. Several ladies in Oakland have obtained babies by means of pills. Mrs. Voorhies took baby-pills and had a baby, and other ladies of your acquaintance did the same. It puzzles me to know how these pills operate, but I have great doubt whether they would produce the desired effect alone. Possibly they might however. Many ladies in San Francisco whose husbands have been absent for years, have babies; probably on account of these pills. For my part, I want no babies compounded originally in drug-stores. Suppose the druggist should make a mistake in the composition and the result should be rattle-snakes or bull-frogs! No, give me the Simon Pure—none of your medicated babies. The precedent is dangerous, to say the least of it. What would be the predicament of a husband, after an absence of a year or two, if his wife should greet him with an enlarged circumference, saying, "Oh, it is nothing, my dear, only a baby! I was a little unwell during your absence and took the wrong medicine." Of course the explanation would have to be satisfactory but in my opinion there would be reasonable ground for doubt. I once read that the great chemist Liebeg succeeded, after various experiments, in composing an egg, out of which a featherless bird was hatched. Why should babies not be hatched out of pills? But the old way is good enough for almost anybody.

This is all I can think of at present. Perhaps you think it is enough.

58

I PAINT THE
TRUTH JUST AS
IT IS

J. Ross Browne

*Humorist Brown (see preceding) was working as a lobbyist in Washington when
he wrote the following letter to James A. Garfield, then a congressman.*

Washington, D.C.,
June 20th, 1866
Dear Sir:
Hon. James A. Garfield of Ohio.
I sent you the other day a few bottles of our native
California wine, merely for the purpose of showing you that
we are not, like the old fogy, looking out from behind the
times; though it is possible we may get knocked in the head
by a passing event.

Such wine as this is calculated to strengthen the
judgment of the most sceptical gentleman in the Halls of
Congress of the impolicy of taxing an interest of such vast
prospective utility to the human race. Why, Sir, it would be
murder in the first degree to strangle this infant giant of
temperance, now innocently disporting himself in his cradle.
Tax crinoline if you please; tax the light of woman's eye;
tax the light of other days; tax your own ingenuity; tax
human forbearance; tax Patience on a monument smiling at

Grief; tax wax, hacks, sacks, backs, tacks, tack a tax on all attacks on tax; but don't, I beseech you, tax such a beverage as this—the generous grape—with which you may be shot every day of your life, yet never hurt.

Sir, I hope it is not in your heart to crush this innocent babe when it comes back to the House, appealing in plaintive accents to the tenderest sympathies of your nature. I hope you will take it by the hand with fatherly care, and say—"go forth, little one, and grow and flourish and give health and happiness to the human race!"

Sir, the tears stand in my eyes when I picture to myself the stunted and wretched little hunch-back that gentlemen in your House would make this infant prodigy. Think of it yourself—as a father and a man! Staggering with five cents a gallon on its back through the desolated vineyards of California! Think of it as a Christian; "In the morning it groweth up like a flower; in the evening it withereth away."

I will not believe you can do such violence to human nature. No. Sir; it is not in that genial eye and generous face to do it.

I take it for granted you have tried the Port. Sailors tell you, "any Port in a storm"; but I can assure you amid the storms of legislation, there is no Port like Wilson's native brand. Go into that, Sir, and you will find it a haven of rest—

> "A balm for the sickness of care
> A bliss for a bosom unblest."

Lest you should doubt what I say, I send you a copy of my travels in the East as a kind of certificate of character. Read that and you will find that a strict adherence to facts is my strong point. I never stretch the truth, but paint it just as it is—"Strange, stranger than fiction."

59

THE BUFFALO CORRAL AND MILKING PEN

James Stevens

James Stevens, the biographer of Paul Bunyan, produced other tall-tale epics. This one, about the nutritional value of buffalo-milk pancakes and a remarkably cold winter, had floated around Oregon long before Stevens reported it.

The great logger's first move in the He Man country [of Oregon] was to build a great buffalo corral and milking pen. When it was completed the buffalos were brought from the old home camp, and a gang of scissor-bills came along to herd and milk them. After their first breakfast of the new man food the loggers got some of their old swagger back, and Paul Bunyan was a picture of cheerfulness as he cruised the sage trees and planned the work of his men. . . .

The timber in this high, wide valley reached from the Eastern slopes of the Cascade Hills to the Western slopes of the Rockies. These sage trees resembled the desert sagebrush of to-day. They were not large; few of them were over two hundred feet in height, and not one of them could give a butt log over nine feet in diameter. But they all had many massive limbs which were crowded with silver gray leaves, each leaf being the size of a No. 12 shoe. The brown bark of the sage trees was thick, loose and stringy; it would have to be peeled from the logs before they were snaked to the landings by the blue ox. . . .

The first day of logging in the He Man country seemed to justify the great logger's best hopes. The men came out from breakfast with a swinging, swaggering tramp, loudly smacking their lips over the lingering flavors of buffalo milk hot cakes. This potent food made them vigorously he in every action. Each man chewed at least three cans of Copenhagen and a quarter-pound of fire cut during his first twelve hours in the woods. "P-tt-tooey! P-tt-tooey! P-tt-tooey!" sounded everywhere among shouted oaths and coarse bellowing. Every ax stroke buried the bit deeply in the tough sage wood, and brown dust spurted and gushed constantly from every singing saw. Crash! Crash! Crash! The thunder of falling trees sounded like a heavy cannonade. On all the loggers' backs gray sweat stains spread from under their suspenders, and their hair hung in dripping strings over their red, wet faces. They had got up steam for the first time since leaving the Hickory Hill country, and they were rejoicing in it. Even after the eleventh hour had passed their eyes were bright, though red-rimmed from stinging sweat, though wrinkles of weariness had formed around them. The men were tired indeed; the fallers and swampers were now panting through open mouths, and they were chewing nervously on their tongues, as is the habit of men when they are wearied out; but they never missed a lick, and when Paul Bunyan called them home they could still walk springily. . . .

The rafters and beams of the great cookhouse shook at this supper, so savagely did the loggers tackle the platters of bear meat. Even the bones were crushed, ground, and devoured; and Hot Biscuit Slim and his helpers were delighted when all the dishes were left slick and clean. . . .

Now, this was the year which is mentioned in history as the Year of the Hard Winter. But the bitterest cold could not now chill the blood of Paul Bunyan's He-Men. . . .

On the last night of the old year the mercury in the great thermometer which hung on the camp office had dropped to four hundred degrees below zero. Then the tube burst, and no one could tell the temperature, but it got appreciably colder. The next morning the boiling coffee froze on the stove, despite the desperate stoking of the kitchen firemen, and the loggers had to drink hot brown ice for their morning's breakfast. But they tramped cheerfully to work, nevertheless, cracking their mittened hands together and stamping the ground as they went along. They worked so hard to keep warm on this day that they talked and swore but little. This was fortunate. For on this incomparable New Year's Day every spoken word froze solidly in the air as soon as it was uttered. The next day the temperature rose, but the words remained frozen, and many a logger bumped his mouth by walking into the HELLOS and DAMNS which were solid in the air. But the hardy victims only laughed through their split lips at such accidents. These words all thawed out at once on a warmer day; they melted in one long-drawn-out, mournful echoing shout so unhumanly humorous in sound that the loggers rolled with laughter to hear it.

60

THE GREASEWOOD
GOLF COURSE

Dick Wick Hall

Dick Wick Hall ran a gas station at Salome, Arizona, and gave away a mimeographed newspaper to tourists, which made him famous among desert rats. Here he tells how Salome got its golf course.

Salome [Arizona] always has kept up its Average Annual Growth of 100% a Year—19 People now in 19 Years—but after going through the Panic of 1907, the World War and 3 Democratic State Asphyxiations without a Slump, it looks as if this here Greasewood Golf Course was going to depopulate the Town. We felt all swelled up at 1st when Eastern Tourists going through all said they never saw Nothing Like It nowhere before—a Golf Club where Everybody in Town had their Own Hole, but we've either got to close up the Town or the Golf Course or else get somebody in here to work.

How come it all Happened was this way. The Chuckawalla Kid had been out prospecting and coming in for grub, down in Granite Wash where the Main Highway is, he found a sack of clubs some Tourist had lost off his car, jolting over the Rocks on his way to Pasadena. Nobody knew what they was until Another Tourist saw them hanging up at the station and told us and said this was Just the Place for a Golf Course and that every Live town had one. He was in a Big Hurry to get to California, like all

207

Tourists, but he stopped long enough to make a Map of a Golf Course for us, with how the Holes ought to be and the Distances between Holes, More or Less, which he said didn't matter So Much as long as they was Enough.

We talked it over and decided that that would be a Good Way to get the Laugh on Buzzard's Roost, the little Side Track a few miles up the line which has been laboring for Fifteen Years under the Delusion that it was a Rival of Salome and that a Post Office printed on a Map always means a Town.

Buzzard's Roost might be able to fool some of Uncle Sam's clerks back in Washington but all of us out here know that the only way they have been able to keep the Cancellation of Stamps up to the $2.50 a Month required by the government to keep the Post Office on the Map is by all of them writing letters to themselves. We figured if we got a Golf Course started at Salome the Folks up at Buzzard's Roost would all be so busy talking about it some of them might forget to write—and then they would lose the Post Office and that would mean 8 or 10 more people coming to Salome for their mail.

It looked like a Good Plan and I said they could use my Dry Ranch, or as many Townships as was needed, and Shorty Burroughs and the Chuckawalla Kid agreed to Boss the job for nothing and their Grub if the rest of us would pay the Mexicans to cut the Sage Brush and Greasewood along the Far a Ways between the Holes. The Man that made the Map for us was in a Hurry and not a Good writer and Shorty had carried the old envelope around in his pocket so long it was blurred and we couldn't make out whether the distances was yds. or rds. but finally decided it must be rds. for rods.

So we made the First Hole 614 Rods, up the other side of the Centennial Arroya. Some of the Holes we only made 135 Rods and Up- wards, like the Man said, some long and some shorter. The Longest Hole is the 14th, 847 Rods, not quite Three Miles, running from the Old Adobe Cabin and across the Ghietta Flats to Mesquite Wells and all told the whole Greasewood Golf Course is 6,429 Rods long—just a little over Twenty Miles.

It took us over 3 months to get all the Brush cut along the Far a Ways and the tin cans fixed in the Holes, but it was Well Worth it and Salome now has the only Natural Nineteen Hole Greasewood Golf Course in the Whole World.

They say Some Folks play Golf just for Fun and Exercise. It's Exercise all right all right but I wish I could get somebody that thinks it's Fun to come and do a Few Days' Real Work for me, if Playing Golf is their idea of having Fun. Starting out to play a Round on Our Course is an Event that requires Time and previous planning, and we generally hire an extra man to Work in our place while we are gone or put a notice on the Door that we will be back Next Week sometime. The only time I ever did get clear around, it took me three days and a half and I used 31 Balls. We keep a Commissary and Supply Wagon for the convenience of Members. I got a letter the other day from Red Katem, who owns the Bermuda Ranch and is just learning. He was out at the 11th Hole and wrote in asking me to send him out a Barrel of Water, a slab of Bacon, some Beans and 3 dozen more Balls. Red never has got all the way around yet, but he keeps on trying.

He generally gets Bill Jackson to caddy for him. Bill is a good Rider and carries a couple of canteens of water along and can pick up a Golf Ball without getting out of the saddle. The Commissary Wagon hauls water around to the different Holes where there ain't any Wells handy so Folks can camp overnight wherever they get to.

One thing that's been puzzling us is these Golf Scores printed in some of the Papers, where it says some made it in 72 or 78 Etc.

The Man that made our Map for us was in such a Hurry he forgot to tell us how or what to count and we can't figure out whether a score of 72 means that he Made it in 72 Hours or 72 Days or used up 72 Balls Going Around.

All our Bunkers and Hazards are Natural. Anything that don't move or is dead, like a Sand Wash or a Mesquite Thicket or a Dead Steer on the Far a Way, we call a Bunker. If it's Alive, like a rattlesnake or a Cow, we call it a Hazard—and if She is Young and Has a Calf it's Extra Hazardous.

That's why our Caddies all go horseback. Lizards don't count, unless they get above your Knees.

The other day a Missus Delancy from Maine en route to California stopped over to Rest, she said, and play a Little Golf. The first day She was Playing, along in the afternoon out between the 3rd and 4th Holes, she stood on a Lizard Hole while she was swinging her Club, and the Lizard crawled up Her Knickerbockers just as she was making a Big Swing. She missed the Ball but she knocked the Caddy off his horse and when she started towards Mexico the War Whoop she let out was heard in Buzzard's Roost and the Caddy had to run her Three Miles horseback to catch her and then wrap her in his saddle blanket to get her Home Again. She went on to Pasadena next day.—DICK WICK HALL, Editor and Garage Owner, Lately Long Distance Amateur Golfer

March 29, 1924

61

THE BADGER
FIGHT

Bill Oden

*Out in the boonies where there wasn't much entertainment, making newcomers
look silly evolved into an art (if not a fine one). I remember as a boy growing
up in Sacred Heart, Oklahoma, the delight caused among the local grown-ups
when an urbanite from Shawnee was lured down into our dry end of the county
to see imaginary rice paddies. Here Bill Oden, in a passage from* Early Days
on the Texas–New Mexico Plains, *relates a badger game pulled on tenderfeet
in the Texas panhandle.*

Every new comer to town was a prospective victim. Even though he had
seen badger fights in kind, they were so well organized and made such a
lavish display of money, he would think this must be a real honest-to-
goodness fight. . . .

"If it was all a choke, vy did youse vant to bet so much money?" It
was funny to everyone but the neophyte. He would be down-cast about
like he would be if some fellow had stolen his best girl. He couldn't even
grin to say nothing of a smile. He would usually hie to the bar and buy the
drinks for those that cared to indulge, which would cost anywhere from
ten to twenty dollars.

After the drinks were disposed of and the crowd disappeared, Uncle
John Scarbauer would be seen headed for the Western Union office to wire

his connections, whatever that was. That the Midland Badger Club had a very successful fight between a very fierce bull dog and a very large yellow badger, and your honorable representative pulled the bell cord. One victim I remember got mad, pulled his hair, cussed and raved. Said he was a graduate of most of the universities in the United States and had finished his education in Europe, and to think he would come to Texas and be made a fool of by a lot of damn ignorant cow-punchers made him sick. He reluctantly bought the drinks for the topers but the next morning he was gone. I presume he gave Midland a wide berth in his travels after that.

Sometime about '96 or '7 my honored friend, Charlie Watson, came to town from down Arkansas way and bought a little newspaper. Charlie was a mere boy at that time, well educated and a fluent writer. In his first issue he stated that he had come west to make a permanent home and was very anxious to cooperate in every way possible with the good people he had chosen to settle among, or words to that effect. Uncle John Scarbauer happened to come to town about the time the ink was dry on the first issue. He was telling the boys what a big fine fat yellow badger one of his cowboys had caught on the 5WLS ranch the day before and he was going to bet one hundred dollars he could whip any dog in town. His bet was called and the time was set at 3 P.M. at D. C. McCormick's Livery Stable.

Of course the new editor was invited as a matter of courtesy to report the fight by rounds, if there by any chance should be more than one round. Along with Charlie's invitation went an invitation by grapevine telephone to all the male inhabitants of the town and nearby ranches. At the appointed hour they were all there and they all had both hands full of money and betting was brisk. Time was up and several was selected to pull the badger, but as each one had money bet on the dog or badger, that debarred them from the honor of pulling the badger. It finally developed that Charlie was the only one in the crowd that didn't have up a bet. As usual it was agreed that Uncle John was to introduce the victim and instruct him just how to yank him to be fair to both badger and dog. He began by saying the young man elected to do the most important part in the contest now about to take place was a man of exemplary habits, attested to by the fact that he hadn't wagered a penny on the fight about to take place—a man of high ideals and a gentleman in every sense the word implied.

Then would follow his instructions how to pull the cord. He would tell him to pull with all his might, then to pull as easy as possible, then to give him a kind of medium jerk. With all the tumult and excitement he wouldn't just know how he wanted him pulled. He would usually jerk with all the strength at his command and as they had him stand in the back end of a hack or wagon to keep the badger from biting him, the badger would usually roll under the wagon. . . .

["The badger" invariably proved to be an old bedroom chamberpot—much to the chagrin of the man who "pulled" the "ferocious beast" out for the fight. The penalty was to "set everybody up for the drinks."]

But they wasn't through with Charlie yet. They found—as Charlie thought—another victim, and Charlie was selected to hold the dog. When all was ready the supposed victim asked Charlie if he had the dog. When answered in the affirmative, he told him to hold him til suppertime, and threw the rope down and walked off. And Charlie had to buy another round of drinks. In the next issue of the paper he said if there was a third part to the badger game he wanted to know it beforehand as his money was running low.

The badger fights were attended by the entire male population of the town. The teller in the bank would walk out without locking the money drawer. The store-keepers and clerks would do the same. The saloon-keeper would leave his whisky bottle on the bar. The gambler never bothered to put his money away but left it stacked on the table. Nothing was ever bothered that I ever heard of.

62

"ANYTHING THAT WILL MAKE MONEY"

An anonymous author, surviving the depression in the Federal Writers Project of the Works Progress Administration, came across this combination of tall tale, treasure yarn, and practical joke and preserved it in Idaho, a Guide in Word and Picture.

An insurance salesman, down at heel and scurvy of disposition, was sitting in unspeakable melancholy one morning, wondering how he could make a living now that no one in Boise ever died, when he had a thought. He leapt to his feet and kissed his wife, a circumstance sufficiently strange, inasmuch as no one in Boise had kissed his wife in months. He remembered that a wealthy man had come from the East to buy land, and with him he vanished into the lava domains, not stopping for blowouts (of which there were none) and running over several pedestrians, all of them from California. 'Now here,' said the salesman, 'is the chance of your life—of a dozen lives like yours, in fact. Are you from Boston? Anyway, you're looking at the greatest unexploited stretch of land on earth—on any earth, and I don't care where your earth is. In fact, you're looking at ground that is practically worth its weight in gold—and it's heavy ground. Will you lift a hunk of it? Try that pile of basalt. Try that hill. Or don't you Easterners lift hills any more?'

'But what,' asked the wealthy Easterner, 'would I do with this ground? What could a man grow on land like this?' And he fell to his knees and looked with singular earnestness into the lidless gaze of a horned toad. He rose and knocked a pile of basalt from his knee. 'What?' he said.

'Anything. Cocoanuts and bananas and avocados, grapes and oranges, melons and grapefruit and pecans. Or orchids. Or even wheat. The question is: what do you want to grow?'

'Well, now,' said the Easterner cannily, 'anything that will make money.'

'Very well. Up there is a reservoir to irrigate it. There is the sun. You need only sun and water to make anything grow. And it never freezes here.'

'Not here?' said the Easterner, politely amazed. 'Not in this land,' he said, looking around him, 'which I should judge to be in Idaho?'

'Never. It never freezes and it never thaws.'

'I don't understand,' said the Easterner urbanely. And he sneezed. 'Pardon me,' he said.

'It's a secret. You see all these piles of lava? Or what,' asked the salesman, 'are you looking at? Now this lava absorbs the heat from the sun in the daytime and holds it all night and when it's fifty below in Boston it's like the middle of June here.'

'I can't believe it,' said the Easterner, and sneezed again.

'Place your hand on that rock.' And the Easterner did, and it curled up like a bacon rind on a hot stove.

'It is rather warm,' he said. But to make sure he sat on a stone and his flesh began to steam, and he added, 'It is very comfortable here. How much do you want for this land?'

'A thousand dollars an acre—and that includes fifty boulders to the rod. A hundred boulders to the rod will cost you more.'

The Easterner rose and looked around him happily for he had never seen such a bargain. He bought two hundred acres and set to work, and before he had plowed up the first acre of stone he uncovered $125,000 in gold that was buried here by Bitch Creek McDade and his gang after they had robbed the Arco stage. He averaged thereafter a buried treasure to the acre and started drilling and in the second month sank a shaft right through the center of the Lost McElmore Mine. He turned up the John R. Rudd Mine next, a very rich vein that had vanished in 1871 and had never again been heard of; and then took the Lost Bonanza, the Lost Gilpin McCreary, and both Lost Rivers in turn. A town, the Winnie Mae, sprang up overnight and within a year had a population of 15,000. Lost mines were yanked to the surface all over this terrain, and buried treasures stood around as thick as bags of potatoes in a field in October. Winnie Mae is a ghost town now between Shoshone and Arco, but persons still go to the area and dig up minor treasures, though they usually do not average more than $50,000 to the pot.

Part Eight

◆

CHARACTERS

Whatever the reason (my theory is that our empty places attracts some and the loneliness modifies others), the West is rich in odd, eccentric or otherwise unusual characters. In the recent past, for example, I have in my wanderings encountered:

• a motel clerk who had left his Los Angeles law practice to find peace in the desert
• a freckle-faced Irish cook in a greasy-spoon cafe who tried to convert me to Shintoism
• a middle-aged college graduate who built himself a cabin in the mountains, lives off the land and odd jobs, and measures his success annually by how little money he needs. Last year he earned $778 and spent $594, down from $840 and $672 the previous year.

The West has always been hospitable to such people.

63

"GENIAL IF RAMBUNCTIOUS"

Marthy "Calamity" Jane Cannary

Hardly a word in this biography she handed out at her shows can be verified. But we know Marthy "Calamity" Jane Cannary (1852–1903) was a teenager in Montana and that Daniel Thrapp, an authority on the period, described her as "an alcoholic, but a genial if rambunctious one; unruly, but not particularly lawless; filled with deviltry, but not evil."

LIFE AND ADVENTURES

OF

Calamity Jane

BY HERSELF

My maiden name was Marthy Cannary, was born in Princeton, Missouri, May 1st, 1852. Father and mother natives of Ohio. Had two brothers and three sisters, I being the oldest of the children. As a child I always had a fondness for adventure and out-door exercise and especial fondness for horses which I began to ride at an early age and continued to do so until I became an expert rider being able to ride the most vicious and stubborn of horses, in fact the greater portion of my life in early times was spent in this manner.

In 1865 we emigrated from our homes in Missouri by the overland route to Virginia City, Montana, taking five months to make the journey. While on the way the greater portion of my time was spent in hunting along with the men and hunters of the party, in fact I was at all times with the men when there was excitement and adventures to be had. By the time we reached Virginia City I was considered a remarkable good shot and a fearless rider for a girl of my age. I remember many occurrences on the journey from Missouri to Montana. Many times in crossing the mountains the conditions of the trail were so bad that we frequently had to lower the wagons over ledges by hand with ropes for they were so rough and rugged that horses were of no use. We also had many exciting times fording streams for many of the streams in our way were noted for quicksands and boggy places, where, unless we were very careful, we would have lost horses and all. Then we had many dangers to encounter in the way of streams swelling on account of heavy rains. On occasions of that kind the men would usually select the best places to cross the streams, myself on more than one occasion have mounted my pony and swam across the stream several times merely to amuse myself and have had many narrow escapes from having both myself and pony washed away to certain death, but as the pioneers of those days had plenty of courage we overcame all obstacles and reached Virginia City in safety.

Mother died at Black Foot, Montana, 1866, where we buried her. I left Montana in Spring of 1866, for Utah, arriving at Salt Lake city during the summer. Remained in Utah until 1867, where my father died, then went to Fort Bridger, Wyoming Territory, where we arrived May 1, 1868. Remained around Fort Bridge during 1868, then went to Piedmont, Wyoming, with U. P. Railway. Joined General Custer as a scout at Fort Russell, Wyoming, in 1870, and started for Arizona for the Indian Campaign. Up to this time I had always worn the costume of my sex. When I joined Custer I donned the uniform of a soldier. It was a bit awkward at first but I soon got to be perfectly at home in men's clothes.

Was in Arizona up to the winter of 1871 and during that time I had a great many adventures with the Indians, for as a scout I had a great many dangerous missions to perform and while I was in many close places always succeeded in getting away safely for by this time I was considered the most reckless and daring rider and one of the best shots in the western country.

After that campaign I returned to Fort Sanders, Wyoming, remained there until spring of 1872, when we were ordered out to the Muscle Shell or Nursey Pursey Indian outbreak. In that war Generals Custer, Miles, Terry and Crook were all engaged. This campaign lasted until fall of 1873.

It was during this campaign that I was christened Calamity Jane. It was on Goose Creek, Wyoming, where the town of Sheridan is now located. Capt. Egan was in command of the Post. We were ordered out to quell an uprising of the Indians, and were out for several days, had numerous skirmishes during which six of the soldiers were killed and several severely wounded. When on returning to the Post we were ambushed about a mile and a half from our destination. When fired upon Capt. Egan was shot. I was riding in advance and on hearing the firing turned in my saddle and saw the Captain reeling in his saddle as though about to fall. I turned my horse and galloped back with all haste to his side and got there in time to catch him as he was falling. I lifted him onto my horse in front of me and succeeded in getting him safely to the Fort. Capt. Egan on recovering, laughingly said: "I name you Calamity Jane, the heroine of the plains." I have borne that name up to the present time. We were afterwards ordered to Fort Custer, where Custer city now stands, where we arrived in the spring of 1874; remained around Fort Custer all summer and were ordered to Fort Russell in fall of 1874, where we remained until spring of 1875; was then ordered to the Black Hills to protect miners, as that country was controlled by the Sioux Indians and the government had to send the soldiers to protect the lives of the miners and settlers in that section. Remained there until fall of 1875 and wintered at Fort Laramie. In spring of 1876, we were ordered north with General Crook to join Gen'ls Miles, Terry and Custer at Big Horn river. During this march I swam the Platte river at Fort Fetterman as I was the bearer of important dispatches. I had a ninety mile ride to make, being wet and cold, I contracted a severe illness and was sent back in Gen. Crook's ambulance to Fort Fetterman where I laid in the hospital for fourteen days. When able to ride I started for Fort Laramie where I met Wm. Hickock, better known as Wild Bill, and we started for Deadwood, where we arrived about June.

During the month of June I acted as a pony express rider carrying the U. S. mail between Deadwood and Custer, a distance of fifty miles, over one of the roughest trails in the Black Hills country. As many of the riders before me had been held up and robbed of their packages, mail and money that they carried, for that was the only means of getting mail and money between these points. It was considered the most dangerous route in the Hills, but as my reputation as a rider and quick shot was well known, I was molested very little, for the toll gatherers looked on me as being a good fellow, and they knew that I never missed my mark. I made the round trip every two days which was considered pretty good riding in that country. Remained around Deadwood all that summer visiting all the camps within an area of one hundred miles. My friend, Wild Bill, remained in Deadwood during the summer with the exception of occasional visits to the camps. On the 2nd of August, while setting at a gambling table in the Bell Union saloon, in Deadwood, he was shot in the back of the head by the notorious Jack McCall, a desperado. I was in Deadwood at the time and on hearing of the killing made my way at once to the scene of the shooting and found that my friend had been killed by McCall. I at once started to look for the assassin and found him at Shurdy's butcher shop and grabbed a meat cleaver and made him throw up his hands; through the excitement on hearing of Bill's death, having left my weapons on the post of my bed. He was then taken to a log cabin and locked up, well secured as every one thought, but he got away and was afterwards caught at Fagan's ranch on Horse Creek, on the old Cheyenne road and was then taken to Yankton, Dak., where he was tried, sentenced and hung.

I remained around Deadwood locating claims, going from camp to camp until the spring of 1877, where one morning, I saddled my horse and rode towards Crook city. I had gone about twelve miles from Deadwood, at the mouth of Whitewood creek, when I met the overland mail running from Cheyenne to Deadwood. The horses on a run, about two hundred yards from the station; upon looking closely I saw they were pursued by Indians. The horses ran to the barn as was their custom. As the horses stopped I rode along side of the coach and found the driver John Slaughter, lying face downwards in the boot of the stage, he having been shot by the Indians. When the stage got to the station the Indians hid in the bushes. I immediately removed all baggage from the coach except the mail. I then took the driver's seat and with all haste drove to Deadwood, carrying the six passengers and the dead driver.

I left Deadwood in the fall of 1877, and went to Bear Butte Creek with the 7th Cavalry. During the fall and winter we built Fort Meade and the town of Sturgis. In 1878 I left the command and went to Rapid city and put in the year prospecting.

In 1879, I went to Fort Pierre and drove trains from Rapid city to Fort Pierre for Frank Witc [sic] then drove teams from Fort Pierre to Sturgis for Fred. Evans. This teaming was done with oxen as they were better fitted for the work than horses, owing to the rough nature of the country.

In 1881 I went to Wyoming and returned in 1882 to Miles city and took up a ranch on the Yellow Stone, raising stock and cattle, also kept a way side inn, where the weary traveler could be accommodated with food, drink, or trouble if he looked for it. Left the ranch in 1883, went to California, going through the States and territories, reached Ogden the latter part of 1883, and San Francisco in 1884. Left San Francisco in the summer of 1884 for Texas, stopping at Fort Yuma, Arizona, the hottest spot in the United States. Stopping at all points of interest until I reached El Paso in the fall. While in El Paso, I met Mr. Clinton Burk, a native of Texas, who I married in August 1885. As I thought I had travelled through life long enough alone and thought it was about time to take a partner for the rest of my days. We remained in Texas leading a quiet home life until 1889. On October 28th, 1887, I became the mother of a girl baby, the very image of its father, at least that is what he said, but who has the temper of its mother.

When we left Texas we went to Boulder, Colo., where we kept a hotel until 1893, after which we travelled through Wyoming, Montana, Idaho, Washington, Oregon, then back to Montana, then to Dakota, arriving in Deadwood October 9th, 1895, after an absence of seventeen years.

My arrival in Deadwood after an absence so many years created quite an excitement among my many friends of the past, to such an extent that a vast number of the citizens who had come to Deadwood during my absence who had heard so much of Calamity Jane and her many adventures in former years were anxious to see me. Among the many whom I met were several gentlemen from eastern cities, who advised me to allow myself to be placed before the public in such a manner as to give the people of the eastern cities an opportunity of seeing the Woman Scout who was made so famous through her daring career in the West and Black Hill countries.

An agent of Kohl & Middleton, the celebrated Museum men came to Deadwood, through the solicitation of the gentleman whom I had met there and arrangements were made to place me before the public in this manner. My first engagement began at the Palace Museum, Minneapolis, January 20th, 1896, under Kohl and Middleton's management.

Hoping that this little history of my life may interest all readers. I remain as in the older days, Yours, MRS. M. BURK, better known as Calamity Jane

64

HOW THE SKI CAME TO SNOW COUNTRY

Robert Laxalt

The gold rush of '49 and the fabled Comstock Lode of Nevada seemed to expand everything into epic proportions. Here, from Robert Laxalt's Nevada, a Bicentennial History, *is a mailman.*

A man named Snowshoe Thompson was one of those cast in the truly heroic mould, with a giant frame and courage to fit it. A Norwegian who had come to California in the gold rush and Nevada in the silver rush, he became an instant legend as a mail carrier over the snowbound winter Sierra. Until he arrived upon the scene, mail service between western Nevada and northern California was almost nonexistent. A few men had ventured the winter passage on webbed snowshoes as we know them today. But the task proved to be too arduous and dangerous, and there were long periods of time when Nevada simply went without news from the nearest centers of civilization.

Recalling the skis of his childhood, Thompson fashioned what he called a Norwegian snowshoe. Hence the nickname he acquired. Made out of fir planking, his skis were ten feet long, five inches wide, and nearly two inches thick at their center of balance. Only a man with prodigious strength could have climbed mountains with such ponderous contraptions on his feet and a mailbag weighing sixty to eighty pounds on his back.

Snowshoe Thompson was such a man. For three long winters, he carried the mail between Genoa in western Nevada and Placerville in California's mother-lode country. The one-hundred-eighty-mile round trip took him from three to five days, depending upon the severity of storms. With neither overcoat nor blanket, he traveled day and night, stopping only for short periods of rest or for refuge from blizzards. In these pauses, he would find dead stumps of pine and set fire to them to keep from freezing to death. It was said of him that he never lost his way through deep forests and the wildest of storms.

Finally, however, exhaustion took its toll and his giant strength abandoned him. He fell sick and died before he was yet fifty years old, leaving behind him an heroic legend and a grave in Genoa, which has become a shrine of the modern ski world.

65

THE EMPEROR OF
CALIFORNIA

Joshua Norton

Joshua Norton decided that about the middle of the nineteenth century that he was the Emperor of California and the Protector of Mexico. Here's how his decision was described in Lights and Shades in California.

. . . He was born in England, and from there went to the Cape of Good Hope, where he entered the military service as a member of the colonial riflemen. How long or how well he served in that capacity we are not informed.

In 1847 or '48 he came to San Francisco, and is remembered by the early pioneers as having been a shrewd, safe and prosperous man possessing more than ordinary intelligence, fertile of resource and enterprising. His business pursuits were varied. At one time he was buying partner for three or four mercantile houses in the interior of the State, and in this capacity manifested great business ability. Then he engaged in the real estate business, in which he continued with apparent prosperity a number of years. . . .

It appears that his business career culminated in a grand effort to get a "corner" on rice, which staple was, some ten or twelve years ago, a favorite article for speculation. He purchased all that was in the city and (as rumor has it) all that he could ascertain was in transit, paying large prices with a view of controlling the future market; [however] . . . the market was so "flat" that he could not meet his contract, and a protracted law suit followed, during which the mania that he was "Emperor" first became manifest. . . .

His hallucination is that he is Emperor of California and Protector of Mexico. . . . San Francisco, his favorite city, he calls the "Queen of the Pacific," and the world pays tribute to her. The municipal authorities receive his praise or condemnation as their administration pleases or offends him. By proclamation (sometimes to humor his whim published in the city press) he communicates to his subjects his ideas of progress and justice, and never fails to attach his signature with the imperial seal, "Norton I. Emperor of California and Protector of Mexico. *Dei Gratia.*" . . .

Emperor Norton may be known by his dress, as he pays no attention whatever to the varying fashions. His coat is navy blue, cut in the military style, and lavishly trimmed with brass buttons. On the shoulders are heavy epaulettes usually tarnished from exposure to weather, though sometimes brilliantly polished. His hat, the regular Jehu style, is trimmed with some brass ornament, from which extends two or three waving cock-plumes. His boots are notorious for their size, and are less frequently polished than otherwise. . . .

Of evenings he may be found at the theatre or in the lecture room, a cool observer and attentive listener. His face is a free ticket for him to all places of amusement and public gatherings, and oftentimes he makes quite extended journeys by rail and other public conveyances without expending a dollar. . . .

His living is very inexpensive. He occupies a cheap room, is temperate in his habits, boards at cheap restaurants, which, with many privileges granted him that others have to pay for, reduces his expenditures to a very small sum. When he wants money he will draw a check on any of the city banks, take it to an acquaintance who humors his delusion, and get it cashed. . . . Some of the merchant Jews contribute to his support, and he is much better cared for than many who labor hard every day for a livelihood. Thus does his affliction secure him a comfortable living, happy today, without care for the morrow, and free from all the annoyances that to many renders life a burdensome existence.

66

SCHLATTER THE HEALER

Agnes Morley Cleaveland

He called himself Francis Schlatter. Nobody knew where he came from but he captivated reporters and the public as the nineteenth century ended, and then he vanished. Here, from No Life for a Lady, is Agnes Morley Cleaveland's remembrance of his arrival at the family ranch in New Mexico.

In the summer of 1895, a golden-bearded, blue-eyed, six-foot-tall Alsatian cobbler named Francis Schlatter appeared in Albuquerque. He had just walked from California across the Mojave Desert, living on little but bread made from unleavened flour which he baked himself, and almost no water. This walk is considered impossible, yet the fact that he made it is amply authenticated.

Arrived in Albuquerque, he announced that as a final act of spiritual preparation for his life mission, 'the Father' had bade him fast for forty days. This fast took place in the home of people we knew, and, according to them and scores of others, including newspaper reporters, was genuine. At its finish, one who was present recorded that he ate a substantial meal of 'fried chicken, beefsteak, and fried eggs.' No ill effects followed.

His fame became of headline importance, but it was not until he appeared in Denver later in the same summer that Mother saw him. She was one of thousands who stood in line to receive his blessing, one that was reputed to carry healing.

Lest the conclusion be jumped at that it was only the weak-minded who stood for hours waiting to touch the hand of this peasant cobbler with his little-understood powers, let me say that on the special trains that were run into Denver to accommodate the throngs who believed in him were many intelligent and well-to-do people. A person who was at the end of the line which formed daily and stretched out for many city blocks at 6 A.M. counted himself lucky to stand in Schlatter's presence by noon. As many as five thousand in a day passed before him. In good journalistic style the newspapers gave accounts of healings claimed and miracles performed. In the line three stations ahead of my mother, a crippled negro woman inched painfully forward, hour after hour. Arrived at last where Schlatter stood in the gateway of the yard to a modest home, where he was being harbored, the negro woman stretched forth her hands to grasp those of the man before her. An instant later she threw her arms in the air and shouted, 'Praise Gawd, he done healed me, and he done give me back my dollar!'

Yes, he gave back all money proffered. That was never disputed. He took no pay.

Day after day he received the lame, the halt, and the blind, the rich and the poor, the educated and the ignorant. I refer you to the Denver daily press of the period, to the press of the whole United States, for details, and for claims of cures.

It was a reporter's paradise.

Then Schlatter disappeared, leaving behind him thousands of disappointed people. It was a disappearance that seemed miraculous, for he vanished on a big white horse. For weeks the boys of the press vied with one another in efforts to find him—solely for his news value. He was reported seen here, there, everywhere, only to have every clue fail. From the newsgatherers' standpoint it was exasperating and the determination to find him grew apace. The hunt assumed incredible proportions. Every white horse within a radius of several hundred miles was held suspect, but none of them was Schlatter's horse, Butte.

Then one winter night, seven weeks after he had seemingly vanished from the earth, a man who was doing some temporary work for Mother in Datil came to where she sat before an open fire reading, with the startling report: 'There's a man lying beside the barn and he had the gall to put his horse in the haystack corral. It's a great big white horse that'll sure make a hole in that stack by morning. I told the man to come over to the house or he'd freeze to death and he answered that he must be invited. He's *poco loco*, I guess, but he'll sure freeze if he stays where he is.'

A few moments later, Mother met the stranger with the cry, 'Francis Schlatter!' He nodded gravely. 'The Father has directed me to a safe retreat. I must restore my spiritual powers in seclusion and prayer.'

He had ridden the seven hundred miles between Denver and Datil in midwinter, much of the way in desolate rugged country, the last stretch across forbidding Putney Mesa, where snow lay over a foot deep. Yet Butte had arrived in exceedingly good condition.

For almost three months, Schlatter remained in an upstairs room, venturing out only when the coast was unmistakably clear. Two occupations engrossed him during this time: he dictated to my mother a manuscript of considerable length, which she later published under the title he gave to it, *The Life of the Harp in the Hand of the Harper.* The rest of the time he spent in swinging a bronze club very like a forty-pound baseball bat, as a drum major might swing a baton. It was a feat requiring prodigious strength, but he did it tirelessly. He said that it was a practice imposed upon him by 'the Father' and he must obey or lose his power.

Mother read him the newspaper accounts of the search still being made for him, to all of which he replied, 'When the time has come for me to reveal myself, the Father will tell me.' . . .

Again he vanished, and for a decade impostors in unbroken succession appeared throughout the country claiming to be the original Schlatter, but all differing from him in the detail of returning any money proffered. A Los Angeles court sent one false Schlatter to jail, and all others were discredited. Meanwhile Mother waited with unfaltering faith. Nothing mattered any more. Schlatter would return and the world would be freed from its shackles. . . .

It was in Old Mexico that, ten years later, the newspapers thought they had discovered him. A clipping was handed to my mother which told that under a tree in Chihuahua had been found a man's skeleton, a peculiar metal rod, a weather-faded Bible with the name Francis Schlatter on the fly-leaf.

'He told me to expect this,' Mother said quietly. 'He is not dead. He will return.'

67

LAW WEST OF THE PECOS

C. L. Sonnichsen

C. L. Sonnichsen, a Harvard man, came to the University of Texas, El Paso, to teach English, fell hard for the desert west, and became its eminent grass-roots historian. Here's a bit from his excellent biography of Judge Roy Bean.

Fifty years ago most of the male passengers on the Southern Pacific westbound from San Antonio to El Paso used to perk up a little as they approached the high bridge over the Pecos River. They knew that twenty miles beyond was a small oasis named Langtry where they would have fifteen or twenty minutes to stretch their legs, buy a drink, and pass the time of day with Judge Roy Bean.

Long before the coaches jarred to a halt in the shadow of the Langtry water tank, the greenhorns in the smoking car would have full information, some of it true, about the Law West of the Pecos, as Roy Bean called himself. With their curiosity already on edge they would take in the handful of adobe buildings which was Langtry, the little station and the big water tank, and finally the small frame shack twenty steps north of the tracks with a covered porch in front and signs plastered over it: THE JERSEY LILLY. JUDGE ROY BEAN NOTARY PUBLIC. LAW WEST OF THE PECOS.

Someone would say, "There he is!" And there he would be—a sturdy, gray-bearded figure with a Mexican sombrero on his head and a portly stomach mushrooming out over his belt, waiting on his porch for the swirl of business and excitement which always came at train time. You could see at a glance that he was as rough as a sand burr and tough as a boiled owl, but you realized also that he was a genuine character with plenty of salt in him.

If you came back more than once and really got to know the old man, you found that he was a curious mixture of qualities. First you noticed that he was almost innocent of book learning, that he was egotistical and opinionated, that he regarded cheating you as good clean fun, and that he drank too much and washed too little. Once you got used to these drawbacks, however, you found that you had to like and even admire him. He was really a tough old rooster and had been a godsend to the ranger force when in 1882 they got him his commission as justice of the peace to help clean up the railroad construction camps. At the same time he concealed under his horny hide a heart which was not without soft spots. Children and animals liked him, and that is supposed to prove something. Then too, he was often generous in his own high-handed, tyrannical way. The poor Mexicans in the neighborhood would not have known what to do without his benevolent bullying. Finally, he had a color and flavor, authentic and attractive, which made people take an interest in him and forget about his profanity, unscrupulousness, and dirt.

The "best people," of course, have always been puzzled by a phenomenon like Roy Bean. Some of them still ask bitterly why such an old rapscallion should get so much attention when better men have lived and died unknown. The boys in the smoking car who piled off the train at Langtry and hot-footed it for the Jersey Lily never asked that question. They knew deep down among their instincts that Roy Bean, with all his faults and shortcomings—perhaps even because of them—was made out of the stuff of America. So they drank with him, played poker with him, laughed when he gypped them, and told epic tales about him which still go marching on.

They told about the time he held an inquest over a dead body on which he had found forty dollars and a pistol. He fined the corpse forty dollars for carrying concealed weapons.

They told about the Irishman who was brought into court for killing a Chinaman. Roy turned him loose, remarking that he had gone through his law book and found that it was homicide to kill a human being. "But," he said, "I'll be damned if I can find any place where it says it's against the law to kill a Chinaman."

They told about his habit of divorcing couples he had married, though he had no legal right to do so, explaining that he only "aimed to rectify his errors."

They told about his long-range platonic affair with Lily Langtry, the actress.

They told about the time he pulled off a heavyweight championship prize fight in his own back yard.

They told fifty yarns to show that he was too cagy to be taken in, too smart to be bluffed, and too tough to be damaged, and most of the stories were at least half true.

What they could not tell about, because they were not aware of it, was the real, deep-seated reason for Roy Bean's notoriety. They were not aware that the American people were examining old Roy as a candidate for hero worship—finding out if he could stand up to Davy Crockett and Mike Fink and Paul Bunyan; experimenting to see whether good folk stories could be made up about him; testing his quality to see if it was true frontier American.

This may seem like an eccentric and over-subtle way of looking at the old man, but there are arguments to justify it. No one doubts that older races than ours have been better able than we to evolve Robin Hoods, Siegfrieds, Rolands, and Arthurs to embody the national ideals. It is almost as plain to anyone who tries to understand our country that America has missed these symbols—has yearned for them —has even gone out and kidnapped some likely prospects and made heroes of them by main force. Jesse James is one example. Billy the Kid is another. With the help of Hollywood we have constructed shrines for such drunken old tarts as Calamity Jane and have burned incense before such homicidal exhibitionists as Wild Bill Hickok. It looks as if the American People have gone shopping for heroes and come home with whatever they could find.

Perhaps we have to put up with so little because we have not wanted much. The fact is we demand less of our folk heroes than we do of our street sweepers and ditch diggers; the specifications for the type are almost shockingly simple. First of all we ask for a certain amount of ignorance. It makes our man seem more like one of us, and besides we have a dim superstition that too much education is destructive of horse sense. The real wise man, we think, is a child of nature. All he knows is what he reads in the papers; but he offers advice to kings and presidents just the same.

Early struggles and a background of poverty are a great help. It is even better if the candidate proves to be an orphan or if he ran away from home at an early age.

"Smartness" is necessary. Nobody wants to idealize a person who can be beaten in a horse trade.

Bravery—even pugnacity—is another essential. The only alternative is to be a master of the game of bluff. If a man we admire can fool his foes, we don't insist that he shoot them.

Most important of all, the aspirant to greatness must do things in a big way, even if he only lies in a big way about the things he does. If he can't rope a cyclone, use the new moon for a powder horn, or outrun a prairie fire, he has to be overwhelming in some other fashion—like calling himself the Law West of the Pecos and making it stick.

Most of the great Americans who had had enough vitality to start a run of legends about themselves have come close to this formula. If we take a liking to a strong personality who doesn't come close enough, we make him over almost before he is quiet in his grave. Even imaginary heroes like Pecos Bill and Paul Bunyan and Strap Buckner fit the pattern.

Roy Bean fits it too. He was not as big of bone as the great ones, but he belonged to the breed. And the most remarkable thing about him is the fact that he knew he belonged. Somehow he discovered that he was the kind of person Americans like to make something of, and he spent the last years of his life helping them make something of him. There were times when ambition burned low in him. His youth was full of color and adventure but he reached middle age without attracting much notice. When he began to crowd sixty, he was just another disreputable old tough living on the wrong side of town in San Antonio. There had been twenty years of this, and he was discouraged; but he never quite gave up the notion that he was a marked man. Then, at the beginning of the final quarter of his life, he went west with the railroad and found his place at last. In a few months he became the Law West of the Pecos, and a minor immortal.

Only one man in a million could have done it. His official residence was a one-room frame shack in which he held court, sold beer, slept, and cultivated his soul. His town was a hamlet of a few dozen inhabitants almost lost in the scorching wastes of the West Texas desert. His friends and acquaintances were cowboys and laborers and men on the dodge. What of it? He wanted to be the biggest man in the country and this was the sort of country in which he could be the biggest man.

For a while he lived the epic he imagined. He really was the Law in those parts for a few years. It was two hundred miles to the nearest justice court and naturally he had things his own way. Before long civilization and lawyers moved in on him, but by that time his saga was started and his position was assured. He became in the minds of other men a sort of Ulysses of West Texas—a man of craft and action combined—a figure of colorful peculiarities and great resourcefulness. His fame was no surprise to him, though it was to a great many other people, for he had been convinced all along that he was no ordinary citizen. He probably thought his recognition was, if anything, considerably overdue.

And so when the train pulled into Langtry, there he was on his porch. He always exposed himself at train time so people could see him. He was sure they would want to.

68

HOW PHOENIX
GOT ITS NAME

Lawrence Clark Powell

Phoenix has become the metropolis of the desert west, filling the Salt River Valley with modern architecture, suburbs, smog, and traffic jams. "You're going to Phoenix us," has become the warning cry shouted in planning commission meetings up and down the Rockies. From Arizona: A History, *by Lawrence Clark Powell, is a story about how two oddballs helped get it started.*

The time was 1868 in the fifth year of the territory. The major [Arizona] army forts were in the center—Whipple at Prescott and McDowell on the Verde near its junction with the Salt, located there to keep a gun on the Tonto Apaches. Although the valley of the Salt could serve for agricultural development, it was not then a place to attract many people as residents. Its scenic attractions were nil: a fickle riverbed, a desert of creosote, cactus, and runty mesquite, and a few barren ranges, more hill than mountain. Also scant rainfall and windblown sand and a summer sun that baked the valley in furnace heat. There was no one there, its first inhabitants had long since gone and been forgotten.

How did it happen that the phoenix arose there? Who waved the wand? How pleasing to civic pride if Phoenix could claim a founder as selfless as Kino, as brave as Anza! Alas, its founder was John W. (Jack) Swilling, a tricky adventurer willing to serve whoever paid him the most,

Confederate or Union. He was also an Indian hunter and highwayman who came to a sad end in jail at Yuma. No wonder the statue in front of the capitol is that of Lieutenant Frank Luke, Jr., that daring young flyer of World War I instead of Swilling's.

Swilling was a South Carolinian who came to Arizona in 1857 as a hand on a government party to improve the Gila Trail. He then joined a gold rush to Gila City and led a militia party called the Gila Rangers to chastise raiding Yavapais. Lust for gold led him back to the domain of Mangas Coloradas at Piños Altos. It was he who treacherously delivered the Mimbreño chieftain to the Union troops to be murdered. Next we meet Swilling prospecting for gold near Prescott. After squandering the profits of a rich strike, he drifted down to the Salt River Valley and became a hauler of hay to the post at Fort McDowell. It was a dangerous job, the last three haulers having been killed by the Tontos.

This man was aware of the land's lay and the wind's direction. He saw that the ancient farmers had canalled water to the drier reaches. Vestiges of their ditches were still visible. Swilling knew naught of the Hohokam. He knew only what he needed to know: that when watered, the sun-baked soil would yield crops; and furthermore that the United States Army paid cash for barley and would provide a market for other crops.

And so there at the crossing of the Salt where Phoenix and Tempe now meet and merge, the enterprising adventurer, together with Henry Wickenburg and others, grandly inaugurated the Swilling Irrigating Canal Company. Following the Indians' example, the company dug a ditch north and west from what is today 44th and Washington streets. Along it settled thirty farmers. They soon grew to a hundred, and by 1872 they had increased sevenfold.

As Swilling prospered, he took to wife a Mexican girl, one Trinidad of Tucson, and at what is today the east end of the parking lot at Grey-hound Park he built an adobe house. With his wife's aid he enrolled the neighboring Mexicans to vote in newly organized Maricopa County's elec-tion to locate the county seat. Their vote was for the site to be centered at Swilling's home and the farming settlement now included in the site of the state hospital. Alas, a rival group of real estate developers paid more for the Indian vote, and so the seat was set where it is today, in downtown Phoenix, west of the original settlement.

This setback plus a native restlessness led Swilling to take up land along the Agua Fria in Black Canyon country up toward Prescott. His career had peaked. From then on his way ran downriver. Because of pain from a head injury suffered in a fight before coming to Arizona, Swilling had become addicted to laudanum and alcohol, neither of which improved his character. He moved outside the law. His fall from grace came with his indictment for the holdup of the Wickenburg stage. Although friends joined in his protest of innocence, circumstantial evidence damned him. He was being held in the Yuma jail awaiting trial when he died in 1878 at the age of forty-eight.

In a last letter he penned these true words: "I will be remembered long after the names of my persecutors have been forgotten." . . .

The naming of Phoenix is owed to yet another eccentric Arizonan, an English wanderer born in France, where his father was in the diplomatic service. With a ready assist from himself, custom conferred upon him no less than a lordship. He was, in fact, descended from the minor nobility, born Bryan Philip Darrel Duppa of Hollingbourne House, County Kent. His early years remain shrouded. They apparently included classical schooling in France and Spain and fluency in the continental languages. Later he suffered shipwreck, explored South America, and then joined his prosperous Uncle George in developing a sheep station at St. Leonards, New Zealand, where in time he accumulated his own flock and property.

Duppa next appeared in Prescott, N.M.T., in 1862 where he is said to have come to investigate some mining shares owned by his uncle. While prospecting and Indian fighting, he managed to receive via the Bank of California remittances from New Zealand from the sale of his sheep. It was enough to keep him in beans and beer.

Then in 1867 those two oddballs, D. Duppa and J. Swilling, rolled together, we know not how. Was the Englishman the "angel" who staked the Carolinian in that venture on the Salt? We only know Duppa turned up as one of the first Phoenicians who claimed land at what is now 116 West Sherman Street.

The new settlement needed a name if for no other reason than to tell shippers where to send supplies. Some favored Pumpkinsville. Others wanted to call it Mill City after Helling's mill at the asylum site. Salina was still another preference—from the salt marshes along the stream. Swilling's Southern sympathies led him to choose Stonewall.

The erudition of "Lord" Duppa settled the argument. According to the recollections of old Charles T. Hayden, father of the even longer lived politician, a bunch of the boys were gathered convivially one day in 1869 at the Pueblo Grande—the Indian ruin restored in our time by Dwight B. Heard as a museum-monument along the Grand Canal of East Washington Street—when the perennial question was asked, Where *are* we?

Whereupon Duppa clambered to the top of the ruined wall and, raising his cultured voice, proclaimed to somewhat short of a multitude, "As the mythical phoenix rose reborn from its ashes, so shall a great civilization rise here on the ashes of a past civilization. I name thee Phoenix!" It is almost too good to be true, and yet who would dispute the memory of the old miller? Phoenix it was and Phoenix it is.

If one will go there today and stand on the wall where Duppa stood and gaze northeast to Papago Park, he will see in apt conjunction the white-tiled tomb of George Wiley Paul Hunt and the monumental head-quarters of the Salt River Project. Far to the southeast at Florence on the Gila, apparent to only the mind's eye, is a rougher tomb, where that other dreamer—Charles Poston—takes his long rest.

Again for reasons unknown Duppa followed Swilling to the Agua Fria, and there on the road to Wickenburg he operated an unofficial stage station. Then and now that region is "an uncompromising piece of desert." Along the same highway stands another modern miracle—Del Webb's Sun City, an "instant city" harboring more than 30,000 fugitives from colder climes.

His lordship's station was a squalid place. Drawing on an early news-paper account, Edward Peplow gave this description:

> The roof was constructed of willows, and the thin, unplastered walls were of ironwood interlaced with rawhide. A few sticks of unpainted furniture were scattered throughout the inside. Guests, when there were any, slept on the dirt floor on blankets taken from a pile stacked in a corner. Guns, ammunition, sad-dles, whips, and spurs were suspended from the joists and cross-beams. Dogs and mules roamed the establishment. A dwarfish, hairy, and gutteral-voiced cook, whose name is lost in history, prepared the meals for Duppa and guests. They were unusual and surprisingly delicious. When the meals were ready, the hirsute cook would rattle pots, pans, and dutch ovens and bellow out, "Hash pile! Come a'runnin'!"[3]

Duppa's final years were spent, as Poston's were, back in Phoenix, drinking in the back room of Doctor Thibodo's drugstore, and yarning with other old-timers, or loafing under the cottonwoods along the canal. He was described as tall, thin, and very dark, wearing brogans and blue denims, a silver-buckled belt, navy-blue shirt, and black, wide-brimmed hat with flat-topped crown. Except for his speech and lordly manner he would have passed for a typical frontier Arizonan.

He died of pneumonia in 1892. Eighteen years later the Maricopa chapter of the Daughters of the American Revolution, overlooking his national origin, reburied him in Greenwood Memorial Park. There on his gravestone are these words:

IN MEMORY OF DARREL DUPPA,
ENGLISH GENTLEMAN AND A PIONEER OF ARIZONA,
WHO NAMED THE CITIES OF PHOENIX AND TEMPE.

69

UNCLE DICK
WOOTTON

Agnes Morley Cleaveland

Few have left more of the impact of their personality on an area than did Wootton. This is from Satan's Paradise, *another of Agnes Morley Cleaveland's recollections.*

One of the men most responsible for the development of Maxwell's *rancho* into the town of Cimarron was Richens Lacy Wootton. At the age of fifteen, he had left his family home in Kentucky and pushed toward the setting sun. Into Mississippi first, thence toward the Rocky Mountains, he followed the river courses, dependent solely on his rifle to keep him alive. He finally reached Westport Landing at Independence, Missouri, head of the fate-laden Santa Fé Trail. His next objective was Bent's Fort on the Arkansas River.

The time was to come when Dick Wootton, no longer ragged or young, would build a toll-gate in Raton Pass as closely identified with the Santa Fé Trail and the "Opening of the West" as Bent's Fort itself, and his nickname of "Uncle Dick" would be known throughout the Southwest. But before that came about, Dick Wootton was to make a name for himself as scout and Indian fighter—in adventures which carried him on trading expeditions with Sioux, Arapahoes, Pawnees, Utes, Comanches, and various other Indian tribes. Some of these expeditions proved profitable, others ended in disaster. There was always that uncertainty, as when Wootton's party stumbled into an inter-tribal war between Utes and Arapahoes and paid the price demanded of unwitting intruders. His party had found an all-but-starved old squaw, sole survivor of an attack by Utes upon an Arapahoe camp. Reviving the half-dead woman, they made a special expedition to return her to her tribe. In gratitude, the chief presented her rescuers with a number of good ponies, a welcome and sorely needed gift. Indian and white man shook hands in friendship.

Cordiality lasted a couple of days. When they were on their way again, a roving band of Pawnees attacked Wootton's party from ambush. Young Dick's horse was shot from under him and he barely escaped being scalped alive. Seventeen Pawnees were killed, but the precious ponies were stampeded and lost.

Indian warfare of that day was a succession of such incidents. Dick Wootton's record for fair dealing with the Indians is one of the best, but he suffered for the sins of the less well-disposed with whom he was bracketed. In the white public mind of the day, all Indians were "savages," and to the red public mind, all whites were bloodthirsty intruders, come to despoil them of their land. The delicate point of whose land it really was remained a detail lost in a broad generality: the sundry tribes who ranged the illimitable spaces of the West had never settled that issue between themselves.

There have always been men who ardently wished that brotherly love might reign in human hearts. Few have succeeded in demonstrating, in their own lives, the completeness of it. But in all ages, there have appeared personalities who exemplify the "little leaven" which leaveneth the whole lump. Dick Wootton was one of them. He fought and killed Indians when to deal with them on any other terms seemed impossible, as did his close friends, Kit Carson, Lucien Maxwell, and almost everybody else who survived in that day and place.

The thick-walled adobe house which Uncle Dick in 1865 built at the foot of the Raton grade, not far beyond Trinidad, Colorado, marked the end of an era. The Raton Pass had been one of the dreaded hazards of the Santa Fé Trail. The bones of draft animals—oxen, horses, and mules—bleached along its tortuous curves. With prodigious labor, Uncle Dick built a zigzag wagon road up and over the northern face of the escarpment. The Territorial Governments of both Colorado and New Mexico granted him a franchise to operate a toll-road.

The first massive gate of logs, which opened only for a price, was an object of wonder and resentment to the Indians until Uncle Dick promised that it would always be opened free of charge for them and their livestock.

Posses in line of duty also passed free, probably because Uncle Dick figured that collecting toll from them would be too difficult and dangerous.

Uncle Dick would greet all other travelers, count them, and collect on a basis of twenty-five cents for horsemen, ten cents for pedestrians, five cents a head for animals and a dollar or a dollar and a half for wagons. Then he would remove the barricade. The sum a given wagon should pay was often a matter for difference of opinion, occasionally accompanied by violence. Collecting toll was a lively business.

Ed Howe, a blacksmith of Wagon Mound, New Mexico, remembers the trip he made as a child over Uncle Dick's toll-road. Mr. Howe's father had brought along not only his family and wagons but also many cattle. Uncle Dick counted, and collected the toll, and the Howe family traveled on up the road.

Then Uncle Dick, mentally rechecking, decided that he was short a nickel, the toll for one cow. So he sent one of the boys after the Howe party, by this time some distance away. The boy had instructions to round up all the cattle and recount them. When the recount showed that the original figure had been correct, the Howes were allowed to proceed over the Pass.

Everybody who traveled the route came to know Uncle Dick. Knowing him served as a credential. Inevitably, his establishment developed into one of the original superservice stations, supplying a traveler's every need: food, beds, hay and grain, fresh animals, and even personally conducted tours over the Pass. He was in due course to serve Henry Lambert in that capacity when commissioned to transport over his toll-road much of the furniture which was to make the St. James Hotel notable: marble-topped tables, four-poster beds, velvet draperies, beveled glass mirrors, and English china, all traveling by ox cart.

Uncle Dick more than once played a part in the destiny of the Morley family. My mother stopped at his fortress-like house on her wedding journey from her Iowa home to share her husband's life in that New Mexico about which Messrs. Miranda and Beaubien had written so disparagingly. She shrank from the vision of such a place becoming the permanent home for her family, but Uncle Dick was kind and reassuring and she took heart. Perhaps, she thought, there were people who managed to live and carve out worth-while careers in this raw and violent land.

She was to stop overnight at Uncle Dick's again, after several years in Cimarron. Her confidence had been badly shaken by the events that lay between that first meeting and this one. I must have been about six years old, but I remember falling asleep before the huge stone fireplace with its blazing *piñon* logs while my elders talked. I wish I could have remained awake and heard (and remembered) that conversation. It dealt, of course, with the trip of the first locomotive-drawn train over the Pass, and of the part my father had played in that achievement; but it also dealt with the empire that Lucien Maxwell had built.

I do remember that Uncle Dick finally carried me off to bed. By that gentle act, he changed our lives. As she walked beside his towering figure, carrying the inert form of her little girl, my mother brushed aside the determination to give up which had been growing in her of late, especially with the birth of each child. Cimarron had brought her face to face with the realization that her children must submit to, or force their way out of, conditions which she had decided Miranda and Beaubien had not exaggerated. The scales seemed weighted against them.

But there were also others like Uncle Dick, she had discovered; men whom she would not protest as models for her own son, her second child. Of course, in the case of the girls! But where, she asked herself, in any place or any age, had girls been safer? It is to the undying glory of the pioneer that women were safe even when they stepped outside of the current code for "good women." She resolved then to say no more about taking the family away from New Mexico.

Could she have looked but a little way into the future, she would undoubtedly have decided otherwise. Fortunately, she did not realize that a web had already been woven about her and her children, a web which she was powerless to break. The spider that wove it was the Maxwell Land Grant.

70

CULTURE COMES
TO VIRGINIA CITY

R. D. Miller

*Shady ladies sometimes played an unusual role on the frontier. Witness Julia
Bulette, as described in R. D. Miller's* Shady Ladies of the West.

The greatest bonanza in precious metals ever to be uncovered in modern
times was the Comstock Lode of Nevada. Close to three quarters of a
billion dollars poured out of the region. In the space of a few short years,
two of its mines alone produced $190,000,000 in gold and silver. Its richest
mine was situated directly beneath Virginia City.

During the last half of the nineteenth century the Comstock Lode
and Virginia City dominated the Western scene. They produced a prodigious number of multimillionaires and madames. Virginia City's first and
greatest madame was Julia Bulette, who braved the wilderness camp in
1860. During her brief but breathless life she found herself to be the toast
of the richest mining community in the United States and the pride of the
Comstock fire companies. Julia has become one of the imperishable legends
of the West.

The *Territorial Enterprise* reported that Julia was a native of London
and had come to the California camps by way of New Orleans in 1853.
After residing in various west-coast towns until 1860, she followed the rush
to the Comstock. Little is known of her true background. Most historians

agree that she was undoubtedly a Creole who had migrated from New Orleans' Rampart Street. This mysterious lady rose with the wealth of the Comstock to be the ranking madame of Virginia City. Her rococo establishment was known as "Julia's Palace."

Julia Bulette lived alone in her house at the corner of Union and D Streets. This establishment was the cultural center of the community. During her "entertainments" she permitted no rough-housing as was found in other houses. She offered good conversation, taught the men to recognize fine wines and champagnes and served skillfully prepared French dishes.

When epidemics swept Virginia City, Julia passed from tent to tent, administering medicine and restoring hope with her mere presence. Poor families on the Comstock received anonymous gifts of food and clothing. Julia was the first to contribute food and money for the widows of men who died in the mines. She was the town's most spirited contributor to the Sanitation Fund, forerunner of the Red Cross. In the very early days of the camp, when Virginia City was threatened with attack by the Paiutes, Julia refused to seek safety with the other women in Carson City and remained with the men to nurse them.

All of these generous acts brought Julia Bulette the highest homage possible for the miners to present her. She was elected an honorary member of the Virginia Engine Company Number One. She was the only woman in history to be so honored, and she took it seriously. No holiday or parade was complete without Julia riding enthroned on the gleaming brass and silver fire engine. When the town was threatened by fire, she was on hand with food and coffee for the fire fighters. Upon at least one occasion, she even assisted at the pumps.

Additional honors were heaped upon the lovely madame of Virginia City. The Virginia and Truckee Railroad boasted a club car named "Julia Bulette." The "Julia," one of the Comstock Mines, was named for her.

To the horror of the later female arrivals to the town, Julia became something of a social leader in the community. When Nevada became a state in 1864, it was learned that the newly-elected Governor Nye was expected to visit Virginia City. Julia proposed and helped build a huge floral arch over the main street.

The "good" women of the town peeked from behind their lace curtains, with what might have been a touch of jealousy, when Julia took her daily ride along C Street in her lacquered brougham. The doors of this fancy rig were decorated with a crest of four aces. She attended the productions at the Opera House accompanied by Tom Peasley, her favorite lover. There, she would sit in her own loge, wearing an opera hood of white silk and purple velvet in the summer. In winter, she would appear in a sable cape with sable muff and wristlets. It was clear that her star was on the ascendent.

The wives of Virginia City were soon given opportunity to nod to each other and whisper of divine retribution. On Sunday morning, January 20, 1867 at 11:30 A.M., Gertrude Holmes, a neighbor lady of the line, entered Julia's house by the open back door. She had come to call her friend to a prearranged breakfast. Receiving no response to her call, Gertrude walked into the bedroom and found the corpse of Julia Bulette in the bed.

Julia's body was lying with the head in a normal position on the pillow. However, her legs and feet protruded from under the covers to one side. It was evident that no one had occupied the bed with her, since the undersheet on both sides of the body was smooth. On the floor, beside the bed, lay her clothes. It appeared as though she had simply dropped them and stepped out of them.

Dr. Bronson and Dr. Gaston examined the body at noon and testified that Julia had been dead six or eight hours. They discovered deep bruises on her forehead and splinters of wood in her hair. Julia had been struck with a stick of wood, which was later found in the room. Death, however, was completed by strangulation.

At five that morning, a newsboy had heard a loud scream from the vicinity of Julia's house. As he made his rounds, he heard nothing more. He even delivered a paper at her door and saw nothing unusual. A Chinaman entered the house early, bringing wood, and lighting the fire. Thinking that Julia was asleep, he left without disturbing her. It had not been until Gertrude Holmes tried to awaken her that the body of the beautiful madame was found.

Julia Bulette was given the finest funeral the Comstock had ever seen. A band, eighteen carriages, and the marching men of Virginia Engine Company Number One escorted her body to Flowery Hill Cemetery. Julia rested in a special silver-handled coffin which was borne by a black-plumed, glass-walled hearse. As the cortége departed from the fire house on B Street, the good wives of the town closed their shutters or drew their shades. They were fearful of seeing their husbands in the procession. The band played a funeral dirge on the way to the grave, but the rollicking strains of "The Girl I Left Behind Me" rocked the town on the return route.

Julia's murder had not been committed because of sex. The motive had been robbery. The murderer had systematically looted the house. Some three months after the funeral, it looked as though the murderer had been found. His name was John Millain. Although he denied all knowledge of the crime, he was found with some of the stolen goods in his possession.

Millain had sat up with the corpse at the funeral parlor all the night following the murder. He also had marched in the funeral cortége wearing a crepe armband. However, the damning evidence of his possession of Julia's jewelry convinced the men of Virginia City that he was the best candidate for a hanging. A group of local architects assembled in the Virginia Hotel bar and drew up plans for a king-sized scaffold.

Although Millain steadfastly denied any knowledge of Julia's murder, he had been recognized by Martha Camp, another lady of the line, as the man she had earlier surprised in her own room. This time, Millain, who had been carrying a knife, escaped. However, Martha saw him a few days later on C Street and had him arrested on a charge of robbery and attempted murder.

It was while he was being held on these charges that new evidence was found connecting Millain with the death of Julia. On May 23, 1867, it was discovered that a Mrs. Cazentre of Gold Hill had paid him forty dollars for a dress pattern, which had initially been sold to Julia. Further investigation uncovered the fact that Millain had sold to Nye, the jeweler, a diamond pin which was known to have been hers. Searching Millain's possessions, the police found a trunk filled with Julia's belongings. . . .

Even though he had informally admitted the murder when faced with the evidence, Millain pleaded not guilty to the charge at his trial. He did, however, admit participation in the robbery. Accusing a man named Blair of the murder, he claimed that he had remained outside the house during the crime and knew nothing of Julia's killing until told of it afterward. However, when placed in a room with Blair, Millain failed to recognize him.

Julia Bulette, Virginia City's first prostitute, was much loved by the town's citizenry. Feelings along the Comstock are perhaps best expressed by the summation of the prosecution. District Attorney Bishop told the jury:

> Although this community has, in times past, seen blood run like water, yet in most cases there was some cause brought forward in justification of the deed, some pretext. But on the morning of the 20th of January last, this community, so hardened by previous deeds of blood, was struck dumb with horror by a deed which carried dread to the heart of every one—a deed more fiendish, more horrible than ever before perpetrated on this side of the snowy Sierra. Julia Bulette was found lying dead

in her bed, foully murdered, and stiff and cold in her clotted gore. True, she was a woman of easy virtue. Yet hundreds in this city have had cause to bless her name for her many acts of charity. So much worse the crime. That woman probably had more real, warm friends in this community than any other; yet there was found at last a human being so fiendish and base as to crawl to her bedside in the dead hour of the night, and with violent hands, beat and strangle her to death—not for revenge, but in order to plunder her of these very articles of clothing and jewelry we see before us. What inhuman, unparalleled barbarity!

The good wives of Virginia City may have abhored murder, but they viewed Millain as an instrument of Providence. He had, after all, rid their community of its most infamous painted lady. They visited him in his jail cell, bringing him gifts of pâté de foie gras, wines and other delicacies. They even went so far as to circulate a petition for the commutation of his sentence to life imprisonment. This action was stopped by the *Territorial Enterprise*. In an editorial the paper issued this blunt statement: "We believe that the man will be hung. If he is not, we do not know where a fit subject for hanging is to be found."

John Millain was convicted of Julia's murder, but his lawyer, Charles E. DeLong, appealed the case to the Supreme Court of Nevada. However, a rehearing was refused, and on February 27, 1867, Millain was sentenced to be hanged on the twenty-fourth day of April between ten in the morning and four in the afternoon.

Julia Bulette's funeral had been a grand affair. The hanging of her murderer made it look tame. Crowds had gathered from all over the state to view the execution. Virginia City took on the attitude of a holiday. Picture postcards of Millain were sold. The gallows had been erected in a natural amphitheater one mile from town, and a parade route to it from the jail had been prepared.

At eleven-thirty on the morning of the twenty-fourth of April, a heavily curtained carriage left the courthouse. Surrounding it were two squares of armed men. Forty special deputy sheriffs, armed with Henry rifles composed the inner ring. The second circle of guards was formed by about sixty members of the National Guard, marching in full uniform with loaded and bayoneted rifles. Inside the carriage rode John Millain, accompanied by Father Clarke of Carson, and Father Manogue of Virginia City.

As the police cleared the line of march, the carriage and its double guard were joined by two other vehicles. One carriage carried the physicians and the other the press. A hearse carrying a black-draped coffin came last.

Upon arrival at the gallows, Millain heard the death warrant read by Sheriff Leconey. He then read a prepared statement in his native French and, in perfect English, thanked the ladies of Virginia City for their concern and food. The noose was adjusted. The black hood was pulled over his face. John Millain, murderer of Julia Bulette, passed into eternity.

John Millain was buried in the Catholic Cemetery, but the exact location of his grave is no longer remembered. Although Julia Bulette's funeral services were allowed in the Saint Mary's Church, her body was not permitted to be placed in the same hallowed ground as that of her murderer. Julia was, after all, a prostitute. She was buried on Flowery Hill. Among the weather-beaten and crumbling headstones of the cemetery one may still find her well-kept grave with its freshly painted picket fence. The people of Virginia City still remember Julia Bulette.

Well they might. Julia was more than a common prostitute. She was more than a common woman. Julia acted as a lady in manners as well as dress. This tall, dark-eyed beauty possessed those deeper feminine characteristics necessary for the civilizing of the West—sympathy, generosity, understanding and compassion. She was, indeed, a great lady of the line.

Part Nine

◆

THE MINES

In economic terms the early West had little to attract European-Americans. There was no demand for its plentitude of timber or its oceans of grass. The climate was (and is) dry enough to discourage cultivation, and only a small percentage of its river valleys could be irrigated. But it did offer gold and silver, plus the illusion that their harvest would be easy. Thus much of the motivation for the Western movement, for the "Manifest Destiny" of the United States to extend its domain through the Rocky Mountains to the Pacific, was the itch to find the metals that would turn a poor man into a rich one.

71

GOLD ONLY
WAITING TO BE
GATHERED UP

Paul Horgan

As Paul Horgan *wrote in* The Great River: The Rio Grande in North American History, *"illusion was the very nourishment of treasure seekers." The book won the Pulitzer Prize in History in 1955 and the lasting envy of historians who lacked Horgan's genius for bringing the dead past to life. In the following passage he provides a glimpse of Creede, Colorado, and Socorro, New Mexico, when the illusion there was bright.*

Illusion was the very nourishment of treasure seekers. Watching westward in 1858 for their first sight of mountains a party of prospectors entering Colorado saw on the horizon what one of the company said looked "like a thunder cloud." What he saw were the Spanish Peaks in the Sangre de Cristo range. His party turned north and followed the base of the mountains to the camps of Pike's Peak and Cherry Creek, where first discoveries of gold were followed by disappointment. Early stories in guidebooks and newspapers, all too often written by men who had never been west, told how gold was lying "on the plains, in the mountains, and by the streams, only waiting to be gathered up." The realities were different. Mineral treasure was present, but it had to be found in its secret lodgments and taken out by hard work. Many immigrants turned away homeward in disgust, making a wish in a popular jingle to

"Hang Byers and D. C. Oakes
For starting this damned Pike's Peak hoax,"

and some drifted southward to New Mexico, where one couple, "with wagon and mess," settled at Taos when the wife was offered a position teaching school. But others persisted, and the Colorado gold fields soon flourished. For about its first decade Colorado mining was located in the great central ranges of the Rockies, far removed from the Rio Grande and the San Juan Mountains of its source.

For though the New York *Herald* declared in 1857 that in "the Sierra San Juan, where, if we recollect rightly, both Pike and Frémont lost their way, gold, silver, cinnabar and precious stones are found in immense quantities," there was no mining of any significance in the Rio Grande basin of Colorado until after the Civil War. Settlement was limited to a few farming communities in the grand San Luis Valley, whose mild slopes and level floor recalled its origin as a huge lake. Through it the river ran a gentle course along which a handful of Mexican families established themselves in 1853 distant from the most northerly New Mexican settlements by only a few days' march. Using the river to irrigate their little fields, and the wide grassy valley to graze their small herds, they recreated the scene of slow water, bounteous cottonwood tree and earthen house that was so familiar in the river's New Mexican passage. They looked no farther for treasures of the earth.

In 1860, as though re-enacting in miniature an earlier pattern of conquest, a small party of Americans passed through the Mexican settlements of the San Luis Valley and followed the Rio Grande out of sight into the mountains of the source. They were looking for gold in the San Juan. Their search took them through summer and autumn, until they were caught in the snows of winter. In the following spring they were joined by other prospectors and all spent the next summer in the San Juan Mountains, but without finding gold. Before another winter could trap them they returned eastward to Fort Garland, where they heard that the Civil War had broken out; and the leader of the prospectors hurried to Virginia to enlist.

At the end of the decade other attempts were made to find the riches of the San Juan, and scattered strikes led to the establishment of mines on the western slope of the continental divide. By 1870 there was enough traffic along the headwaters of the Rio Grande to call alive the town of Del Norte as a supply point, at the gateway of the river between the San Luis Valley and the mountains. In the same year gold was found at Wightman's Gulch and other sites in the Del Norte region, the most thriving of which was Summitville to the southwest. The population of the district grew to six hundred. Stamp mills were set up at the largest camps. During the short summers pack trains bringing ore came from over the divide by way of Stony Pass which was over twelve thousand feet above sea level. On the eastward road out of the mountains a new town was founded in 1878—Alamosa.

It came as the new western terminus of the Denver and Rio Grande Western Railroad. The town itself came by rail, for from the old terminus of Garland City houses, churches, stores and other buildings were hauled on flat cars to be set up at the new end of the line. With heavy transportation now available, a new commercial interest was developed in the San Luis Valley that soon overshadowed mining as the main business of the region. Large-scale irrigation projects were organized and supported by foreign capital—principally British. Between Alamosa and Del Norte a huge grid of irrigation canals reached out from the Rio Grande for thirty or forty miles north and south. A land boom resulted. Speculation in land values and water rights went wild. As in so many other Western localities toward the end of the nineteenth century, company promoters preached a new paradise and trainloads of colonists came in response to the dazzling promise. For a little while, so long as competition was fresh and vigorous, the San Luis prospered in the vision of a future nourished by inexhaustible resources. Monte Vista, a third railroad town, was founded in 1887. But within a decade the vision began to pale, for what ended so many other organized Western dreams elsewhere presently took effect in southern Colorado—there was not enough water. Sapped by the greatly overextended system of canals, the river could not supply all. The euphoria of the pioneer faded, many immigrants abandoned their hopes and went away, and those who remained came to a regulated sharing of the waters whose stabilized flow was made possible by the building of reservoirs at the head of the valley. In the same period the mining ventures of the San Luis Valley began to lose energy. The camptowns of the Summitville region were left to the weather, and turned into silvered ghosts. Raw pine boarding turned gray, and weeds climbed the rusting machinery, and the character of the wide valley became wholly agricultural, supplied and drained by the railroad in a stabilized economy.

But farther up the river a major find of precious minerals was made in 1889 that suddenly brought the Rio Grande source country into the national news. For several years prospectors had been scratching at the rocks beyond Wagon Wheel Gap—where Kit Carson had once fought the Ute Indians—but without making significant discoveries. In that country they saw diamond clear creeks that were shadowed all day by narrowing mountains but for a little while at noon, when straight fingers of sunlight reached down through forest. On slopes open to the sun in summer, groves of quaking aspens showed here and there, creating little gardens of their own within immense wild parks. In winter the only green was that of the evergreens, solemn and frowning amidst the silver and brown of lichens— the colors of age—set off by heavy banks of snow. Far above, at timberline, like fixed images of the winds on the inhumane peaks, the last trees clutched the naked rock with gestures of agonized survival. Emerging from between two flat-cliffed mountains of flesh-colored stone streaked with olive lichens came a little stream which the prospectors named Willow Creek. They saw that it was a tributary of the Rio Grande, and that it had its own smaller tributary which they called West Willow Creek.

On a summer day in 1889 two experienced prospectors who had made successful discoveries elsewhere walked up Willow Creek through its formidable gateway. Presently one of them—Nicholas C. Creede—saw in the stream what surely seemed to be evidence of silver ore on the washed sandy bottom. He followed the creek and turned into its west branch, and when he reached the head of it, found rocks flecked with quartz and stippled with silver. Creede and his partner George L. Smith staked a location and went to work sinking a shaft at the spot. They were soon rewarded, for they struck a silver vein so rich that Creede on first making certain of it, exclaimed, "Holy Moses!" The mine was given that name. Winter would soon close in. Creede and Smith gathered specimens of their mine, and went to Denver where word of the discovery presently reached David H. Moffat, president of the Denver and Rio Grande Western Railroad. With other investors, Moffat bought shares in the Holy Moses after inspecting it when travel became possible the next spring. Creede was retained to continue prospecting for the new syndicate. In the summer of 1890 a rush began to Willow Gap, and by October there was a town of tents ready to survive the winter.

A year later the Denver and Rio Grande Western tracks reached Creede, as Willow Gap was now called, and by December trains ran regularly up the Rio Grande canyon past Wagon Wheel Gap and the confluence of Willow Creek, which entered the river along a peninsula of heavy gravel. Twenty months after it was founded, Creede displayed an energy that reached far beyond its own rock-bound limits. A gentleman journalist felt it in Denver on his way to examine the new camp. The word Creede "faced you everywhere from billboards, flaunted at you from canvas awnings stretched across the streets, and stared at you from daily papers in type an inch long." In Denver shops there were photographs of Creede, and "the only correct map of Creede," and ore specimens from the Holy

Moses. Miners' outfittings were advertised everywhere. A druggist pleaded in the newspapers for an investment of five hundred dollars with which to start a drugstore in Creede. Wherever the visitor met other people—in hotel lobbies, or the Denver Club—"Creede" was in the air. On the train from Denver to Creede every passenger "showed the effect of the magnet that was drawing him—he was restless, impatient, excited." The daily train had fifteen or twenty cars, and even so there were not enough seats for all its two or three hundred passengers. Some of the men sat on the others, while women of a certain class "smoked with the men and passed their flasks down the length of the car." As the train pulled into Creede the journalist jumped from his car "into two or three feet of mud and snow," and saw that "the ticket and telegraph offices on one side of the track were situated in a freight car with windows and doors cut out of it." The next thing noticed by the incoming passenger was that Creede already had electricity. A single electric light burned high against the pink cliff of Willow Gap at whose base huddled the town, and incandescent carbon "glow-lamps" shone in white, red and blue brilliance along the street front.

As a familiar of the great clubs and smart restaurants and polite drawing rooms of the world's capitals, the journalist was entranced by the simple rudeness of all he found in the mining camp. The approaches and slopes of Willow Gap were "covered with hundreds of little pine boxes and log cabins." It was "a village of fresh pine." There was "not a brick, a painted front, nor an awning in the entire town," which looked "like a city of fresh cardboard." The street was all confusion and movement. He saw "oxteams, mules, men, and donkeys loaded with ore . . . sinking knee deep in the mud," and "furniture, and kegs of beer, bedding and canned provisions, clothing and half-open packing cases, and piles of raw lumber . . . heaped up in front of the new stores—stores of canvas only, stores with canvas tops and foundations of logs, and houses with the *Leadville front,* where the upper boards have been left square instead of following the sloping angle of the roof." At the base of the superb rock panels rising above the town, all such clutter looked to him "impudent and absurd"— more like a "gypsy camp in a canyon," really, than a town. And the nomenclature of the establishments!—The Holy Moses Saloon, The Théâtre Comique, The Keno, The Little Delmonico. . . .

And the accommodations!—there were dozens of hotels, most of which afforded the traveller only a cot in a common room teeming with other sleepers. Beds were so scarce that the railroad company often left a number of Pullman cars on a siding to provide a lodging for the night. The population by now was about ten thousand, and included every type of commercial frontier character. The journalist saw gamblers, prospectors, miners, engineers, bankers, bartenders, itinerant evangelists, actors, prostitutes, schoolteachers, family men and women, jobbers, merchants, and confidence men to whom in his observations he could condescend with easy bad manners, and adventurous younger sons of rich Eastern families, with whom he was more at home. Luckily, he was able to find a bed for the night with a group of these young men who, like him, had come just for the lark. To go West to see such a spectacle as Creede was a gallant and correct thing for them to do, and he was their prophet, for his career had been full of just such fashionable exploits.

The night life, even though at the moment Creede was "not at all a dangerous place," with a lawlessness that was "scattered and mild," was worth an amused glance. There were things to see—a prize fight at Billy Woods's, a pie-eating match at Kernan's, a Mexican circus in the bottom near Wagon Wheel Gap, a religious service in Watrous and Brannigan's saloon where two electric lights hung in the middle of the room and a stove stood below them. The prayer meeting over, the house resumed its own character, and took in three hundred dollars an hour, while the women of the establishment, wearing "sombrero hats and flannel shirts and belts" above their long skirts, "were neither dashing and bold, nor remorseful and repentant." Actually, people seemed to use the gambling houses as clubs where they might keep warm and talk business and find company and gossip. One night Nicholas Creede was offered $1,250,000 for his share in the Holy Moses Mine, and refused. The journalist winced. How could anybody choose this life over what that much money would buy back East? But if the visitor read the Creede *Candle*—the local newspaper—he saw self-critical and outspoken opinion. Some of the citizens, it said, "would take the sweepstake prize at a hog show," and from time to time, it documented examples of the usual murderous antics of official "bad men" who in Creede as elsewhere on the recurrent American frontier enacted the dreariest convention of character in United States history.

The journalist went by day into the canyon to observe mining operations. Now he saw the prosperous, well-developed shafts, and again, "a solitary prospector tapping at the great rock in front of him, and only stopping to dip his hot face and blistered hands into the snow about him, before he began to drive the steel bar again with the help which hope gave to him." Long lines of burros went down the gulch "carrying five bags of ore each, with but twenty dollars' worth of silver scattered through each load." The voice of the driver echoed on the upright stone walls and the tinkle of the little burro bells carried far in the enclosed air. Other loads, often of ten tons, were brought down in sleds drawn by horses. The trail was slippery with packed snow and once their momentum was released, the sleds came flying heavily down the twisting canyon course and into town, where all scattered out of their way, for they must not stop until they stopped by the railroad tracks, which they reached in a great circle on the flat land where their cargo would be removed to freight cars.

Within a year after the mines were opened in Creede and its near-by camps of Sunnyside, Bachelor and Spar City, six million dollars' worth of silver was shipped out. In its sudden rise to fame and prosperity, Creede was typical of any mining town of the period in the West—and so it was, too, in its early fall to decay. After 1893 the price of silver declined, many mines were abandoned, and others if they were kept running were greatly reduced in operation.

Socorro on the river in central New Mexico knew much the same history. Silver was found in the Socorro mountains in 1867, and for over a decade was hauled upriver by mule train. When in 1880 the Santa Fe line went down the river toward El Paso, the Socorro region drew a new population of exploiters until Socorro itself was the largest town in New Mexico—one estimate fixed the total at thirty thousand. Magdalena, twenty-seven miles west of the river, was established by silver miners in 1884, and a railroad spur soon reached it. But again, in the familiar cycle of such mining towns, decline followed until both Socorro and Magdalena were primarily local towns for agriculture—here, the supply and shipping points for cattle and sheep raisers. Only an occasional die-hard among prospectors continued to go alone with his burro, his pick, his skillet and his coffeepot into the blue rocks of his visions, determined, if he had one, to be faithful to his secret until the end.

One such was found in after years near Socorro when a group of students on a Saturday exploration came upon a jug pit or cave whose open mouth, invisible from a very little distance across flat ground, was narrower than its interior. The students knew that the cave like others in the area must be a repository of an ochreous dust so dense and fine that to breathe it freely was dangerous. Equipped with a respirator and a flashlight, one of the students was lowered into the pit by the others. In a few moments he was hauled up to tell what he had seen. His find was awesome. When he landed in the pit he disturbed from its floor a swiftly billowing cloud of yellow dust. It roiled in the air shutting off the sight of anything about him. He peered with his lamp toward the pit walls and suddenly through the suspended motes he was shocked to see at his very side the figure of a man that seemed to be molded of the dust, leaning on a sloping wall of earth with its brow on its forearm. It was the body of an old prospector, wearing a short coat hanging open and trousers poked into high boots, and over all a softening layer of dust. Half buried near his feet was his pick. It seemed probable that he had gone alone into the pit with no protection against the dust that instantly rose to choke the air about him. Leaning his head upon his arm against the wall as he struggled to breathe he had died of suffocation. Through the years he had been mummified by the dry air and the little desert whirlwinds that having created the pit must have continued to spin in and out of it now and again. In his open grave he was a classic rendering of dust to dust itself, and a symbol of solitary man, killed by the country of his love, faith and work.

72

"SOMETHING SHINING IN THE BOTTOM OF THE DITCH"

James W. Marshall

As far as California was concerned, the Great Gold Rush began in January 1848. Here is James W. Marshall's personal account, from Sketches of Early California, *of how it happened.*

"In May, 1847, with my rifle, blanket, and a few crackers to eat with the venison (for the deer then were awful plenty), I ascended the American River, according to Mr. Sutter's wish, as he wanted to find a good site for a saw-mill, where we could have plenty of timber, and where wagons would be able to ascend and descend the river hills. Many fellows had been out before me, but they could not find any place to suit; so when I left I told Mr. Sutter I would go along the river to its very head and find the place, if such a place existed anywhere upon the river or any of its forks. I traveled along the river the whole way. Many places would suit very well for the erection of the mill, with plenty of timber everywhere, but then nothing but a mule could climb the hills; and when I would find a spot where the hills were not steep, there was no timber to be had; and so it was until I had been out several days and reached this place, which, after first sight, looked like the exact spot we were hunting.

"I passed a couple of days examining the hills, and found a place where wagons could ascend and descend with all ease. On my return to the fort I went out through the country examining the cañons and gulches, and picking out the easiest places for crossing them with loaded wagons.

"You may be sure Mr. Sutter was pleased when I reported my success. We entered into partnership; I was to build the mill, and he was to find provisions, teams, tools, and to pay a portion of the men's wages. I believe I was at that time the only millwright in the whole country. In August, everything being ready, we freighted two wagons with tools and provisions, and accompanied by six men I left the fort, and after a good deal of difficulty reached this place one beautiful afternoon and formed our camp on yon little rise of ground right above the town.

"Our first business was to put up log houses, as we intended remaining here all winter. This was done in less than no time, for my men were great with the ax. We then cut timber, and fell to work hewing it for the framework of the mill. The Indians gathered about us in great numbers. I employed about forty of them to assist us with the dam, which we put up in a kind of way in about four weeks. In digging the foundation of the mill we cut some distance into the soft granite; we opened the forebay and then I left for the fort, giving orders to Mr. Weimar to have a ditch cut through the bar in the rear of the mill, and after quitting work in the evening to raise the gate and let the water run all night, as it would assist us very much in deepening and widening the tail-race.

"I returned in a few days, and found everything favorable, all the men being at work in the ditch. When the channel was opened it was my custom every evening to raise the gate and let the water wash out as much sand and gravel through the night as possible; and in the morning, while the men were getting breakfast, I would walk down, and, shutting off the water, look along the race and see what was to be done, so that I might tell Mr. Weimar, who had charge of the Indians, at what particular point to set them to work for the day. As I was the only millwright present, all of my time was employed upon the framework and machinery.

"One morning in January,—it was a clear, cold morning; I shall never forget that morning,—as I was taking my usual walk along the race after shutting off the water, my eye was caught with the glimpse of something shining in the bottom of the ditch. There was about a foot of water running then. I reached my hand down and picked it up; it made my heart thump, for I was certain it was gold. The piece was about half the size and of the shape of a pea. Then I saw another piece in the water. After taking it out I sat down and began to think right hard. I thought it was gold, and yet it did not seem to be of the right color: all the gold coin I had seen was of a reddish tinge; this looked more like brass. I recalled to mind all the metals I had ever seen or heard of, but I could find none that resembled this. Suddenly the idea flashed across my mind that it might be iron pyrites. I trembled to think of it! This question could soon be determined. Putting one of the pieces on a hard river stone, I took another and commenced hammering it. It was soft, and didn't break: It therefore must be gold, but largely mixed with some other metal, very likely silver; for pure gold, I thought, would certainly have a brighter color.

"When I returned to our cabin for breakfast I showed the two pieces to my men. They were all a good deal excited, and had they not thought that the gold only existed in small quantities they would have abandoned everything and left me to finish my job alone. However, to satisfy them, I told them that as soon as we had the mill finished we would devote a week or two to gold hunting and see what we could make out of it.

"While we were working in the race after this discovery we always kept a sharp lookout, and in the course of three or four days we had picked up about three ounces—our work still progressing as lively as ever, for none of us imagined at that time that the whole country was sowed with gold.

"In about a week's time after the discovery I had to take another trip to the fort; and, to gain what information I could respecting the real value of the metal, took all that we had collected with me and showed it to Mr. Sutter, who at once declared it was gold, but thought with me that it was greatly mixed with some other metal. It puzzled us a good deal to hit upon the means of telling the exact quantity of gold contained in the alloy; however, we at last stumbled on an old American cyclopedia, where we saw the specific gravity of all the metals, and rules given to find the quantity of each in a given bulk. After hunting over the whole fort and borrowing from some of the men, we got three dollars and a half in silver, and with a small pair of scales we soon ciphered it out that there was no silver nor copper in the gold, but that it was entirely pure.

"This fact being ascertained, we thought it our best policy to keep it as quiet as possible till we should have finished our mill. But there was a great number of disbanded Mormon soldiers in and about the fort, and when they came to hear of it, why it just spread like wildfire, and soon the whole country was in a bustle. I had scarcely arrived at the mill again till several persons appeared with pans, shovels, and hoes, and those that had not iron picks had wooden ones, all anxious to fall to work and dig up our mill; but this we would not permit. As fast as one party disappeared another would arrive, and sometimes I had the greatest kind of trouble to get rid of them. I sent them all off in different directions, telling them about such and such places, where I was certain there was plenty of gold if they would only take the trouble of looking for it. At that time I never imagined that the gold was so abundant. I told them to go to such and such places, because it appeared that they would dig nowhere but in such places as I pointed out, and I believe such was their confidence in me that they would have dug on the very top of yon mountain if I had told them to do so.

"The second place where gold was discovered was in a gulch near the Mountaineer House, on the road to Sacramento. The third place was on a bar on the South Fork of the American River a little above the junction of the Middle and South forks. The diggings at Hangtown [now Placerville] were discovered next by myself, for we all went out for a while as soon as our job was finished. The Indians next discovered the diggings at Kelsey's, and thus in a very short time we discovered that the whole country was but one bed of gold. So there, stranger, is the entire history of the gold discovery in California—a discovery that hasn't as yet been of much benefit to me."

73

"MEN LIVING LIKE COYOTES"

J. Ross Browne

The queen of the mining boomtowns was Virginia City, Nevada, described here as it was before it had prospered into brick edifices and an opera house by J. Ross Browne in a letter home to his wife. Browne (1821–1875) was a journalist, artist, lobbyist, adventurer, and artist. His satirical style is reminiscent of Mark Twain, another Virginia City journalist of the time.

To Lucy, Carson City, U.T., Apr. 5, 1860. I would leave today but the mountains are covered with snow and the trails are impassable. The Express will no doubt push through, but I do not think it worth while to risk my life to save a few days delay.

Provisions are getting very scarce, and there will be some suffering. Meals $1.25; hay $400 a ton; flour $50 a sack; barley 40¢ lb.; sugar 80¢ brown; bacon $1 lb.; etc. Every shed, tent and stable crowded. California in '49 was nothing to it.

I am now sitting in a little shanty, with my back to a stove, and about twenty people huddled around scheming, speculating and talking of the everlasting dollar—nothing else but "leads claims"—"A hundred dollars a foot, etc." I write on a dry-goods shelf and have to poke my head in to get a sight at what I am writing.

Of all the places on the face of the earth, I have never seen any quite so bad as Virginia City. It is perched up amongst desolate rocks and consists of several hundred tents, holes in the ground with men living in them like coyotes, frame shanties and mud hovels. The climate is perfectly frightful, and the water is so bad that hundreds are sick from drinking it. Alkali and arsenic are among the mildest ingredients found in it. The people as they rush about wild and frantic after silver, unwashed and unshaved as they are, with haggard and bloodshot eyes, look like the inmates of Bedlam.

Some are making fortunes rapidly, but many are sick and dying. I yesterday helped to bury a poor fellow who was shot a few weeks ago, without cause or provocation as I was told. His murderer was pointed out to me, swaggering around unmolested. The same man has shot two others since, and yet goes at large.

The richest man in Washoe (Col. Raymond), has been separated from his family for 11 years trying to make money. He has made it at last, but does it give him back 11 years of life?

74

SUTRO'S TUNNEL

The first big mines tapping the Comstock Lode at Virginia City dug down from the top of the mountain and raised the ore. Adolph Sutro proposed the wild idea of tunneling into the base of the mountain and letting gravity move the ore.

Among the earliest comers to the Comstock in the white heat of its first fame in 1859 was Adolph Sutro, a Jewish cigar maker from San Francisco. A contemporary, in Washoe chronology at least, with such future nabobs as George Hearst and John Mackay, Sutro was possessed of an orderly and practical mind to which waste was anathema and the useless and unscientific dissipation of energy an abomination.

Upon arriving in Virginia City Sutro set out on a tour of inspection of the mines then in operation. Profit-taking started at the very roots of the sagebrush on the slopes of Sun Mountain, and such easy access to riches had banished all thought of anything even approximating scientific mining from the intelligence of the first miners. Ophir was little better than a cut in the hillside. Gould & Curry was being worked with Mexican peons under contract labor and no attempt was being made to reclaim any but the richest ores. The waste of less valuable ores was stupefying and they lay abandoned in the dumps to the value of hundreds of thousands of dollars.

Sutro's whole being was outraged. Here, he reflected, was a profile specifically created by nature for the easy, orderly and scientific working of its resources. The ore deposits lay on a hillside whence gravity, only slightly implemented by human ingenuity, would take them with an absolute minimum of waste labor down to the millsites along the Carson River. Obviously instead of sinking shafts straight down to follow the leads and fissures in their underground progress and then timbering up enormous chambers underground, the original shafts should be supplemented by a tunnel or tunnels dug in to meet them at right angles from lower down the hillside. Through this tunnel ore could be carried by gravity rather than by the expense of vast quantities of fuel to hoist it hundreds of feet vertically to the surface. Via the agency of a tunnel, too, it would be anywhere from five to six miles nearer Carson Water when the ore emerged to the light of day and all that distance would have been eliminated by a simple, gravity-activated underground tram instead of by costly teaming down the side of the mountain. The thing was so obvious as to be almost laughable.

But Sutro's tragedy was that to the easily satisfied miners of the Comstock's early years, his project *was* laughable. Why in heaven's name, they asked, should they be put to the trouble of digging a tunnel six miles long, even if such a project were practicable, which of course it wasn't, to ventilate shafts that were now practically open to the sky and carry out ore that already lay on the surface? The miners, who at this stage were recovering surface values, never foresaw that in a few weeks or months their shafts must sink to levels where their digging and maintenance would prove increasingly costly and hazardous and where their depth would easily justify a lateral tunnel dug in to meet them. Nor did they or even Sutro foresee the floods of boiling water which, at increased depths, could be removed only by the most powerful and costly surface pumps, yet easily could have been drained by the very tunnel Sutro proposed at but a fraction of the expense of tremendous pumping plants working night and day on a year around basis.

Five years after the Comstock's first excitements, its name was beginning to lose its power. The greedy manner in which the mines had been operating was having its effect and, more than anything else, their output was emperiled by water. Shortly thereafter it was to be entirely suspended. Perhaps the most dramatic example of the manner in which subterranean floods were able to defeat the shrewdest and most resolute superintendents was at Ophir. Ophir was the first to experiment with steam pumps in the hope of abating the seepage which, with every foot its shaft was sunk, became stronger and less controllable. A fifteen horsepower steam-activated pump was erected in San Francisco and installed while the Comstock held its breath. The pump functioned magnificently but it was soon apparent that, despite its satisfactory performance, it would require more and bigger pumps than existed anywhere to make an impression on the underground floods. Half of the mines along the Lode were closed and Virginia was in the midst of its first great panic.

Again Adolph Sutro came forward with his proposal of a tunnel to the Carson. His arguments now seemed more valid than they had before because, besides ventilating the mines and facilitating the economical, easy removal of ore, such a bore would perhaps drain off the waters that were plunging every shaft on Sun Mountain into borrasca. But there was powerful opposition to Sutro among the mine operators who were determined never to pay the two dollars a ton royalty that Sutro proposed to charge to defray the tunnel's cost of construction and operation. Sutro obtained articles of incorporation from the Nevada Legislature in 1865 but funds were not forthcoming from any source at all. Sutro pleaded with Congress in Washington for funds. In vain. He submitted prospectuses to Commodore Vanderbilt and William B. Astor in New York. In vain. He received encouragement in France but the approach of the Franco-Prussian War put an end to that hope.

It remained for one of the Comstock's periodic disasters to do more than all his own efforts had availed to promote Sutro's tunnel. In 1869 there occurred the terrible fire in the Yellow Jacket Mine which cost scores of lives and it became apparent to everyone that, had Sutro's tunnel been in operation as a subterranean fire escape, the holocaust need never have exacted so frightful a toll in life and treasure. With the united opinion of the Comstock miners behind him, Sutro scraped enough funds to begin work on his tunnel a short distance up the slope from Carson River in the fall of 1869.

Work on the tunnel was slow. Sutro had to meet a score of crises, most of them of a financial nature. The mines were booming again and a period of bonanza was earning unheard-of wealth for the operators of the mines while employment, too, was up and Sutro experienced difficulty in recruiting workmen for the construction of his project. The construction of the Virginia & Truckee Railroad was also a threat since its completion materially cut the cost of freighting ore down to the mills along Carson River, a boon which Sutro had planned to confer on the Comstock himself.

But, despite all opposition of man and nature, Sutro by May of 1878 was working at a depth of 2,000 feet under Virginia City and only 640 feet from the nearest operations of the Lode. Sutro was personally peddling small blocks of tunnel stock to anyone he could interest but relief was closer at hand than he had dared to imagine. At the 2,000 foot level all the mines of the Comstock were again encountering floods of hot water and no pumps on earth could avail to pump these steaming tides from such depths. Four of the biggest mines, Hale & Norcross, Best & Belcher, Savage and Crown Point suddenly capitulated and agreed to pay Sutro his two dollars royalty if he could finish his tunnel before they were irrevocably ruined. Only the mines producing the Big Bonanza, the California and Consolidated Virginia, held out.

On July 8 Sutro himself fired the final charge of dynamite which demolished the last underground barrier between his tunnel heading and the Savage shaft and, stripped to the waist and sweat-grimed as any laborer, stepped through the breach. After thirteen years of continued battle he had triumphed over his enemies in the ranks of the mine operators and over the implacable hostility of the forces of nature deep underground in the approaches to Sun Mountain.

Ironically the great Sutro tunnel was completed at the precise moment when the fortunes of the Comstock and Virginia City started the last great decline from which they never recovered. But there were still many years of unspectacular activity ahead on Sun Mountain and the tunnel, which had cost more than $5,000,000, paid off handsomely and remained in useful operation until the forties of the present century when deep mining on the Comstock was entirely suspended. In one year it drained more than 2,000,000,000 gallons through its laterals and connecting passages.

Sutro sold out his interest in the property at a profit and left Nevada to become one of San Francisco's most respected public citizens and a benefactor of many good causes, while the tunnel of which he dreamed, although of scant moment by comparison to the titanic feats of engineering which the twentieth century was to evoke, will remain for all time an integral part of the Comstock story.

75

GROWING UP IN BONANZA TOWN

John Taylor Walford

John Taylor Walford spent his boyhood, from ages three to sixteen, in booming Virginia City. Here's a glimpse, from his A Kid on the Comstock, *of what it was like for a youngster.*

To be raised in a mining camp means an experience as full of thrills and wounds and scars as going to the wars. You who have tried it and have survived its perils deserve service medals. If I ever meet Andy Carnegie I'm going to speak to him about it. I want a piece of that kind of junk myself.

It would be easier for me to tell what didn't happen to me in Virginia City than to tell what did. I wasn't more than 10 years of age when I got my first peep into the barrel of a revolver. Behind the artillery—it looked like a cannon to me—was a somewhat excitable gentleman from the Azores.

There had been a fire the night before, and, kid-like, I was poking around among the remains of what had been a second-class shanty looking for something to play with. I surely didn't want to play with the owner. He didn't want to play, either. He borrowed the speed of one of his bull-fighting ancestors and came at me. As he closed in he obligingly lifted the gun so that I could see into it, uncoiled a string of Portuguese oaths and topped it off with as vigorous an invitation to "Get out" as I ever heard.

I got. Was I frightened? Maybe not. Frightened didn't mean anything to me in those days. I was scared. As far as I know I still hold the white ten year old championship record for climbing close-boarded seven-foot fences.

About two years later I helped myself to a worse scare than that. Some of my grown up friends were prospecting in an old tunnel that in a wandering, drunken way had sought to touch the heart of the mountain. One morning they yielded to my "Lemme go with you" and into the tunnel we went. For several hundred yards it was fine. Whenever I wanted to I could turn my head and see daylight.

Then the tunnel turned and got smaller and smaller until even I had to stoop to keep from bumping my head. The candles threw a bilious light a few feet ahead of us and we had no trouble in keeping to the car track that ran the length of the tunnel.

I turned my head to look for that circle of sunshine. All was blackness. A wall of coal couldn't have matched it. Dark nights were noonday compared to it. I stepped on the heels of the man in front of me in my eagerness to keep up.

After the dark had followed us along that sluice-like tunnel for a few minutes we reached a station, a widened-out place where two other tunnels joined ours. One of the men told me that if I took the tunnel to the left, which came in at a deceptive angle, making it seem a part of the main tunnel, I would walk straight into the Savage shaft, which didn't go more than 2,000 feet below the level on which we stood.

We moved on, with me in the center of the group, and in perhaps ten minutes we reached another scooped out place. Here we took a ladder route and reached the gallery in which my friends had been working. It wasn't bad there, except when I was foolish enough to think that the earth above us might decide to cave in. With much difficulty I made this thought keep its distance.

After a while I grew hungry. The men weren't going out for two hours yet, they said. I dreaded to make the trip alone, but I couldn't wait that long. One of the men hinted that I was afraid to go by myself. That settled it. He lent me two inches of candle, and I said, "So long, fellers," and went down the ladder.

After I got into the tunnel I never looked back, but stooped and hurried on whistling as hard as I could. A whistle wasn't much against a big silence like that, but I had to do something. I got along fine for about five minutes, and then my light went out. My heart gave a great thump. My hand went feverishly into my pocket. Not a match! My knees shook. If I groped on in the dark I might get into the wrong tunnel and be dashed to death in the Savage shaft. If I stayed where I was and waited for the men to come out, like as not they would have a car ahead of them and it would come speeding along the down grade, drowning my cries of alarm, and crushing me to death when it reached me.

Perhaps there would be room for the car to pass if I hugged the timbers close, but I didn't dare to risk it. Then, again, I felt that two hours in that black silence would make me an old man. I muttered prayers, and stammered as I prayed. I thought of my prized possessions—twenty-seven marbles, including nine crystals and two agates; two tops, a boxwood and a "Frenchy"; a "red-head" baseball and 20 cents in money. I would have given them all for a match. Shivering, I went through all my pockets. In a corner I found half a match. Joy unimaginable! It was the wrong half. Despair unspeakable! I dug into the pocket again, and found a hole. In that hole, stuck deep in the lining, I found the other half. The hand that held it flapped like a bird's wing.

Finally I steadied down a little, and then I tried the match. The flame flickered. I could hardly hold it to the candle. The candle flickered. The flame steadied, and I gave a deep sigh that almost put it out. With nervous joy I went on again. That light was my life, and I guarded it carefully.

I reached the station. That black hole to the left was the Savage tunnel. I breathed easier after I passed it. At last I came to the turn. It was all easy now. I could see that circle of light again. I dropped my candle and never stopped running until God's sun was shining on me. I didn't go into another tunnel for a week, and then I had matches in sufficient quantity to make a candle merely a convenience.

As to the wounds and scars, they came from climbing around ore houses and up the beams of trestles and over the great waste dumps. A fall a week was a fair average. It seemed as if we were trying to see who could fall the farthest and live. When it was reported that Jimmy Dillon had fallen forty feet, "Spider" Walker measured the distance with his eye and remarked disgustedly, "He ain't done nothin' to brag about. 'Taint more'n twenty feet."

I had more than my share of falls. The oddest mishap of all occurred one afternoon when the wind was busy carrying loose shingles from the town to any old place down the canyon. I had a sack of shavings from the Savage carpenter shop and as I came down the dump dared to walk in the teeth of the wind out on the roof of the G Street tunnel, intending to drop the sack into the road below, and thereby save carrying it a little part of the distance. That sack of shavings served as a sail. The wind caught it. I held on, and the sack and I took a trip together.

I landed on the rocks, and a neighbor's boy carried the shavings home—to his home, not mine. After I got well I had many an argument with the boys over that fall. The tunnel was sixteen feet high. I explained that I fell about four feet sideways before I began to drop, but they would never give me credit for falling more than sixteen feet.

Virginia City and its famous Comstock Lode were responsible for half a dozen millionaires, including the quartet of Bonanza Kings—Mackay, Fair, Flood and O'Brien. We children of the camp heard of them all, but only two of the "awfully rich" made any impression upon us. These two were James G. Fair and John W. Mackay. The others might better have been myths as far as we were concerned. In that event we would have given them at least an occasional thought.

In my day Mackay and Fair were familiar figures on the Comstock. Neither came to town any oftener or stayed any longer than business demanded. Fair had a mansion up on B Street. If Mackay ever had a residence in the camp in my time I never knew it. Fair's visits were frequent, those of Mackay were few and at long intervals, but we children learned to dislike Fair and to look upon Mackay as the kindest man in the world.

The millionaires were known to us by their first names. Like our fathers, we spoke of Jim Fair and John Mackay. By keeping our ears open while our elders were talking among themselves we heard much that was not to the credit of the one and formed our opinion on those tales. Our opinion of the other was based on the personal experiences of numerous small boys.

It didn't matter where one went if the object was to learn what the kids thought of John Mackay. The Divide Gang, the Andes Gang, the First Ward Gang, and the C. C. Gang differed on a great many things, but every member of all four gangs would tell you that John Mackay was all right.

We used to envy Fair his wealth. Mackay couldn't have too much to suit us. We naturally supposed that each had more than a million in good hard coin. If any one had told us that about all their wealth was the mines, on the dumps of which we wore out our shoes, we wouldn't have believed it. Millions with us meant actual money aside from such trifles as mines and mills.

This view of things gave that mansion on B Street an attractiveness that it should have not possessed. We believed that it contained heaps of twenty dollar pieces. Just where the heaps were located was a favorite subject of speculation. All of us had at one time or another got a peek into some of the big rooms with the great chandeliers and rich carpets and gorgeous furniture, but the money wasn't in sight. As none of us had ever been in either the cellar or the garret, we concluded that it was in one of those two places. This narrowed the scope of the argument, but whenever as many as three of us took up the subject there was no chance of agreement.

I shall never forget two of the many stories that were told of the master of the mansion. There was a poor old miner who had injured his back so badly that he could work no more and became a charge on the county. He lived in a little cabin and was able to do his own cooking and washing. For firewood he depended on the carpenter shop of the nearby Savage Mine. The foreman of this shop, a man named Jim, always responded to the old man's request for blocks and shavings, sending them over to the cabin.

One day when word came that the old man was out of firewood, Fair happened to be "nosing" around the works. The foreman, being something of a diplomat, dispatched a carpenter to find Fair and lay the matter before him. Fair stroked his beard as he listened to the story of misfortune. When it was ended he did the right thing, but in a way that robbed it of the charm of benevolence. He took his own good time to get around to the carpenter shop, and when he reached the foreman he said, "Jim, send a load of blocks to that broken-backed pauper."

The other story is still worse. There was a strict rule against smoking underground. No one objected to the rule, for the reason that a fire in a mine generally meant the loss of many lives, but still not a few of the miners were willing to menace their safety and their jobs to get a few pulls at a pipe.

One day while Fair was on one of his lower level inspection tours his keen nose caught the smell of tobacco. Without making any remark as to his discovery he turned to the miner at his side and said longingly, "I'm dying for a smoke. I'd give anything for a pipeful of tobacco." The miner looked up, but Fair's face gave no hint of suspicion. Fair spoke of his longing again and again. Finally the miner took pity on him, reached behind a timber and brought forth a pipe and tobacco.

Fair took a smoke, but when he got above ground he made it his business to see the foreman and say, "Fire that man; he's smokin' down there." It wasn't so much what Fair used to do as the way he did it. I don't wonder that we kids didn't like him.

It won't take long to tell why we used to think so much of John Mackay. In the first place he had a pleasant pastime habit of scattering money among the gangs of small boys who used to hang around the mines. This, however, wasn't the main thing. His claim to our affections was based principally on what he did whenever he went to the theater in Virginia City.

Each performance in Piper's Opera House meant forty or fifty penniless small boys hoping for miracles as they stood outside the entrance. Old
John Piper would sit in the box office and scowl at us until his fat face was
all wrinkles. Then Mackay would come along, nod his head toward the
gang and say, "John, how much for the bunch?"

A heavenly smile would wreath John's face as he counted us and
announced the result. At fifty cents a head it generally came to about $20.
Mackay would say, "Let the kids see the show," and John would deal out
our tickets with one hand while he gathered in the twenty with the other.
We would enjoy the show, and what is more we would think better of all
mankind because John Mackay had remembered that he was once a boy
and had given us something from his great store.

That is why we never envied John Mackay. We wanted him to live
forever and always be rich. When he died we children of the Comstock,
although most of us had not seen him for years, felt that we had lost a near
and dear friend.

It takes a mining camp to get the full measure of joy out of a picnic.
You who have great parks almost at your doors can't imagine what a picnic
means to the small boy who is surrounded by sagebrush. I was that kind
of a small boy, and I know. In Virginia City we looked on picnic days as
second in importance only to such days as Christmas and Fourth of July
and circus days. If there was even a slight chance of going, we drew heavily
on the bank of anticipation, and then if we were disappointed, we were
bankrupt indeed.

One great feature of those picnics in the golden days was the opportunity it gave us to partake of that notorious forbidden fruit known as the
green apple. Whenever we read in the paper or saw on the bill boards a
flaring advertisement that started off, "Ho, for Treadway's!" we realized
anew that life had much in store for us.

Treadway's was the picnic park down in Carson, and as it was thirty-
two miles away by the crooked Virginia & Truckee Railway, a bully ride
would come before and follow after the feast of green apples. Then there
was the falling into the pond with your clothes on, and the target-shooting,
and the footraces, and the trips to town to see what you could see. Surely
this was a program of the kind that the small boy would have thought out
and suggested, if he had been given the opportunity.

Cynical grown-ups used to say that picnics were all alike. That was
all for effect. I had been to Sabbath-school jubilations, and I had seen the
Emmet Guard stack arms and help themselves to a good time. Therefore,
no peddler of second-hand philosophy could convince me that they were

quite the same. If he had said something intelligent, such as, "A poor picnic is better than none," I might have agreed with him.

The great picnic of the year was given by the Miners' Union. What a time that used to be! Families that sent no representative to Carson that day insured themselves against being on speaking terms with their neighbors. Only one of three things could keep one in town. If it wasn't force of circumstance, it was lack of intelligence; if it wasn't either of those it was a desire to make way with unguarded valuables. Force of circumstances got me once or twice, but there is one particular time that it didn't. I mention this particular time because it brought about my progression from playing faro for matches to putting real money down on the red and black.

For many weeks before the picnic I had been doing business with the junk man. After I had sold all the white glass, bits of brass and copper and old iron that I could pick up, I turned my attention to rags, which commodity was bringing half a cent a pound. This seemed a fair price, and but for unexpected interference I might, in my enthusiasm, have denuded our house of all clothing not in immediate use. Despite obstacles, I did fairly well, and the morning of the picnic found me with $2.75 knotted tightly in the corner of a handkerchief. I was rich—and greedy. I didn't want to pay my way to the grounds and back.

A few passenger coaches and a long string of flat cars, fenced around and provided with seats, made up the picnic train, or, rather the first section; for the great crowd got away in installments that day. I slipped away from my big sisters, knowing that they would make me pay fare, and got in with a gang of kids who couldn't have paid if they wanted to. As the train was running through town and every mine whistle in the camp was screeching "Good bye!" I was looking for a place to hide. That was easy. When the conductor passed by I was under a seat. So was the rest of the gang.

At last we reached Treadway's, which I am beginning to suspect was a poor excuse for a park, but that is now. It looked like heaven then. After eating four green apples and three green pears I hurried over to the pond, jumped on a raft, took a ride, upset the raft and got wet enough to attract everybody's attention. The sun warmed up to his work and dried me in two hours. Afterwards I was sorry he hurried so.

No sooner was I dry than I followed the crowd to where a big man in his shirt sleeves gave a pretty wheel a twirl and shouted "Round she goes! Where she stops nobody knows!" Occasionally, he added, "Even money on the red and black; six to one on the green. Step up, gentlemen. Here's a chance to make your expenses."

I still had all of my $2.75, and the expense argument couldn't have appealed to me, but when I saw a man in front of me win four straight times on the red I tremblingly dropped a quarter of a dollar on the black. The black won; I "pinched" a quarter; it won again; I "pinched" another quarter; another win and another "pinch." I was six bits ahead! Like the greenhorn in the story, I wanted to know right away how long that sort of a thing had been going on. I kept on trembling and betting, and "pinching"—sometimes. At one time I had hopes of winning the bankroll. It was when I was $1.75 to the good.

Pride trips over its own feet. What got me going the wrong way was sticking to the red. After it had lost nine straight times, I concluded that warm colors were not for me. My money went on the somber, and then the gay had a run of luck. My heart sank with my pile. When I reached the lone quarter stage I had one of those cold chills. I held that quarter in my hand and watched the red win twelve times running. Then I put my quarter on the black. The green won!

One of my big sisters gave me money enough to buy dinner, but, alas! nothing for ice cream, or soda, or popcorn, or peanuts, or cigarettes. The only thing I got besides dinner money was a real saucy lecture about gambling. All I can remember of it now is that she spoke of "big thieves" and "little fools." I didn't even answer her back. I was too miserable.

That wasn't a good afternoon. Something was the matter with the baseball game, and the target-shooting, and the foot races. Nobody seemed to know how to do anything right. From every place on the grounds I could hear an awful voice shouting, "Round she goes!" I kept figuring up what that $2.75 would have got me. I even regretted that I had not bought a ticket for the picnic, instead of smuggling my way. My conscience was thoroughly aroused.

On the way home I didn't try to hide, but somehow the conductor overlooked me. There was my luck coming back to me, and me broke! A minute later the easiest member of all the gang wanted to match me for a quarter. That's always the way.

76

BOYHOOD AT THE CHLORIDE FLAT

James K. Hastings

James K. Hastings was thirteen when his family moved to a mining camp in a more desolate area of New Mexico. Compare his life with that of John Walford (preceeding selection) in Virginia City, Nevada.

In April, 1880, we were living in southern Colorado, at Trinidad. Father was in New Mexico at Silver City, near the Mexican border, and it was decided that we should join him. . . . We reached Silver City on May 1, 1880, and father met us there.

Father was the superintendent of a quartz mill that crushed the silver ore from two mines, named the '76 and Baltic, located a few miles above town in a small valley on the Continental Divide, known as Chloride Flat. The ore was hauled down from the mines by 4 and 6 mule teams, in giant wagons with boiler plated beds. Silver reduction in a stamp mill is much like any other manufacturing business. The mill ran 24 hours a day for 7 days a week, for about ten months in the year; in the heat of summer they laid off for repairs. The men worked 12 hours a day and drew good wages. The ore was first crushed to a fine dust with powerful stamps that rose and fell hour after hour, with deafening noise, and this dust was washed into massive pans where it was ground still finer in between or under the monster shoes that worked like the "upper and nether millstones." In the last set of pans, quicksilver was added and it picked up the silver in amalgam, the same that some dentists once used for filling teeth. This silver amalgam was poured into a conical sack of strong canvas and drained of much of the quicksilver in it, just as a farmer's wife of the olden days used to make cottage cheese by twisting the sack until the whey, or quicksilver in this case, was mostly removed. The resulting amalgam was called a "goose egg" and when a batch of these were obtained they were heated in a retort where the fumes were run into a tank of water that chilled the rest of the quicksilver to a fluid state. There was constant weighing of the amalgam to show any losses. We laughed at one man working on the pans once, for he asked when being discharged, "I haven't been stealing anything have I"? The silver on coming from the retort was pure and was in danger of being stolen before being cast into the great bricks. It was often moved to our house in the night for safe keeping. I can remember walking beside my father carrying his Colt's revolver as he and a trustworthy man carried the silver in a hand barrow. Of course if we had been attacked father, and not I, would have used the gun. One night some one evidently drunk tried with a steel bar to pry off our front door and get at our cache of silver. Father stood at the head of the stairs ready to shoot if the man gained entrance. After the quicksilver was roasted from the amalgam the pure silver was cast into monster bricks of 300 pounds or more in weight. These were unwieldy and much smaller ones would have been more convenient, but also more easily stolen. Two express companies, the Adams and the Wells-Fargo, ran Concord coaches from our town to carry the mail, express and passengers to the railroad at Deming, where it had reached within 50 miles of our town. The morning after we had cast a brick, one of these would stop at the mill and take it to the railroad. Once a 350 lb. brick broke through the coach floor on the desert and all the driver could do was to drive off and leave it. It was safe there for no pack mule could carry it away and a wagon could be tracked by a fast posse. The abandoning of a $5,000 silver brick in the road did not bother us any, for when it was once signed for by the Wells-Fargo driver, it was their baby. . . .

Our mill being so far from the others had a complete shop attached, with a carpenter, blacksmith and molder. Stamp shoes were always wearing out with the incessant pounding, and so we ran a cupola to melt our scrap iron with charcoal made back in the hills. One of my jobs, when they melted, was to man the hose on the roof to see that no sparks started a fire. The men generally drenched me down first so as to not get the shirt burned off me. Sometimes they let me help load the cupola furnace with successive layers of charcoal and iron.

I realize now that I must have been a pest about the mill; with no school to go to I was there much of the time, although I was supposed to study some old school books at home. Once, when I had been too much of a nuisance, Dad asked, "Where are you in arithmetic young man?" I answered, "I have finished it," only to hear him say, "Go home and go through it again." Well I started at common fractions that time.

I had a fine assortment of friends in that camp. We had school for only a month or so, when a traveling school master taught a few of us long enough to get money to move on with. . . .

The carpenter, though old enough to be my father, was my special chum. When I saw him come down the street, trailed by a Chinese, carrying some long iron rods, I beat it to him. His first question was, "Did you ever read Robinson Crusoe, Jim?" Of course I admitted it, and he replied that he was Crusoe, and that his rear guard was Friday. From that hour, the man answered to that name. On the Chinese New Years, which comes in the Spring, he deluged us with presents. My brother and I got firecrackers, and the girls Chinese candy, while Dad who never used tobacco got a box of what in China must correspond to "Wheeling Stogies." I tried one once and quit for life.

I can remember, when we made a survey of the surface of some of those mines, how father marked them by hewn stones a foot square and 4 feet long. They stuck like a sore thumb and were easily seen from a distance, so there was no question where property lines were. . . .

Near the quartz mill that father used to run, he owned a garden plot of a few acres, irrigated from the same stream that supplied the mill boilers with water. This he rented to some Cantonese Chinese who used it for a truck garden and raised vegetables for the camp. The first season they had it, they carried their produce to market in baskets hung from yokes over their shoulders. They made a picturesque sight in their conical hats as they went along in single file, sing-songing to each other like a lot of grackle black birds. The next season, they got a decrepit horse and an old market wagon, so that one could sell the stuff and leave the rest at home to work. The driver knew about as much about horses as I do about atomic energy. One day, when the salesman had reached our house on his return trip from market, he discovered that the horse had something in a hind hoof. Instead of picking up the hoof to investigate, he crawled under the wagon and began working on the hoof, when the horse kicked him in the head, laying him out cold. My older sister, just a kid, was doing the dishes in the kitchen, but hearing the wagon stop, came to the door to investigate, when she saw that the man was out, she hurried back into the house, got the water pail, pulled the man from under the wagon by his feet and drenched

him with cold water. In time he recovered and getting on the wagon went
on home. The next day after selling his load, he stopped at our house and,
on his knocking, mother went to the door and the Chinese said, "Me
tankie you boy." Lord Chesterfield himself could do no better.

The sister, when grown to womanhood, won an education and became a Doctor of Medicine. Haven't we read somewhere about the boy
being father to the man? Wouldn't that apply to the girl also? . . .

One night the camp put on a celebration of some event of more or
less importance, the reason for which I have forgotten. They likely had
absorbed more or less liquid refreshment from the commissary and were
duly exhilarated and had built a huge campfire near the camp's center
among the lofty pines. They had gotten out three blacksmith anvils and
would pour a handful of black powder on one and stack the other two on
top of it and then fire the powder with a long half inch rod that had been
heated in the fire. The anvils would bounce into the air with a roar and
the process would be repeated. The noise made was a good imitation of
the firing of a cannon.

There were only two women in the camp at that time. One ran the
tiny boarding house where we ate. The racket that the men made that
night must have disturbed the women a lot.

The boarding house keeper was no cook, much as we needed one,
perhaps because she had nothing to do with, for her biscuits were always
undone inside and caused the engineer, who had drunk his share and some
other man's portion of whisky, much pain. I got away with the grub, for
I was young and tough. When I could not get enough at the table, I
haunted a nearby turnip patch and so survived. . . .

As this draws to a close I must say in defense of the Indians that most
of the white men of that day and area were as fine as one could ask for,
but some to my knowledge were just scum and they by their actions caused
the Indians to hate the Whites and that hatred was often taken out on
defenseless people.

77

THE SUN RIVER
STAMPEDE

Robert Vaughan

In a recent poll, a volume entitled Then and Now *published by Robert Vaughn in 1900 ranked among the one hundred most popular books in Montana. In the following item from Vaughn's reminiscences he reports how a rumor caused a 1,500-man stampede.*

In the years 1865–66 there were from fifteen to twenty thousand people in the various mining camps of Montana, and its mountains were swarmed with daring prospectors. In those times nearly every day had its new discovery, and the slightest whisper of a new "find" would create a stampede, in which instances the most extraordinary endurance and courage were displayed. There is no animal on earth that will stampede quicker, keep on going with the same stubbornness and determination, as a fortune hunter; they are worse than Texas cattle. For one instance, I will relate the following: McClellan, an old mountaineer and prospector, and who was the discoverer of the "McClellan Gulch," but sold his claim in that renowned mine for a song, and, after having two or three weeks' good time in town, he began laying his plans for another prospecting tour.

In the following fall (1865) he decided to go to the Sun river country, that was about one hundred miles north of Helena, and hunt for more mines. He was considered a lucky prospector in finding gold, and when a report came from him it could be relied upon.

After having prospected for two or three months the cold weather began to set in, and, as he had already found some gold, he decided to build a cabin and keep on prospecting till spring. In a week or so he had his house up and everything in apple-pie order, except one thing, and that was to have some one to have his meals ready after returning from the hills where he had been working hard all day. As there was a Piegan camp not far off he went there one day and engaged a squaw to come and cook for him. As the new employe had many relations, who became her frequent visitors, it was not long before the proprietor discovered that a few extras in the line of groceries had to be gotten, an extra sack of flour, a few pounds of soap, and so forth; besides some calico, beads, brass ear rings and bracelets for the new housekeeper, who was trying her hand for the first time in her life at house-keeping.

One day Mac mounted his pony, and, with another pack horse, struck for Helena to get the goods. On his arrival he met many of his old friends, and of course they were anxious to learn what success he had prospecting. He said that so far he had not discovered anything that would pay, although he had found what he called good indications. For all that a close watch was kept on the old prospector during the few days he was in town, and a suspicion was aroused among many that on account of the fact that he was buying considerable goods he must know of something greater than he wanted to tell. To one of his confidential friends he told of the pleasant home he had in the Sun river country, and, in a whisper, his last sentence was: "I have got as good a thing as I want," meaning his new housekeeper and the household outfit that he had just purchased. Two of the anxious ones stood near and overheard him saying, "I have got as good a thing as I want." They decided at once that a new find was meant. The news spread like wild fire to every camp in the vicinity, and, like the story of the "three black crows," something was added to the first report as it went from camp to camp. A tremendous stampede followed, and, although it was in the month of January and the thermometer stood thirty-five degrees below zero, and there was over a foot of snow on the level, this did not check the rush. From twelve to fifteen hundred rugged miners participated in this stampede; some went on horseback, others on foot, and, after traveling about one hundred miles, the new Eldorado could not be found. Before returning home several suffered severely from cold and hunger and two died from exposure. Some threats were made against the one giving the false report, but no foundation could be found that McClellan had said that a discovery of gold had been made, but to the contrary it was proven that he had said that no diggings had been found. And, when the particulars of what started the stampede were learned, no further complaint was made.

All returned home except a few who had supplied themselves with enough provisions; they stayed and prospected.

Mr. Thomas Moran of St. Peter, who was on this stampede, told me only a few days ago that at least seven hundred men were one night in camp in a bend of the Missouri river and near where the St. Peter's Mission was then. He said that Father C. Imoda, who was in charge of the Mission, treated them kindly and gave assistance to many that were suffering from cold and hunger. Mr. Moran said that the thermometer registered forty degrees below zero that night.

All of the old timers remember this event, and it is known at the present time as the "Great Sun river stampede in the winter of 1866."

78

THE POST-HOLE BANKS

J. Frank Dobie

J. Frank Dobie's Coronado's Children *is his most famous work and the best "lost treasure" book of the West. People still hunt post-hole treasure in the Southwest, the best source being the abandoned corrals of small farms that were consolidated into big ones.*

"The methods of business were in keeping with the primitive conditions of society," says a chronicler of the open range of southern Texas. "There were no banks in the country. Consequently every ranch home was the depository of more or less money. The coin, if of considerable amount, was put in saddle bags, morrals, etc., and secreted in remote corners of the house or up under the roof or it was buried; it could be brought forth from its hiding place as occasion demanded. . . . In buying stock the ranchmen brought the money in gold and silver to where the animals were to be received and there paid it out dollar by dollar. They generally carried the gold in leather belts buckled around their waists, but the silver, being more bulky, was carried in ducking sacks on a pack horse or mule. . . . It was a matter of current knowledge that one thousand dollars in silver weighed sixty-two and one-half pounds. . . .

"One time a rancher near the line between Karnes and Goliad counties decided to bury a considerable amount of money that he had on hand.

Choosing an especially dark night, he went down to the cowpen and, after removing one of the fence posts, dropped his bag of gold in the post hole. He then replaced the post and went to bed satisfied that he had put his treasure where moth and rust could not corrupt nor thieves break through and steal. After a year or two had gone by, he needed the money and went to get it. He had failed to mark the particular post under which it was buried and time had obliterated all trace of his work. There was but one thing for him to do and he did it. He dug up post after post until he came to the right one, and by that time half his pen was torn down."

I don't know whether old Tolbert forgot his post hole or not. He ranched on the Frio, and, as the saying goes, was "stingy enough to skin a flea for its hide and taller." He would never kill a maverick no matter how hungry he was for meat, but would always brand it. He never bought sugar or molasses; "sow bosom," even of the saltiest variety, was a rare luxury; he and his men made out on "poor doe"—often jerked—javelina meat, and frijoles. When he "worked" and had an outfit to feed, he always instructed the *cocinero* to cook the bread early so that it would be cold and hard, and thus go further by the time the hands got to it. He distrusted banks, and during a good part of his life there were no banks to trust. The practice of keeping money on the premises suited him finely.

When he died, none of his money could be found. So, even till this day, people dig for it around the old ranch house. . . .

Berry got that—and he never hunted for it either. Years ago Berry bought the Tolbert ranch and went to live on it. One day when he had nothing else for his Mexican, Pedro, to do, he told him to put some new posts in the old corral fence. Pedro worked along digging holes and putting in new posts until near ten o'clock. Then at the third post to the east from the south gate he struck something so hard that it turned the edge of his spade. He was used to digging post holes in rocky soil with a crowbar to loosen it and a tin can to dip it out, and so he went to a mesquite tree where the tools were kept and got the crowbar.

But the crowbar would no more dig into the hard substance than the spade would. The sun was mighty hot anyhow; so the Mexican went up to the house where *el señor* Berry was whittling sticks on the gallery and told him that he couldn't dig any more. "Why, *señor*," he said, "in that third hole from the south gate the devil has humped himself into a rock that nothing can get through."

Berry snorted around considerably at first, but directly he seemed to think of something and told his man, very well, not to dig any more but to saddle up and go out and bring in the main remuda. . . .

After Pedro had saddled his horse and drunk a *cafecita* for lunch and fooled away half an hour putting in new stirrup-leather strings and finally had got out of sight, Berry slouched down to the pens. He came back to his shade on the gallery and whittled for an hour or so longer until everything around the *jacal*, even the road-runners and Pedro's wife, was taking a siesta. Then he pulled off his spurs, which always dragged with a big clink when he walked, and went down to the pen again. The spade and the crowbar were where the Mexican had let them fall. Berry punched the crowbar down into the half-made hole. It almost bounced out of his hand, and he heard a kind of metallic thud. No, it was not flint-rock that had stopped the digging.

Berry went around back of the water trough to the huisache where his horse was tied and led him into the pen. Then he started to work. He began digging two or three feet out to one side of the hole. The dry ground was packed from the tramp of thousands of cattle and horses. He had to use the crowbar to loosen the soil. But it was no great task to remove a patch of earth two or three feet square and eighteen or twenty inches deep. Berry knew what he was about, and as he scraped the loosened earth out with his spade he could feel a flat metal surface that seemed to have rivets in it.

It was the lid of a chest. When he had uncovered it, Berry placed one of the new posts so that he could use it as a fulcrum for the crowbar. With that he levered up the end of the chest. As he suspected, it was too heavy and too tightly wedged in the soil for him to lift. He worked a chunk under the raised end of the chest and then looped a stout rope over it. Next, he mounted his horse and dallied the free end of the rope around the horn of his saddle. He had dragged cows out of the bog on that horse, and he knew that the chest was not so heavy as a cow. He had but fifty yards to drag it before he was in the brush, where undetected he could pry the lid off.

When the Mexican got back that night his *mujer* told him that Señor Berry had gone to San Antonio in the buckboard and that he had left word for the remuda to be turned back into the big pasture and for the repair of the corrals to be continued.

"They say" that the deposit Berry made at the Frost National Bank was a clean $17,000, nearly all in silver.

79

THERE'S GEMS IN THEM THAR HILLS

Randall Henderson

Since riches were involved, and since it was the West, there had to be hoaxes. Randall Henderson recounted this "diamond" salt hoax in On Desert Trails, Today and Yesterday. *The con men netted $660,000 in the swindle.*

One February morning in 1872 two roughly dressed miners appeared at the window of a San Francisco bank. They carried a heavy canvas bag, which they wanted to leave in the bank vault for safe-keeping. When they were asked about the contents of the bag they untied the cord and dumped on the counter a dazzling cascade of uncut diamonds, rubies, emeralds and sapphires, and referred vaguely to a mine they had found "up in the hills." They gave their names as Philip Arnold and John Slack.

The display of so much sparkling wealth, by two men who obviously were prospectors from the back country, caused a flurry of excitement among employees in the bank. A report of the incident was soon passed along to William C. Ralston, head of the banking firm, and one of the best known financiers in California. He asked to talk with the men.

There were several conferences in the days following. The men admitted they needed capital to develop their jewel mine, but they were cagey with their information. Quite by accident, they said, they had found what they believed to be an extensive area of placer ground containing precious stones, but they were unwilling to give the exact location, and they did not want to relinquish control of the property without ample safeguards as to their personal equity.

Finally it was agreed they would accompany Ralston's personal representatives to investigate the discovery, with the stipulation that the men would be blindfolded before approaching the field.

The two men selected by the banker to accompany the discoverers carried out their mission, and returned with glowing reports of the richness of the field, and another bag of diamonds to confirm their findings. Ralston was delighted. Perhaps this was a fabulous new diamond field which would rival the fame and fortune of the great South African gem deposits discovered five years previously and widely known as the Kimberley diamond field.

News of the diamond strike spread rapidly, and Ralston's associates in other financial ventures were eager to invest with him in what might prove to be the world's greatest producer of precious gem stones. As an extra precaution samples of the uncut diamonds were sent to Tiffany of New York for expert appraisal. A mining engineer of high standing was sent into the field to make a full report as to the extent of the deposits. To all these arrangements the discoverers gave ready assent. They asked only that an advance payment of $100,000 be deposited in escrow as evidence of good faith on the part of the men who were to invest in the property.

Tiffany confirmed the genuineness of the diamonds, and the mining engineer returned with an enthusiastic report. "Twenty laborers could wash out a million dollars' worth of gems in a month," he said.

Ralston and his associates then organized the San Francisco and New York Mining and Commercial Company, with a capitalization of $10,000,-000. They paid Arnold and Slack a total of $660,000 for all their rights to the claims, giving the money to Arnold, who had a power of attorney from his partner.

In the meantime, Clarence King, an engineer who had long been in the employ of the federal government, and had done much surveying along the 40th parallel, became suspicious. Piecing together what information he could gather, he became certain the reported diamond field was located in the mountainous area of northeastern Utah, west of what recently became the Dinosaur National Park. He knew the mineralogy of this region, and was unwilling to believe it contained gem stones of any value. Unknown to any of the interested parties, he found his way into the field to make a personal appraisal.

A few days later the president of the newly formed mining syndicate received a telegram from King stating flatly that the deposits were a fake—that the gem stones had been planted there for fraudulent purposes, and the investors had been duped. He had found diamonds in the soil, but some of them bore the marks of lapidary tools.

Investors in the property were stunned. They again sent a mining engineer into the field. He confirmed King's report, that the area had been "salted" and the alleged discovery was a gigantic swindle.

Then the story unfolded. Arnold and Slack had acquired $50,000 through the sale of some mining property. Arnold had made two trips to various lapidary establishments in England and Europe and invested $35,000 in uncut stones, many of them culls known in the trade as "niggerheads." With an iron rod the partners had planted the stones over an area of 30 or 40 acres, where the first rainstorm would wash away all evidence of their chicanery.

The diamond episode had a tragic sequel for some of those who played leading roles in the hoax. Slack disappeared and was never heard from again. Arnold, who had retained most of the money, was located in Kentucky. The wounds of the Civil War had not begun to heal, and the state refused to extradite a man who had outwitted the Yankees. Arnold agreed, however, to surrender $150,000 of his loot for immunity from further prosecution. Later he opened a bank and the following year was killed in a gun fight with one of his competitors.

Ralston personally made good the losses of his associates in the diamond venture. But this and other ventures so depleted his resources that his bank closed its doors three years later. Two days after the bank closing, his body was found floating in the bay at San Francisco. The verdict of an autopsy was that he had died from natural causes.

Part Ten

◆

WOMEN

Western movies and a lot of popular fiction give the impression that the West was populated by about eleven women. One was the madam of the boom town's house of ill repute, and the other ten were all demure and wore sunbonnets. Of course the number and variety were greater. In fact, the empty country seemed to attract women who were both remarkably literate and incredibly durable—which should surprise no thoughtful person.

80

"A PRETTY
HOORAH PLACE"

Nannie Alderson

Nannie Alderson was a young bride from an upper-class Southern family when she helped her husband found a remote cattle ranch a hundred miles out of Miles City, Montana. Here she describes her first month on the ranch in a passage from A Bride Goes West.

The site Mr. Alderson chose for a ranch was near the mouth of Lame Deer Creek where it runs into the Rosebud, some sixty miles above the place where the Rosebud joins the Yellowstone. Crook had fought the Indians on the Rosebud only six years before, and Custer had marched up it, to cross over the divide and be slaughtered with all his command at the battle of the Little Big Horn. I had read about all this when it happened, and had seen a picture of Custer with his long yellow hair in one of our Southern papers, when I was just a young girl. I had been terribly and painfully impressed, never dreaming that I should some day live so near the battle-field, even visit it, and walk on ground that had been stained by his blood.

    With the ranch selected and the cattle bought, Mr. Zook sold the race horse in Kansas and went out to the ranch to take over, while Mr. Alderson spent his share of the proceeds on coming East. We were married at my mother's house in Union, on April 4, 1883. . . .

                              *   *   *

295

I had been prepared for Miles City ahead of time, so I was not surprised by the horses hitched to rails along the store fronts, the wooden sidewalks and unpaved streets, nor was I surprised that every other building was a saloon. Mr. Alderson had told me it was a pretty hoorah place. He didn't want me to go out alone, even in the daytime—not that I wouldn't be perfectly safe, but I might run into a drunken crowd or a fight.

We stopped at the Macqueen House, which was headquarters for cattlemen and for men who were planning to become cattlemen. It was homey enough in one way, but it was a poorly built, wooden structure; and as the only bath was off the barber shop, I had to bathe in the wash basin just as I did later at the ranch. The walls were so thin that you could hear every sound from one end to the other, with the result that I overheard several masculine conversations which both fascinated and embarrassed me. Once I heard a man say: "You know, there isn't a decent waitress in this house"—which shocked me because the waitresses had been very kind. I could hardly believe it.

Miles City was teeming with men who were going into the cattle business; many were friends of my husband, and they came from all parts of the United States. Among those whom Mr. Alderson brought upstairs to introduce to me I remember men from Chicago, from Pennsylvania, from Maryland, and several from Texas. One was a lawyer from Boston, Mr. Loud—or Judge Loud as he later became; he was planning to raise cattle until he had saved enough money to keep him during the lean years while he was building a practice. They were all gallant enough to be greatly interested in a wife who was planning to live on a ranch with her husband.

I must have bragged of my one accomplishment—hot rolls—for they all declared they were tired of baking powder biscuit and sour dough bread, and they all announced: "We're coming to see you." So part of our preparation for the ranch was going to a bake shop the night before we left and buying a bottle of starter for my yeast. We went to bed leaving the bottle corked, and in the middle of the night it exploded with a loud "Pop."

Mr. Alderson's first thought was that someone had fired off a gun; and he jumped up and took his six-shooter and started out to investigate. The next moment we heard the sizzle-sizzle-sizzle of the yeast running out of the bottle. In a moment it was all over the room, and even on the dress I'd been planning to wear.

But when we told about the catastrophe in the morning, one of the stockmen said: "I'm still coming for those hot rolls and you're not going out there without that yeast." So he went out and got a tin bucket full, which we took with us.

Mr. Alderson had assured my mother and grandmother that I could go on to Bozeman where he had bought the cattle, and stay with friends there while our new house was being finished. I had different ideas, however, and on the train I had told him that I wanted to go on with him. He was very ready to be convinced.

So we left Miles City April seventeenth, with a hundred-mile journey ahead of us which would take two days. We were driving behind two horses in a spring wagon, which was like a buckboard but very much more comfortable. Already the grass had started, and the country was prettily tinged with green. But it was a big and bare country, with only scattering pine trees and the cottonwoods in the river bottoms to break its vast monotony. In all the years of my marriage, I never had trees over my head; they could have been planted, but we never lived long enough in one place for them to grow.

We made our first noon halt at Piper Dan's, a road ranch thirty-five miles out of Miles City, where the Tongue River mail stage changed horses. . . .

The second day of our trip was beautiful when we started out, though before we arrived it had clouded over and begun to snow. After coming sixty-five or seventy miles up Tongue River, we crossed over the divide to the Rosebud, then went on down a long gulch to Lame Deer. One of my first lessons as a western wife was that location in that almost uninhabited country was not a matter of cities and roads, but of rivers and divides. Rivers, like women, were few, and they gained in importance proportionally, while the location of every tiny creek might be a matter of life-and-death importance to men and animals alike. . . .

In the late afternoon we came out of the mouth of a gulch down which we had been traveling. A huddle of log buildings lay below us on the flat, and as I watched, a man on horseback burst out of it, galloping across the valley. I was told that it was one of our cowboys, and that he was probably going after the milk cow. Two men climbed down from a partly completed log house—our house-to-be. Then a fourth man whom I recognized as Johnny appeared in the door of a low cabin. So this was home.

In a minute I was unfolding my cramped limbs and being helped out of the spring wagon, and then I was being introduced to "Old Uncle—the best logger in Montana," and to "Baltimore Bill—the best man ever seen on the end of a whipsaw." They were building our new house. Then the cowboy, Brown Taliaferro, came riding back and greeted me as "Miss Tiffany," which made everybody laugh and eased the stiffness.

The first sight of my temporary home was not reassuring—a dirt-roofed cabin, hardly any taller than a man, with one door and only *one window*! In this country where windows had to be hauled many miles they were usually used sparingly, one being made to do the work of two—a half to each room. An immense pair of elk antlers hung over the door, one prong supporting a human skull which was perforated with bullet holes. The skull, I later learned, had been picked up on the battle ground of Lame Deer; whether it was Indian or white no one knew, but most of the bullet holes had been put there in the course of target practice by the boys.

Indoors waited a pleasant shock. On our arrival in Miles City Johnny Zook had met us, expecting to take my husband back to the ranch with him while I went on to Bozeman. As soon as he learned of my intention of coming to the ranch, he went on out ahead of us to fix things up for my coming. He had said merely: "I'm going out to take down the variety actresses off the walls." But when I saw what a home he had made of that little shack, I had to admit that few women could have done as well.

A bright fire was burning in the stone fireplace, and the dirt floor was covered with a clean new wagon sheet of white canvas. Over that were laid several beautifully tanned skins—a buffalo robe, a mountain lion, a gray wolf, a coyote and two red fox pelts more worthy to be used for a lady's neckpiece than for rugs. (Later I hung those fox skins on the wall.) Johnny had even found a white bedspread—as I later had cause to regret, for our bedroom was also the family living room, the bed did double duty as a couch, and I never could keep that bedspread clean. A gray army blanket, hung across an opening in the logs, made a door between the bedroom and the kitchen. I was told to lie down and rest while the men got supper ready. I gratefully did so, but was too excited and tired to sleep.

Just before supper my husband came in, to explain that Uncle and Baltimore Bill (so called because he talked so much about Baltimore, where he had once been), had been worrying because neither possessed a coat other than the kind worn in winter for warmth. Going coatless was a custom of the country; would I excuse the boys if they came to the table in their shirtsleeves?

I said Yes, of course I would. But when I did go out and sit down to table in the dirt-floored kitchen, with those grizzled coatless men in their grimy-looking flannel work shirts they had worn all day, a wave of home-sickness came over me.

It soon disappeared in enjoyment of one of the best suppers I ever ate—hot biscuits, venison and bacon, potato chips, evaporated fruit and coffee. That men could cook was something new under the sun to me, but the men in Montana could and did, and most of what I learned during my first years as a housewife I learned from them.

This first meal was a product of bachelor team work in the kitchen, and as such was typical. My husband was the biscuit maker and meat cook; Brown made the gravy and the coffee, while our partner's specialty was saratoga chips, on which he spent all the care and artistry of a French chef, putting one or two in the fat at a time, and bringing them on the table piping hot.

The table was the let-down lid of a chuck box, such as was used on roundup wagons. This crude kitchen cabinet, the stove, and some home-made three-legged stools were the sole furnishings of the kitchen that night, but next day Uncle was turned over to me, to build a table and benches. I had brought enough white oilcloth to cover the top, and when it was set for our supper the second night with bright red doilies, my grandmother's silver, an old-fashioned "lazy Susan" in the center with vinegar, salt, pepper and mustard bottles; and two delicate china cups and saucers to raise the tone, I felt I had made a real stride toward home-making in the West. . . .

One question had troubled me all the way out to Montana: Would the ranch be equipped with a certain humble but necessary structure in the back yard? I had heard somewhere that men living alone and very primitively weren't apt to bother with such a nicety. And I was terribly afraid that now, with a woman coming, they might not think to build one. I worried over this during all those days on the train, but I had been brought up with such modesty that I couldn't bring myself to mention it to my husband. Finally, after we were in Miles City, I did screw up the courage to ask him about it one night. I don't know whether I was more shocked or relieved when Mr. Alderson laughed out loud.

"I knew all the time you were worrying about that," said the unfeeling man. "I just wouldn't help you out!"

I'm sure mine was the most wonderful structure of the kind ever built. It was made of boards which Uncle and Baltimore Bill had whipsawed out by hand; a most delicate and difficult operation, and one resorted to only in the absence of sawmills. All the lumber for our new house had to be whipsawed. The log is laid over the top of a pit, and two men at either end of a long saw cut out the planks one at a time. Uncle thought so much of his precious lumber that he couldn't bear to have a foot of it wasted, and so refused to trim off the ends of the boards used in the out-house— though, as Mr. Alderson told him, he wasn't saving anything that way, because the long ends would be sure to warp. This they did, and curled in all directions. No roof could be put over such a crazy thing, and all that summer and fall it stood open to the sky. . . .

*   *   *

The ignorance of brides has been a subject of jokes probably ever since the days of Mother Eve. My own ignorance as I look back upon it seems incredible—and like Eve I had to learn housekeeping in a wilderness. If I had married at home in West Virginia I should at least have had kindly neighbor women to turn to for advice, and I should have had stores where I could buy things to cover a few of my mistakes. As it was I was a hundred horse-and-buggy miles from a loaf of baker's bread or a paper of pins. And with one unpleasant pair of exceptions, I didn't see a white woman from April to July. . . .

The next week when my husband was away on Tongue River buying horses I announced to the rest of the "family" that I was going to do the washing, and even invited the boys to put in their soiled things. I had never done a washing in my life and supposed, in my ignorance, that all it required was willing hands and soap. I knew nothing about hard water— but I soon learned.

For a guide to housekeeping in the West I had brought a cook book and housekeeping manual which our dear old pastor at home had given me for a wedding present. This book, written by a Southern gentlewoman for Southern gentlewomen, didn't contain a single cake recipe that called for fewer than six eggs. I now opened it to the section on laundry, and the first sentence that met my eye was as follows: "Before starting to wash it is essential to have a large, light, airy laundry with at least seven tubs."

I had one tub, a boiler and a dishpan. But for air and light at least I was well off, since my laundry was the shady north end of the shack and took in the whole of Montana. I threw the book under the bunk bed and put all my best clothes in the boiler. I didn't use half enough soap, and the water was very alkaline. My white under-things turned a dingy yellow and came out covered with gummy black balls of alkali as big as a small pea and bigger, which stuck to the iron. I shall never forget that washing as long as I live.

The boys did their best to help. One of them got dinner, and the others helped me to wring the clothes out of the hot water. I was grateful for their efforts and their sympathy, but as they didn't know any more about laundry than I did, it was a case of the blind leading the blind. I had so little sense, I didn't even know enough to pour cold water over the boiling clothes to cool them, and neither did the rest of them. We wrung them out hot, until my fingers were bleeding around the nails. There was no clothesline, so one of the boys stretched a lariat in the yard, but there

were no clothespins either, and when a wind came up it blew down half
of the wash into the sawdust which covered the premises. In the midst of
all this Sadie, the neighbor's daughter-in-law, came to call, I think to find
out why I hadn't sent the washing that week. Humiliation was forgotten
in the relief of being able to sit down.

81

NOW THE PRAIRIE
LIFE BEGINS!

Susan Shelby Magoffin

*Susan Shelby Magoffin was an eighteen-year-old bride, the daughter of a promi-
ent Eastern family, when she became one of the first women to cross the Santa
Fe Trail from Missouri to Santa Fe in 1845. Her diary,* Down the Santa Fe
Trail and into Mexico, *is one of the classics.*

Thursday 11th. Now the Prairie life begins! We soon left "the settlements"
this morning. Our mules travel well and we joged on at a rapid pace till
10 o'clock, when we came up with the waggons. They were encamped just
at the edge of the last woods. As we proceeded from this thick wood of
oaks and scrubby underbrush, my eyes were unable to satiate their longing
for a sight of the wide spreading plains. The hot sun, or rather the wind
which blew pretty roughly, compelled me to seek shelter with my friends,
the carriage & a thick veil.

All our waggons were here, and those of two or three others of the
traders. The animals made an extensive show indeed. Mules and oxen
scattered in all directions. The teamsters were just "catching up," and the
cracking of whips, lowing of cattle, braying of mules, whooping and hallow-
ing of the men was a novel sight rather. It is disagreeable to hear so much
swearing; the animals are unruly tis true and worries the patience of their
drivers, but I scarcely think they need be so profane. And the mules I

believe are worse, for they kick and run so much faster. It is a common circumstance for a mule (when first brought into service) while they are hitching him in, to break away with chains and harness all on, and run for half hour or more with two or three horsemen at his heels endeavouring to stop him, or at least to keep him from running among the other stock. I saw a scamper while I sat in the carriage today. One of the mules belonging to Col. Owens scampered off, turning the heads of the whole collection nearly by the rattling of the chains. After a fine race one of his pursuers succeeded in catching the bridle, when the stubborn animal refused to lead and in defiance of all the man could do, he walked backwards all the way to camp leading his capturer instead of being led.

82

THE PREGNANT
PRIVATE

William Gilpin

While the regular Army was fighting Mexico to the south, a makeshift battalion was formed under William Gilpin to fend off the Indians who had the effrontery to defend their homes. The following, about a lieutenant who enlisted a friendly private, is from Gilpin's William Gilpin, Western Naturalist.

In the summer of 1847 the Indians concluded that they could strike with impunity almost anywhere along the road from the settlements on the Missouri to Santa Fe. Nearly every company of merchants and travelers was attacked; and since small groups were in Santa Fe or scattered along the Arkansas trying to get home safely, Missourians estimated that hundreds of whites would be killed if the government did not act quickly.

The only available military force was the army occupying Santa Fe, which gave such help as it could, but was badly weakened by having to send companies into the Navajo country. . . .

President Polk and his advisors concluded that controlling the Plains Indians required the use of a military force distinct from those engaged in fighting the Mexicans—a unit with one purpose, organized outside the normal channels of command. On July 24, 1847, the federal government asked the state of Missouri to raise the Separate Battalion of Missouri Volunteers, composed of two companies of cavalry, two of infantry, and one of artillery.

William Gilpin's personal recollection was that one day late in August he was sick in bed, attended by a physician, when Governor John
Edwards came to his home and urged him to accept command of the
new battalion. . . .

As William and the cavalry forged ahead toward Bent's Fort (about
two hundred miles up the Arkansas), a more unusual problem was about
to brighten the gray Kansas winter for the troops at Fort Mann. Unbelieva-
bly, back in September at Leavenworth, First Lieutenant Amandus Schnabel had recruited into Company "D" a young woman named Caroline
Newcome. Caroline used no such old stratagem as calling herself a laundress; she was enrolled as a genuine soldier—Private Bill Newcome. How
many men were in on the game is a company secret, but she traveled with
the troops to Fort Mann. Schnabel disguised Caroline in soldiers' clothing
and helped her escape detection by sending her "off from duty in the
Company under different pretexts . . . [Schnabel meanwhile] tenting,
sleeping and cohabiting with the said female . . ."

The fraud was revealed when Private Bill Newcome became pregnant and went absent without leave. Schnabel had already been repri-
manded in October for spreading a rumor that Company "E" was planning an attack on the two German companies ("C" and "D"). William,
disgusted, initiated court-martial proceedings against the artful lieutenant. William's charges would indicate that he was neither shocked by the
immorality nor amused by the cleverness of the trick. For he alleged
"gross fraud upon the United States" in his specifications. Schnabel, he
said, was guilty of "defrauding the United States of the service of a good
and competent soldier. . . ."

83

GREAT WESTERN, THE ARMY'S AMAZON

Arthur Woodward

The late Arthur Woodward had more fun with history than most historians and took the time to track down this affair and do a paper on it.

Out of the ruck of the years new personalities constantly emerge. One of these is a woman known to hundreds of her fellow men in the years 1841 to 1866 as "The Great Western."

She was, in the parlance of the army, a "camp follower." She was born apparently in 1813, but whether in Tennessee, as the United States Census of Arizona for 1860 shows, or in Clay County, Missouri, as recorded in her burial certificate, is not known. We do not know her maiden name. Apparently her given name was Sarah, and that she used until her death. My belief, not shared by all others, is that she was a woman of many aliases and many amours.

She herself stated in 1847, just after the Battle of Buena Vista, that she and her first "husband" (not named) were enlisted into the army in the 8th Regular Infantry at Jefferson Barracks, Missouri. Another unverified source places her in the army in Florida in the latter years of the Seminole Wars (1835–1842).

Be that as it may, she first attracted national attention when she stood the test under fire during the bombardment of Fort Texas (renamed, on

May 17, 1846, Fort Brown), which stood on the bank of the Rio Grande opposite the Mexican town of Matamoros. This scrap was mainly an artillery duel that lasted for 160 hours. In the heat of the bombardment "The Great Western" served hot coffee and soup to the artillerymen. Her position with the army at this time was as cook for an officers' mess in the 7th Infantry.

A woman to obtain permission to travel with the troops had to be married to a soldier and was usually signed on as a regimental laundress. Hence the redoubtable Sarah was called by a variety of names. During 1846–1848, she was known variously as Mrs. Bourdett or Bourjette, Mrs. Bouget, Mrs. Borginnis, and possibly as Mrs. Sarah Foyle. She became "Mrs." Davis in 1848; later she was known as Mrs. Philips-Bowman or Booman, and was buried under the name of Sarah A. Bowman.

In appearance, Sarah was about six feet tall, her hair was reddish, her complexion fair, and she had blue eyes. By nature she was kindhearted. Apparently she operated a restaurant or hotel in Saltillo, the city five miles north of the Buena Vista battlefield, and, according to a Texan in Taylor's army, "She was a great nurse and went with Taylor's army. She stood six feet two . . . would always get up at night at any time to get one something to eat . . . kept sort of a restaurant; they all knew her. The boys tell about one of the Indianans that when they broke through, two of Minon's cavalry made a dash for them on horse back." He continues that the Indianan was so scared he "rushed right down to 'The Great Western's' headquarters, yelling that the army was all cut to pieces and the Mexicans under full way for Saltillo."

"She just drew off and hit him between the eyes and knocked him sprawling, saying, 'You son-of-a-bitch, there aint Mexicans enough in Mexico to whip old Taylor. You just spread that report and I'll beat you to death.'" Probably Sarah would have kept her word.

When the major part of the army moved, she moved with it. In the field she cooked for the officers, or, when in town, opened a restaurant, coffee house, bar, and hotel. She catered to officers and gentlemen and tolerated no rough stuff. If anyone was going to get rough it was Sarah. On the march, she usually wore two pistols strapped to her ample waist.

I suspect that when she traveled with the army she signed on with any man who took her fancy. This may account for her numerous married names. When she ran into old acquaintances she was probably known by the name of the last man she took into her blankets. When she set up business in town she may, or may not, have used the name of her last "husband." She was shrewd in a business way, and probably the reason she catered to officers only was that she knew a lieutenant who made $70 or

$80 a month, or a captain who made more, or a major who had more than a captain offered better financial returns than a lowly buck private at $7.

After peace was declared, Madame Sarah left Mexico City and headed north with the army. Young Sam Chamberlain, relating his experiences in the American Army in Mexico, tells how a combined outfit of dragoons and artillery was organized for the march to California at Walnut Springs, on the northern outskirts of Monterrey, and at Arista Mills, not far from El Obispado. Three Chihuahua wagons caught up with the command as it was ready, on the morning of July 19, 1848, to begin its march. On horseback with the wagons was Mrs. Sarah Borginnis, who requested permission to accompany the troops.

Sarah was informed she could go provided she would marry a dragoon and sign on as a laundress. The inimitable "Great Western" replied, with a salute, "All right, Major, I'll marry the whole squadron and you thrown in but what I go along." Then she rode down the line of halted troops shouting, "Who wants a wife with fifteen thousand dollars and the biggest leg in Mexico! Come my beauties, don't all speak at once—who is the lucky man?" At first there were no takers, but finally a man by the name of Davis agreed to marry her providing there was a clergyman to tie the knot. Sarah, however, laughed uproariously and said, "Bring your blankets to my tent and I will learn you how to tie a knot that will satisfy you, I reckon."

Thus, without more ado, Sarah Borginnis, alias Bouget, alias Burdette, Bourjette, Foyle, etc., became "Mrs. Davis" and was off to California. One thing I would like to bet is that neither Davis nor any of her "husbands" ever laid a hand on a single dollar of her money.

"The Great Western" wound up in the Mexican town of El Paso (now Juarez) and then shifted across to the American side sometime in late 1848 or early 1849. She moved on to Fort Yuma in 1852. In 1854, she bought property in the newly laid out town of Colorado City, where she erected a restaurant and was the first American woman to settle in what is now the flourishing city of Yuma.

When the 1860 United States Census was taken in Arizona City, now Yuma, among the inhabitants was Albert J. Bowman, age 32, originally from Brunswick, Germany, an upholsterer by trade. His wife was Sarah, "The Great Western," who gave her age as 47, and her birthplace as Tennessee. She had property valued at $2,000.

On December 23, 1866, Mrs. Sarah A. Bowman was buried in the lonely cemetery on the northwest slope of the hill on which Fort Yuma stood. Her burial was the first in the new settlement and the military from the post gave her a splendid funeral, with a band and full military honors.

This graveyard was badly neglected and by June 1890, was overgrown with brush and weeds. In August 1890, the Quartermaster's Department undertook the removal of all the bodies from the old post cemetery to the San Francisco National Cemetery. This work was completed on September 9, 1890. Some 159 bodies were disinterred in eight days of hard work. Among them was that of "The Great Western." Her remains now rest among those of the military men she knew so long ago.

84

DOING THE WASHING

Eleanor McGovern

At least one of Washington's social elite was not born with a silver spoon. Here, in Uphill: A Personal Story, *Eleanor McGovern, wife of U.S. Senator and Democratic presidential nominee George McGovern, describes doing laundry in South Dakota.*

Grandma Stegeberg taught me all I know, and a great deal I wish to forget, about laundry. She was fastidious about the laundry, even though it took us literally days of hard physical labor to produce crisp, white, sweet-smelling, absolutely faultless linen and wearing apparel.

We soaked the clothes overnight. Then early in the morning we gathered wood for a fire and heated water for the washing machine and for a huge oblong iron boiler and as many pots and pans as we could fit on top of the stove. Into the washing machine went the first load: dishtowels, pillowcases, sheets, hand towels, and all the least grimy odds and ends. The machine was operated by pushing a lever back and forth to agitate the clothes, and the wringer was turned by hand. After the wet wash rolled out of the wringer, it was rinsed at least twice in tubs of clear water carried in from outside and then boiled in the pans of soapy water on top of the stove for about half an hour; the wringer again; a warm rinse; the wringer again; and another rinse, cold this time because there would be no soap left to "set." The soap was made by Grandma with lard rendered at the time of the annual slaughtering when one pig was taken from the crop and butchered, the fat stripped away, melted, mixed with lye, hardened, and cut into chips. It was strong enough to take the skin off our hands.

Today, when I see a family clothesline strung with washing, I usually think of Grandma Stegeberg. She did not hang things on the clothesline helter-skelter; she created a tableau. It was unthinkable, for instance, for her to reach down into the bushel baskets and grab what was on top so that the overalls might land next to, say, the sheets. No, our laundry went where it was meant to go—into some mysterious, interlocking, master plan.

The ironing took longer. Again at dawn we garnered fuel for the stove, lots of it, enough to keep the irons hot for hours and hours. Grandma showed us how to sprinkle the night before, to roll things up as tightly as possible so they would stay damp, and to tuck the pieces carefully like sardines into bushel baskets. It often took more than a day to iron the hand-embroidered flatwork, sheets, pillowcases, towels; and the dresses, gathered, ruffled, tucked, and pleated; the work shirts and the endless little rolls of spotless linens that came out of the seemingly bottomless baskets.

Willa Cather once wrote: "The one education which amounts to anything is learning how to do something well, whether it is to make a bookcase or write a book. If I could get a carpenter to make me some good bookcases, I would have as much respect for him as I have for the people whose books I want to put on them. Making something well is the principal end of education. I wish we could go back, but I am afraid we are going to become more and more mechanical." I do not wish, as she did, that we could "go back." But I am sorry that my daughters did not have the chance to observe a farm woman who did well and proudly what had to be done.

85

"A BALL PUT IN YOUR CARCASS"

Caroline Nichols Churchill

Caroline Nichols Churchill began teaching school at fourteen and subsequently became an author and Colorado newspaper publisher. She founded The Queen Bee, *in 1879, one of America's first feminist publications. Here (referring to herself always in the third person) she illustrates how to deal with intrusive males.*

The first time Mrs. Churchill was at Georgetown, Colorado, she had an unpleasant affair, that bore far-reaching effects. It was ten o'clock P.M. when the stage reached the interesting little city. The guests were shown to their rooms, Mrs. Churchill being left to the last; so it was discovered that she was unattended by another. She protested against being left to the last one located. She was put in room fourteen, upstairs, a forbidding looking top floor. At two in the morning a couple of men came to the door, presumably landlord and clerk. As one confirmed what the other said it was known that there were two individuals. They stated that they were railroad men, and "you have our room," they said. "You leave that door instantly or you will have a ball put into your carcass, if not more than one," was the rejoinder. They answered, "Fire away." Mrs. Churchill did not wait for the second invitation, but fired three balls into the door. As there was no thud she concluded the gallant U.S.A. man, woman's protector, had stepped aside at the invitation, and sneaked noiselessly downstairs after hearing the shots. There was no more disturbance that night. In the morning, as soon as the clerk was at the office to get pay unjustly for a night's lodging, Mrs. Churchill took her departure for a private boarding house. Here she told her grievance. Never thinks it her duty to keep a man's secrets for him. This was not her secret. The landlady where she had private board was well protected herself, as she had a vacation college girl rooming with her, besides an immense dog, which laid at her door upon a rug. Besides, she had a big six-shooter, which could be introduced to her legal protectors if things became dangerous.

86

RAGS TO RICHES
TO RAGS

Robert Laxalt

In Virginia City the stereotype of the gold miner was a reality. This is from Robert Laxalt's Bicentennial History of Nevada.

The story of the [Nevada] Comstock's first millionaire and his wife was of the rags-to-riches substance of which every fortune seeker dreamed.

Sandy Bowers was an unlettered working miner who managed to save enough of his wages to buy a small claim in Gold Hill on the outskirts of Virginia City. He lived in a boardinghouse operated by Eilley Orrum, a hard-working woman who cooked meals and washed clothes for her boarders. When one of them could not pay his bill, he blithely signed away a small mining claim that he owned. By coincidence, the claim happened to adjoin that of Sandy Bowers. This fact of neighboring claims prompted the boarders to the perpetration of a good joke—urging Sandy Bowers to marry Eilley Orrum. He did so, and, as predicted, the union caused much amusement among the miners. They did not laugh quite so hard when rich deposits of gold and silver were found on the two claims.

Money poured into the laps of slow-witted Sandy Bowers and his wife in such quantity that at first they did not know what to do with it. They soon learned. After buying a new home and attiring themselves in fine clothes, they decided to build a mansion in the verdant valley that lay between the Virginia Mountains and the Sierra. While it was being erected, Sandy and Eilley yielded to the advice of their practical-joker friends that they should go to Europe to get "polished" enough to live up to their new station in life. And while they were there, they should drop in on the queen of England.

Sandy and Eilley never got to see the queen, but they saw practically everything else. They also went on a spending spree for their new mansion. Ornate furniture, fireplaces of Italian marble, chandeliers and mirrors from France, all made their way by boat to San Francisco and then by wagon over the Sierra.

Sandy Bowers, at least, tasted the full fruits of his fortune. Bowers's mansion in Washoe Valley became the setting for the fanciest parties Nevada has probably ever known. At the Bowerses' expense, caravans of fine carriages made their way down from Virginia City to banquets and balls at the mansion. Imported wines, French champagne, seafood from the Pacific Ocean, orchestras, and liveried servants were all part of the grand display.

And then, Sandy Bowers died, and the swindlers and the cheaters descended upon Eilley to strip her of her fortune. Her mine and mill went into debt, and she was left with nothing but a silent, unwanted mansion in which to eke out her remaining years. For Eilley Orrum Bowers, her Nevada adventure had come full circle from rags to riches to rags.

8 7

AND FROM RAGS
TO RICHES TO
STARVATION

Marshall Sprague

For Baby Doe, the rise and fall of the golden meteor took thirty-six years, as described by Marshall Sprague in his Colorado, a Bicentennial History.

Because of the increasing difficulty of removing gold from its ore, dozens of the [Colorado mining] camps that had boomed in 1860 were almost ghost towns by 1865. Disappointed miners on Blue River and the Upper Arkansas and in South Park thought of returning to the comfort and dull security of their homes back East but found themselves held by the appeal of their giddy environment, the spaciousness, the violence and serenity of the climate, the brightness of stars, and the gorgeous sunups. The hangers-on believed that their luck would turn, maybe tomorrow. Horace Tabor was typical of this irrational optimism—a Vermonter in his mid-thirties who mortgaged his Kansas homestead in 1859 to climb the beanstalk of hope with his wife Augusta and small son Maxcy. The trio crossed the plains to Denver and moved on to Colorado City at Pikes Peak, to Oro City in California Gulch near the head of the Arkansas, and finally over that frightening Mosquito Pass (at 13,188 feet still the highest road in North America) to a camp tucked like a bird's nest in a cleft under Mount Bross. Tabor christened the camp Buckskin Joe while serving as postmaster there before moving his family back to have another go at California Gulch.

Tabor was an engaging human being of average size and mind and looks, gregarious, outgoing, moderately hardworking, honest as the falling rain. He found time to play poker, to dabble in county politics, to organize volunteer fire departments. Augusta was thin and small, smelling of starch and Calvinism. Hers was not a loving nature. She lacked sex appeal, preferring balanced budgets to the techniques of romance. But she was incredibly industrious, capable, and loyal. Though Horace wasted money grubstaking any miner who came to his general store for a loan, Augusta kept the household better than out of debt. As the years of high-altitude striving and hardship passed, she realized that her overgenerous husband was not apt to strike it rich. She did not complain. She gave him all she had to give because she knew that he was a good man. . . .

And the leader of the Leadville boom, its dynamic core, was—of all people—the forty-six-year-old storekeeper with the drooping handlebar moustache, Horace A. W. Tabor, whom we saw last in Oro City apathetically celebrating statehood and wondering why success had escaped him during his eighteen years in Colorado. It has been told how Tabor and his antiseptic wife, Augusta, moved their dying store business from Oro City to the shack-town under Fryer Hill and found themselves, by the spring of 1878, grossing a thousand dollars a day. "If," the no longer apathetic Tabor announced in newspaper ads, "you want anything from a small-sized needle to a large-sized elephant, come and see me." In addition to acquiring a modest affluence, Tabor had been elected mayor of Leadville and treasurer of Lake County during the winter of 1878.

A phenomenon could be described as a series of extraordinary coincidences producing miraculous results. The phenomenon of Horace Tabor began on April 20, 1878, when a shoemaker named August Rische and his companion George Hook trudged over Mosquito Pass from Fairplay, where they had been trying to learn how to tell ore from rock. They stopped at the Tabor store in Leadville, received from the kindly and popular mayor a basket of groceries in exchange for a third interest in whatever they found as miners, walked up Fryer Hill, and began to dig. Eight days later, at a depth of twenty-seven feet, they hit a rich vein of silver carbonate. They called their strike the Little Pittsburg, and it became during its brief career one of the most famous lodes in the history of silver-mining.

In a few months, George Hook sold his third interest in the bonanza to Tabor and Rische for one hundred thousand dollars. As word of the mine's richness leaked out, a pack of lawyers began suits alleging that Tabor's vein surfaced in other claims, infringing the law of apex. Tabor had watched such suits for two decades and knew what to do. The Little Pittsburg was earning eight thousand dollars every day, and he could afford to buy out the claimants. As a further safeguard, Tabor and Rische paid

Senator Jerome Chaffee $125,000 for his half interest in another Fryer Hill bonanza, the New Discovery. A bit later Chaffee bought out Rische, which led to a combine of Chaffee, Tabor, and David Moffat in a firm owning most of Fryer Hill, called the Little Pittsburg Consolidated Mining Company.

A feature of the phenomenon of Tabor in this period was his management skill under enormous pressure. He accepted his sudden imperial status calmly, switching from penny profits in the sale of "needles and elephants" to the handling of sums large enough to buy much of Colorado. His shambling, apologetic style did not change when he found himself to be the largest single stockholder of Chaffee's First National Bank of Denver—which meant, in effect, that he had become the state's top financier. He remained diffident when he was elected the Republican lieutenant governor of the state, an honor which he deserved because he had raised Leadville from infancy, and his child had grown so fast that it came to hold the balance of political power in the Republican party of Colorado. . . .

Though the Little Pittsburg bonanza was exhausted soon, Leadville's Croesus kept buying more Fryer Hill mines like the Matchless, and countless others along the Continental Divide—the Tam O'Shanter near Aspen, for instance, and several in the Park County and San Juan districts. It is probable that the value of the state as a whole owed much of its tenfold increase through the 1880s to the stimulus provided by Tabor's compulsive buying as he scattered his own and borrowed millions on everything from gas and insurance companies to streetcar lines, ranches, irrigation ditches, toll roads, and uniforms for the Leadville police department. It is said that he spent $200,000 trying to become U. S. senator in 1883. The state legislature elected Thomas Bowen to the post, but Tabor was made a senator briefly—filling the thirty-day unexpired term of Henry Teller, who had resigned to become President Arthur's secretary of the Interior.

The popular appeal of this diffident creature with the drooping moustache was of the broadest kind. Whereas other Colorado kingpins like John Evans and General Palmer maintained themselves as models of propriety, Tabor went out of his way to show that he was both bad and good. He divorced the admirable but unappetizing Augusta in 1882 at a cost of $350,000 and took up with a ravishing divorcee from Wisconsin, described as "the Belle of Oshkosh" and "a Dresden doll" by her biographer Caroline Bancroft. Her maiden name was Elizabeth McCourt, but she was called Baby Doe after her marriage in her teens to Harvey Doe. Baby Doe was small, blue-eyed, and possessed of a fetching plumpness when, at the age of twenty-eight, she met Tabor. She was neither a dance-hall girl nor a prostitute but one of a number of respectable young women who, after their marriages soured, popped up in Central City or in Leadville demurely on the prowl for a replacement spouse, preferably a bonanza king.

Tabor installed his mistress in Denver's new Windsor Hotel and married her at the Willard in Washington during his thirty days as senator. President Arthur was among the guests gasping at the most sumptuous nuptials that the nation's capital had ever seen. Tabor's gift to his bride was a $75,000 diamond necklace that was alleged to have been pawned by Queen Isabella of Spain in 1492 to finance the first voyage of Columbus to America. Later Tabor paid $54,000 (the equivalent of half a million today) for a Denver mansion at Thirteenth and Sherman, and the couple set up housekeeping while the town's elite ladies, the whist-playing "Sacred Thirty-Six," ignored them utterly, and talked of nothing else.

What nobody knew until Tabor went bankrupt during the Panic of 1893 was that this ignoble affair had a noble twist. The wicked old man and his gold-digging paramour had fallen deeply and permanently in love. After Tabor's death in 1899, his penniless widow, shorn even of Queen Isabella's jewels, remained faithful to his memory for thirty-six years by standing guard alone at his played-out Matchless Mine on Fryer Hill until her death by freezing and malnutrition in a shack near the shaft-house of the Matchless.

While legends grew about Tabor's lack of culture, he began using some of his wealth to help Denver emerge from the planless chaos of its pioneer days into a city of aesthetic distinction. As a first step he went East in 1879 and hired Chicago's best young architects, the brothers Frank and W. J. Edbrooke, to design an office building worthy of the city's new status as beneficiary of the treasure pouring out of Leadville. The resulting Tabor Block on Larimer Street was a sensation. When newsmen of the day called it "a Temple to Progress, worthy of any city in the world," they were inaugurating the custom of exalted hyperbole that Denverites have followed ever since. The Tabor Block cost $365,000, soared five stories, and was built of carved limestone, perhaps in honor of Tabor's work as a youthful stonemason back in Vermont. Before residents could catch their breath, Tabor and Frank Edbrooke were touring the East gathering ideas for a far greater project, the million-dollar Tabor Grand Opera House at Sixteenth and Curtis. It opened on September 5, 1881, to a first-night throng who came to hear the soprano Emma Abbott in the Irish opera *Maritana.*

88

BISCUITS, COFFEE
AND BEANS

Annie D. Tallent

Annie D. Tallent was the first woman in the Black Hills, joining the Gordon expedition's invasion of Sioux territory in search of gold. In her memoirs, she left us a report on wagon-train cooking.

Perhaps some of my readers may like to know how we fared during our long journey over the plains. Well, until the settlements were left behind, we lived on the fat of the land through which we passed, being able to procure from the settlers along the route many articles which we were after compelled to do entirely without.

From that time to the end of our journey, or rather until we returned to civilization, the luxuries of milk, eggs, vegetables, etc., could not, of course, be had for love or money.

Our daily "bill of fare," which, in the absence of menu cards, was stereotyped on memory's tablets, consisted of the following articles, to wit: For breakfast, hot biscuit, fried bacon, and black coffee; for dinner, cold biscuit, cold baked beans, and black coffee; for supper, black coffee, hot biscuit, and baked beans warmed over. Occasionally, in lieu of hot biscuits, and for the sake of variety, we would have what is termed in camp parlance, flapjacks. The men did the cooking for the most part, I, the while, seated on a log or an inverted water bucket, watching the process through the smoke of the camp fire, which, for some unexplainable reason, never ceased for a moment to blow directly in my face, shift as I might from point to point of the compass. I now recall how greatly I was impressed with the dexterity and skill with which they flopped over the flapjacks in the frying-pan. By some trick of legerdemain, they would toss up the cake in the air, a short distance, where it would turn a partial somersault, then unfailingly return to the pan the other side up. After studying the modus operandi, for some time one day, I asked permission to try my skill, which was readily granted by the cook, who doubtless anticipated a failure. I tossed up the cake as I had seem them do, but much to my chagrin, the downcoming was wide of the mark. The cake started from the pan all right, but instead of keeping the perpendicular, as by the laws of gravitation it should have done, it flew off, at a tangent, in a most tantalizing manner, and fell to the ground several feet away from the pan, much to the amusement of the boys. I came to the conclusion that tossing pancakes was not my forte.

To relieve the monotony of our daily fare, our tables(?) were quite frequently provided with game of various kinds, such as elk, deer, antelope, grouse, etc., large bands of antelope being seen almost daily along the route over the plains. Each outfit had their own hunters, who supplied, for the most part, their respective messes, with game, but Capt. Tom. Russell, who was the real "Nimrod" of the party, and a crack shot, bagged much more game than he needed, which surplus was distributed among the camps. Besides being a good hunter and skillful marksman, Capt. Tom Russell ever proved himself a brave and chivalrous gentleman, during the long, trying journey, and somehow I always felt safer when he was near.

There were several others in the party, too, who won the reputation of being skilled hunters, and judging by the marvelous stories told of the great number of deer, elk, and other animals killed, which could not be brought into camp, they deserved to stand at the head of the profession. If there is anything in the wide world, more than another, of which the average man feels proud, it is of the quantity of game he captures.

Speaking of game brings to mind an experience, the very remembrance of which always causes an uprising and revolution in the region of the principal organ of digestion. Some of the boys, in their very commendable desire to provide the camp with game, one day captured an immense elk, bringing in the choicest parts for distribution among the different messes, and judging from the flavor and texture of the flesh of the animal it must have been a denizen of the Hills since the time of the great upheaval, and to make a bad matter worse, our chef for the day conceived the very reprehensible idea of cooking the meat by a process called "smoth-ering."

Having a deap-seated, dyed-in-the-wool antipathy to smothered meats of all kinds, I employed all the force of my native eloquence in trying to persuade him to adopt some more civilized method of cooking, but no, he was determined to smother it or not cook it at all, as by that process, he said, all the flavor of the meat would be retained, and he continued: "If my way doesn't suit you, cook it yourself." Accordingly it was cooked his way and brought to the table—the word table is here used figura-tively—and truth compels me to admit that it looked very tempting, so, as I was abnormally hungry that night, I conveyed to my mouth, with a zeal and alacrity worthy of a better cause, an exceedingly generous morsel of the meat; but, oh, ye shades of my ancestors! it was speedily ejected and then and there I pronounced it the most villainous morsel I had ever tasted in all my checkered career, and the cook was compelled to concur in that opinion. "Ugh!" although more than two decades have passed since then, I can taste it yet. The trouble, however, was more in the elk than in the cooking.

All formality was thrown to the winds at meal time, each one helping himself or herself with a liberality and abandon, that was truly astonishing and, I might add, alarming, in view of the fact that our larders were becoming rapidly depleted, and that we were completely cut off from our base of supplies. Our coffee was drank from tin cups and our bacon and beans eaten from tin plates. Yes, we had knives and forks—not silver, nor even silver-plated, yet we enjoyed our meals, for with appetites whetted with much exercise and fresh air we were always ravenously hungry, and could eat bacon and beans with the keenest relish.

Strange as it now seems, while journeying over the plains I was for the most time blessed, or cursed, with a voracious, almost insatiable appe-tite—in fact, was always hungry during my waking hours, and what is most remarkable, none of the others were afflicted with the malady.

At the outset of the journey I had protested strongly against the kind of food on which we were being regaled, declaring that I never could be tempted to eat such abominable stuff, and prophesying my own demise from starvation within a month. Later, however, as I trudged along on foot in the rear of the wagon, I would often, between meals, stealthily approach the wagon, surreptitiously raise the lid of the "grub" box and abstract therefrom a great slice of cold bacon and a huge flapjack as large around as the periphery of a man's hat—and a sombrero hat, at that—and devour them without ever flinching or exhibiting the slightest disgust.

89

GREASY MEALS, INFESTED WITH LAZY FLIES

Isabella Bird

Isabella Bishop wrote under the name Isabella Bird and was perhaps the greatest world-traveller of the nineteenth century. Here she describes an 1873 Pullman car journey eastward from Truckee.

Cheyenne, Wyoming, *September 8.* Precisely at 11 P.M. the huge Pacific train, with its heavy bell tolling, thundered up to the door of the Truckee House, and on presenting my ticket at the double door of a "Silver Palace" car, the slippered steward, whispering low, conducted me to my berth—a luxurious bed three and a half feet wide, with a hair mattress on springs, fine linen sheets, and costly California blankets. The twenty-four inmates of the car were all invisible, asleep behind rich curtains. It was a true Temple of Morpheus. Profound sleep was the object to which everything was dedicated. Four silver lamps hanging from the roof, and burning low, gave a dreamy light. On each side of the centre passage, rich rep curtains, green and crimson, striped with gold, hung from silver bars running near the roof, and trailed on the soft Axminster carpet. The temperature was carefully kept at 70°. It was 29° outside. Silence and freedom from jolting were secured by double doors and windows, costly and ingenious arrangements of springs and cushions, and a speed limited to eighteen miles an hour.

As I lay down, the gallop under the dark pines, the frosty moon, the forest fires, the flaring lights and roaring din of Truckee faded as dreams fade, and eight hours later a pure, pink dawn divulged a level blasted region, with grey sage brush growing out of a soil encrusted with alkali, and bounded on either side by low glaring ridges. All through that day we travelled under a cloudless sky over solitary glaring plains, and stopped twice at solitary, glaring frame houses, where coarse, greasy meals, infested by lazy flies, were provided at a dollar per head. By evening we were running across the continent on a bee line, and I sat for an hour on the rear platform of the rear car to enjoy the wonderful beauty of the sunset and the atmosphere. Far as one could see in the crystalline air there was nothing but desert. The jagged Humboldt ranges flaming in the sunset, with snow in their clefts, though forty-five miles off, looked within an easy canter. The bright metal track, purpling like all else in the cool distance, was all that linked one with eastern or western civilisation.

90

CONTEMPT OF COURT

Ellen Jack

In her memoirs, Fate of a Fairy, *Ellen Jack described herself as a fairy-like bride, but she became a nineteenth-century boomtown businesswoman adept with axe, pistol, or shotgun. Here she describes an incident at court.*

In Gunnison once I was very busy when one of the help came to me and said: 'There will be trouble in the bunkhouse, for Jim is full and has a gun, and is abusing one of the carpenters.'

I said, 'Well, go and throw him out.'

He said, 'Not me, by gosh, I don't want to be killed by that drunken whelp.'

I went in my room, got my gun, went to the bunkhouse, and said, 'What are you growling about? Get out of this.'

He said, 'Not till I have settled with this son of a b———' and pulled his gun to fire at the man. I pulled mine and shot the gun out of his hands and part of his hand with it.

I said, 'Now, go, or I will wing off the other hand.'

He began to yell, but got afraid that I would give him another shot, so he went; and as soon as he had gone the carpenter said, 'Words are empty, for you have saved my life and I have a wife and two children depending on me for a living.'

325

I said, 'What was the trouble?'

He said: 'Jim wanted to borrow five dollars of me and I told him I didn't have it. Then he began his abuse, and I am afraid that he will do something yet, for the very old Satan is in that lad.'

I said: 'No, he is a coward, for he knew that he had the drop on you, that you were unarmed, but he did not think of me being so quick and taking such a straight shot. He will never try to come at me.'

That night the officers told me that I was under arrest, so I went and got Frank Gowdy and gave a bond for $1000, and I would not let the justice try the case, but took it to the county court, before Judge Smith. When the trial came off, we all went to court and the jury was all sworn in. The man had Ike Stevens, and both the young attorneys began their case. All at once Stevens called Gowdy a liar, and Gowdy struck him a paster on the nose and the blood streamed down his face. When they both began to fight, all the jurors jumped from their seats and began scrapping too, and old Judge Smith jumped upon his desk and yelled out, 'I fine you both for contempt of court.' Then some one struck him with a chair and knocked him off the desk. The sheriff tried to grab some one and old Jack Seamon struck him and sent him head foremost over some chairs; the chairs were fastened together, and when I saw him go over, his coattails opened behind and his ears sticking up as he went on all fours over the backs of the chairs, I thought I would die laughing. But as soon as the men got out of the fight they made for the door and out. I never heard anyone say court adjourned nor anything more about fining for contempt, nor that any one was arrested. They all got out as fast as they could, and when I got out on the main street three old deadbeats that I had fired out of my place stood on the corner. Those men saw the bloody handkerchief and the black eyes of the two men, then saw me laughing. One of them said, 'There, I told you she had done it.'

Just then Frank McMaster, who had just got a little newspaper, came up to the men and said, 'What's up?'

The man, who did not know anything only what he had surmised, said, 'Why, that yellow-haired girl has cleaned the court room up with a gun and licked both judge and jurors, and then turned loose on both lawyers and sheriff. They all have bloody faces and one a black eye, and the poor old judge is getting his wrist set, as she must have broken it with the butt end of her gun.'

The newsman went back to his office with all this, and as it was press time he put it all in the paper, with big headings how 'MRS. CAPTAIN JACK, THE DARE-DEVIL OF THE WEST,' had cleaned out the county court room, and a lot more that the man told him, when the truth was that I was the only one that was not in the fight. The only part I took was to laugh at George Hues, the sheriff, going over the chair backs.

Well, that paper went to Denver, then all the papers in the U.S.A. had me as one of the worst and most daring women that had ever lived. It seemed that every paper added a little more to it. They even sent agents from New York to get pictures of me to put in the Police Gazette and all this was through the vicious tongue of old man Kirkbe.

My trial did not come for several weeks after, and when it did I was fined $15 and costs for saving a man's life and at least $1000 expense to the county for prosecuting the murderer, but the game was to get what they could out of me, and they knew if they made the fine too large I would carry the case up. I was very angry at being fined, but paid it, and a few weeks after Judge Smith came to me to see about some land I had got, and after he got through with the land business he said, 'You see if you had not shot that man I would not have got my wrist sprained, and it gives me a great deal of pain and trouble.'

I said, 'Is that why you fined me for saving a good man's life and disarming a ruffian?'

He said, 'Well, no, not that.'

I said, 'Judge, you should have been in your grave ten years ago. You are not fit to judge between right and wrong. You remind me of an old piece of parchment that has done its work, and when election day comes I do mine. I cannot vote, but I let the boys vote for me.'

And when election day came there were stickers with names on them, and we cut off the name we wanted and stuck it over the name we didn't want. I was very busy fixing up my tickets and getting the boys to vote them, and the Judge was beaten. He started to sell out everything he had, and got his wife to help him, and when he had got all he could he took a seventeen year old girl and disappeared, leaving his poor old wife and daughter without home or money. That is a sample of the officers we had in those days.

91

GOLDFIELD BOOMS

Anne Ellis

Anne Ellis (1878–1938) called her memoirs The Life of an Ordinary Woman. *She was hardly that, prospering in the gold boom, running for public office, and winning wide respect. Here she describes Goldfield, Nevada.*

We arrived in Goldfield soon after the Gans-Nelson prize fight [in 1907]. People were wild over it and made a hero of Joe Gans. I wish I had tried to write then and tell of the stirring times; but there was no time for writing in this mad but thrilling search for gold. (I have heard that Peter B. Kyne first started to write in Goldfield.) The cost of everything was soaring; wages were also high. Whiskey was cheaper than water, and used more. We had a time getting into a hotel (a thrown-together frame building), and I remember it was alongside the 'Velvet Bar' Saloon. After standing in line for a long time, we find there are no more rooms. A man who had a room reserved said he 'could sleep on a billiard table,' and gave the room to me, to be shared with two women who were in line back of me. They turned out to be a nurse and a fast woman, and these two and myself took this tiny room. Necessity does make strange bedfellows! I use coats and things and make a bed for the girls on the floor; Herbert takes Earl and goes to the 'bull-pen,' a large tent full of cots, running over with all sorts and conditions of men. The next day I look for some kind of shelter, and while the sound of hammers fills the air, and houses and shacks are going up day and night, still there is no place for us. I walk, coax, and beg for a place till both my feet and heart ache. It is three days before I find one. During this search, I am passing the Mohawk Saloon, where there is a greater crowd than usual, although the streets are all so crowded you could hardly walk. Two men are fighting; some one in the crowd calls, 'Look out for the knife, kid.' I don't know whether this was a plan to stop the fight or not; at any rate, it did, both men letting go at once and backing off in opposite directions.

When almost desperate, I find two tiny rooms for forty dollars per month, and we move into this, promising to give it up in case of a sale, which happens on the third day, so again we are out in a cold, cruel world. After searching, we find a small one-room tent which had been boarded up, then covered with tar paper. For this we give three hundred and seventy-five dollars and move in. Our beds are made of bed springs which during the day can be closed against the wall; in one corner is a tiny inkstand stove; between the foot of the bed and table is one trunk, which two children can sit on while they eat. (On wash days this trunk is used for a bench.) The big box is unpacked and used for a dresser, lending quite an air when it is draped with a piece of Battenberg on top, with the old mirror hanging above. I hemstitch curtains for the one window and door, and after the books are unpacked and put on a shelf, and the few pictures tacked up, we are quite cosy.

Now I am seeing life in big gobs; fortunes made or lost each day on the stock exchange, in the saloons, at the mines, or at stealing, buying, and selling high-grade. I knew men who made, in addition to their wages, from twenty to fifty dollars per day, depending on how rich the ore was where they were working. The ore was a dark porous formation, no gold showing till it was roasted. In almost every family, either in the oven or on the back of the stove, there were pieces of this ore roasting; then, when you poured water over the hot ore, blisters of gold came out. Gold does not glitter, only the baser metals do. Mark Twain knew this, and said, 'However, like the rest of the world, I still go on underrating men of gold and glorifying men of mica.' After selling the house, we put all the money we had left, not much, into mining stock—United Mines. Each day after we buy it, it drops, till it is taken off the board. This was our luck. Other people around us, with seemingly no more judgment, were buying stock and making money. We are forced to be honest, as there is no high-grade on the Kewanas Mine where Herbert works (nor low, either, for that matter). Wages are very high, prices accordingly. We find that we must all work and I get a place in a laundry, five dollars per day. . . .

Goldfield was discovered, so I heard, by some cowboy prospectors (I believe George Winfield was one of them) riding into Tonopah. Their horses kicked rich gold-bearing quartz from the side of the trail. This is all desert country, covered with tufts of yucca, Joshua palms, and, in the spring, beautiful flowers. Low hills rise to the east, and on the northwest is the Malapai—this is in the form of a plateau, desert on top, with a rocky, steep rim.

In the lower part of town some one was fortunate enough to find and stake a small spring, and from this they made more money than if they had found the Mohawk or the Little Florence. Water was hauled around on wagons in big tin tanks, a short hose which could be unhooked giving you a pailful for fifteen cents. Never was water so precious. One never used more than one could help, the family all bathing in the same tubful, then using it to mop with, then pouring it, very sparingly, on a small patch of wheat planted beside the door. Many tired and dusty men would stop and look at this little bunch of green, but it did not last long, as the sun soon burned it up. I know of one woman who kept a boarding-house, who would boil the dishwater, then skim it, and strain it, in this way using it time and time again.

We lived on High-Grader's Hill, looking down Hall Street, across Sundog Avenue. On the upper end of this avenue the prominent people lived. There were many lovely homes, some of stone, a great many on the bungalow order. Later they built stone schoolhouses, banks, churches, hotels, and business blocks, that, one would think, might last for ages.

At that time there was a population of thirty thousand. To-day, eighteen years later, I understand only two buildings are left standing, one, the Goldfield Hotel, a seven-story brick structure covering one block. When it was built it was considered the finest building between Denver and the Coast. . . .

Looking down toward town one saw tents like mushrooms, all in orderly rows, the largest the Rotunda Hotel, which looked like a circus tent. All lots were on mining ground, so, first come, first served. This led to jumping lots, and this to many fights and shooting scrapes.

One day I heard a big racket, and in these times a commotion meant there was something doing, so I ran to the door, and just below me saw a woman throwing the foundation off a lot. The moment the last stick was off, a mule team was driven in on the run, drawing a tent house on skids—smoke coming out of the stovepipe. So Mrs. Enright jumped and held her lot, a gun in her hand in case of trouble. Later her gentleman friend (to-day we call them 'Sweet Papas') moved in with her, both of them fine-looking, well-dressed people. Comes a day when they fight; he fires her out, she pounds on the door, screaming and swearing. Finally he opens it a crack, sticks a gun out, and shoots a few times, just to show her he means business. We are glad, as she is a tough citizen, having killed her man before this.

Fuel is very scarce and expensive; at one time there is a real famine and people suffer. Coal and timbers are stolen from the mines; a car of coal is taken right off the tracks, and guards are put out to take care of it. During this time Herbert is sick, and we try in every way to get fuel, but there is none, only promises from day to day, then talk of the coal being shipped elsewhere, or of other towns taking over whole trainloads. Finally, through the influence of some one in power, a car does come to Goldfield—I just have to have some of this, so go early in the morning to the Tonopah freight yards, over a mile through slush and mud, to find a huge crowd—all of the same mind—before me, all talking and arguing. We form in some kind of line, trying to slip and squirm nearer. After standing for hours, I come to where the man is doling it out, only to find that there is none left. I tell him, 'There is no use in talking, I just have to have coal; a sick husband at home,' etc., and make it pretty strong. He gives me a gunnysack full—supposed to be one hundred pounds, for which I pay three dollars and a half. Then begins the search for an expressman to take it home. . . .

One would see coming out of small shacks or tents the most beautifully dressed women. This was the time of the Merry Widow hat, a large wide-brimmed sailor covered with flowers. Maude Adams was playing in 'Chanticleer,' and there were little red roosters on hatpins, embroidered in ties, in fact, everywhere.

Each store had its counter for wines besides all the hotel bars and saloons. One day a grocery store advertised a sale, unheard of, and the first sale in Goldfield. By daylight—I know, because I was there—the crowd reached several blocks, their money tightly held for fear of pickpockets. The congestion near the door is so bad that finally it crashes in, policemen are called, and a good time is enjoyed by all. In the mean time, all who can crowd in, rush madly and buy everything in sight, only to find when they got it home that it was spoiled. 'They said' (not the grocers) that these were goods shipped to the sufferers from the San Francisco earthquake, and held up, intentionally, in Nevada. . . .

Every saloon had its side entrance to the winerooms, where women went. There were also several places for both men and women. The Rendezvous is the only one I remember now. Here one could drink and gamble. Most of the women did lay bets on the roulette wheel, but I never did, as there was no money to lay. Once I did go in one of the back rooms with Billie and his wife, and have beer and club sandwiches, but considered it a very tame affair, as I didn't like beer, and you got only a rumble from the front, where things were really doing.

A big theater was built, The Hippodrome. I don't think it was quite finished before it was condemned, but they had good shows in it. (My first and last shows, and how I revelled in them, taking the last cent to go!) There I saw Nance O'Neil, Nat Goodwin, Grace George, Weber and Fields, Kolb and Dill. The latter sang, 'I don't like your familie-e, I don't think your Uncle John ever had a collar on,' etc.; also, 'Thursday always was my Jonah day. If I bet my money on a Thursday's race, you could see the smile on the horse's face.' Some of the chorus girls remained in Goldfield, and married miners, and some stayed without marrying. Here I saw 'The Wolf' played, and from somewhere they had brought small pine trees to decorate the stage, which was a show in itself. I enjoyed this play because it was so human and real.

'The Mikado' and 'Pinafore' were put on by local talent, with no expense spared—hand-painted Chinese lanterns for programmes, lovely embroidered Chinese costumes, and startling decorations.

Part Eleven

◆

LAW AND DISORDER

In the popular mythology of Clint Eastwood and John Wayne movies, those clouds on the Western horizon in the nineteenth century were the smoke of gun battles. That's a gross exaggeration, of course. A lot of the notorious lawlessness of the West was no more violent than the modern practice of looting savings and loan institutions. For example, the effort of J. A. Reavis to steal much of Arizona and New Mexico was the work of penmanship instead of pistols. But where there's smoke, there's at least a little fire. And there was plenty of smoke at Frisco, New Mexico, when the cowboys came after Elfego Baca.

92

MISSED FOUR THOUSAND TIMES

Elfego Baca

Elfego Baca was a young Hispanic cowboy when he decided to insert a bit of law into the disorder being caused by Slaughter Ranch cowboys over the mountains at Frisco. He survived to become a sheriff, a lawyer, a prominent politician, and to tell his own story in The Political Record of Elfego Baca.

About the middle of October, 1884, I was working with José Baca, a big merchant at Socorro. He was paying me $20 a month, together with board and room, for my services. At that time there was a whole lot of shooting and killing at Socorro, but the worst spot was west of Socorro: [a place] called Frisco. Frisco was divided into Upper, Middle and Lower Francisco. We didn't have any newspapers then; there were only a few in the country.

About the middle of October, 1884, a man by the name of Pedro Sarracino, brother-in-law of José Baca, owner of the store where I was working [came in]. He had a big deputy's badge. He came to talk to me frequently at that time, and he told me that he was deputy sheriff at Lower Frisco, because the cowboys at the time were raising all kinds of disturbances. He told me that if he arrested anybody his life would become thereafter in danger.

He told me that before he left Frisco for Socorro about six or seven cowboys got hold of a Mexican called "El Burro." They laid him down on the counter: one of the boys sat on his chest and arms and the other one on his lap, and that right then and there poor Burro was alterated in the presence of everybody.

Then a man by the name of Epitacio Martinez who happened to be present objected and begged them not to do that. The result was that after they were finished with Burro, the same cowboys got hold of Epitacio Martinez and measured about twenty or thirty steps from where they were and tied him. Then they used Epitacio as a target, and they betted the drinks on who was a better shooter. Martinez was shot four different times, but still he didn't die. He finally died in Gallup about two years ago [c. 1942]. He also has a brother by the name of Tomás Martinez, who is still living.

I told Sarracino, the deputy sheriff, that he should be ashamed of himself, having the law on his side, to permit the cowboys to do what they did. He told me that if I wanted to, I could take his job. I told him that if he would take me back to Frisco with him I would make myself a self-made deputy.

We left for Frisco about two or three days after that, on a buckboard with a big mule. Half of the time we had to help the mule climb every steep hill. When in Frisco he took me to his house. I was expecting to run up against anything any minute.

Three days after we arrived there we went over to what is called the Upper Plaza or Milligan's Plaza. Milligan was the owner of a big store together with Whiskey Bar, where the cowboys had a lot of fun. I was talking to the Justice of the Peace of that precinct, named Lopez, when here comes a couple of cowboys shooting up the town. Afterwards they went into Milligan's place where there were plenty of cowboys drinking.

I asked the J.P. why that should be allowed there. The judge told me that it couldn't be stopped, because the Slaughter outfit had about 150 cowboys. When a bunch of them came into town they shot dogs, chickens, cats, etc. Just then I saw a cowboy butt another on the head about three or four times. I walked up to the fellow using the gun, and he had already fired five shots. I commanded him to quit; that I was a self-made deputy in order to keep order. He turned around and shot my hat off.

That started the rest of the performance. He got away from me, and I went over to the ranch where he was working. He got out of the ranch [house] through the back door. There must have been about thirty cowboys. I had one man with me, by the name of Francisquito Naranjo, a very brave man. Then I put this cowboy under arrest and took him to Lower Frisco, where deputy Sarracino was living. That night twelve cowboys demanded the release of the man I had under arrest. They were armed to the teeth. I told them that instead of releasing the prisoner I was going to give them time enough to count from one to three before I shot.

They undertook to draw their weapons; then I started "one, two, three" and fired. When I fired they ran. I killed one man and horse on the run. I hung on to my supposed prisoner.

Next morning about 8:00 o'clock there were two men on horseback that I knew, one of them by the name of Clement Hightower and Gyrone [Jerome] Martin. They stood about two hundred yards away from me. I commenced to play with my two guns in their direction, and they made me a proposition to take the prisoner up to the Upper Frisco. I was informed that there were about one hundred men in the cañon waiting for me to go by there.

I went and got almost everybody in the small settlement. Told all the children and women who didn't want their lives in jeopardy to get into the church. When I left, there must have been about one hundred and twenty-five people in the church.

When I came to the Upper Frisco I talked to the Justice of the Peace, and while I was talking to the Justice of the Peace here comes a big bunch of cowboys. The testimony in court [later] showed that there must have been about eighty cowboys. I knew two of the cowboys, and I walked up to them and threw their guns on the ground. By that time I saw another man by the name of Wilson. I said, "Hello, Mr. Wilson." His answer was, "Hello, you little Mexican," etc., etc. By that time a man behind him fired a shot at me. I don't think he intended to shoot me, because there were some more people in back of me. I drew my guns and backed up to a picket house called a *jacal,* belonging to a man by the name of Geronimo Armijo. Molo Armijo, his son now living in Magdalena, was on the roof of the so-called *jacal,* husking corn. He and another boy went down in a hurry. I went into the house and put the lady and children out.

Then the fight started. One man got off his horse in a hurry, by the name of Kearns [Herne?]. He said, "I'll get the little Mexican out of there." I could see him when he got off his horse, through the cracks of the door. I shot at him with both guns at the same time. A man by the name of Jim Cook was leading the fight against me. He is now in Nebraska. He was in charge of Slaughter's outfit. That started the fight well and good. I was hungry while I was there, but I found some beef and made beef stew, coffee and tortillas. The court evidence shows that over four thousand shots were fired at me within thirty-six hours. At the *jacal* the only big object was *Nuestra Señora Santa Ana,* a statue supposed to be over six hundred years old. And neither the statue nor I was hit.

Finally a deputy sheriff by the name of Ross showed up there, a deputy whom I knew at Socorro. He and Jim Cook asked me to surrender. I told deputy Ross, "I am your prisoner, but I will not surrender my guns." We went into an understanding with Mr. Ross and Mr. Cook: that Mr. Ross was to have six cowboys from Frisco to Socorro, about 165 miles, but the guards had to be at least thirty long paces or steps ahead of me. They were to ride horseback, and I was to be behind with Ross on a buckboard.

At that time they were building a jail in Socorro, and I was put in it while they were putting the roof on it. The place where they put me was a cell about four feet square with iron doors. They kept me there for four months, then brought me to Albuquerque for my first trial on a change of venue. When they brought me to Albuquerque they put two pairs of handcuffs [on me], one pair welded by a blacksmith, and also two pairs of shackles for my legs. When they arrived with me in Albuquerque, the first thing the Albuquerque sheriff did was to take me to the blacksmith to take off the handcuffs.

I was tried for murder and found innocent.

9 3

THE MARQUIS
DE PERALTA

The biggest land fraud in the history of the United States, if not of the planet, was organized by James Addison Reavis, who claimed about 7,500 square miles of Arizona and New Mexico and almost got away with it. This account was originally published in Arizona Magazine.

J. A. Reavis, a young law clerk in St. Louis, came across an old Spanish document one day which referred to a land grant. This young fellow then conceived the idea to create a Spanish land grant for his own benefit. He first created, in his mind, a Spanish nobleman, made him go to Mexico and render conspicuous military services, for which he was created a marquis and a grandee of Spain. In some way Reavis obtained access to the royal archives in Madrid and there fabricated ancient documents (patent of nobility, commissions in the military services, etc.) in a most perfect way. All such documents were written on ancient paper and with ink which resembled that used in the time which the papers were supposed to have been written. He obtained ponderous looking seals of the state and attached these to his papers. Then the papers were deposited among the ancient records.

When all the work of constructing the "Marquis de Peralta" was in perfect order, Reavis returned to the United States and then prepared to produce a direct heir to his fictitious marquis. He went to California and there, in the vicinity of Ukiah, selected a small half-breed Indian girl of doubtful parentage and took her away and put her in a private school. Then Reavis set about to produce a lineal descent of the girl from the Marquis de Peralta. To this end he got access to the records of several churches, forged and altered certain records, tore out sheets from old record books and replaced these with others from his own manufacture. All forgeries or new creations were so perfect in regard to style of writing, phraseology, paper and ink, as to deceive the best experts.

When all was prepared to demonstrate the existence of a Marquis de Peralta and his descendants in an unbroken line, backed up by apparently authentic records, on file in the royal archives in Madrid, and in several old churches in California, Reavis began to interest some backers to assist him financially, and by the prominence of their names, to launch his scheme. He was successful in convincing some of the brightest men in the United States that he had a valid title. But Reavis was patient and went at his work in a thorough and systematic way. He waited about fifteen years, until his little Indian girl, the descendant and heiress of Peralta, had grown to womanhood, and then he married her. From this time on he called himself Peralta Reavis. Others styled him the Red Baron. The backers of Reavis must have furnished an unlimited amount of money, for Reavis henceforth lived as became the heir of an empire; he took some of his dupes to Madrid, traveling like a king, and there showed them the many ancient documents which the attendants dug from the records, where they had reposed for about thirty years. They were convinced.

In 1893, when the United States court of private land claims was established, for the purpose of finally disposing of the many Spanish land grants in New Mexico, Arizona and California, Reavis filed an application for the confirmation of a grant of land, made by the king of Spain to the Marquis de Peralta. He gave the approximate boundaries of the alleged grant and stated that he would have the complete records, supporting his claim, on file with the court within a short time.

At about that time I was chief draughtsman in the United States surveyor-general's office at Santa Fé, N. M., which office was located in the federal building, where also the court of private land claims was located. One day, Mr. Reeder, the clerk of the court, and Mr. William Tipton came into my office; they had a paper, which, they said, was an application for the confirmation of a land grant; that they thought the grant was unusually large, and asked me if I could make them a sketch, showing approximately the extent of the grant. I consented and began at once. After a while I became interested and after having obtained a start at the western most boundary, near the coast, in California, kept extending the boundaries eastward, in accordance with the description given in the application. When I had finally completed the sketch, it showed a broad strip of territory extending from the coast across the state of California, thence across Arizona and far into New Mexico. If I remember correctly, the east boundary of the Peralta Grant was some distance east of Deming, New Mexico.

When I brought my sketch of the grant to the court, everybody laughed. They thought Reavis was trying to practice a joke on the court and considered the claim preposterous and unworthy of serious consideration. But nobody laughed when an express wagon drove up to the federal building some time afterwards and unloaded an array of boxes and packages, all addressed to the court and marked "Peralta Grant." When all was unpacked there were three large tables, placed end to end, filled with documents, ancient books, pictures, including a large oil painting of the Marquis de Peralta, in his robes as grandee of Spain. There were documents, with large leaden seals attached and signed by the king of Spain. There was a complete history of the marquis, letters to him and from him. There were authenticated copies of the patent of nobility, copies of military commissions, copies of church records, showing the marriage of the Marquis to an Indian girl and a record of all the descendants of the marquis in California, up to the last one, the wife of Reavis, the claimant on behalf of his wife and children. The members of the court threw up their hands in despair. Never was there a more elaborate and complete record of proof filed in support of a claim. There was apparently nothing to be done but to refuse confirmation, but the very immensity of the territory claimed made it imperative that something must be done to save this large tract of the public domain from passing from the people to private ownership. The United States then employed one of the most renowned lawyers as assistant to the United States Attorney.

During this time the people living within the affected territory became alarmed at the situation and threats were made to assassinate Reavis, who at that time lived in Tucson, Arizona. Reavis employed several detectives for protection and never ventured out except accompanied by two of these guardians. It was William Tipton, an attache of the court of private land claims, who discovered the first flaw in the proofs submitted by Reavis. Will Tipton was a student of ancient Spanish, he was also an expert on paper used at different periods and ink, and in order to pursue his investigations of old documents, had provided himself with a powerful microscope. One day, while examining one of the ancient Spanish documents, filed by Reavis, he detected an erasure. Some words and dates had been skillfully erased and replaced by others. The work done was, however, so perfectly executed that it would have been impossible to detect the forgery without the aid of a powerful microscope. This discovery started something in the court. Other erasures were discovered. Then the government got busy. High-priced special agents were employed to visit every place where Reavis had obtained records or copies of records and finally the court itself adjourned to Madrid, there to examine the records in the royal archives, assisted by experts.

The result was that every document submitted by Reavis was either an altered original or a certified copy of a document, placed by Reavis, more than thirty years before, among the archives of the place, where the copy was obtained. Reavis' case fell with a crash; his high-priced attorneys left him, his financial backers withdrew their support, and Reavis and his family were without means. But this man, who had devoted some forty years of his life to a romance, which makes the story of Monte Cristo, a kindergarten tale, did not give up and continued the case before the court himself, unaided. It was really pitiful to watch the man, as one by one his proofs were pronounced forgeries; I believe that Reavis, having devoted his whole life to the consummation of his romantic dream, really had come to believe in the reality of his claim. But the end came at last and the claim was rejected. Reavis was a broken man; from early youth until ripe age he had devoted all his energies, all his brain power, to his wild dream. Had he devoted a part of his efforts which he made to accomplish the most gigantic fraud to something legitimate, he surely would have accomplished something worth while.

When this famous trial was ended, which cost the government a large sum of money, the government decided to put Reavis on trial for an attempt to defraud. He was found guilty and was sentenced to a year in the penitentiary at Santa Fé, New Mexico, where he served his term and then moved to Arizona. Not long after his defeat he died.

I have often wondered how the case would have come out had not Will Tipton discovered the alteration in the old document. Until that time, the court simply had to make a show to resist such a gigantic claim, but had practically given up hope to reject the claim, as all the documentary proof was apparently unimpeachable.

The reader may remember about this case, which created quite a sensation in 1893. I witnessed the hearings and remember all vividly.

"IT BEGAN WITH WRONG AND OUTRAGE"

Eugene Manlove Rhodes

Billy the Kid and the Lincoln County War have produced a huge cult of followers, a bunch of scholars, a shelf-load of books, and disagreements that still cause hard feelings in New Mexico. Eugene Manlove Rhodes (a genuine cowboy in Lincoln County country) did a lot to turn lore of the West into literature and looked on the struggle as a neutral. In these comments in The Rhodes Reader *he reflects on those who made a hero of Billy the Kid.*

The Lincoln County War started with the murder of [John Henry] Tunstall, February 13, 1878. It ended with the fight at Lincoln in July. It began with wrong and outrage, and it was carried on with outrage and wrong—by both sides, but not by all men on both sides. That is the way with wars. *The Saga* records, fairly enough, the murder of Baker, Morton and McClosky, the killing of Dick Brewer and Buckshot Roberts, the ambushing of Brady and Hindman, the killing of Frank McNab; and the final battle, in which Crawford and Beckwith were killed on the Murphy side, Morris, Semora and Romero on the other. These were fighting men, and they were killed. But for the death of McSween, who had tried to check the fighting from the first, an avowed non-combatant and unarmed, there is no other word than murder. And I agree with Mr. Burns that Colonel Dudley's part was the shabbiest chapter of that heart-breaking history.

It is generally thought that the Lincoln County War was a conflict between opposing gangs of desperadoes from Texas. Nothing could be farther from the truth. There were Texans on both sides, but of the principals only John Chisum was from Texas, and he took little part in the war. Tunstall was English, McSween from Prince Edward Island. Murphy, Dolan, Riley—don't ask. (Murphy came from California during the Civil War.) Billy the Kid was born in New York City, Frank Baker came from Syracuse, Morton from Virginia. What is true is this: that, after four months of civil war and eighteen months of anarchy, the men who finally brought the law to the Pecos were, without exception, men from Texas; and all but one from a little town—Tascosa. (You will not find Tascosa on any map.) I, who am not a Texan, may say this with good grace. And it is here that I part company from Mr. Burns. His man-hunters—"Poe was a veteran man-hunter." "Frank Stewart, with a posse of man-trailers in the employ of a cattleman's association." Frederick Bechdolt, writing of the same men, called them "The Law Bringers." I string along with Bechdolt.

This was submitted to Jim East, the only surviving member of the posse that captured Billy the Kid at Tivan Arroyo. His comment is illuminating. He says:

> "After all these years I do not believe that the posse were thinking very much about bringing the law to the Pecos. We were common, every day, thirty dollars a month cowboys. We were sent out to recover stolen cattle and to get the thieves, if possible. We got some."

There you have the west. It was all in the day's work. The outlaws got the headlines and the working man got the outlaws. On every ranch you would find some one who would go up against any man in the world, if the affair in hand was part of his proper business.

There was no fighting after the July battle in Lincoln. Murphy died in Santa Fe before McSween was killed. General Lew Wallace became Governor in August. He "made proclamation of amnesty to all who had taken part in the war, except those under indictment for crime, on the understanding that they would lay down their arms." For the most part, the fighting men went back to work gladly enough. From first to last it had been a sorry business. Billy the Kid, Charlie Bowdre, Tom O'Folliard, with five others, declined to quit. They made the deliberate choice to live by the trade of outlawry.

Governor Wallace came to Lincoln and arranged an interview with Billy the Kid. He made a definite offer. If Billy would surrender and stand trial on whatever charges might be brought against him, the Governor made this promise: "If you are convicted, I will pardon you and set you free." The offer was rejected.

95

THE REAL BILLY
THE KID

Howard Bryan

In 1880, the final winter of his lethal career (some say as many as twenty-one killed in twenty-one years, some say as few as four), Billy the Kid and three of his associates were captured. En route to Santa Fe for trial, the party stopped at Las Vegas for the night, creating a stir of excitement in the town, partly because one of the group, Dave Rudabaugh, had killed the city jailer a few months earlier. The following is from Wildest of the Wild West, *Howard Bryan's delightful biography of old Las Vegas, New Mexico. It provides an unusually imtimate look at America's most famous gunman.*

THE PRISONERS

Kid is about 24 years of age, and has a bold yet pleasant countenance. When interviewed between the bars at the jail this morning, he was in a talkative mood, but said that anything he might say would not be believed by the people.

He laughed heartily when informed that the papers of the Territory had built him up a reputation second only to that of (Apache chief) Victorio. Kid claims never to have had a large number of men with him, and that the few who were with him when captured were employed on a ranch. This is his statement and is given for what it is worth.

346

DAVE RUDABAUGH

looks and dresses about the same as when in Las Vegas, apparently not having made any raids upon clothing stores. His face is weather-beaten from long exposure. This is the only noticeable difference. Radabaugh [sic] inquired somewhat anxiously in regard to the feeling in the community and was told that it was very strong against him. He remarked that the papers had all published exaggerated reports of the depredations of Kid's party in the lower country. It was not half so bad as has been reported.

TOM PICKETT

Tom, who was once a policeman in West Las Vegas, greeted everybody with a hearty grip of the hand and seemed reasonably anxious to undergo an examination. Pickett is well connected, but has led a wild career. His father lives in Decatur, Wise county, Texas, and has served as a member of the Legislature. All the home property was once mortgaged to keep Pickett out of prison, but he unfeelingly skipped the country, betraying the confidence of his own mother.

BILLY WILSON,

the other occupant of the cell, reclined leisurely on some blankets in the corner of the apartment and his meditations were not disturbed by our Faber pusher.

The *Gazette* reporter wrote that he arrived at the jail as Mike Cosgrove, a mail contractor, was delivering a good suit of clothes to each of the four prisoners, saying that he wanted "to see the boys go away in style," knowing that they soon would be transported to a Santa Fe jail. The *Gazette* said the Kid looked and acted a mere boy, adding:

> He is about five feet eight or nine inches tall, slightly built and lithe, weighing about 140; a frank open countenance, looking like a school boy, with the traditional silky fuzz on his upper lip; clear blue eyes, with a rougish snap about them; light hair and complexion. He is, in all, quite a handsome looking fellow,

the only imperfection being two prominent front teeth slightly protruding like squirrel's teeth, and he has agreeable and winning ways.

"You appear to take it easy," the *Gazette* reporter said.

"Yes. What's the use of looking on the gloomy side of everything," the Kid answered. "The laugh's on me this time."

Then, looking around the walled jail yard, the Kid asked, "Is the jail in Santa Fe any better than this? This is a terrible place to put a fellow in."

That afternoon, December 27, the Kid, Rudabaugh, and Wilson were taken from the jail by Garrett, Stewart, and others and escorted to the railroad depot, where they were placed aboard a westbound passenger train for conveyance to Santa Fe. An angry crowd gathered at the depot, demanding that Rudabaugh be left behind. The *Optic* reported the disturbance:

> As the train was ready to leave the depot, an unsuccessful attempt was made by Sheriff Romero to secure Radabaugh [sic] and return him to the county jail. The engineer of the outgoing train was covered by guns, and ordered not to move his engine. If the sheriff had been as plucky as some of the citizens who urged him forward, the matter would have been settled without any excitement whatever. The prisoner, Radabaugh, the only one wanted, was virtually in the hands of the United States authorities, having been arrested by deputy United States marshals, and they were in duty bound to deliver him to the authorities in Santa Fe. The sheriff and a few picked, trusty men might have gone over to Santa Fe with the party, and, after Radabaugh's delivery, brought him back to Las Vegas, where he is badly wanted, not only by the Mexicans, but by all Americans who desire to see the law vindicated.

The excitement at the depot delayed the departure of the train for about forty-five minutes, but Garrett held on to his prisoners, threatening to arm them if that proved necessary for their own protection. Billy the Kid seemed to enjoy the commotion, pointing a make-believe gun out a car window at some children standing alongside the tracks and saying "Bang, bang, bang."

"As the train rolled out," the *Gazette* said, "he (the Kid) lifted his hat and invited us to call and see him in Santa Fe, calling out adios."

96

BILLY'S ALIVE, AND SO IS JESSE

C. L. Sonnichsen

In the West, it has become almost axiomatic that bad men, if they are bad enough to capture public fancy, never really die. Given time for the bones to moulder, an impostor appears. An old man declaring himself to be Jesse James showed up in Lawton, Oklahoma, in 1949. Belle Starr apparently reincarnated herself. And so did Tom Horn, John Wilkes Booth, Butch Cassidy and many others. History says Billy the Kid was shot to death by Sheriff Pat Garrett at old Fort Sumner, New Mexico, in 1881. But in 1949, a Texan named Brushy Bill Roberts announced to the world that he was Billy. Here is the pertinent part of his story he told as related by C. L. Sonnichsen, one of the West's most literate historians.

"I RODE into Fort Sumner from Yerby's a few days before Garrett and his posse rode in. When they rode in that day, I had spent the day with Garrett's brother-in-law, Saval Gutierrez. Nearly all the people in this country were my friends and they helped me. None of them liked Garrett.

"Garrett and his posse came in that night while we were at a dance. Silva saw Garrett in Fort Sumner a little while before we rode in from the dance. He knew I was staying with Gutierrez, so he went over there to warn me to leave town. Gutierrez told him we were out to a dance.

"When my partner, me, and the girls rode into town, we stopped at

Jesus Silva's. Jesus told Celsa that Garrett was in town looking for the Kid. About midnight the girls left and I began asking him about Garrett. He got excited and told us to leave before Garrett found us there. I thought Garrett would go to Gutierrez', and I had better stay away that night. I told Silva that we was not going to leave till we had something to eat. He agreed to fix a meal for us.

"He was cooking the meal for us to eat when my buddy asked for fresh beef. Silva said if one of us would go over to Maxwell's and get beef, he would cook it for us. I sensed a trap, but my partner insisted that we go get the beef. He started out to Maxwell's after I refused to leave Silva's house. I thought that Garrett might still be in town, and I wanted to meet him in the daytime so I could beat him to it.

"In a short time we heard pistol shots. I ran through the gate into Maxwell's back yard in the bright moonlight and started shooting at the shadows along the house. One of their first shots had killed my partner on the back porch. After entering the yard, their first shot struck me in the lower left jaw, taking out a tooth as it went through my mouth. As I started over the back fence, another shot struck me in the back of my left shoulder. I had emptied one of my .44's when another shot struck me across the top of my head about an inch and a half back of the forehead and about two inches in length. This shot knocked me out and I stumbled into the gallery of an adobe behind Maxwell's yard fence. A Mexican woman was living there, and she pulled me in through the door. When I woke up, she was putting beef tallow on my head to stop the flow of blood. I told her to reload my .44's, which she did.

"I started to go back out after them when Celsa came running in and said that they had killed Barlow and they were passing off his body as mine. She begged me to leave town. She said that they would not leave Maxwell's house for the night. They were afraid of being mobbed.

"About three o'clock in the morning Celsa brought my horse up to the adobe. I pushed my .44's into the scabbards and rode out of town with Frank Lobato. We stayed at the sheep camp the next day. Then I moved to another camp south of Fort Sumner, where I stayed until my wounds healed enough to travel.

"Around the first of August I started for El Paso, where I had lots of friends. I crossed the Rio Grande north of town and went into Sonora, Mexico, where I was acquainted with the Yaqui Indians. I lived with them nearly two years."

97

THAT FAMOUS SHOOTOUT AT THE O.K. CORRAL

The most famous gunbattle in American legend happened October 26, 1881, when the Clantons, known around Tombstone as "The Cowboys" came to town to settle an old score. The Tombstone Epitaph *reported it.*

Sometime Tuesday Ike Clanton came into town and during the evening had some little talk with Doc Holliday and Marshal Earp but nothing to cause either to suspect, further than their general knowledge of the man and the threats that had previously been conveyed to the Marshal, that the gang intended to clean out the Earps, that he was thirsting for blood at this time with one exception and that was that Clanton told the Marshal, in answer to a question, that the McLowrys were in Sonora. Shortly after this occurrence someone came to the Marshal and told him that the McLowrys had been seen a short time before just below town. Marshal Earp, now knowing what might happen and feeling his responsibility for the peace and order of the city, stayed on duty all night and added to the police force his brother Morgan and Holliday. The night passed without any disturbance whatever and at sunrise he went home and retired to rest and sleep. A short time afterwards one of his brothers came to his house and told him that Clanton was hunting him with threats of shooting him on sight. He discredited the report and did not get out of bed. It was not long before another of his brothers came down, and told him the same thing, whereupon he got up, dressed and went with his brother Morgan uptown. They walked up Allen Street to Fifth, crossed over to Fremont and down to Fourth, where, upon turning up Fourth toward Allen, they came upon Clanton with a Winchester rifle in his hand and a revolver on his hip. The Marshal walked up to him, grabbed the rifle and hit him a blow on the head at the same time, stunning him so that he was able to disarm him without further trouble. He marched Clanton off to the police court where he entered a complaint against him for carrying deadly weapons, and the court fined Clanton $25 and costs, making $27.50 altogether. This occurrence must have been about 1 o'clock in the afternoon.

Close upon the heels of this came the finale, which is best told in the words of R. F. Coleman who was an eye-witness from the beginning to the end. Mr. Coleman says: I was in the O. K. Corral at 2:30 P.M., when I saw the two Clantons (Ike and Bill) and the two McLowrys (Frank and Tom) in an earnest conversation across the street in Dunbar's corral. I went up the street and notified Sheriff Behan and told him it was my opinion they meant trouble, and it was his duty, as sheriff, to go and disarm them. I told him they had gone to the West End Corral. I then went and saw Marshal Virgil Earp and notified him to the same effect. I then met Billy Allen and we walked through the O. K. Corral, about fifty yards behind the sheriff. On reaching Fremont street I saw Virgil Earp, Wyatt Earp, Morgan Earp and Doc Holliday, in the center of the street, all armed. I had reached Bauer's meat market. Johnny Behan had just left the cowboys, after having a conversation with them. I went along to Fly's photograph gallery, when I heard Virg Earp say, "Give up your arms or throw up your arms." There was some reply made by Frank McLowry, when firing became general, over thirty shots being fired. Tom McLowry fell first, but raised and fired again before he died. Bill Clanton fell next, and raised to fire again when Mr. Fly took his revolver from him. Frank McLowry ran a few rods and fell. Morgan Earp was shot through and fell. Doc Holliday was hit in the left hip but kept on firing. Virgil Earp was hit in the third or fourth fire, in the leg which staggered him but he kept up his effective work. Wyatt Earp stood up and fired in rapid succession, as cool as a cucumber, and was not hit. Doc Holliday was as calm as though at target practice and fired rapidly. After the firing was over, Sheriff Behan went up to Wyatt Earp and said, "I'll have to arrest you." Wyatt replied, "I won't be arrested today. I am right here and am not going away. You have deceived me. You told me these men were disarmed; I went to disarm them."

This ends Mr. Coleman's story which in the most essential particulars has been confirmed by others. Marshal Earp says that he and his party met the Clantons and the McLowrys in the alleyway by the McDonald place; he called to them to throw up their hands, that he had come to disarm them. Instantaneously Bill Clanton and one of the McLowrys fired, and then it became general. Mr. Earp says it was the first shot from Frank McLowry that hit him. In other particulars his statement does not materially differ from the statement above given. Ike Clanton was not armed and ran across to Allen street and took refuge in the dance hall there. The two McLowrys and Bill Clanton all died within a few minutes after being shot. The Marshal was shot through the calf of the right leg, the ball going clear through. His brother, Morgan, was shot through the shoulders, the ball entering the point of the right shoulder blade, following across the back, shattering off a piece of one vertebrae and passing out the left shoulder in about the same position that it entered the right. This wound is dangerous but not necessarily fatal, and Virgil's is far more painful than dangerous. Doc Holliday was hit upon the scabbard of his pistol, the leather breaking the force of the ball so that no material damage was done other than to make him limp a little in his walk.

Dr. Matthews impaneled a coroner's jury, who went and viewed the bodies as they lay in the cabin in the rear of Dunbar's stables on Fifth street, and then adjourned until 10 o'clock this morning.

The moment the word of the shooting reached the Vizina and Tough Nut mines the whistles blew a shrill signal, and the miners came to the surface, armed themselves, and poured into the town like an invading army. A few moments served to bring out all the better portions of the citizens, thoroughly armed and ready for any emergency. Precautions were immediately taken to preserve law and order, even if they had to fight for it. A guard of ten men were stationed around the county jail, and extra policemen put on for the night.

98

THE SOLDIER
OF FORTUNE

Thompson M. Turner

Political chaos in Mexico and Central America in the nineteenth century inspired several efforts by entrepreneurs to organize private Armies and grab a piece of the country for themselves. The fate of the "Crabb Filibuster" in 1857 is described in Thompson M. Turner's Latest from Arizona: The Hesperian Letters.

Henry A. Crabb, former California state senator and Know Nothing party candidate for the United States Senate, had married into a prominent Sonora family. While visiting his wife's relatives in 1856, he conceived a scheme to take advantage of the Pesqueira-Gándara conflict and ultimately to put himself in control of the state. His objective is implied in a letter one of his men wrote from Fort Yuma: "Future generations, perhaps, will bless us as they did the Marquis de Lafayette in the early history of our glorious republic."

How he planned to attain this objective remains a matter for conjecture. In one version, he had verbal agreements with Pesqueira for mining concessions and large land tracts along Sonora's northern border, in exchange for support against Gándara; with the anti-American feeling in Mexico, it is hard to believe that Pesqueira made such agreements. Men who left the expedition at Fort Yuma said they had been recruited to colonize the Gadsden Purchase but dropped out when they learned the destination to be Sonora; these men thought Crabb expected to join Gándara.

In any case, Crabb's actions seem so unaccountable that, to believe him sane, one must assume he depended upon sources of information which proved disastrously mistaken.

The proposed filibuster was no secret, although Crabb himself continued to speak about peaceful colonizing. In anticipation, Pesqueira arrested Crabb's brother-in-law, Augustin Ainsa, and this news reached San Francisco before Crabb sailed for San Diego on January 21, 1857. Gándara had already been defeated, his forces dispersed, by the time Crabb entered Arizona to assemble his group at Filibusters' Camp, about forty miles from Yuma.

Correspondents at Fort Yuma wrote that 150 men made up the initial party and that another thousand were expected by way of Guaymas. These estimates exaggerated, but evidently Crabb expected reinforcements. Indeed, all through March, coastal steamers from San Francisco brought men on their way to join him. Although a week's delay might have doubled his force, he did not wait and even left twenty men to follow more slowly while he set out with the main party of about seventy.

At Sonoita, learning that the Prefect of Altar had organized resistance, Crabb decided to march through Caborca. Near that town he met Mexican troops whose officer advanced for a parlay. The filibusters shot him dead. The troops retreated to Caborca with Crabb's men in pursuit, but in town the filibusters soon found themselves besieged. Five days later, they surrendered. On April 7 all were executed except for a boy of sixteen whose youth saved him.

In California, feeling ran high over the executions; well into 1860, newspapers, which originally condemned the filibuster, spoke of "avenging Crabb." More intense emotions prevailed among Arizonans, some of whom just missed sharing Crabb's fate. From Filibusters' Camp, he sent representatives to enlist recruits in Tucson and twenty-four men, led by Granville Oury, nearly reached Caborca before Mexican soldiers appeared. Distrusting an offer of safe conduct to the border upon surrender, the Arizonians fought their way out. Two were killed and several wounded.

99

"NO COMPLAINT WAS MADE AGAINST HIM"

Thompson M. Turner

In Tucson in 1860 having a bad reputation and being "overbearing and insulting" could be a capital offense. Thompson M. Turner, a Tucson editor, described the fate of such a person in newspaper accounts, now collected in The Latest from Arizona: The Hesperian Letters.

On the afternoon of the 30th October, William Beattie was shot in the principal thoroughfare of Tucson by Miller Bartlett. He received five balls from a six-shooter in his breast, and expired immediately. Much excitement prevailed at first in consequence of Beattie having been shot down without weapons of defense about his person; but public opinion underwent a rapid change on learning about his conduct just prior to receiving the shots. It seems that the deceased was compelled to exile himself from California on account of some difficulty which occurred at Murphy's Bar, Calaveras county. He arrived hereabout two months since, and during this brief sojourn won the unenviable reputation of being the most unprincipled desperado in the country. He evidently delighted in fomenting quarrels, and scarcely a day passed without his being either a principal or accessory in some disturbance. He pawned several articles of borrowed property, and was insulting and overbearing in his general demeanor. At length some of his friends, among whom was Mr. Bartlett, assured him that he had rendered himself so unpopular that his life was not safe in Tucson, and prevailed upon him to leave town. He was aided with means by Bartlett, who parted with him on the most friendly terms. On Wednesday afternoon he returned, and evinced the same quarrelsome disposition. He had declared on his way in that he was returning to Tucson for the purpose of killing Bartlett and Mr. Wheat, who had given him employment part of the time while here, and assisted in getting him off. Mr. Bartlett was made acquainted with these threats, and deliberately shot him dead as described. Beattie was buried on the succeeding day. . . . Bartlett remained in town without attempting to escape, and as no complaint was made against him, he has not been arrested.

100

TAKING POLITICS
SERIOUSLY

Ralph Emerson Twitchell

The plaza of Old Mesilla is quiet now, with the village having lost its population and prominence to booming Las Cruces, New Mexico. Such was not the case in 1871 when Republicans and Democrats chose the same day to hold rallies for their candidates for territorial delegate and decided to circle their parades in opposite directions. What happened became one of The Leading Facts of New Mexico History *as written by Ralph Emerson Twitchell. While Twitchell doesn't mention it, a detachment of U.S. Cavalry restored order.*

During [the 1869] campaign, which was a very bitter one, a riot occurred in the streets of Mesilla, resulting in the killing and wounding of a number of people. A meeting had been held on the 27th of August, 1871. After the meeting was over the democrats and republicans formed in two processions and marched around the town of Mesilla; coming from opposite directions the two processions met in front of the store of Reynolds and Griggs. I. N. Kelley, a democrat, and John Lemon, a republican, engaged in angry political discussion as the processions came together. In the excitement Apolonio Barela, a prominent citizen, intentionally or otherwise fired his pistol in the air. Immediately Kelley, who carried a heavy pick-handle, struck Lemon a fierce blow upon the head, felling him to the ground. The next instant Felicitas Arroyas y Lueras shot Kelley, inflicting a mortal wound. The fighting now became general. Nine men were killed and forty or fifty wounded in this fight. Judge Hezekiah S. Johnson, of the 2d district, was sent for, there being no judge in the district. He came from Alburquerque, stayed three days and returned without taking any action. No indictments were ever returned and no one was punished.

101

THE HANGING
WINDMILL

Howard Bryan

It is hard today, even with the advent of crack houses and gang warfare on city streets, to imagine law enforcement by vigilante mobs. But in the 1880s in Las Vegas, New Mexico, where the lawmen themselves tended to be bandits and horse thieves, a windpowered water pump adjoining the jail was so commonly used for lynching that it was known as "Hanging Windmill." The following extracts are from Howard Bryan's Wildest of the Wild West.

Manuel Barela walked into the Flores Saloon in Las Vegas at sundown on June 4, 1879, one month before the railroad arrived in town, and asked for a pint of wine. He was in charge of a wagon train owned by his brother, Mariano Barela, a prominent merchant of Las Cruces in southern New Mexico, which had been camped just outside Las Vegas for several days. During that time, Barela had been whooping it up in Las Vegas, visiting the various saloons and gambling dens, and, as the *Las Vegas Gazette* reported, becoming very "demonstrative and disagreeable."

As the bartender was drawing Barela's pint of wine, the Las Cruces resident turned and noticed two men standing and talking just outside the saloon door. According to one report, Barela bet the bartender that he could shoot the third button off the vest of one of the men. At any rate, Barela drew his six-shooter and fired out the door. The bullet struck one of the men, Jesús Morales, in the face, inflicting a severe but not fatal wound.

Benigno Romero, seventy-year-old companion of the wounded man, was shocked by the unprovoked shooting of Morales, and when Barela came to the door, Romero asked him why he had shot his friend. Barela answered by firing two shots into Romero's body, killing him instantly. Moments later, Las Vegas officers arrived on the scene, arrested Barela, and took him to jail. Many bystanders had witnessed the double shooting, and a large crowd of citizens followed the policemen and their prisoner to the jail, making angry threats to lynch the prisoner. The officers got Barela safely to jail and locked him in a cell. The angry citizens stood outside the closed doors of the jail for a while, hurling insults and threats at the prisoner, but the crowd soon melted away.

Referring to Romero, the man who had been slain, the *Las Vegas Gazette* said:

> The person killed was a hardworking old man. He had stopped before the saloon to talk of his work next day. He was an entire stranger to Barela, and neither he nor his companion had given him the slightest pretext for offense. The shooting was entirely without provocation, a devilish and crazy freak which should not go unpunished.

All available officers were placed on guard duty at the jail that night to safeguard the prisoner from any lynch mob. The evening passed quietly, however, with no sign of trouble. Then, at midnight, the silence was broken by the sounds of gun shots on a nearby hill. Somebody called for the police, and the policemen on guard duty at the jail rushed to the scene of the supposed trouble.

As soon as the officers had left, a large crowd of citizens moved silently upon the jail and overpowered the few guards left on duty. Two of them knocked at the door of the jail and informed the jailer that they had come to deliver a prisoner. When he opened the door, the mob moved in and overpowered him.

The citizens forced the jailer to hand over the keys to Barela's cell. They took Barela from his cell, and, apparently on second thought, also took custody of another prisoner, Giovanni Dugi, an Italian held on a murder charge. The two men were dragged to the barren plaza in the center of town.

Standing near the center of the plaza was an odd-shaped windmill, erected in 1876 over a well. Built entirely of wood, the windmill consisted of two parts, a large platform held about twenty feet above the ground by four sturdy posts and a narrowing superstructure that rose about another twenty feet from the platform. Wood ladders led up to the platform and on to the top.

In bright moonlight, Barela was hanged from the windmill, and when he expired, Dugi met the same fate. "In half a minute after the hanging was accomplished," the *Gazette* reported, "the plaza was perfectly clear of people and the town was as quiet as a graveyard."

MORE ACTION AT HANGING WINDMILL

Howard Bryan

Shortly thereafter the windmill figured in another bizarre incident. A mob estimated at one hundred citizens descended on the jail and extracted three horse thieves who, the previous night, had killed town marshal Joe Carson (himself associated with the notorious Hoodoo Brown gang) in a dance hall gun battle. The trio, nooses around necks, stood on the windmill platform and had just said their last words (according to the Las Vegas Optic the last words of J. J. West were: "Please button my pants.") when the widow of Joe Carson began blazing away at them with her rifle. The following jury verdict and afterthought is from Howard Bryan's Wildest of the Wild West *(copyright © 1988 Howard Bryan).*

We, the justice of the peace and jury, who sat upon the inquest held this day, Feb. 8, 1880, on the body of three men whose names are Tom Henry, John Dorsey and James West, found on the public plaza, find that the two former persons came to death by several shots in their heads, and the latter one by signs of being hanged by the neck by some person or persons unknown, at about 2 or 3 o'clock in the morning on the day as above stated. We also found that the doors of the jail were broken open and from investigation we learn that the above men were taken out of their cells by a mob, unknown to this

jury. (Signed) Arthur Morrison, J. P., Charles Ilfeld, M. White-
man, Theodosio Lucero, H. Romero, Antonio José Baca, J.
Felipe Baca.

Another brief item in the *Optic* the same day said: "There is a petition
in circulation to have the windmill torn down. It is too great a temptation."
The "hanging windmill" was torn down that same day, not only because
it was a great temptation but also because it was a bad influence on the
children of Las Vegas. As *The Las Vegas Gazette* reported on February 10:

> The windpump in the plaza by the repeated tragedies ex-
> acted thereon became of such bad memory that the citizens
> determined that it should come down, and a purse was raised
> and a carpenter sent to work yesterday who took down the
> scaffold close to the foundation. The bad effects of such sights
> on children cannot be realized. Yesterday boys were hanging
> dogs all over town and many a poor dog had his neck stretched
> just by force of example.

103

THE JOHNSON COUNTY WAR

T. A. Larson

There was also the Lincoln County War, the American Valley War, and others in which competing commercial interests fought it out for control of grazing, water rights, or other economic advantages. But the 1882 conflict between small ranchers and farmers and the cattle barons who controlled public lands in Wyoming is the one that provoked Jack Schaefer's classic novel Shane, *and, subsequently, the classic film. Here, from T. A. Larson's* Wyoming, *is what the war was all about.*

In 1891–1892 a handful of big cattlemen had become so infuriated by cattle thieves in northern Wyoming's Johnson County that they secretly organized a search-and-destroy mission. The expedition included nine big cattlemen, thirteen ranch foremen, five stock detectives, twenty-two mercenaries from Texas, two newspaper reporters, and four observers. No Wyoming cowboy below the rank of foreman participated.

Fifty-two members of the party loaded a special train with horses and equipment and set out from Cheyenne early in April at the end of the annual WSGA convention. The train took them to Casper, where they mounted their horses and rode north. They were joined by three other men along the way. The "Invaders," as they were later called, hoped to surprise and assassinate twenty or more "rustlers." After they had killed only two of the marked men, the Johnson County sheriff's posse surrounded the Invaders until they surrendered to federal troops, thus ending the "Johnson County War." Some of the captives were charged with murder, but the case against them was dismissed in Cheyenne eight months later. Key witnesses who had been spirited out of the territory could not be found by the prosecution. The Invaders had too many powerful friends in high places, too much money, and too much legal talent.

Before the dust settled, the Invaders and the WSGA, whatever its role may have been, drew much criticism and some ridicule all over the country. The importation of hired gunmen from Texas drew special scorn because it was inconsistent with the cattlemen's vaunted self-reliance. Some aspects of the affair, such as the extent of the WSGA's involvement, are still obscure and disputed because the 1892 records of the association include no mention of it. Many Wyoming citizens who assumed that the invasion was an official function of the association applauded editor Hayford's comment that "of all the fool things the stock association ever did this takes the cake." Association members have maintained ever since that the invasion was an unofficial project of some of its members.

Part Twelve

♦

TRAVEL

It is difficult for Europeans and residents of the American East to conceive of Western distances—or how mountain ranges affect travel. When I was a wire-service reporter, our New York office would casually dispatch a newsman from Dallas to El Paso to cover an event. The distance is 636 miles—about the same as from New York to Indianapolis. Recently, NBC-TV, dispatching a camera crew to Canyon de Chelly in Arizona for some early-morning shooting, made reservations at an Albuquerque hotel for the previous night. The crew had a 240-mile drive ahead. When the map makes it look easy, terrain often complicates matters. For example, getting from Kaibab to Tusayan in Arizona is thirty miles by helicopter but more than two hundred miles by road.

How did prehighway humans get from Santa Fe to San Diego? The Spanish missionary friars bent on converting the natives to Christianity did it on foot. Later horse trails were explored and established. Then came wagon roads and railroads. For generations, travel in the West was tough enough to provoke a lot of writing.

104

OVER THE OREGON TRAIL

Bernard DeVoto

Today, on an interstate highway, it is a long, long way from Dodge City to Denver. I have tried to imagine, without much success, how long it must have seemed to those first westward pioneers crossing the sea of grass and the mountains before roads existed. In Across the Wide Missouri, *Bernard DeVoto gave us a remarkable description of the first wagon train headed for Oregon over the South Pass gateway in 1846. The book won the Pulitzer Prize for history in 1947.*

South Pass, July 4, 1836. The annual pack train of the American Fur Company, commanded by Thomas Fitzpatrick; a considerable outfit, seventy-odd engagés, upwards of four hundred horses and mules. Fitzpatrick's adjutant is Black Harris, the specialist in solitary and winter travel. Harris rides at the end of the Company train to keep an eye on the technique of the march and to enforce trail discipline. A Company cart (a 'charette' as in Miller's drawings) is going through the Pass this year—and with it a light wagon which will presently establish itself in American history forever. At the head of the train Fitzpatrick is the familiar figure of the partisan, thin-faced, gaunt, eyes sweeping the land, Hawken rifle unslung and held across the saddle. He looks in fact like a Ranney painting of the next decade or a Tait lithograph of the following one. Beside him on a superb black horse rides his hawk-nosed, mustached friend of three years' standing now, Captain William Drummond Stewart. Stewart is making another trip to the mountains and has outfitted himself with two fast horses which he commissioned Bill Sublette to buy for him for the sole purpose of racing mountain men and Indians. He has two new Manton guns, imported by way of New Orleans, and he started West with so many luxuries that they required two light wagons, but the wagons have been left behind at Fort Laramie and pack mules substituted. The Captain has a companion this year, 'Mr. Sillem, a German gentleman' and his two blooded horses.

We may assume that the train camped for the night of July 3 at the last tangential touch of the Sweetwater, in the greenery of its shallow gully where it comes down out of the hills, and we know that it camped for the night of July 4 at Pacific Spring or at the little Sandy. From camp to camp this was a tremendous day for any westering party—any party, that is, which had newcomers in it, for it was just a day's drive, and a dry one, to veterans. But it crossed the parting of the waters, the fundamental divide of the continent, and it marked the end of the United States. From water to water was twelve miles and somewhere in that stretch you left home behind and came to Oregon. Frémont, who had Kit Carson to help him, found the true height of land only with great difficulty and no doubt incorrectly, for he had no instruments sensitive enough to make sure. He estimated that the final rise where the continent parted and fell away on both sides was about equal 'to the ascent of the Capitol hill from the Avenue at Washington.' But it was enough for any traveler that somewhere in that twelve-mile stretch of dun and olive sagebrush he crossed the fundamental watershed and the frontier of fable. No one ever more momentously than some of those who crossed it with Fitzpatrick on Independence Day of 1836.

So large a train must stretch out for the better part of a mile. From that impalpable divide, looking southward for eight or ten miles across seemingly unbroken level of sage, one's gaze rested at last on a low ridge, a little greener than the aching plain, a fragmented prolongation of the Antelope Hills. Northward the sage stretched with the same illusion of smoothness for perhaps five miles, then hills thrust up, detached, rounded, mesalike, grouped in a formal composition and leading to the last peak of the Wind River range, a lesser peak but higher than the flat perspective of this empty air made it out to be, prowlike, abrupt, with a side falling away. At the utmost extent of one's vision southwestward, a slate-blue vagueness which seemed to float above the earth meant mountain peaks that were in neither the United States nor Oregon but Mexico. In this vast emptiness the sage and greasewood seemed level as a surveyor's bench but that was another illusion of thin air, for actually the plain undulated and thrust up sizable buttes. Actually also the baked, heat-quivering surface was not so dry as it seemed; there were gullies with snow water in them and even an occasional, incredible small patch of marsh.

The composition opened outward to the West, and westward into that widening vista Fitzpatrick's caravan plodded under the weight of sun, under the steel-white zenith, under the rippling canopy of brown and bitter dust. Eyes narrowed by the glare were red-rimmed with alkali. Alkali smelled too, like the vague nastiness of a chemistry laboratory, but not enough to overcome the reek of turpentine and resin from the hot sage—yet when the wind coming up from Green River drove the dust momentarily away, one's lungs took in a clean, electric air. Voices were microscopic in space, cursing the demoniac cussedness of mules. . . . Fitzpatrick and Stewart and the unexplained Sillem in the lead, an outrider or two on each flank, three-quarters of a mile of diabolism and dust, then the Company cart and Black Harris with a headful of trail cunning.

But behind Harris the momentous thing: a light four-wheeled wagon without springs, fourteen horses and six mules, fifteen head of beef and milch cattle—and the missionary party. The new missionary party that was a revolution. Marcus Whitman and the two Nez Perce boys who had gone East with him last year and a third one inexplicably found at Liberty. A dubious hired hand named (or spelled) Dulin and a nineteen-year-old youth named Miles Goodyear who was hellbent to be a mountain man—and soon made the grade. Also William H. Gray, a 'mechanic' of attested piety and proved malice whom the American Board had added to the party for no sound reason. Also the Reverend Henry Hart Spalding. Also, and here was the difference, Mr. Spalding's wife, Eliza, and the wife whom Marcus Whitman had married during the winter.

Fitzpatrick had sent the usual express to tell the clans that he was approaching the rendezvous, which was to be at Horse Creek again this year. So now, past midafternoon, above the crawling heat-mirage to the westward there was a flurry of moving dots, at the appearance of which the reflexes of Fitzpatrick, Harris, and Stewart were instantaneously activated. The figures running through illusion might be elk, which at a distance looked like horsemen, but they might be mountain Indians and hostile ones. Shouted commands from partisan and lieutenants; rifles slipped from the saddle loops and their priming renewed; the gaps closing; tranquil tension, eyes fixed on that motion in deceptive light. It resolved itself into men on horseback, about fifteen of them at a dead gallop. As the distance lessened they could be heard yelling—the piercing ululation of the war shout. They were Indians and white men mixed but Fitzpatrick saw a piece of shirting tied to one of the brandished gun-barrels and told his charges these were friends. Friends, however, who probably awed the women as much as any hostiles could have done and who at that moment fired a volley over the heads of the caravan. They galloped down its whole length, yelling, jumping their horses over clumps of sage, rolling round their necks, making them buck, spinning them in the zigzag of an Indian charge. Still at the gallop they came back the whole length of the caravan, which by now was firing its own guns in welcome. Nez Perces and trappers flung themselves to the ground and shook hands with their friends—but only for a moment. They had to gape at the most inconceivable sight ever seen here, the first white women who had come to the mountains.

Two of them. In heavy boots and swathed with yards of skirt. Riding sidesaddle. Eliza Spalding, tall, naturally thin and emaciated by travel and illness, dark-haired, sallow under her tan, frightened and appalled by the uproar of hospitality. And Narcissa Whitman who was neither frightened nor appalled—she was delighted. A smaller woman than Eliza but by no means emaciated, the period's ideal in womanly curves, blue-eyed, tanned now but memorably blond. Men always remembered her face and her red-gold hair. Men in fact remembered Narcissa, and though she was dedicated to God's service she was charged with a magnetism whose nature no one could mistake. The Nez Perces had never seen a white woman. Joe Meek and the three equally gnarled trappers who rode here with him had not seen one for years. They had their memories and their fantasies and Narcissa fulfilled them.

There are significant scenes in Western history but few so significant as this moment of uproar and wonder in a sagebrush sea. A Sioux chief is supposed to have once said that his people were not alarmed till they saw plows in the emigrant wagons and his remark has served innumerable chroniclers who may forget that the Sioux had no way of knowing what a plow was. A truer symbol for the chief would be these two women surrounded by Indians and men in buckskin, in Oregon, west of the Continental Divide.

105

THUS THE FIRST
MAIL WAS
BROUGHT ON
CAMELS

Edward F. Beale

Lieutenant Edward F. Beale's assignment in 1857–58 was to test the use of camels in the Southwest. In these pages from his diary he reports how his dromedaries performed.

April 18.—While we were busily engaged in digging out a large basin at the spring this forenoon, I heard exclamations of surprise from the men, and looking down the valley saw two men approaching rapidly on dromedaries; I recognized at once the white Egyptian dromedary, my old friend of last year; as they came nearer I saw that one of the men was S. A. Bishop, esq., and the other Ali Hadji, who accompanied me on my former expedition; they had glorious news to tell me; I had sent my clerk, F. C. Kerlin, by El Paso, to California, to say that I should take only provisions to last me to the Colorado, and expecting Colonel Hoffman with the troops would be there to pack my camels with provisions and meet me at my crossing of that river; Colonel Hoffman had gone to the river to reconnoitre, but the Indians having attacked him he returned to the settlements for reinforcements; Mr. Bishop knowing I would be at the river about the time set, and that Colonel Hoffman with his seven hundred troops could not get there in time to meet me, as they intended to travel to Beale's crossing *via* Fort Gaines, fitted out an expedition of forty men, and boldly came on to the river; here he was met by a thousand warriors flushed with their successes over the emigrants, and rendered confident by their skirmish with the troops; they immediately attacked him, but did not calculate on the character of the men he had, or the deadly efficiency of the frontier rifles in the hands of frontier men; he killed two out of every three aimed at, and, in a brilliant battle, completely routed them; he then crossed the river and remained in their village for a number of days defying them; then so completely was the spirit of this formidable tribe broken, that he divided his party, sending back twenty, leaving a strong garrison of six at the river, and with the remainder came on to meet me. On the second day after leaving the river he was again attacked by two hundred choice warriors, anxious to wipe out the disgrace of their late defeat. These, with his small party, many of whom were beardless boys, but *frontiersmen,* he routed, killing four at the first fire. As he approached the river, four men of the mail party, which has been making fruitless attempts for nearly a year to get a mail over the road, joined him, but on seeing the number of the Indians their hearts failed them, and two turned back. The mail was brought on my camels and delivered to the agent, Mr. Smith, who was travelling with my party; and having no means of sending back the mail he brought, and as the camels after meeting me turned back to the Colorado, it was transferred to the back of one of them, and now returns with us. Thus the first mail of the 35th parallel was brought on my camels both ways, and never would have come until the establishment of a post, as the men who accompany it affirm, but for Bishop coming under my direction to meet me. In the evening we hitched up and came over to Bear spring, about four miles further on. This is a fine locality for emigrants to lay by and recruit their stock, as there are several fine springs within a mile or two around the base of the mountain which afford abundance of water; and the grass cannot be surpassed, and the forest filled with game in plenty. Little Axe killed two antelope, and the Delaware a deer.

April 19.—Leaving Bear spring we came to Cedar creek in eight miles, where we found plenty of water in the same large pool in which we found it in our first journey of exploration. Here we remained three hours and a half, and then coming ten miles further, stopped for the night near King's creek. The Delaware killed an antelope.

April 20.—We came in three miles and a little over to King's creek, where we found a pool of water of some hundred yards length by fifteen in width, and about four feet deep. Our camels with their solemn faces make our camp look like old times again. The Delaware and Little Axe killed two antelope. Leaving King's creek, and travelling eighteen miles, we encamped without water, but in good green grass; cedar and pine abundant.

106

AUBRY'S
GREAT RIDE

J. Frank Dobie

J. Frank Dobie, author of the following, is beloved in the West as a writer-historian and for his suggestion that the skyscraper library that defaces the University of Texas in Austin campus should be laid on its side and a porch built around it.

For sustained endurance, speed and distance, I rank a ride made by François Xavier Aubry as supreme in the whole riding tradition of the West. "Little Aubry," they called him. He was small, only five feet and two inches tall, weighing hardly more than a hundred pounds. Every ounce of his body was distilled energy. He was quiet and modest; he loved fame and adventure. He led wherever he went.

A French-Canadian by birth (in 1824), he came to St. Louis at eighteen and went to clerking in a big store of general merchandise. He heard talk of bull trains and pack outfits. He sold goods consigned to Independence, the jumping-off place for the West, up the Missouri River. The stuff in his body was not compounded of clerkly tameness. He bought goods on credit from his employers, went to Independence, and joined one of the freight trains setting out for Santa Fe. He prospered as a trader and soon had extensive interests.

The year of his great rides was 1848. It generally took three or four weeks to ride the 800 miles between Santa Fe and Independence. The schedule of the military mail was thirty days; ox wagons required from two to three months. Early in January, Aubry arrived in Independence after having been on the road only fourteen days. Five men who started with him had dropped out. Mexican robbers, Indians and a blizzard had delayed him; he had killed three mules and covered the last 300 miles in three days. The *Daily Missouri Republican* (published in St. Louis) declared the ride "unprecedented in Prairie life."

For Aubry it was merely a warming-up exercise. As soon as the first weeds of spring were greening for oxen to graze upon, he loaded his wagons for Santa Fe. By the time they reached their destination the whole country was on a boom; the United States had defeated Mexico in a war of conquest and taken from her an immense territory that included New Mexico. Aubry sold his goods at 100 per cent profit and determined to return to Missouri and bring out a second cargo the same season. This procedure was "unprecedented." The freight outfits in Santa Fe could not get back in time to haul for him, but there were always oxen and bull whackers on the Missouri.

He announced that he would make the ride in eight days—and bets ran high. Before he had gone 300 miles, six men who set out with him had fallen behind. The remainder of the trip Aubry performed alone. He killed three horses and two mules. Indians took his baggage, his food, even letters he was carrying; but he contrived to slip away from them. He walked forty miles, went three days without a bite to eat, slept—off his horse—only four or five hours on the whole route. It took him eight days and ten hours to make the trip; but, counting out the time lost to Indians and on the walk they made him take, his actual traveling time was about seven days.

When Aubry got back to Santa Fe in late summer, the plaza was buzzing over his record. "I can do better," he said. "I'll bet $1000 that I can make the ride within six days." The money was covered. Aubry at once began making preparations. He sent men ahead to have horses in readiness at Fort Mann on the Arkansas, Council Grove and another point or two. Over certain stretches of the route he would drive extra mounts, California style. It was to be a lone ride over an empty land.

Before dawn on September 12 he left Santa Fe in a swinging gallop, and he ate only six meals on the ground, stopped only once to sleep—for two hours—before he reined up his final horse, heaving and atremble, at Independence on the Missouri. On the way he killed six horses and broke down six others. Several of these he had purchased from wagon trains encountered on the road. He ate a little while riding, and after the first day and night out tied himself to the saddle so that he could doze without danger of falling off. So long as he kept steady in the saddle, a good horse would keep the gait. It was the rainy season of the year; for a whole day and night rain fell on him continuously, and high winds were blowing most of the time. Streams were swimming deep.

Picture Little Aubry as he makes his ride! In the yellow morning sun and under the slant rays of autumn noon he races down the mountains past the village of San Miguel, where he changes horses, and on to another change at the Rio Gallinas, now the site of Las Vegas. For hours and miles and for miles and hours, in twilight and then in darkness, he listens to hoofbeats. In the dead of night he comes to the camp of a Mexican pack train; the boss knows him and lets him have a grullo that has never been tired. The Morning Star is still shining when, nearing Point of Rocks, he gives the long-drawn-out "coyote yell" of the West and the man whom he sent out a week ago stirs the coals around a pot of coffee and draws in the stake rope of a fresh mount.

The mount is "a yellow mare"—without doubt a Spanish dun— named Dolly. One deduces that all the mounts Aubry sent out from Santa Fe were native New Mexican horses.

"I'd kill every horse on the Santa Fe Trail before I'd lose that thousand dollar bet," he says to his man, "but it's not the money I care about. I'm riding to prove that I can get more out of a horse and last longer myself than any other man in the West."

The man by the fire of buffalo chips does not have time to answer. The saddle has been changed, Aubry has gulped down a quart of simmering coffee and sprung onto Dolly's back with a roasted buffalo rib in his hand.

"Adios!"

He rides on. The high, dry country recedes behind him and a chill autumn drizzle hides the sun. He cannot see Rabbit Ear Mounds, but he knows where they mark an edge of the wide, flat plains. At Rabbit Ear Creek he passes Alexander Majors's wagon train "at a full gallop without asking a single question as to the danger of Indians ahead." At roaring Willow Bar he takes off the bridle for a blow and a drink.

But where are the relay horses that were to be here, over one hundred miles from Point of Rocks? Indians? A dead man's scalped head answers. Beautiful Dolly must go on. On, on, until she has carried Little Aubry one hundred and fifty, two hundred, miles in twenty-six hours. So far as I know, this is the world's record for one horse in one day and night, plus two hours, of galloping.

The yellow mare bears him lightly across the Cimarron of the quick-sands and somewhere beyond he delivers her for safekeeping to a wagon-master who knows him and gives him the best horse he can spare. Hidden in timber above the ford on the Arkansas, three fresh horses await him.

He mounts one and cracks his whip over the others. The old church at Santa Fe is still less than four hundred miles behind. He is not quite half way to Independence. He cannot spare horseflesh now. He wears the first of the relays down in ten miles, the second in about the same distance; the third unexpectedly drags his feet. In a minute Aubry has unsaddled, hidden his saddle and blanket in the grass, and, silver-plated bridle in hand, is trotting on east afoot. For twenty-four miles he does not see a human soul. Then he walks into Fort Mann, where he finds one of his own freight trains and has to spend a long while tending to business. Here he lies down for two hours and sleeps while a certain horse is being brought in.

Refreshed now, he skims the ground past Coon Creek and past Pawnee Rock, where so many good men have bit the dust. To detail all the changes of horses would betray Aubry's swiftness. At Council Grove he pauses long enough for coffee to boil, ties himself on a fresh horse, rides on. It is a hundred and fifty miles to Independence yet. He hardly notices the beautiful trees and hills to which the plains have given away; he does not hear the cawing of the crows in the valleys. It takes a full twenty-four hours, most of it in rain, to make that last lap. At Big John Springs, by paying heavy boot, he swaps with a trapper for one of the best mounts on the journey.

At ten o'clock on the night of September 17 he halts in front of the Noland House, called also the Merchant's Hotel. It is bright with lights. Men rush out from the bar and "lift" him from his saddle. It is "caked with blood." The few words he breathes out are in a thin whisper. He has won his bet. He bolts ham, eggs and coffee and tells the proprietor to wake him in three hours. The proprietor waits six hours before rousing him. He bounds up "rather wrathy" at the misjudged kindness. "I like to take my food and rest in broken doses," he says. He is up in time, however, to catch a steamboat just leaving the dock for St. Louis.

The next summer in Santa Fe, Captain R. B. Marcy met Aubry at a supper being paid as a debt to the great rider. At Marcy's request Aubry wrote down and signed a short account of his ride. "I made the trip," he said, "travelling time only counted, in 4 days and 12 hours, though the time spent between Santa Fe and Independence was 5 days and 16 hours. I made a portion of the trip at the rate of 250 miles to the 24 hours; made 200 miles on my yellow mare in 26 hours."

107

"WITHOUT ANY THING TO EAT BUT THE DEAD"

Virginia Reed

Virginia Reed was thirteen in 1846 when her family joined the Donner-Reed party on its doomed journey to California. She lived through the terrible winter in which the party resorted to cannibalism to survive and described this fabled American tragedy in a letter to her cousin.

May the 16 1847
My Dear Cousan
    I take this opportunity to write to you to let you now that we are all Well at presant and hope this letter may find you all well to My dear Cousan I am a going to Write to you about our trubels geting to Callifornia; We had good luck til we come to big Sandy thare we lost our best yoak of oxons we come to Brigers Fort & we lost another ox we sold some of our provisions & baut a yoak of Cows & oxen & they pursuaded us to take Hastings cut of over the salt plain thay said it saved 3 Hondred miles, we went that road & we had to go through a long drive of 40 miles With out water or grass Hastings said it was 40 but i think it was 80 miles We traveld a day and night & a nother day and at noon pa went on to see if he coud find Water, he had not bin gone long till some of the oxen give out and we

379

had to leve the Wagons and take the oxen on to
water   one of the men staid with us and others went on
with the cattel to water pa was a coming back to us with
Water and met the men & thay was about 10 miles from
water   pa said thay git to water that night, and the next
day to bring the cattel back for the wagons any [and] bring
some Water   pa got to us about noon the man that was
with us took the horse and went on to water   We wated
thare   thought Thay would come we wated till night and
We thought we start and walk to Mr doners wagons that
night   we took what little water we had and some bread
and started pa caried Thomos and all the rest of us
walk   we got to Donner and thay were all a sleep so we
laid down on the ground we spred one shawl down we laid
doun on it and spred another over us and then put the dogs
on top   it was the couldes night you most ever saw the
wind blew and if it haden bin for the dogs we would have
Frosen   as soon as it was day we went to Miss
Donners   she said we could not walk to the Water and if
we staid we could ride in thare wagons to the spring so pa
went on to the water to see why thay did not bring the
cattel   when he got thare thare was but one ox and cow
thare   none of the rest had got to water   Mr Donner come
out that night with his cattel and braught his Wagons and
all of us in   we staid thare a week and Hunted for our
cattel and could not find them so some of the companie
took thare oxons and went out and brout in one wagon and
cashed the other tow and a grate manie things all but what
we could put in one Wagon   we had to divied our
propessions out to them to get them to carie them   We got
three yoak with our oxe & cow so we [went] on that way a
while and we got out of provisions and pa had to go on to
callifornia for provisions   we could not get along that way,
in 2 or 3 days after pa left we had to cash our wagon and
take Mr. graves wagon and cash some more of our
things   well we went on that way a while and then we had
to get Mr Eddies Wagon   we went on that way awhile and
then we had to cash all our our close except a change or 2
and put them in Mr Brins Wagon and Thomos & James
rode the 2 horses and the rest of us had to walk, we went

on that way a Whild and we come to a nother long drive of
40 miles and then we went with Mr Donner

We had to Walk all the time we was a travling up the
truckee river   we met that and 2 Indians that we had sent
out for propessions to Suter Fort   thay had met pa, not fur
from Suters Fort   he looked very bad   he had not ate but
3 times in 7 days and thes days with out any thing his horse
was not abel to carrie him   thay give him a horse and he
went on so we cashed some more of our things all but what
we could pack on one mule and we started Martha and
James road behind the two Indians   it was a raing then in
the Vallies and snowing on the mountains so we went on
that way 3 or 4 days tell we come to the big mountain or
the Callifornia Mountain   the snow then was about 3 feet
deep   thare was some wagons thare   thay said thay had
atempted to cross and could not, well we thought we would
try it so we started and thay started again with thare
wagons   the snow was then way to the muels side   the
farther we went up the deeper the snow got so the wagons
could not go so thay packed thare oxons and started with
us carring a child a piece and driving the oxons in snow up
to thare wast   the mule Martha and the Indian was on was
the best one so thay went and broak the road   and that
indian was the Pilot so we went on that way 2 miles and
the mules kept faling down in the snow head formost and
the Indian said he could not find the road   we stoped and
let the Indian and man go on to hunt the road   thay went
on and found the road to the top of the mountain and
come back and said they thought we could git over if it did
not snow any more   well the Woman were all so tirder
caring there Children that thay could not go over that night
so we made a fire and got something to eat & ma spred
down a bufalorobe & we all laid down on it & spred
somthing over us & ma sit up by the fire & it snowed one
foot on top of the bed so we got up in the morning & the
snow was so deep we could not go over & we had to go
back to the cabin & build more cabins & stay thare all
Winter without Pa   we had not the first thing to eat   Ma
maid arrangements for some cattel giving 2 for 1 in
callifornia   we seldom thot of bread for we had not had any
since [blot, words not readable] & the cattel was so poor

thay could note hadley git up when they laid down   we
stoped thare the 4th of November & staid till March and
what we had to eat i cant hardley tell you & we had that
man & Indians to feed   well thay started over a foot and
had to come back so thay made snow shoes and started
again & it come on a storme & thay had to come back   it
would snow 10 days before it would stop thay wated tell it
stoped & started again   I was a goeing with them & I took
sick & could not go—thare was 15 started & thare was 7
got throw 5 Weman & 2 men   it come a storme and they
lost the road & got out of provisions & the ones that got
throwe had to eat them that Died   not long after thay
started we got out of provisions & had to put Martha at
one cabin James at another   Thomas at another & Ma &
Elizea & Milt Eliot & I dried up what littel meat we had
and started to see if we could get across & had to leve the
childrin   o Mary you may think that hard to leve theme
with strangers & did not now wether we would see them
again or not   we could hardle get a way from them but we
told theme we would bring them Bread & then thay was
willing to stay   we went & was out 5 days in the
mountains   Elie giv out & had to go back   we went on a
day longer   we had to lay by a day & make snow shows &
we went on a while and coud not find the road & we had
to turn back   I could go on verry well while i thout we wer
giting along but as soone as we had to turn back i coud
hadley git along but we got to the cabins that night   I froze
one of my feet verry bad & that same night thare was the
worst storme we had that winter & if we had not come
back that night we would never got back   we had nothing
to eat but ox hides   o Mary I would cry and wish I had
what you all wasted   Eliza had to go to Mr Graves cabin &
we staid at Mr Breen   thay had meat all the time & we
had to kill littel cash the dog & eat him   we ate his head
and feet & hide & evry thing about him   o my Dear
Cousin you dont now what trubel is   yet a many a time we
had on the last thing a cooking and did not now wher the
next would come from but there was awl wais some way
provided

there was 15 in the cabon we was in and half of us had
to lay a bed all the time   thare was 10 starved to

death   there we was hadley abel to walk   we lived on little
cash a week and after Mr Breen would cook his meat we
would take the bones and boil them 3 or 4 days at a
time   ma went down to the other caben and got half a
hide carried it in snow up to her wast

it snowed and would cover the cabin all over so we
could not git out for 2 or 3 days   we would have to cut
pieces of the loges in sied to make a fire with   I coud
hardly eat the hides and had not eat anything 3 days   Pa
stated out to us with providions and then came a storme
and he could not go   he cash his provision and went back
on the other side of the bay to get compana of men and the
San Wakien got so hye he could not crose   well thay Made
up a Compana at Suters Fort and sent out   we had not ate
any thing for 3 days & we had onely a half a hide and we
was out on top of the cabin and we seen them a coming

O my Dear Cousin you dont now how glad i was, we
run and met them   one of them we knew   we had traveled
with them on the road thay staid thare 3 days to recruet a
little so we could go   thare was 20 started   all of us started
and went a piece and Martha and Thomas giv out & so the
men had to take them back   ma and Eliza James & I come
on and o Mary that was the hades thing yet to come on
and leiv them thar   did not now but what thay would
starve to Death   Martha said well ma if you never see me
again do the best you can   the men said thay could hadly
stand it   it maid them all cry but they said it was better for
all of us to go on for if we was to go back we would eat
that much more from them   thay give them a littel meat
and flore and took them back and we come on   we went
over great hye mountain as strait as stair steps in snow up
to our knees   litle James walk the hole way over all the
mountain in snow up to his waist   he said every step he
took he was a gitting nigher Pa and something to eat   the
Bears took the provision the men had cashed and we had
but very little to eat   when we had traveld 5 days travel we
met Pa with 13 men going to the cabins   o Mary you do
not nou how glad we was to see him   we had not seen him
for months   we thought we woul never see him again   he
heard we was coming and he made some seet cakes to give
us   he said he would see Martha and Thomas the next

day   he went to tow days what took us 5 days   some of
the compana was eating from them that Died but Thomas
& Martha had not ate any   Pa and the men started with
12 people   Hiram O Miller Carried Thomas and Pa caried
Martha and thay wer caught in [unreadable word] and thay
had to stop Two days   it stormed so thay could not go and
the Bears took their provision and thay weer 4 days without
anything   Pa and Hiram and all the men started one of
Donner boys   Pa a carring Martha Hiram caring Thomas
and the snow was up to thare wast and it a snowing so thay
could hadley see the way   they raped the chidlren up and
never took them out for 4 days & thay had nothing to eat
in all that time   Thomas asked for something to eat
once   those that thay brought from the cabins some of
them was not able to come and som would not
come   Thare was 3 died and the rest eat them   thay was
10 days without any thing to eat but the Dead   Pa braught
Thom and pady on to where we was   none of the men was
abel to go   there feet was froze very bad so they was a
nother Compana went and braught them all in   thay are all
in from the Mountains now but five   they was men went
out after them and was caught in a storm and had to come
back   thare is another compana gone thare was half got
through that was stoped thare sent to their relief thare was
but   families got that all of them got   we was one

    O Mary I have not wrote you half of the truble we
have had but I hav Wrote you anuf to let you now that you
dont now what truble is   but thank the Good god we have
all got throw and the onely family that did not eat human
flesh   we have left every thing but i dont cair for that   we
have got through but Dont let this letter dishaten anybody
and never take no cutofs and hury along as fast as you can.

108

"GOODBYE, DEATH VALLEY"

The wagon train left Salt Lake City in September 1849, headed for the town of Los Angeles. But the Jayhawkers split off to try a shorter route and got lost. The outcome gave Death Valley its name.

The first whites to pass through Death Valley and live to give it its sinister name were a party of gold seekers and settlers who crossed it in '49. Their disastrous story was told by Lewis Manly, a survivor, in 'Death Valley in '49,' a vivid description of wagon-train life and of suffering and death in a desolate land.

In September of 1849 a wagon train left Salt Lake City with Jefferson Hunt of the Mormon Battalion as its guide. Hunt said he would take the party over a new southern route that avoided the Salt Desert, where many travelers had come to disaster. There were in that train approximately 200 persons, 110 wagons, and 500 horses and oxen. Captain Hunt was to receive ten dollars a wagon for his services. The train rolled slowly south, ten miles a day. The immigrants had heard of a shorter way west and complained of the months this southern route would cost them, precious time lost from the gold fields. Some had read Frémont's book describing his trip from California to Salt Lake City; others had heard that Captain Joe Walker had guided a wagon train from Salt Lake City to a lake in

Nevada (that later bore his name), then down Owens Valley and through the pass that Frémont had named for Walker. When another party caught up with the first and displayed a map that vaguely indicated Walker's route, the immigrants' wrath boiled over. Near Mountain Meadows in Nevada, party after party broke off and swung to the west, the owners sure that they could find their way without a guide. Many returned to follow the tracks of the main party a few days later, when the country they had attempted to cross became impassable. Discussion of a shorter route, however, did not die. There were arguments and fights. Again the train swung west, leaving only seven wagons to follow Captain Hunt. When the west-bound wagons were halted by a narrow canyon, feeling still ran high. Two men sawed in half the wagon they owned jointly, because neither hothead would give in to the other as to the route. The party divided once more; in the end the majority turned back to rejoin Hunt and the few that had gone on with him. They overtook Hunt and reached San Bernardino after an arduous trip.

Among those who had stubbornly continued west were three groups. The Jayhawkers, thirty young men from Illinois, found a route through the mountains for their twenty wagons. A man named Brier, with his wife and their three small boys, pulled out after them; the Jayhawkers resented this addition to their party but the Briers refused to leave them. The last group, the Bennett-Arcane party, was made up of two women, four children, and thirteen men—among them Manly. After some scouting about, the three parties turned in the same direction and traveled in loose contact, sometimes camping together. Lewis Manly, who later wrote the Death Valley saga, did not have a wagon to drive, but ranged ahead each day, hunting water to camp by and a route that the wagons could travel. It was not difficult to keep ahead of a train that could travel only ten miles a day at best.

The travelers slowly worked their way through the rough mountains, and then for weeks crawled across the upland deserts, a little cloud of dust in the vast expanse. Springs were few and the fall rains did not come as early as usual; cattle feed was scarce. The way grew rougher; each time a mountain was breasted another range was seen ahead.

One day Manly, disheartened, reported that an immense plain lay ahead with no signs of water; although a snowy mountain was in sight on its far side and he could see what looked like a pass, he did not believe they would be able to reach it. There was nothing, however, they could do but keep on; the way back was too long. The Jayhawkers decided on a final burst of speed to reach the pass, sure that the rich valleys of California must lie just beyond it. But the Bennetts and Arcanes, hoping to find water along the way, decided to continue southward for a while.

For five days the Jayhawkers fought their way across the waterless plain. A fall of snow gave them respite and on the following day they reached the Amargosa River. Both stock and men drank the bitter water; the men did not know that the bitterness was caused by Epsom and Glauber's salts, though they were soon to learn it to their further distress. Weak and exhausted they reached what is now called Furnace Creek, where for the first time in many weeks they had more water than they could drink. Refreshed and strengthened, they urged their oxen down the wash, only to find—not the rich California lands they had hoped for, but the barren desolation of a narrow, salt-encrusted valley surrounded by towering ranges.

Moving more slowly than the Jayhawkers, the seven wagons of the Bennett-Arcane party went down a long, dry valley in Nevada, today named Emigrant Valley, between the Skull Mountains and the Spotted Range, and crossed the Amargosa Desert, where they picked up the Jay-hawker trail not far from Furnace Creek Wash. Manly, moving ahead down the wash, on Christmas Day found the Briers by the springs in Furnace Creek Wash. The children sat forlornly sucking bits of bacon rind, while their father, a clergyman, discoursed to them on the beauties of education. The Briers, traveling alone, had made a halt in Forty-Mile Canyon in Nevada, some twenty miles east of Beatty, had burned their broken wagons, and had loaded their possessions on their oxen. 'It was a mistake,' Mrs. Brier wrote later, 'as we were about five hundred miles from Los Angeles and had only our feet to take us there.'

From the Brier camp, Manly followed the trail of the Jayhawkers to their camp near Salt Creek. He found the formerly self-confident Jayhawk-ers badly frightened. They had decided to abandon their wagons and equipment and proceed on foot. The meat of their slaughtered oxen was drying over fires made from the wagons. (Bits of iron and burned wood were found here later.) Doty, their captain, told Manly that they intended to divide their food equally, and then it would have to be each man for himself. Young and strong, Manly was sure his best chance of surviving was to go with the Jayhawkers, but he also was sure that without his help the Bennetts and Arcanes would perish; and so he went back to them. On the way he met two of the men from his party who had decided to join the Jayhawkers. One of these Manly was to see again—dead in the Slate Range.

The Jayhawkers started up Emigrant Wash and crossed the Pana-mints, planning to go west and then south; the Briers trailed after them. Moving in small parties over the rugged mountains west of Death Valley, they had almost incredible meetings with one another. Some of the older men, unable to endure the exhaustion of hunger and thirst, died on the way, but the others, without guide or trail, stumped doggedly on till they reached Los Angeles.

After Manly had rejoined them, the wagons of the Bennett-Arcane party rolled slowly down Furnace Creek Wash, the oxen so feeble they could hardly pull the wagons down the rough grade. Ahead was the snowy mountain Manly had seen, but the immigrants could not see any pass. They tried to go south around the tall, steep mountains, but the oxen could not drag the wagons over the rough salt. So the party crossed to the west side of the Valley and forced the wagons up a long wash into a canyon of the Panamints in the hope that they could surmount them there. A cliff ended that attempt. They toiled back down to the floor of the Valley. An ox died on the way. Four men deserted to follow the Jayhawkers on foot. The pitiable little group camped in exhaustion and despair; their food was almost gone, the scanty water was bitter, and the Valley was hemmed in by steep mountain barriers. It was finally decided that Manly and John Rogers should go ahead alone to find a way out and bring back food. Bennett believed that at the longest they would be back in fifteen days. An ox was killed, so poor and thin that it took seven-eighths of its dried flesh to fill the two knapsacks. The two men started in the early morning, and those left behind waved hats and bonnets to them as they disappeared from sight.

For a few days the party rested in the Valley. Then the single men, both those with their own wagons and the drivers of the Arcane wagons, became restless. They doubted that Manly and Rogers would be so foolish as to return; they said that when the oxen were gone they would all die. Before long they too left to follow the Jayhawkers. Only two families with four little children remained here. Captain Culverwell, one of the men who left, changed his mind somewhere on the trail and started back to the Bennett camp; he was later found dead, on his back with outstretched arms, not far from the camp of those he had deserted. Not a morsel of the food he had carried was left, and the two little powder cans he had taken to hold water were dry.

The Bennetts and Arcanes, anxiously awaiting deliverance, had only a little rice and tea left with which to vary the meals of stringy ox meat. At night they dreamed of crusty loaves of fresh bread, and woke to hear their children crying in hunger. The two-year-olds, Charlie Arcane and Martha Bennett, suffered most from the restricted diet; little Martha, who had been able to climb in and out of the wagons so spryly that she reminded Manly of a quail, became sick. Lacking medicine and medical aid, her parents had no hope that she would live. But her fever finally waned, and, though pitifully thin, she did recover.

The allotted fifteen days passed after the departure of Manly and Rogers, but neither returned; though the others had little hope, Bennett firmly believed that Manly would come back if he were alive. Days dragged on. Determined to make a last attempt before they died, the members of the party prepared to leave. The wagons, they decided, must be left; the remaining oxen should be used to carry the women and children. The men tore the canvas tops from the wagons to make pack harnesses and the women sewed two hickory shirts together to form saddle-bags that would hold the two small children.

They worked slowly, with little hope, sitting in the shade of the wagons. Charlie and Martha fretted, and Melissa and George played listlessly with their few toys and with Cuff, the dog. Manly and Rogers had been gone twenty-five days when the desert stillness was broken by a crash. In the silence that closed in again after the shot, the travelers scrambled from beneath the wagons. Not far away was Manly holding a smoking gun, and Rogers leading a little black mule with a pack on its back. Bennett, Arcane, and Mrs. Bennett rushed towards the scouts to embrace them hysterically. As they walked back to the wagons, Manly said, 'they stopped two or three times, and turned as if to speak, but there was too much feeling for words; convulsive weeping would choke the voice.'

As Manly unpacked flour and beans from the mule he told them that he and Rogers had crossed more than two hundred miles of desert mountains and found a 'native Californian' ranch, thirty miles from Los Angeles. The people there had fed them and sold them some food and two horses for thirty dollars; they had bought the mule and another horse from a freight train. But the horses had not been able to endure the rough, waterless going on the way back to Death Valley; one had died, and the other two had become so weak the men had had to leave them in a canyon. The little mule, on the contrary, had trudged on, nosing out water, snatching at every bit of green.

Among other things Manly took four yellow balls from a sack and handed one to each child; these, the first oranges the children had seen, had been sent to them by the Mexican woman at the ranch.

After a few delicious meals of bread and beans, the little train started out of the Valley with Rogers leading the mule, and the oxen following; Charlie and Martha stood in the hickory shirt pockets hung across the back of Old Crump, and George and Melissa sat on his back. Each woman rode an ox. Mrs. Arcane, wearing her best dress and beribboned hat, made a brave appearance until a strap on the ox slipped and he began bucking and bawling. The other animals caught the excitement and bounced about, shaking off their packs. Someone snatched the children to safety, but Mrs. Arcane, with ribbons and skirts flying, clung desperately to her seat until the ox bucked her to the ground. When the men found that she was not hurt, they rolled on the ground, holding their sides and whooping hysterically. It had been long since any of them had laughed.

The travelers camped for the night and the next morning reloaded with care. When the party reached the top of the Panamints on the second day, it halted and the men climbed a peak to look back at the brilliantly colored mountains and the shimmering valley floor where they had spent a bitter month. Someone said, "Good-bye, Death Valley." It has borne the name ever since.

109

"FIFTEEN-HUNDRED HATS WERE LOST YEARLY"

Raphael Pumpelly

Raphael Pumpelly was a remarkably well-traveled man for the 1860s, and his Across America and Asia *is a remarkable example of nineteenth-century travel writing. His account of crossing the West in the Butterfield stage illustrates why more people stayed home.*

In the autumn of 1860 I reached the westernmost end of the railroad in Missouri, finishing the first, and, in point of time, the shortest stage in a journey, the end of which I had not even attempted to foresee. My immediate destination was the silver mines of the Santa Rita, in Arizona, of which I was to take charge, as mining engineer, for a year, under the resident superintendent.

Having secured the right to a back seat in the overland coach as far as Tucson, I looked forward, with comparatively little dread, to sixteen days and nights of continuous travel. But the arrival of a woman and her brother, dashed, at the very outset, my hopes of an easy journey, and obliged me to take the front seat, where, with my back to the horses, I began to foresee the coming discomfort. The coach was fitted with three seats, and these were occupied by nine passengers. As the occupants of the front and middle seats faced each other, it was necessary for these six people to interlock their knees; and there being room inside for only ten

391

of the twelve legs, each side of the coach was graced by a foot, now dangling near the wheel, now trying in vain to find a place of support. An unusually heavy mail in the boot, by weighing down the rear, kept those of us who were on the front seat constantly bent forward, thus, by taking away all support from our backs, rendering rest at all times out of the question. . . .

Before reaching Fort Smith every male passenger in the stage had lost his hat, and most of the time allowed for breakfast at that town was used in getting new head-coverings. It turned out to be a useless expense, however, for in less than two days we were all again bareheaded. As this happens to the passengers of every stage, we estimated that not less than fifteen hundred hats were lost yearly by travellers, for the benefit of the population along the road. . . .

Here we were constantly exposed to the raids of this fierce tribe, which has steadily refused to be tamed by the usual process of treaties and presents. They were committing serious depredations along the route, and had murdered the keepers at several stations. We consequently approached the stockade station-houses with considerable anxiety, not knowing whether we should find either keepers or horses. Over this part of the road no lights were used at night, and we were thus exposed to the additional danger of having our necks broken by being upset.

The fatigue of uninterrupted travelling by day and night in a crowded coach, and in the most uncomfortable positions, was beginning to tell seriously upon all the passengers, and was producing a condition bordering on insanity. This was increased by the constant anxiety caused by the danger from Camanches. Every jolt of the stage, indeed any occurrence which started a passenger out of the state of drowsiness, was instantly magnified into an attack, and the nearest fellow-passenger was as likely to be taken for an Indian as for a friend. In some persons, this temporary mania developed itself to such a degree that their own safety and that of their fellow-travellers made it necessary to leave them at the nearest station, where sleep usually restored them before the arrival of the next stage on the following week. Instances have occurred of travellers jumping in this condition from the coach, and wandering off to a death from starvation upon the desert. . . .

Over the hard surface of this country, which is everywhere a natural road, we frequently travelled at great speed, with only half-broken teams. At several stations, six wild horses were hitched blind-folded into their places. When everything was ready, the blinds were removed at a signal from the driver, and the animals started off at a run-away speed, which they kept up without slackening till the next station, generally twelve miles distant. In these cases the driver had no further control over his animals than the ability to guide them; to stop, or even check them, was entirely beyond his power; the frightened horses fairly flying over the ground, and never stopping till they drew up exhausted at the next station. Nothing but the most perfect presence of mind on the part of the driver could prevent accidents. Even this was not always enough, as was proved by a stage which we met, in which every passenger had either a bandaged head or an arm in a sling.

At El Paso we had hoped to find a larger stage. Being disappointed in this, I took a place outside, between the driver and conductor. The impossibility of sleeping had made me half delirious, and we had gone but a few miles before I nearly unseated the driver by starting suddenly out of a dream.

I was told that the safety of all the passengers demanded that I should keep awake; and as the only means of effecting this, my neighbors beat a constant tatoo with their elbows upon my ribs. During the journey from the Rio Grande to Tucson my delirium increased, and the only thing I have ever remembered of that part of the route was the sight of a large number of Indian campfires at Apache pass. My first recollection after this, is of being awakened by the report of a pistol, and of starting up to find myself in a crowded room, where a score or more of people were quarrelling at a gaming table. I had reached Tucson, and had thrown myself on the floor of the first room I could enter. A sound sleep of twelve hours had fully restored me, both in mind and body.

110

THE GREAT
WAGON-TRAIN
SWINDLE

William Miles

Captain Parker H. French may well have been the original "black-hearted scoundrel." William Miles ran afoul of this early travel agent when he joined a California-bound wagon train French was organizing. French shipped his tourists to Texas, got off with their money, left them deeply in debt, sold off the mules that pulled their wagons, and then tried to rob them when they bought more mules. This excerpt of Miles's memoirs does not include the happy ending: later French and his bandidos attacked the wagon train, French was killed, and the tourists got to California—one of the few groups to safely cross the Southern route.

September 1 [1851]—General dissatisfaction in camp; no water, crackers nor bacon. Horrible feelings! not knowing how or where to obtain water! At length came to the dry bed of a small stream and by digging obtained some; miserable indeed, but quenches thirst. 2d—Pass a marble mountain; stop on the way; while here Capt. French challenged Duran, the wagon master, to fight a duel, but he did not accept. 4th—Express comes back from ahead and reports 900 Indians in ambush! This news created quite a consternation; every gun and pistol was examined and loaded ready for defence. We pushed forward and arrived at our camp ground pleased with the disappointment, the enemy having fled. 5th—Friendly Indians came into camp to trade; twelve of them, a few squaws. The captain gives them liquor and exchanges dry goods for a horse; some of the passengers trade clothes for deer skins. 6th—The captain orders all off early in the morning with the train, to get rid of us, expecting a party of Indians to come into camp, at the usual time of starting, to monopolize the trading; but none came after we left, so that he was compelled to drive up, having gained nothing by this well-contrived operation. His disappointment created a great deal of laughter. Reached the Rio Grande river and marched up along its banks until we arrive at El Paso, after having already been on our way from 13th of May until 18th of September; mules very much emaciated, wagons broken and not safe to carry us farther. Believing that we could not get to the place of our destination this winter with such a broken down and worn out train, and now hearing, at this point, that Captain French had committed heavy forgeries, on Sunday, Sept. 22, the train crossed the Rio Grande into Mexico and encamped near the town. On the 19th inst. Mr. Boyd, assistant commissary, came from town to camp and related the following thrilling intelligence: That an express had arrived from San Antonio with the news that Howland & Aspinwall's credit had been used by Parker H. French without any authority or their signatures! French, according to this report, had contracted debts to a large amount on the way hither, for mules and supplies, presenting always a letter of credit unlimited in amount, but limited in time to six months. No such man as French was known to the firm, which was soon confirmed; first, by an order sent for McGaffin's mules, to save them from execution; and afterwards, by the sheriff making a levy for satisfaction on the protested draft and bill of sale. Now all comes to light; from us this infamous transaction was kept hid until our arrival at El Paso. It appears, from reliable information, that when we passed through San Antonio, Texas, 600 miles from this place, French gave a Mr. Fisk a bill of sale of the whole train, and here, at this station, obtained a warrant to arrest French, and went in pursuit to El Paso. He was driven over the Rio Grande into El Paso, or rather pursued here, and kept a body guard to save him from arrest. Here again came the "tug of war!" This sad news spread like an electric shock; we stood amazed, dumb! As the whole train was under the supervision of Mr. North West, French's first officer, and French being unwell at town, I, in company with others, called on this West, and proposed to give the property into the hands of the passengers and hold it for French; but this was refused, he considering French in no such difficulty, when he had already received information of the forgery from an assistant officer, Mr. Boyd. What was to be done at this crisis? His credit was gone at the very point where he was to lay in a whole winter's provision, as well as a large number of mules and wagons! In order that 230 men (passengers and hired men) might be furnished with the means to get to California, 1,000 miles distant, in general meeting assembled Hugh C. McGuire, Esq., of Illinois, was duly elected sheriff, and three assistants, Joseph Fertner, William Hazeltine and Mr. Johnson, to make a levy on all the property belonging to the train, in behalf of the passengers, whereby their respective claims might be paid.

A general call was now made for all hands to help to *carrel* the mules and guard the cattle; all was formally taken possession of by the company. A note is sent by Captain French for us to let Mr. McGuffin have his mules, that he (French) had just purchased in connection with 28 wagons, numbering in all over one hundred. Now that the old stock of French's had been reduced to skeletons by hard driving we conceived that self-protection required us to hold on to McGuffin's purchase. The bearer of the note returned to French, who was in El Paso, with the refusal; then another note was sent, demanding all the mules and cattle, without reserve, and another refusal returned by the company. And now that French had no flour with us for our support, and his credit was gone, we concluded as soon as possible to dispose of all the property, reserving the mules for transportation or distribution. Accordingly, on Saturday, September 21, the whole was again put in motion, back to El Paso, from the camping ground, on the Rio Grande. Not yet having disposed of anything, all was confusion. Fathers now five months from home, some 5,000 miles, out of means to carry them on or to return home, many having put into the hands of French $250 passage money, and some of them having also loaned him hundreds of dollars, expecting, as he told them, that at El Paso he would refund it. Not only passengers, but still poorer men, who had by hard labor saved $100, put that, each of them, about fifty men, into his hands, as a pledge that they would stay and labor six months. What was to be done in this extremity, His pledges had all been broken. The time to carry us to San Francisco was sixty days. Seeing now as their only hope to get to California, to divide all the property useful to them, sell the balance to purchase provisions and proceed.

A committee was elected to effect sales day after day; some goods were sold to the Sheriff of El Paso, three wagons to the Mexican Consul and so on, until when all was summed up, only 20 per cent. could be realized. The claims were from $100 to $700. Thus, the reader can judge of our destitute and helpless condition. All over, parties consisting of various numbers started; first procuring a mule to carry baggage and scant provisions; others more careful of their money were able to purchase two mules, one for riding, at rates from $15 to $50 each. When arrangements had been made by French, for hands to go with him ahead of our train of pack mules through Mexico to California, and when 70 miles on his way commenced the work of a *Guerilla*. Not being satisfied with the time and money of all, he commenced robbing with his band of desparadoes, of guns, mules and money. First he and his party intimidated with harsh words, and then Colt's revolvers are buckled on, ready to assassinate any who would show resistance. Here is an evidence of his barbarity and lawlessness. He found one who had been a guide, useful in helping us onward to our destination; from him he took his blankets, and sold his clothes to his assistant pirates at public auction.

111

HORACE GREELEY'S WILD RIDE

Artemus Ward

The West has always had an inferiority complex concerning the effete East, which complex is soothed by putting down Easterners. Here's an account by noted nineteenth-century humorist Artemus Ward of how Horace Greeley, editor of the New York Tribune, fared on a California trip from Folsom to Placerville.

When Mr. Greeley was in California ovations awaited him at every town. He had written powerful leaders in the *Tribune* in favor of the Pacific Railroad, which had greatly endeared him to the citizens of the Golden State. And therefore they made much of him when he went to see them.

At one town the enthusiastic populace tore his celebrated white coat to pieces, and carried the pieces home to remember him by.

The citizens of Placerville prepared to fête the great journalist, and an extra coach, with extra relays of horses, was chartered of the California Stage Company to carry him from Folsom to Placerville—distance, forty miles. The extra was in some way delayed, and did not leave Folsom until late in the afternoon. Mr. Greeley was to be fêted at 7 o'clock that evening by the citizens of Placerville, and it was altogether necessary that he should be there by that hour. So the Stage Company said to Henry Monk, the driver of the extra, "Henry, this great man must be there by 7 to-night."

And Henry answered, "The great man shall be there."

The roads were in an awful state, and during the first few miles out of Folsom slow progress was made.

"Sir," said Mr. Greeley, "are you aware that I *must* be at Placerville at 7 o'clock to-night?"

"I've got my orders!" laconically returned Henry Monk.

Still the coach dragged slowly forward.

"Sir," said Mr. Greeley, "this is not a trifling matter. I *must* be there at 7!"

Again came the answer, "I've got my orders!"

But the speed was not increased, and Mr. Greeley chafed away another half hour; when, as he was again about to remonstrate with the driver, the horses suddenly started into a furious run, and all sorts of encouraging yells filled the air from the throat of Henry Monk.

"That is right, my good fellow!" cried Mr. Greeley. "I'll give you ten dollars when we get to Placerville. Now we *are* going!"

They were indeed, and at a terrible speed.

Crack, crack! went the whip, and again "that voice" split the air. "Git up! Hi yi! G'long! Yip—yip!"

And on they tore, over stones and ruts, up hill and down, at a rate of speed never before achieved by stage horses.

Mr. Greeley, who had been bouncing from one end of the coach to the other like an india-rubber ball, managed to get his head out of the window, when he said:

"Do—on't—on't—on't you—u—u think we—e—e—e shall get there by seven if we do—on't—on't go so fast?"

"I've got my orders!" That was all Henry Monk said. And on tore the coach.

It was becoming serious. Already the journalist was extremely sore from the terrible jolting, and again his head "might have been seen" at the window.

"Sir," he said, "I don't care—care—*air*, if we *don't* get there at seven!"

"I have got my orders!" Fresh horses. Forward again, faster than before. Over rocks and stumps, on one of which the coach narrowly escaped turning a summerset.

"See here!" shrieked Mr. Greeley, "I don't care if we don't get there at all!"

"I've got my orders! I work for the Californy Stage Company, I do. That's wot I *work* for. They said, 'git this man through by seving.' An' this man's goin' through. You bet! Gerlong! Whoo-ep!"

Another frightful jolt, and Mr. Greeley's bald head suddenly found its way through the roof of the coach, amidst the crash of small timbers and the ripping of strong canvas.

"Stop, you————maniac!" he roared.

Again answered Henry Monk:

"I've got my orders! *Keep your seat, Horace!*"

At Mud Springs, a village a few miles from Placerville, they met a large delegation of the citizens of Placerville, who had come out to meet the celebrated editor, and escort him into town. There was a military company, a brass band, and a six-horse wagon-load of beautiful damsels in milk-white dresses, representing all the States in the Union. It was nearly dark now, but the delegation were amply provided with torches, and bonfires blazed all along the road to Placerville.

The citizens met the coach in the outskirts of Mud Springs, and Mr. Monk reined in his foam-covered steeds.

"Is Mr. Greeley on board?" asked the chairman of the committee.

"*He was, a few miles back!*" said Mr. Monk; "yes," he added, after looking down through the hole which the fearful jolting had made in the coachroof—"yes, I can see him! He is there!"

"Mr. Greeley," said the Chairman of the Committee, presenting himself at the window of the coach, "Mr. Greeley, sir! We are come to most cordially welcome you, sir————why, God bless me, sir, you are bleeding at the nose!"

"I've got my orders!" cried Mr. Monk. "My orders is as follers: Git him there by seving! It wants a quarter to seving. Stand out of the way!"

"But, sir," exclaimed the Committee-man, seizing the off leader by the reins—"Mr. Monk, we are come to escort him into town! Look at the procession, sir, and the brass band, and the people, and the young women, sir!"

"*I've got my orders!*" screamed Mr. Monk. "My orders don't say nothin' about no brass bands and young women. My orders says, 'git him there by seving!' Let go them lines! Clear the way there! Whoo-ep! KEEP YOUR SEAT, HORACE!" and the coach dashed wildly through the procession, upsetting a portion of the brass band, and violently grazing the wagon which contained the beautiful young women in white.

Years hence grey-haired men, who were little boys in this procession, will tell their grandchildren how this stage tore through Mud Springs, and how Horace Greeley's bald head ever and anon showed itself, like a wild apparition, above the coach-roof.

Mr. Monk was on time. There is a tradition that Mr. Greeley was very indignant for awhile; then he laughed, and finally presented Mr. Monk with a bran-new suit of clothes.

112

WHAT THE TRAVEL AGENT DOESN'T TELL YOU

H. M. Chittenden

In 1877 George Cowan took a party of tourists to visit the Yellowstone country.
It wasn't a good idea. He was captured by Indians, robbed, shot in a leg, climbed
a tree, was shot in the back, crawled away to escape, and was caught in a forest
fire. When he was finally rescued, the wagon wrecked; and when he finally
reached safety, his sickbed collapsed under the weight of friends sitting on it. The
author of this selection, General H. M. Chittenden, was the first important
historian of Yellowstone country.

Going back to the morning of August 24th [1877], when Chief Joseph and
his people arrived at the Lower Geyser Basin, we will record the experiences of the two parties of tourists. . . . The party from Radersburg, Mont.,
was composed of the following persons: George F. Cowan and wife, Frank
and Ida Carpenter, brother and sister of Mrs. Cowan, Charles Mann,
William Dingee, Albert Oldham, A. J. Arnold, and a Mr. Meyers. . . . The
party was to start home this morning and Arnold and Dingee had arisen
before sunrise to make a fire and prepare breakfast. Soon after, Mrs. Cowan
aroused her husband and told him there were Indians outside. . . .

By this time the Indians had collected in large numbers and Cowan
became thoroughly alarmed. He ordered the teams hitched up and camp
to be broken at once. Everything was soon ready. There was a double-
seated covered spring wagon, and a half spring baggage wagon. Such of

the party as could not find seats in the wagons rode saddle horses. Cowan ordered the drivers to pull out, and he himself mounted his horse and rode alongside the wagon in which his wife was seated. The two women were crying, for the situation seemed to them hopeless. The start was made and the little stream crossed, when the wagons came to an abrupt stop. Directly in front, completely blocking the way, was a line of mounted warriors, like a platoon of cavalry, with guns against the thigh as if ready for action. . . .

Here, then, was a situation. Cowan was "up against" Chief Joseph himself, and Looking Glass and the whole Nez Percé army. Joseph was painted in vermilion, but Looking Glass not. Joseph was the better looking man of the two. Cowan did not hesitate, but carried his petition promptly and unfalteringly to the throne itself. Joseph looked him straight in the eye, but never deigned a word. Charley then came up and said to Cowan: "Look here, now; we're going to take your party right along." Cowan protested, but Charley made no reply except to order the party to move on.

Forced to accompany the army of Chief Joseph, the hapless party felt that their hopes of escape were slender and that they would all be massacred at the first favorable opportunity. They were wretchedly armed and could offer no effective resistance. They moved on up the valley of Nez Percé Creek, and when about a mile and a half above the present bridge were stopped by the timber. Charley ordered the wagons abandoned, and the passengers to mount the horses. The provisions were all confiscated and the spokes cut out of the wheels of the spring wagon. Charley rushed matters and in a little while the party were again on their way.

Nothing of importance transpired on the march up Nez Percé Creek, and the noon camp of the Indians was reached in a beautiful spot in the edge of the timber at the foot of Mary Mountain. Here the party were ordered to dismount. Off a little to one side were the squaws preparing something to eat. The chiefs and some other principal men were seated in a half circle in a lovely little grass-covered opening among the trees and it was evident that a council was to be held to decide the fate of the whites. In fact, the council commenced at once, an Indian by the name of Poker Joe acting as spokesman for the chiefs, who could not speak English. Cowan answered for his party.

Poker Joe opened up by asking several questions about where the tourists were from, the purpose of their visit, and where they desired to go. . . . The chiefs had decided to take the horses and firearms of the party, and give them broken down horses and let them go home. This was their only salvation; otherwise all would be killed.

To this deliberate ultimatum there was evidently only one reply—

acceptance. Resistance was out of the question. The proposition of the chiefs gave at least a hope, slender though it was, and after consultation with his people, Cowan gave his consent.

The council at once broke up and the Indians made a rush for the confiscated outfit. . . . The whole camp then moved up the trail. Poker Joe told the captives that they were free and directed them to take the back trail. They started back entirely alone. To this time they had not suffered the slightest indignity from the Indians.

After retreating some three-quarters of a mile, a force of about seventy-five Indians came galloping back uttering warwhoops, and evidently bent upon mischief. They ordered the little party to stop, and Charley (who again appears on the scene) asked, in apparent anger, what had become of two of the men who had discreetly taken to the brush. Cowan replied that he did not know before that they were gone. After a little delay the party were countermarched and taken back up the trail. It was evident that their situation was now desperate. An occasional stop was made to give the Indians time for consultation. The party proceeded back past the council ground and perhaps three-quarters of a mile beyond, when two Indians were sent on in great haste, with the probable purpose of finding out if the chiefs were at a safe distance ahead. A few minutes later, as the party were passing over a little knoll, these two Indians came riding back at full speed. Seeing the party they stopped, and one of the Indians fired at Mr. Cowan, striking him in the right thigh. The firing then became general and most of the whites scattered into the woods. Carpenter and his two sisters were taken prisoners. Carpenter's life was saved by an involuntary act which has won for him the undeserved credit of showing great presence of mind. An Indian leveled his gun at him, when Carpenter, believing that his time had come, made a sign of the cross. The religious nature of the Indian instantly responded to the familiar movement, and he dropped his gun and told Carpenter that he would save him.

When Cowan was shot he slid from his horse, but his leg was paralyzed and he fell upon the steep side hill and rolled down against a log. Mrs. Cowan instantly leaped from her horse, ran to her husband's side, enveloped his head in her arms, and tried to baffle the efforts of the Indians to kill him. The Indians endeavored to pull her away, but she resisted strenuously, begging them to kill her instead. Cowan himself held fast to her, preferring that she be killed there with him than be left to the mercy of the savages. Charley then came up, asked where Cowan's wound was, and seeing that it was not fatal, made a desperate effort to get a shot at his head, but Mrs. Cowan was too alert for him. Finally, Charley drew Mrs. Cowan back and another Indian held a pistol almost in Cowan's eyes and fired. Mrs. Cowan was pulled away, and with her brother and sister was taken along with the Indians. Some stones were thrown upon Cowan's head, and he was then left for dead.

Singularly enough, neither the bullet wounds nor the blows from the stones had been fatal to Mr. Cowan and he presently recovered consciousness. The attack had taken place about 2:30 P.M., and when he opened his eyes the sun was just dropping below the western hills. He recalled what had happened, examined himself, made up his mind that there was hope yet, and concluded to save himself if he could. He drew himself up by the branch of a tree, when, lo! a little way off, he saw a mounted Indian in the act of drawing his rifle to fire at him. Cowan tried to get away, but the Indian dismounted and fired and struck him in the back. He fell to the ground and momentarily expected the Indian to come up and dispatch him, but for some reason he did not come.

After waiting awhile, and seeing no other Indians, Mr. Cowan commenced a pilgrimage on his knees which continued for several days and probably has no parallel in history. He was wholly without food, with three bullet wounds and dangerous bruises on his person, and in a neighborhood that was still thronging with hostile Indians. He crawled along on the back trail in a bright moonlight until about midnight, when he thought he saw something. Stopping and looking closely, he saw an Indian rise up from his sleep, look around, and then lie down again. Cowan retreated as noiselessly as possible, made a wide detour, and resumed his course. He next passed a bunch of broken down Nez Percé horses, which had been abandoned. He would have caught one, but there was no bridle and it was doubtful if he could have ridden. It was not until noon of the following day that he reached a creek crossing and found plenty of water.

At snail pace Cowan kept on day after day. One morning, about nine o'clock, he heard Indians again. Lying low behind a tree he watched and listened, and presently saw a body of about seventy-five Indians passing up the valley. He thought he saw a white man among them, but was not certain. It was, in fact, a company of friendly Bannock scouts on the trail of the Nez Percés, under the command of an army officer. But Cowan did not know and it would not do to run any risk.

The day after this event he reached the abandoned wagons. There was nothing to be found there in the shape of food, but he did find a bird dog that belonged to the party. The dog had probably been there ever since the wagons were abandoned. At the first sight of Cowan she rushed at him fiercely, but suddenly recognizing him, her fury changed and she pawed and caressed him in a paroxysm of joy.

Cowan next made his painful way to the old camp, where he found about a dozen matches and a little coffee scattered on the ground. With an old fruit can he succeeded, after much difficulty, in making some coffee—the first thing he had had in the way of nourishment since he was shot. Remaining there over night, he started for the valley of Nez Percé Creek, because he would there be more in the route of any force that might be following the Indians. When nearing a point which he had selected for his permanent bivouac, he discovered two horsemen on the edge of some timber and presently distinguished that they were white men. He signaled and they approached, inquiring in much astonishment, "Who in h—l are you?" Cowan gave them his name and they replied that they had expected to bury him that day. They had met Oldham and Meyers, who had told them that Cowan was dead. The two men were scouts from Howard's command. They fixed Cowan up as well as they could, built him a large fire, left him food to last till Howard should come, and then went on their way.

Cowan dropped asleep, but soon fell into another peril which came near proving fatal. The ground on which he was lying was full of vegetable mold, very dry at that season of the year, and the fire burrowed through it with facility. Cowan was awakened by the heat and found himself completely surrounded by fire. With great difficulty and severe burns, he extricated himself from this new danger.

Howard and his command came along on the afternoon of August 30th, and went into camp half a mile above the present bridge over Nez Percé Creek. He named this camp "Camp Cowan." He brought news of the safety of Mrs. Cowan and her sister and brother. Cowan was given surgical attendance, and when camp moved was carried in one of the wagons. He accompanied General Howard's command as far as to Mud Geyser, and was then intrusted to the wagon train in charge of Captain Spurgin.

While descending the valley of Carnelian Creek Mr. Cowan experienced an unnecessary fright and passed an anxious half hour. There was an alarm of Indians and suddenly he found himself and his ambulance entirely deserted. Quite ungenerously, but with some show of reason, his first thought was that his escort had sought their individual safety at the risk of his own. As a matter of fact they had gone to meet the supposed enemy, who turned out to be friendly scouts under Lieutenant Doane, the explorer of 1870.

After many delays and great suffering, Cowan reached Bottler's ranch about twenty-five miles north of the Park, a noted stopping place in those days. Here the military left him to await the arrival of friends. Mrs. Cowan in the meanwhile had returned home. She remained there but one day, when she went to her father's house some twenty miles distant and there received news of Mr. Cowan's safety. She at once went to Helena to learn by telegraph where he was, and then by stage to Bozeman, where she procured a suitable conveyance and started for Bottler's ranch. The day after her arrival they set out on the return journey to Bozeman, Mr. Cowan lying on a bed in the bottom of the wagon. The route lay across the Trail Creek divide between the Yellowstone and Gallatin Rivers. When near the top of his divide, and going down a steep hill, the neckyoke broke, the team ran, and the wagon was overturned down the mountain side. Only the generous supply of bedding on which Mr. Cowan was lying saved him from serious injury. By good luck a man on horseback happened along just then. Arnold impressed the horse, made a forced ride to Fort Ellis, secured an ambulance, and the journey was thus completed to Bozeman. Cowan was taken at once to a hotel, where he remained until well enough to return home.

The fatality which seemed to pursue Mr. Cowan did not yet desert him, but now began to assume a ludicrous phase. As soon as his presence at the hotel became known, friends and others rushed in to see him and tender their congratulations. They gathered around his bed and so many sat down upon it that it gave away and fell in a wreck on the floor. The proprietor jokingly threatened to expel the wounded man, as he could not afford to have such a Jonah on the premises.

113

COLD FEET

Some stagecoaches offered a "lady's footwarmer" but none had heaters. The following account describes how to treat frozen feet with whiskey and melted snow.

The first winter I was in Georgia Gulch I got my feet frozen. I had gone down to the store to buy some supplies which I made into a pack and carried on my back.

The temperature kept falling and long before I got back home, or to the litle log shack we called home, it had reached 40 degrees below. The trail was well traveled and the snow packed hard and I made good time.

When I was about four miles from our cabin I had to cross the creek on the ice. The ice broke under the combined weight of myself and the pack, and before I could get out I got wet to my knees. I yanked off my boots and poured the water out of them and put them on again, but my trousers were wet and in a few minutes were frozen stiff. I picked up my pack and hurried along as fast as I could, but in a very short time my legs were frozen so that there was no feeling in them. Long before the cabin was reached my feet and legs felt like sticks of wood.

Hank Carmen and Calenses Hawkins were watching for me and came to meet me and when I told them of my mishap they took me in hand at once. They got me into the cabin and got my boots off by ripping the outside seam of the boots clear down to the soles.

We had a tub that had been made by sawing a whiskey barrel in two and this tub they filled with snow and set it down by the fireplace for the snow to melt. Then they poured in one or two buckets of water to start the snow melting.

They made me sit on the edge of the tub with my feet and legs in this melting snow. We had a barrel of whiskey in the cabin and from this they filled a pint cup and gave me to drink. My legs were frozen solid like cakes of ice. When the melting snow began to draw the frost out of my legs and the feeling began to come back again the pain was so great that I could hardly stand it. If the two had not stood over me and held me I would have taken my feet out of the snow, but they wouldn't let me.

They built up a roaring big fire. It was very hot in the cabin. I drank another tin cup of whiskey and the sweat rolled off me.

I could not keep from yelling with pain. The frost as it was drawn out formed a film of ice around my legs as thick as a pane of glass. As the snow melted the boys brought in more snow and heaped it around my knees until at last the tub was full of ice cold water and they said the cure was over. But the cure nearly killed me.

But the treatment saved me from losing my feet. It would probably have been necessary to amputate my legs above the knees. After that I suffered no inconvenience. My feet were always easily frosted and would itch and now in my 80th year I think I can still feel the effects of those frost bites.

114

A REVOLVER IS
AN ADMIRABLE
TOOL...

Sir Richard Burton

Sir Richard Burton, perhaps the most famous travel writer of all time, rode the stagecoach from St. Joseph, Missouri, to San Francisco in 1860, and left some tips on the best way to do it.

Unaccustomed, of late years at least, to deal with tales of twice-told travel, I cannot but feel, especially when, as in the present case, so much detail has been expended upon the trivialities of a Diary, the want of that freshness and originality which would have helped the reader over a little lengthiness. My best excuse is the following extract from the Lexicographer's "Journey to the Western Islands," made in company with Mr. Boswell during the year of grace 1773, and upheld even at that late hour as somewhat a feat in the locomotive line.

"These diminutive observations seem to take away something from the dignity of writing, and therefore are never communicated but with hesitation and a little fear of abasement and contempt. But it must be remembered that life consists not of a series of illustrious actions or elegant enjoyments; the greater part of our time passes in compliance with necessities, in the performance of daily duties, in the removal of small inconveniences, in the procurement of petty pleasures, and we are well or ill at ease, as the main stream of life glides on smoothly or is ruffled by small obstacles and frequent interruptions."

True! and as the novelist claims his right to elaborate, in the "domestic epic," the most trivial scenes of household routine, so the traveller may be allowed to enlarge, when copying nature in his humbler way, upon the subject of his little drama, and, not confining himself to the Great, the Good, and the Beautiful, nor suffering himself to be wholly engrossed by the claims of Cotton, Civilisation, and Christianity, Useful Knowledge and Missionary enterprise, to *desipere in loco* by expatiating upon his bed, his meat, and his drink. . . .

We hurried therefore to pay for our tickets—$175 each being the moderate sum—to reduce our luggage to its minimum approach towards 25lbs. The price of transport for excess being exorbitantly fixed at $1 per lb., and to lay in a few necessaries for the way, tea and sugar, tobacco and cognac. I will not take liberties with my company's "kit"; my own, however, was represented as follows:

One indian-rubber blanket pierced in the centre for a poncho, and garnished along the longer side with buttons, and corresponding elastic loops with a strap at the short end, converting it into a carpet-bag,—a "sine quâ non" from the Equator to the Pole. A buffalo-robe ought to have been added as a bed: ignorance however prevented, and borrowing did the rest. With one's coat as a pillow, a robe, and a blanket, one may defy the dangerous "bunks" of the stations.

For weapons I carried two revolvers: from the moment of leaving St. Jo. to the time of reaching Placerville or Sacramento the pistol should never be absent from a man's right side—remember it is handier there than on the other—nor the bowie knife from his left. Contingencies with Indians and others may happen, when the difference of a second saves life: the revolver should therefore be carried with its butt to the fore, and when drawn it should not be levelled as in target practice, but directed towards the object, by means of the right fore-finger laid flat along the cylinder whilst the medius draws the trigger. The instinctive consent between eye and hand, combined with a little practice, will soon enable the beginner to shoot correctly from the hip; all he has to do, is to think that he is pointing at the mark, and pull. As a precaution, especially when mounted upon a kicking horse, it is wise to place the cock upon a capless nipple, rather than trust to the intermediate pins. In dangerous places the revolver should be discharged and reloaded every morning, both for the purpose of keeping the hand in, and to do the weapon justice. A revolver is an admirable tool when properly used; those, however, who are too idle or careless to attend to it, had better carry a pair of "Derringers." For the benefit of buffalo and antelope, I had invested $25 at St. Louis, in a "shooting iron" of the "Hawkins" style,—that enterprising individual now dwells in Denver City,—it was a long top-heavy rifle, it weighed 12lbs., and it carried the smallest ball—75 to the pound—a combina . . . A Stanhope lens, a railway whistle, and instead of the binocular, useful for things of earth, a very valueless telescope—(warranted by the maker to show Jupiter's satellites, and by utterly declining so to do, reading a lesson touching the non-advisability of believing an instrument maker)—completed the outfit.

The prairie traveller is not particular about toilette: the easiest dress is a dark flannel shirt, worn over the normal article; no braces,—I say it, despite Mr. Galton,—but broad leather belt for "six-shooter" and for "Arkansas tooth-pick," a long clasp-knife, or for the rapier of the Western world, called after the hero who perished in the "red butchery of the Alamo." The nether garments should be forked with good buckskin, or they will infallibly give out, and the lower end should be tucked into the boots, after the sensible fashion of our grandfathers, before those ridiculous Wellingtons were dreamed of by our sires. In warm weather, a pair of moccasins will be found easy as slippers, but they are bad for wet places, they make the feet tender, they strain the back sinews and they form the first symptom of the savage mania. Socks keep the feet cold; there are however those who should take six pair. The use of the pocket-handkerchief is unknown in the plains, some people however, are uncomfortable without it; not liking "se emungere" after the fashion of Horace's father.

In cold weather—and rarely are the nights warm—there is nothing better than the old English tweed shooting-jacket made with pockets like a poacher's, and its similar waistcoat, a "stomach warmer" without a roll collar, which prevents comfortable sleep, and with flaps as in the Year of Grace 1760 when men were too wise to wear our senseless vests, whose only property seems to be that of disclosing after exertions a lucid interval of linen or longcloth. For driving and riding, a large pair of buckskin gloves, or rather gauntlets, without which even the teamster will not travel, and leggings—the best are made in the country, only the straps should be passed through and sewn on to the leathers—are advisable, if at least the man at all regards his epidermis: it is almost unnecessary to bid you remember spurs, but it may be useful to warn you that they will, like riches, make to themselves wings. The head covering by excellence is a brown felt, which, by a little ingenuity, boring, for instance, holes round the brim to admit a ribbon, you may convert into a riding hat or night cap, and wear alternately after the manly slouch of Cromwell and his Martyr, the funny three-cornered spittoon-like "shovel" of the Dutch Georges, and the ignoble cocked-hat, which completes the hideous metamorphosis.

And above all things, as you value your nationality—this is written for the benefit of the home reader—let no false shame cause you to forget your hat-box and your umbrella. I purpose, when a moment of inspiration waits upon leisure and a mind at ease, to invent an elongated portmanteau, which shall be perfection,—portable—solid leather of two colours, for easy distinguishment,—snap-lock—in length about three feet, in fact long enough to contain without creasing, "small clothes," a lateral compartment destined for a hat, and a longitudinal space where the umbrella can repose: its depth—but I must reserve that part of the secret until this benefit to British humanity shall have been duly made by Messrs. Bengough Brothers and patented by myself. . . .

Precisely at 8 A.M. appeared in front of the Patee House—the Fifth Avenue Hotel of St. Jo.—the vehicle destined to be our home for the next three weeks. We scrutinised it curiously.

The mail is carried by a "Concord coach," a spring wagon, comparing advantageously with the horrible vans which once dislocated the joints of men on the Suez route. The body is shaped somewhat like an English tax-cart considerably magnified. It is built to combine safety, strength, and lightness, without the slightest regard to appearances. The material is well-seasoned white oak—the western regions and especially Utah, are notoriously deficient in hard woods—and the manufacturers are the well-known coachwrights, Messrs. Abbott of Concord, N. Hampshire; the colour is sometimes green, more usually red, causing the antelopes to stand and stretch their large eyes whenever the vehicle comes in sight. The wheels are five to six feet apart, affording security against capsising, with little "gather" and less "dish;" the larger have fourteen spokes and seven felloes; the smaller twelve and six. The tyres are of unusual thickness, and polished like steel by the hard dry ground, and the hubs or naves and the metal nave-bands are in massive proportions. The latter not unfrequently fall off as the wood shrinks, unless the wheel is allowed to stand in water; attention must be paid to resetting them, or in the frequent and heavy "sidlins" the spokes may snap off all round like pipe stems. The wagon bed is supported by iron bands or perpendiculars abutting upon wooden rockers, which rest on strong leather thoroughbraces: these are found to break the jolt better than the best steel springs, which moreover, when injured, cannot readily be repaired. The whole bed is covered with stout osnaburg supported by stiff bars of white oak; there is a sun-shade or hood in front, where the driver sits, a curtain behind which can be raised or lowered at discretion, and four flaps on each side either folded up or fastened down with hooks and eyes. In heavy frost the passengers must be half dead with cold, but they care little for that if they can go fast. The accommodations are as follows:—In front sits the driver with usually a conductor or passenger by his side; a variety of packages, large and small, is stowed away under his leather cushion; when the break must be put on, an operation often involving the safety of the vehicle, his right foot is planted upon an iron bar which presses by a leverage upon the rear wheels,—and in hot weather a bucket for watering the animals hangs over one of the lamps, whose companion is usually found wanting. The inside has either two or three benches fronting to the fore or placed *vis-à-vis;* they are moveable and reversible, with leather cushions and hinged padded backs; unstrapped and turned down they convert the vehicle into a tolerable bed for two persons or two and a half. According to Cocker, the mail bags should be safely stowed away under these seats, or if there be not room enough, the passengers should perch themselves upon the correspondence; the jolly driver, however, is usually induced to cram the light literature between the wagon bed and the platform, or running gear beneath, and thus when ford-waters wash the hubs, the letters are pretty certain to endure ablution. Behind, instead of dicky, is a kind of boot where passengers' boxes are stored beneath a stout canvas curtain with leather sides. The comfort of travel depends upon packing the wagon; if heavy in front or rear, or if the thoroughbraces be not properly "fixed" the bumping will be likely to cause nasal hæmorrhage. The description will apply to the private ambulance, or as it is called in the west "avalanche," only the latter, as might be expected, is more convenient; it is the drosky in which the vast steppes of Central America are crossed by the government employés.

115

THE DESERT
TRAVELER'S KIT

Joseph P. Allyn

Joseph P. Allyn (1833–1869) was a young Connecticut lawyer appointed by President Lincoln to the first Arizona Territorial Supreme Court. His letters home were published in The Arizona of Joseph Pratt Allyn. *In this letter, he describes his equipment for a horseback ride across the desert from La Paz, on the Colorado River, eastward to Prescott.*

I left La Paz in September, to attend the assemblage of the Legislature and the opening of the District Court here, in company with the expressman and a merchant. We were in light marching order, all that we carried hung upon our horses. When we left La Paz we were quite heavily loaded, carrying food for ourselves and our horses, as well as blankets, firearms and a change of clothes. One never knows what can be packed on a horse until he tries it, and it is these little details that will give you the best idea of traveling in Arizona. From the horn, in front of my saddle, were hung, first, a pair of holsters designed for large pistols, but now holding smoking tobacco, brush, comb, towels and soap; then on one side a huge canteen, holding over a gallon of water; on the other my old tried Spencer rifle, and above all my lariat. The horn of the Spanish saddles you see is far from being ornamental alone. Behind were my saddle bags, with clothes, paper, memorandum books, etc., and above that a large sack containing my and my horse's "grub," to use the vernacular of the country. The "grub" consisted of twenty pounds of barley loose in the sack, and my own comissariat was arranged in a smaller bag, which was dropped into the barley sack, and consisted of still smaller bags, holding coffee, sugar, crackers, *pinoly*, and jerked beef, or "jerky," as it is called, and a bottle of whisky. My blankets were all folded under the saddle, the tin cup that answers all the purposes of coffee pot, wash basin, etc., tied on to the bundle behind, and with hunting knife in the belt, with your pistols, you are "outfitted," that is, supposing you have a good horse, for a trip of 150 miles.

116

HOW EXQUISITELY PLEASANT, HOW COSY AND DELIGHTFUL!

James Rusling

James Rusling, experienced traveler and author of Across America, *preferred steamboats. But going down the Columbia River in one involved switching back and forth from steamboat to trains to avoid the frequent rapids.*

Ding! Dong! Puff! Puff! The steamer had come, and Nov. 28th [1866], we at length embarked for down the Columbia. She was a little stern-wheel boat, scarcely longer than your finger, called *Nez Perce Chief*, Capt. Stump, master. Her fare to Fort Vancouver or Portland, including railroad-portages, was $18 in coin, which at rates then current was equivalent to $25 in greenbacks. Meals were extra, at a cost of $1,50 each, in currency, besides. The distance to Portland was about 200 miles; to the mouth of the Columbia, 100 or so more. We found Capt. Stump a very obliging Oregonian, and obtained much interesting information from him. His boat was part of a line belonging to the Oregon Steam Navigation Company, a gigantic corporation that controlled all the navigable waters of the Columbia, and with far-reaching enterprise was now seeking to connect them with the headwaters of the Missouri. He said, their boats could ascend to Umatilla all the year round, except in mid-winter, when the Columbia sometimes froze over for several weeks together, though not usually. With good water, they could go up to Wallula, at the mouth of the Walla-Walla, 25 miles farther, which they usually did six months in the year. With very high water, they could run up to Lewiston, at the junction of the Snake and Clearwater, about 175 miles more, three months in the year—making about 500 miles from the sea in all. Above Lewiston, there was a bad cañon in the Snake, with shoals, and rapids for a hundred miles or so to Farewell Bend; but after that, he thought, a light-draught steamer might get up at least three hundred miles farther, or within about 200 miles of Salt Lake, as stated heretofore.

Clark's Fork of the Columbia, or the Columbia proper, makes a sharp bend north at Wallula, and for 300 miles, he said, was unnavigable, until you reach Fort Colville near the British line, when it trends east and south, until it disappears in the far off wilds of Montana. Just above Fort Colville, it became navigable again, and a small boat was then running up to the Great Bend region, over 200 miles farther, where good placer mines had been discovered (Kootenay) and worked a little. This boat could connect with another, already plying on Lake Pond Oreille (a part of Clark's Fork), and this with still another then building, that it was believed with short portages would extend navigation some 200 miles more, or into the very heart of Montana, within two or three hundred miles only of Fort Benton—the head of navigation on the Missouri. These were weighty facts, marrying the Pacific to the Atlantic; but Captain Stump thought the O. S. N. company could accomplish them, or anything else, indeed, it seriously undertook. Just now it was bending its energies in that direction, and he said would beat the Northern Pacific Railroad yet. No doubt we have a fine country up there, near the British America line, abounding in lakes and threaded with rivers, and roomy enough for all enterprises, whether railroad or steamboat.

Puff! Puff! And so we were off down the Columbia, at last. How exquisitely pleasant, how cosy and delightful, our little steamer seemed, after 2,400 miles of jolting and banging by stage-coach and ambulance! The staterooms were clean and tidy, the meals well-cooked and excellent, and we went steaming down the Columbia without thought or care, as on "summer seas." Occasionally rapids appeared, of a serious character; but as a rule the river was broad and deep, majestic in size and volume. On the banks were frequent Indian villages, with their hardy little ponies browsing around—apparently on nothing but sage-brush and cobblestones. These Indians fancied spotted or "calico" horses, as the Oregonians called them, and very few of their ponies were of a single color. They spend the summer mostly in the Mountains, making long excursions in all directions; but as winter approaches, they return to the Columbia, and eke out a precarious subsistence by fishing, etc., till spring comes. Timber was scarce, and frequently we saw numbers of them in canoes, paddling up and down the river in search of drift-wood, for their winter's supply of fuel. Past Owyhee rapids and the seething caldron of Hell-Gate, we reached Celilo, eighty-five miles from Umatilla, with its long warehouse (935 feet), and its mosquito fleet of five or six pigmy steamers, that formed the up-river line. Here we disembarked, and took the Railroad around the "chutes" or rapids, some fourteen miles, to still water again below. The shrill whistle of the locomotive and the rattle of the cars were delightful sounds, after our long exile from them, and soon convinced us we were on the right road to civilization again. This portage had formerly been made by pack-mules, and then by wagons; but recently a railroad had been constructed, after much hard blasting and costly wall-work, and now "Riding on a rail," there, with the Columbia boiling and roaring at your side, like the Rapids above Niagara, was exhilarating and superb. At very high water, these "chutes" or rapids somewhat disappear, though they still continue very dangerous. No attempt had been made to ascend them with a steamer; but the spring before, Capt. Stump had safely descended them, much against his will. It was high water in the Columbia, with a strong current, and his boat drifting near the rapids was suddenly sucked in, before he knew it. Clearly, escape was impossible; so he put on all steam, to give her steerage-way, and then headed down stream—neck or nothing. There was a good deal of bumping and thumping—it was a toss and a plunge, for awhile—and everybody he feared was pretty badly scared; but his gallant little boat ran the rapids for all that, and reached still water below safely at last. It was a daring feat, and worthy of this brave Oregonian. Just now, the Columbia was very low, rocks and reefs showing all through the rapids—among, around, and over which the waters boiled and rushed like a mill-race.

The locomotive carried us to the Dalles, at the foot of the Rapids, a town of some two thousand inhabitants, with a maturer civilization than any we had seen since leaving Salt Lake. It was but five or six years old; yet it was already in its decrepitude. A "rush" of miners a few years before, to alleged fine "diggings" near there, had suddenly elevated it from an obscure landing into quite a town; but the mines did not justify their promise, and the Dalles was now at a stand-still, if not something worse. "Mining stock" and "corner lots" had gone down by the run, during the past year or two, and her few merchants sat by their doors watching for customers in vain. The enterprise of the town, however, deserved a better fate. At the Umatilla House they gave us an excellent supper, at a moderate price, and the hotel itself would have been a credit to a much larger town anywhere. The mines on John Day River, and other dependencies of the Dalles, had formerly yielded $2,000,000 per year, and Congress had then voted a U. S. Mint there. We could but sincerely hope it would be much needed, some day or other.

Halting at the Dalles over night, the next morning we took the side-wheel steamer *Idaho,* and ran down to Upper Cascades—some fifty miles—through the heart of the Cascade Mountains. Here we took the railroad again for six miles—to flank more rapids—and at Lower Cascades embarked on the *W. G. Hunt,* a large and elegant side-wheel steamer, that some years before had come "round the Horn," from New York. The Columbia, soon issuing from the Mountains, now became a broad and majestic river, with good depth of water to the ocean all the year round, and larger vessels even than the *W. G. Hunt* might readily ascend to Lower Cascades, if necessary. Our good boat, however, bore us bravely on to Fort Vancouver, amidst multiplying signs of civilization again; and as we landed there, we realized another great link of our journey was over.

1 1 7

THE RACE FOR RATON PASS

James Marshall

Raton Pass has only enough room for one railroad. Both the Santa Fe and the Denver and Rio Grande wanted to squeeze through it. Rights to build the route would go to the first one who started it. The race was won in a single night. This from Santa Fe: The Railroad That Built an Empire, *by James Marshall.*

The fall before the [railroad] battle [for Raton Pass], while Rio Grande surveyors were running new lines on the slopes of Raton Mountain, a slight figure in a Mexican serape, with a black slouch hat pulled down over his eyes, wandered around through the meadows and along the creeks with a band of sheep. At night by the light of a campfire, the figure squatted on a rock and made notes in a dogeared book—figures, grades, curves, sketch maps.

And so, when the battle opened, Ray Morley was able to go back to his scrawled notes and lose little time surveying in the winter snows. . . .

As the [surveyors] talked, another Santa Fe stalwart was hurrying north to join them. It was Kingman. He and his family had wintered at Cimarron and, when he got the message from Strong ordering him to go to Raton to help win and hold the pass, he went into action. He commandeered a government telegraph repair wagon, bribed the driver and galloped up the trail. By daybreak they'd made fifty miles. Changing teams, they picked up Mexican laborers here and there and, by five o'clock on March 1st, had crossed the mountain on the toll road and were four miles down on the Colorado side. Here they camped for the night—and Robinson and Morley, racing up to Wootton's toll house in a pole buggy, saw their campfires far up the canyon.

To go back a little: Santa Fe and Rio Grande telegraph lines connected and the two concerns broke each other's codes and read each other's wires. The Rio Grande, getting wind of the Santa Fe plan, quickly organized a crew of graders, called in J. A. McMurtrie and J. R. De Remer, two of its best engineers, and held them ready at Pueblo for a dash into the pass. . . .

The Santa Fe'ers saw the Rio Granders register for their rooms, yawn and go upstairs. Robinson grinned at Morley.

"Come on, Ray. Where's the livery stable?"

They hired a buggy and a team and drove off in the darkness through Trinidad and up the old trail toward "Uncle Dick" Wootton's toll house and hotel. It was ten o'clock and, as they drove, far up on the mountain, they saw the glow of Kingman's campfires in the cold, still air. . . .

They stopped the buggy at the chain across the road, turned the team into the corral and went in to find Uncle Dick getting ready for bed.

Richens Lacy Wootton was the son of a Mecklenburg County, Virginia, planter. He was born May 6, 1816, and at twenty struck out alone for Independence, Missouri, and joined a wagon train. He never went east again. He became a trader, Indian fighter, scout for Fremont, friend of Kit Carson, rancher, sheepman and toll-road owner. Indian fighting, although he did some, he considered nonsense. . . .

As Robinson and Morley had driven up to Wootton's they had paralleled two surveys from El Moro and Trinidad up to the foot of the pass. But above Uncle Dick's place there was only one road—and two railroads wanted to go over it. Even as the engineers talked with Dick a messenger arrived on horseback from Trinidad. He had been sent by friendly townsfolk who, still mad at the Rio Grande, wanted to help the Santa Fe.

"They told me to tell you, Mr. Robinson, that General Palmer is onto your game and he's got a gang of men coming up here first thing in the morning to start grading. McMurtrie and De Remer are down in the hotel this minute." . . .

They roused out the sleeping freighters and talked to a few of the boys up from Trinidad for the dance. Uncle Dick tackled them all. . . .

Shovels and lanterns were handed out. Dick flung open the door and the cold night air rushed in. In the darkness at 2 A.M. the little party set off up the hill. The campfires had died out now. The lanterns went flickering slowly up the winding road; boots clumped hollowly on the plank bridges over tumbling Raton Creek.

"Wait for me," chirped sixty-two-year-old Uncle Dick. "I'm coming too."

At 4 A.M., still in the darkness, Morley said, "This'll do. One of you boys go on up where you see that red spot of campfire and find out if there's a Lewis Kingman there. If there is, tell him Robinson and Morley say to start grading now."

The boy struck off up the hill. The others stood, breathing heavily in the sharp cold air. Dick Wootton handed his lantern to a freighter and grabbed a shovel. The dirt flew. Others followed his example.

Raton Pass was the Santa Fe's by right of prior construction.

118

THE CONTINENT IS JOINED

Theodore H. Hittell

Historian Theodore H. Hittell gives us his view of that moment, on May 10, 1869, when the lines of the Central Pacific, building eastward, and the Union Pacific, building westward, met at Promontory Point, Utah, and became the nation's first transcontinental railroad.

It was determined that the ceremonies of the meeting of the two [rail] roads at Promontory should be, as far as possible, worthy of the occasion—one of the most important in the history of the United States. The time fixed upon was May 10, 1869. There were about a thousand persons present, consisting of all the officers, directors and employees of the roads that were within reach, including laborers, together with many prominent men and a few ladies who had been invited, delegations from Salt Lake City and surrounding towns, several companies of soldiers, a military band and a number of Indians. The place was a grassy plain between green hills with the Great Salt Lake not far off to the south and with mountains, some nearer and some further and many capped with snow, in various directions to the east, north and west of it. In the middle, between the last rails of the Union Pacific on the east and the Central Pacific on the west, there was a short unclosed gap. About eleven o'clock in the forenoon, everything being prepared for the celebration, a Central Pacific train of cars, drawn by a decorated locomotive, all of which had come from the Pacific coast, approached the gap from the west; and about the same time a Union Pacific train with its equally decorated locomotive from the Atlantic coast approached from the east. As the engines came up, each a ponderous and powerful structure made for scaling mountains and with a whistle that was heard for miles and waked echoes in the furthest mountains, they saluted. It was the salutation, the all-hail of the Orient and the Occident in the middle of the continent. Soon the passengers, pouring from the trains on each side, gathered around the gap; and the last tie was produced. It was from the west and consisted of a beautifully polished stick of Californian laurel, bearing in its center a plate of silver on which were engraved the names of the two companies and their officers. It was soon put in place under the ends of the last rails, which were drawn together and fastened; and the connection was complete with one exception. This was the last spike. It too was soon produced. Like the last tie it also came from the bounteous west. It was of solid Californian gold.

But little time was lost in placing the last spike in position; and it was driven home with a hammer of solid silver in the hands of Stanford, the president of the Central Pacific. Then followed a few addresses, including a prayer, cheers, music and the reading of numerous congratulatory tele-grams, which came flashing over the wires from the far east and the far west, as the news of the driving of the last spike spread. Again the engines saluted; the officers and guests of the Union Pacific boarded their cars; and their train passed over the connecting tie, pressed the Central Pacific rails and then retired back upon its own track. The Central Pacific train in the same manner ran over upon the Union Pacific rails and then back to its own track. The union was complete; the east and west had embraced, and the two lines had become one continuous road across the continent in its widest breadth. Before the sun sank, there was banqueting and feasting— the best that could be afforded on the trains—and the day ended with more saluting, more cheering and more rejoicing, which were repeated in nearly every city of the eastern states and in every city, town and village of the Golden West.

119

THEY DO NOT DRINK, FIGHT, OR STRIKE

Charles Nordhoff

Charles Nordhoff described, in an 1872 travel book, the quality of Chinese laborers employed to build a California railroad.

From Merced, where the railroad company are building a very large hotel to accommodate the Yosemite travel, which here branches off for the famous valley, I had the curiosity to go down to the San Joaquin River, where the railroad people are at work. I wanted to see how Chinamen do as road-builders.

There are about seven hundred Chinese employed in grading and laying track, and perhaps one hundred white men. The engineer in charge, Mr. Curtis, told me that the Chinese make, on the whole, the best road-builders in the world. The contractor, Mr. Strobridge, told me that they learn all parts of the work very quickly; and I saw them employed on every kind of work. They do not drink, fight, or strike; they do gamble, if it is not prevented; and it is always said of them that they are very cleanly in their habits. It is the custom, among them, after they have had their suppers every evening, to bathe themselves all over; not in the stream here, which is too cold, but with the help of small tubs. I doubt if the white laborers do as much.

These Chinese receive twenty-eight dollars per month of twenty-six working days, and for this they furnish all their own supplies of food, tents, cooking utensils, etc., but the contractor pays the cooks. They work in gangs of from twelve to twenty men, who form a mess; and the head-man of the gang receives the wages of all, and divides the money among them.

The Chinaman, except when he is in gala dress, is a dingy-looking creature; he is said to be parsimonious; and to an American his quarters always look shabby. One gets the idea, therefore, that he lives poorly; and I should have said that pork and rice probably made up their bill of fare here on the plains. It will perhaps surprise you, as it did me, to find that they have a greater variety of food than their white neighbors.

They buy their supplies at a store kept in several cars near the end of the track; and this shop was a great curiosity to me. Here is a list of the food kept and sold there to the Chinese workmen: Dried oysters, dried cuttle-fish, dried fish, sweet rice crackers, dried bamboo sprouts, salted cabbage, Chinese sugar (which tasted to me very much like sorghum sugar), four kinds of dried fruits, five kinds of desiccated vegetables, vermicelli, dried sea-weed, Chinese bacon cut up into salt cutlets, dried meat of the abelona shell, pea-nut oil, dried mushrooms, tea, and rice. They buy also pork of the butcher, and on holidays they eat poultry.

Compare this bill of fare with the beef, beans, bread-and-butter, and potatoes of the white laborers, and you will see that John has a much greater variety of food.

At this railroad store they sold also pipes, bowls, chop-sticks, large shallow cast-iron bowls for cooking rice, lamps, joss paper, Chinese writing-paper, pencils and India ink, Chinese shoes, and clothing imported ready-made from China. Also, scales—for the Chinaman is particular, and re-weighs every thing he buys as soon as he gets it to camp. Finally, there was Chinese tobacco.

The desiccated vegetables were of excellent quality, and dried, evidently, by a process as good as the best in use with us.

The cost of these supplies, imported from China, was surprisingly low, and the contractor told me that the Chinese laborers can save about thirteen dollars per month, and, where they do not gamble, do lay by as much as that.

120

THE RAWHIDE
RAILROAD

George Estes

George Estes tended to stretch things a bit in his reporting (for example, the tribes on the Columbia River never had any hope of effecting complete annihilation of the whites), but much of this account from The Rawhide Railroad *is historic fact.*

This is a story of a remarkable steam railroad actually constructed and successfully operated in the beautiful Walla Walla Valley many years ago, on which rawhide, overlaying wooden beams, was used in place of iron or steel rails. This unique road, later modernized, is now operated as part of a large railway. It is doubtful, however, if through the roll of years, the changing managements of the big line have preserved either record or recollection of the once famous rawhide railroad, which was the germ of the present transportation system.

More than a quarter century ago, while in railroad service, it was my good fortune to come in contact with an old Irish section foreman, long since dead, who had been actually employed on the singular railroad. The outlines of the narrative were extracted from him disjointedly and at different times, but the wealth of detail and circumstantial accuracy leaves no doubt of the truth of the story as a whole.

After the catastrophe, which closes the last chapter, the railroad was operated successfully for many years with iron plates fastened on top of the wooden rails.

The question of bringing the locomotives and equipment up the Columbia was one of great moment not unmixed with danger. The red robbers of Wish-ram, if they permitted the locomotives to pass around the rapids at all, would exact enormous tribute, or there would be a great battle which would gradually extend to the neighboring tribes and the result might be the complete annihilation of the whites, who in the whole northwest were at that time greatly outnumbered by the Indians.

When the barges containing the two locomotives, one hundred pairs of car wheels and the thousand plug hats arrived at the rapids of Wish-ram the wisdom of Doc Baker shone out anew. The resplendent breeches of Seekolicks, though with luster now slightly impaired by coatings of salmon scales, still continued to attract the admiring glances of Wish-ram maidens, to the intense disgust of all the other bucks who from necessity were without breeches. This general feeling was, one might say, openly and nakedly displayed without attempt at concealment. Doc Baker had studied this situation from the first and now decided to profit by working with, instead of against, human passions and desires. He called a council of the head villains of Wish-ram and with the astuteness of an oriental peddler in the ancient city of Bagdad, displayed for the first time to the astonished gaze of the assembled robbers the wonders of a dress silk hat, and with consummate cunning bargained at the price of one stove-pipe for each of the doughty warriors of Wish-ram, not only for free passage of the locomotives, but for the combined power of a thousand naked but plug-hatted villians to drag the locomotives around the rapids.

What boots it now that Seekolicks' breeches displayed the glories of a sunset (apologies to the Pacific Monthly)? For influence with an Indian maiden a shiny plug hat will do more than a thousand dollars in stock of the Standard Oil Company, and Seekolicks' breeches fell behind in the mad race of changing fashions along the river.

At last the locomotives and one hundred pairs of car wheels reached Wallula, where Bill Green had built an incline running down to the water in order to bring them up to the roadway.

This he did without difficulty by hitching his great team of forty oxen to each locomotive in turn. It is safe to say that this team of oxen could pull as much as either locomotive, though not so rapidly, perhaps.

When the locomotives were at last on the main line the names "Loco Ladd" and "Loco Blue Mountain" were painted on their cab panels. Thus Doc Baker honored the two greatest objects, to him, in the world. The road was ready for service, the cars having been previously constructed entirely of wood and the car wheels brought from New York had been placed under them.

The chief engineer had conducted all these operations from the saddle of his mule. He galloped back from the leading yoke of the forty-ox team, to where Doc Baker stood near the locomotives, now on the main line, and solemnly announced to his chief that the road was ready for business. Then turning to the train dispatcher, also mounted on a long-legged mule with two big horse pistols hanging low on his hips, the chief engineer formally turned over the completed railroad from the Construction to the Operating Department in these terse terms: "Their your'n. Get to hell out o'here with 'em."

But the most intensely practical side of the train dispatcher was perhaps best illustrated in his conception of the locomotive pilots sometimes called "cowcatchers." When the locomotives first arrived at Wallula the train dispatcher, taking Pat Prunty the source of all railroad wisdom, along with him, proceeded to look them over. He inquired of Prunty the purpose of the "V" shaped combination of slats on the front ends of the locomotives. Prunty explained that these were called "cowcatchers" and were to clear the track of cattle. The train dispatcher remarked that the bunch of corset staves might be serviceable for catching cows in the City of New York, but in the great west cows were harder to catch and more dangerous when caught. His authority in reality being as absolute as the country operator thinks the authority of the average dispatcher is today, he ordered the pilots ripped off the two locomotives and low platforms built in their stead. On each of these platforms he stationed one of his best hunting dogs which he quickly trained, when cattle on the tracks were approached, to leap to the ground and drive them away. The dogs at once grasped the responsibility of their important railroad positions and thirty minutes before departure of each train from their respective terminals at Walla Walla and Wallula, without the service of the caller, they took their positions on their locomotive platforms and, like the great figure heads on the ship prows of the conquering Vikings, they piloted the trains across the Walla Walla Valley faithful to their duties as "cowcatchers" in fact as well as in name.

The Rawhide Railroad, though operating in a cattle country, under the wise direction of Bill Green and Josh Moore paid fewer claims for cattle killed according to its size than any other railroad in the world.

Nor did the two "cowcatchers," "Ponto" and "Thor" ever "bark" on account of their overtime being short on payday. They were watchful of other things besides six o'clock and the pay car.

Soon it was found that the gnawing movements of the tread and flanges of the locomotive drivers quickly wore off the tops and edges of the wooden rails making it necessary constantly to renew them.

The pioneer of the Pacific coast has one favorite "metal" on which he relies to surmount all difficulties—the renowned rawhide. He who understands it can accomplish wonders with it. But its antics are strange to those from eastern lands, unfamiliar with its peculiar properties.

The pioneers delight to tell of the tenderfoot who did not know how rawhide would stretch when wet and contract when dry. He hitched up his team with rawhide harness in a rain storm, and attached a drag chain to a log, intending to pull it to his cabin for fuel. Driving the team to the cabin, he looked back and saw that the log had not moved, the rain causing the rawhide harness to stretch all the way to the house. Disgusted, he unharnessed the horses and threw the harness over a stump. The sun came out, and contracting the harness, pulled the log up to the house.

Possessed of enormous quantities of this durable material, Doc Baker directed that the wooden rails be "plated" with rawhide from Walla Walla to Wallula. It hardened in the summer sun and made the roadway practically indestructible.

In the rainy season the rawhide became soft and the road could not be operated, but there was no occasion to operate it in the winter time, for the reason that there was no traffic, and when the snow melted in the spring, the sun blazing out over the valley quickly put the rawhide railroad in good condition and ready for train service.

Finally there came a winter of terrible severity on the Pacific coast which was long spoken of as the "hard winter."

In the empire of Walla Walla it did untold damage. The snow fell very deep throughout the land. With the first rains and snows the rawhide railroad ceased operation for the winter, according to its usual custom, as the rawhide had become soft as mush.

Provisions became scarce. Great hardships and suffering were experienced. Cattle raisers were obliged to begin feeding their stock earlier than usual and soon the feed ran short. In desperation they turned the cattle out on the range, which was covered with deep snow. Blizzards swept over the prairie lands and many of the cattle froze to death standing erect, a gruesome sight.

The deer in the Blue Mountains were starved and frozen and the wolves from the fastnesses of the distant Rockies on the east and from icebound Canada on the north swept over the country, devouring the carcasses of the frozen deer and after these were all gone, forced on by famishing hunger, and growing bolder as the winter became more and more severe, they crept out over the great valley of Walla Walla in search of food.

Driven at last in desperation, to sustain their lives, the red-throated, ravening monsters, running in great packs, crowded on and on to the very edge of the village of Walla Walla, searching for carcasses of frozen cattle which they pawed out of the snow and quickly devoured.

The beleaguered village now felt that it was only a question of days, perhaps hours, if the storm did not break, when they would have to fight the oncoming horde of famished fiends to preserve their very lives. And everyone was prepared for the final conflict.

One night, late in midwinter, the blizzard was roaring and howling across the prairie and snow was falling in long slanting sheets, when a tremendous disturbance was made at the door of Doc Baker's home.

Grabbing up a loaded pistol, the doctor ran to the door, fearing the last stand against the wolves was at hand. Opening the door cautiously, he saw outside the two faithful Indians, Sapolil and Seekolicks, seeking admission. They hurled their shivering bodies through the doorway and began in a mixture of English and Chinook, a wild effort to communicate some disastrous intelligence to their friend, Doc Baker.

Their excitement was so great that the only word the doctor could catch in the first rush of their attempt to talk, was "wolves."

Without waiting for more, the doctor called to all the men of the household to arm themselves quickly and prepare for a fight against the coming onslaught of the wolves. Then turning to his sideboard he poured a good big drink of strong whiskey for each of the Indians, now trembling with cold and excitement. This disposed of, he pushed them down by the roaring fire-place and forced them to deliver their message slowly and in a manner that could be understood.

In broken English, interwoven with Chinook, Sapolil finally succeeded in disclosing the terrible information, which ran as follows:

"Railroad—him gonum hell. Damn wolves digum out—eatum all up—Wallula to Walla Walla."

121

185 MILES
IN FIFTEEN
HOURS AND
TWENTY MINUTES

Alexander Majors

Few endeavors have produced more phoney stories than the Pony Express. Here are the facts from Alexander Majors's Seventy Years on the Frontier.

In the year 1859 several magnates in Wall Street formed a formidable lobby at Washington in the interests of an overland mail route to California, and asked Congress for a subsidy for carrying the mails overland for one year between New York and San Francisco.

The distance was 1,950 miles. Mr. Russell proposed to cover this distance with a mail line between St. Joseph, Mo., and San Francisco, that would deliver letters at either end of the route within ten days.

Five hundred of the fleetest horses to be procured were immediately purchased, and the services of over two hundred competent men were secured. Eighty of these men were selected for express riders. Light-weights were deemed the most eligible for the purpose; the lighter the man the better for the horse, as some portions of the route had to be traversed at a speed of twenty miles an hour. Relays were established at stations, the distance between which was, in each instance, determined by the character of the country.

These stations dotted a wild, uninhabited expanse of country 2,000 miles wide, infested with road-agents and warlike Indians, who roamed in formidable hunting parties, ready to sacrifice human life with as little unconcern as they would slaughter a buffalo. The Pony Express, therefore, was not only an important, but a daring and romantic enterprise. At each station a sufficient number of horses were kept, and at every third station the thin, wiry, and hardy pony-riders held themselves in readiness to press forward with the mails. These were filled with important business letters and press dispatches from Eastern cities and San Francisco, printed upon tissue paper, and thus especially adapted by their weight for this mode of transportation.

The schedule time for the trip was fixed at ten days. In this manner they supplied the place of the electric telegraph and the lightning express train of the gigantic railway enterprise that subsequently superseded it.

The men were faithful, daring fellows, and their service was full of novelty and adventure. The facility and energy with which they journeyed was a marvel. The news of Abraham Lincoln's election was carried through from St. Joseph to Denver, Colo., 665 miles, in two days and twenty-one hours, the last ten miles having been covered in thirty-one minutes. The last route on the occasion was traversed by Robert H. Haslam, better known as "Pony Bob," who carried the news 120 miles in eight hours and ten minutes, riding from Smith's Creek to Fort Churchill, on the Carson River, Nevada, the first telegraph station on the Pacific Coast.

On another occasion, it is recorded, one of these riders journeyed a single stretch of 300 miles—the other men who should have relieved him being either disabled or indisposed—and reached the terminal station on schedule time.

The distance between relay riders' stations varied from sixty-five to one hundred miles, and often more. The weight to be carried by each was fixed at ten pounds or under, and the charge for transportation was $5 in gold for each half of an ounce. The entire distance between New York City and San Francisco occupied but fourteen days. The riders received from $120 to $125 per month for their arduous services. The pony express enterprise continued for about two years, at the end of which time telegraph service between the Atlantic and Pacific oceans was established. . . .

The day of THE FIRST START, the 3d of April, 1860, at noon, Harry Roff, mounted on a spirited half-breed broncho, started from Sacramento on his perilous ride, and covered the first twenty miles, including one change, in fifty-nine minutes. On reaching Folsom, he changed again and started for Placerville, at the foot of the Sierra Nevada Mountain, fifty-five miles distant. There he connected with "Boston," who took the route to Friday's Station, crossing the eastern summit of the Sierra Nevada. Sam

Hamilton next fell into line, and pursued his way to Genoa, Carson City, Dayton, Reed's Station, and Fort Churchill—seventy-five miles. The entire run, 185 miles, was made in fifteen hours and twenty minutes, and included the crossing of the western summits of the Sierras, through thirty feet of snow. This seems almost impossible, and would have been, had not pack trains of mules and horses kept the trail open. Here "Pony Bob"— Robert H. Haslam—took the road from Fort Churchill to Smith's Creek, 120 miles distant, through a hostile Indian country. From this point Jay G. Kelley rode from Smith's Creek to Ruby Valley, Utah, 116 miles; from Ruby Valley to Deep Creek, H. Richardson, 105 miles; from Deep Creek to Rush Valley, old Camp Floyd, eighty miles; from Camp Floyd to Salt Lake City, fifty miles; George Thacher the last end. This ended the Western Division, under the management of Bolivar Roberts, now in Salt Lake City.

Among the most noted and daring riders of the Pony Express was Hon. William F. Cody, better known as Buffalo Bill, whose reputation is now established the world over. While engaged in the express service, his route lay between Red Buttes and Three Crossings, a distance of 116 miles. . . .

The quickest time that had ever been made with any message between San Francisco and New York, over the Butterfield line, which was the southern route, was twenty-one days. Our Pony Express shortened the time to ten days, which was our schedule time, without a single failure, being a difference of eleven days.

To do the work of the Pony Express required between four hundred and five hundred horses, about one hundred and ninety stations, two hundred men for station-keepers, and eighty riders; riders made an average ride of thirty-three and one-third miles. In doing this each man rode three ponies on his part of the route; some of the riders, however, rode much greater distances in times of emergency.

The Pony Express carried messages written on tissue paper, weighing one-half ounce, a charge of $5 being made for each dispatch carried.

As anticipated, the amount of business transacted over this line was not sufficient to pay one-tenth of the expenses, to say nothing about the amount of capital invested. In this, however, we were not disappointed, for we knew, as stated in the outset, that it could not be made a paying institution, and was undertaken solely to prove that the route over which it ran could be made a permanent thoroughfare for travel at all seasons of the year, proving, as far as the paramount object was concerned, a complete success.

Two important events transpired during the term of the Pony's existence; one was the carrying of President Buchanan's last message to Congress, in December, 1860, from the Missouri River to Sacramento, a distance of two thousand miles, in eight days and some hours. The other was the carrying of President Lincoln's inaugural address of March 4, 1861, over the same route in seven days and, I think, seventeen hours, being the quickest time, taking the distance into consideration, on record in this or any other country, as far as I know.

122

FINALLY, BEHIND THE WHEEL!

Upton Sinclair

In his 1926 novel, Oil!, *Upton Sinclair provided a fine word-picture of a trip through Southern California in an open auto as it might have been experienced by a boy.*

The road ran, smooth and flawless, precisely fourteen feet wide, the edges trimmed as if by shears, a ribbon of grey concrete, rolled out over the valley by a giant hand. The ground went in long waves, a slow ascent and then a sudden dip; you climbed, and went swiftly over—but you had no fear, for you knew the magic ribbon would be there, clear of obstructions, unmarred by bump or scar, waiting the passage of inflated rubber wheels revolving seven times a second. The cold wind of morning whistled by, a storm of motion, a humming and roaring with ever-shifting overtones; but you sat snug behind a tilted wind-shield, which slid the gale up over your head. Sometimes you liked to put your hand up, and feel the cold impact; sometimes you would peer around the side of the shield, and let the torrent hit your forehead, and toss your hair about. But for the most part you sat silent and dignified—because that was Dad's way, and Dad's way constituted the ethics of motoring.

Dad wore an overcoat, tan in color, soft and woolly in texture, opulent in cut, double-breasted, with big collar and big lapels and big flaps over the pockets—every place where a tailor could express munificence. The boy's coat had been made by the same tailor, of the same soft, woolly material, with the same big collar and big lapels and big flaps. Dad wore driving gauntlets; and the same shop had had the same kind for boys. Dad wore horn-rimmed spectacles; the boy had never been taken to an oculist, but he had found in a drug-store a pair of amber-colored glasses, having horn rims the same as Dad's. There was no hat on Dad's head, because he believed that wind and sunshine kept your hair from falling out; so the boy also rode with tumbled locks. The only difference between them, apart from size, was that Dad had a big brown cigar, unlighted, in the corner of his mouth; a survival of the rough old days, when he had driven mule-teams and chewed tobacco.

Fifty miles, said the speedometer; that was Dad's rule for open country, and he never varied it, except in wet weather. Grades made no difference; the fraction of an ounce more pressure with his right foot, and the car raced on—up, up, up—until it topped the ridge, and was sailing down into the next little valley, exactly in the centre of the magic grey ribbon of concrete. The car would start to gather speed on the down grade, and Dad would lift the pressure of his foot a trifle, and let the resistance of the engine check the speed. Fifty miles was enough, said Dad; he was a man of order.

Far ahead, over the tops of several waves of ground, another car was coming. A small black speck, it went down out of sight, and came up bigger; the next time it was bigger yet; the next time—it was on the slope above you, rushing at you, faster and faster, a mighty projectile hurled out of a six-foot cannon. Now came a moment to test the nerve of a motorist. The magic ribbon of concrete had no stretching powers. The ground at the sides had been prepared for emergencies, but you could not always be sure how well it had been prepared, and if you went off at fifty miles an hour you would get disagreeable waverings of the wheels; you might find the neatly trimmed concrete raised several inches above the earth at the side of it, forcing you to run along on the earth until you could find a place to swing in again; there might be soft sand, which would swerve you this way and that, or wet clay which would skid you, and put a sudden end to your journey.

So the laws of good driving forbade you to go off the magic ribbon except in extreme emergencies. You were ethically entitled to several inches of margin at the right-hand edge; and the man approaching you was entitled to an equal number of inches; which left a remainder of inches between the two projectiles as they shot by. It sounds risky as one tells it, but the heavens are run on the basis of similar calculations, and while collisions do happen, they leave time enough in between for universes to be formed, and successful careers conducted by men of affairs.

"Whoosh!" went the other projectile, hurtling past; a loud, swift "Whoosh!" with no tapering off at the end. You had a glimpse of another man with horn-rimmed spectacles like yourself, with a similar grip of two hands upon a steering wheel, and a similar cataleptic fixation of the eyes. You never looked back; for at fifty miles an hour, your business is with the things that lie before you, and the past is past—or shall we say that the passed are passed? Presently would come another car, and again it would be necessary for you to leave the comfortable centre of the concrete ribbon, and content yourself with a precisely estimated one-half minus a certain number of inches. Each time, you were staking your life upon your ability to place your car upon the exact line—and upon the ability and willingness of the unknown other party to do the same. You watched his projectile in the instant of hurtling at you, and if you saw that he was not making the necessary concession, you knew that you were encountering that most dangerous of all two-legged mammalian creatures, the road-hog. Or maybe it was a drunken man, or just a woman—there was no time to find out; you had the thousandth part of a second in which to shift your steering-wheel the tenth part of an inch, and run your right wheels off onto the dirt.

That might happen only once or twice in the course of a day's driving. When it did, Dad had one invariable formula; he would shift the cigar a bit in his mouth and mutter: "Damn fool!" It was the only cuss-word the one-time mule-driver permitted himself in the presence of the boy; and it had no profane significance—it was simply the scientific term for road-hogs, and drunken men, and women driving cars; as well as for loads of hay, and furniture-vans, and big motor-trucks which blocked the road on curves; and for cars with trailers, driving too rapidly, and swinging from side to side; and for Mexicans in tumble-down buggies, who failed to keep out on the dirt where they belonged, but came wabbling onto the concrete—and right while a car was coming in the other direction, so that you had to jam on your foot-brake, and grab the hand-brake, and bring the car to a halt with a squealing and grinding, and worse yet a sliding of tires. If there is anything a motorist considers disgraceful it is to "skid his tires"; and Dad had the conviction that some day there would be a speed law turned inside out—it would be forbidden to drive less than forty miles an hour on state highways, and people who wanted to drive spavined horses to tumble-down buggies would either go cross-lots or stay at home.

123

STEINBECK'S HIGHWAY 66

John Steinbeck

The "mother road" of the West, running two thousand miles from Chicago to Los Angeles, was Route 66. John Steinbeck realized the symbolic importance of this westward-reaching road and referred to it often in The Grapes of Wrath, *his epic work about the Joads, Dust Bowl refugees who attempted to flee from drought and depression. What follows are passages from the book describing the highway.*

Highway 66 is the main migrant road. 66—the long concrete path across the country, waving gently up and down on the map, from the Mississippi to Bakersfield—over the red lands and the gray lands, twisting up into the mountains, crossing the Divide and down into the bright and terrible desert, and across the desert to the mountains again, and into the rich California valleys.

66 is the path of a people in flight, refugees from dust and shrinking land, from the thunder of tractors and shrinking ownership, from the desert's slow northward invasion, from the twisting winds that howl up out of Texas, from the floods that bring no richness to the land and steal what little richness is there. From all of these the people are in flight, and they come into 66 from the tributary side roads, from the wagon tracks and the rutted country roads. 66 is the mother road, the road of flight.

Clarksville and Ozark and Van Buren and Fort Smith on 64, and there's an end of Arkansas. And all the roads into Oklahoma City, 66 down from Tulsa, 270 up from McAlester. 81 from Wichita Falls south, from Enid north. Edmond. McLoud, Purcell. 66 out of Oklahoma City: El Reno and Clinton, going west on 66. Hydro, Elk City, and Texola; and there's an end to Oklahoma. 66 across the Panhandle of Texas. Shamrock and McLean, Conway and Amarillo, the yellow. Wildorado and Vega and Boise, and there's an end of Texas. Tucumcari and Santa Rosa and into the New Mexican mountains to Albuquerque, where the road comes down from Santa Fe. Then down the gorged Rio Grande to Las Lunas and west again on 66 to Gallup, and there's the border of New Mexico.

And now the high mountains. Holbrook and Winslow and Flagstaff in the high mountains of Arizona. Then the great plateau rolling like a ground swell. Ashfork and Kingman and stone mountains again, where water must be hauled and sold. Then out of the broken sun-rotted mountains of Arizona to the Colorado, with green reeds on its banks, and that's the end of Arizona. There's California just over the river, and a pretty town to start it. Needles, on the river. But the river is a stranger in this place. Up from Needles and over a burned range, and there's the desert. And 66 goes on over the terrible desert, where the distance shimmers and the black center mountains hang unbearably in the distance. At last there's Barstow, and more desert until at last the mountains rise up again, the good mountains, and 66 winds through them. Then suddenly a pass, and below the beautiful valley, below orchards and vineyards and little houses, and in the distance a city. And, oh, my God, it's over.

The people in flight streamed out on 66, sometimes a single car, sometimes a little caravan. All day they rolled slowly along the road, and at night they stopped near water. In the day ancient leaky radiators sent up columns of steam, loose connecting rods hammered and pounded. And the men driving the trucks and the overloaded cars listened apprehensively. How far between towns? It is a terror between towns. If something breaks—well, if something breaks we camp right here while Jim walks to town and gets a part and walks back and—how much food we got?

People in flight along 66. And the concrete road shone like a mirror under the sun, and in the distance the heat made it seem that there were pools of water in the road.

Danny wants a cup a water.

He'll have to wait, poor little fella. He's hot. Nex' service station. *Service* station, like the fella says.

Two hundred and fifty thousand people over the road. Fifty thousand old cars—wounded, steaming. Wrecks along the road, abandoned. Well, what happened to them? What happened to the folks in that car? Did they walk? Where are they? Where does the courage come from? Where does the terrible faith come from?

And here's a story you can hardly believe, but it's true, and it's funny and it's beautiful. There was a family of twelve and they were forced off the land. They had no car. They built a trailer out of junk and loaded it with their possessions. They pulled it to the side of 66 and waited. And pretty soon a sedan picked them up. Five of them rode in the sedan and seven on the trailer, and a dog on the trailer. They got to California in two jumps. The man who pulled them fed them. And that's true. But how can such courage be, and such faith in their own species? Very few things would teach such faith.

Joads and Wilsons crawled westward as a unit: El Reno and Bridgeport, Clinton, Elk City, Sayre, and Texola. There's the border, and Oklahoma was behind. And this day the cars crawled on and on, through the Panhandle of Texas. Shamrock and Alanreed, Groom and Yarnell. They went through Amarillo in the evening, drove too long, and camped when it was dusk. They were tired and dusty and hot. Granma had convulsions from the heat, and she was weak when they stopped.

The Joad family moved slowly westward, up into the mountains of New Mexico, past the pinnacles and pyramids of the upland. They climbed into the high country of Arizona, and through a gap they looked down on the Painted Desert.

They crawled up the slopes, and the low twisted trees covered the slopes. Holbrook, Joseph City, Winslow. And then the tall trees began, and the cars spouted steam and labored up the slopes. And there was Flagstaff, and that was the top of it all. Down from Flagstaff over the great plateaus, and the road disappeared in the distance ahead. The water grew scarce, water was to be bought, five cents, ten cents, fifteen cents a gallon. The sun drained the dry rocky country, and ahead were jagged broken peaks, the western wall of Arizona. And now they were in flight from the sun and the drought. They drove all night, and came to the mountains in the night. And they crawled the jagged ramparts in the night, and their dim lights flickered on the pale stone walls of the road. They passed the summit in the dark and came slowly down in the late night, through the shattered stone debris of Oatman; and when the daylight came they saw the Colorado river below them. They drove to Topock, pulled up at the bridge while a guard washed off the windshield sticker. Then across the bridge and into the broken rock wilderness. And although they were dead weary and the morning heat was growing, they stopped.

Pa called, "We're there—we're in California!" They looked dully at the broken rock glaring under the sun, and across the river the terrible ramparts of Arizona.

"We got the desert," said Tom. "We got to get to the water and rest."

The truck took the road and moved up the long hill, through the broken, rotten rock. The engine boiled very soon and Tom slowed down and took it easy. Up the long slope, winding and twisting through dead country, burned white and gray, and no hint of life in it. Once Tom stopped for a few moments to let the engine cool, and then he traveled on. They topped the pass while the sun was still up, and looked down on the desert—black cinder mountains in the distance, and the yellow sun reflected on the gray desert. The little starved bushes, sage and greasewood, threw bold shadows on the sand and bits of rock. The glaring sun was straight ahead. Tom held his hand before his eyes to see at all. They passed the crest and coasted down to cool the engine. They coasted down the long sweep to the floor of the desert, and the fan turned over to cool the water in the radiator. In the driver's seat, Tom and Al and Pa, and Winfield on Pa's knee, looked into the bright descending sun, and their eyes were stony, and their brown faces were damp with perspiration. The burnt land and the black, cindery hills broke the even distance and made it terrible in the reddening light of the setting sun.

Al said, "Jesus, what a place. How'd you like to walk acrost her?"

"People done it," said Tom. "Lots a people done it; an' if they could, we could."

"Lots must a died," said Al.

All night they bored through the hot darkness, and jackrabbits scuttled into the lights and dashed away in long jolting leaps. And the dawn came up behind them when the lights of Mojave were ahead. And the dawn showed high mountains to the west. They filled with water and oil at Mojave and crawled into the mountains, and the dawn was about them.

Tom said, "Jesus, the desert's past! Pa, Al, for Christ sakes! The desert's past!"

"I'm too goddamn tired to care," said Al.

"Want me to drive?"

"No, wait awhile."

They drove through Tehachapi in the morning glow, and the sun came up behind them, and then—suddenly they saw the great valley below them. Al jammed on the brake and stopped in the middle of the road, and, "Jesus Christ! Look!" he said. The vineyards, the orchards, the great flat valley, green and beautiful, the trees set in rows, and the farm houses.

Part Thirteen

THE MILITARY

From the first sixteenth-century Spanish Conquistador to missile research at White Sands Proving Grounds, the military in all its forms—as explorers as well as warriors—has been an integral part of Western life.

124

THE LAST WORD
FROM THE
ALAMO

William Travis

On February 23, 1836 in the opening days of Texas' war of independence from Mexico, General Santa Anna's troops entered San Antonio and began the siege of the Alamo mission, which Colonel William Travis was defending with 187 men. No aid came, and on March 6 the Mexicans stormed the Alamo, killing the last defenders, including Davy Crockett and James Bowie. Travis wrote this letter the second day of the seige.

"To the People of Texas and All Americans in the World."

"Fellow Citizens and Compatriots: I am besieged by a thousand or more of the Mexicans under Santa Anna. I have sustained a continual bombardment and cannonade for twenty-four hours and have not lost a man. The enemy has demanded a surrender at discretion, otherwise the garrison are to be put to the sword, if the fort is taken. I have answered the demand with a cannon shot, and our flag still waves proudly from the walls. *I shall never surrender or retreat. Then,* I call on you in the name of Liberty, of patriotism and everything dear to the American character, to come to our aid with all dispatch. The enemy is receiving reinforcements daily and will no doubt increase to three or four thousand in four or five days. If this call is neglected, I am determined to sustain myself as long as possible and die like a soldier who never forgets what is due his own honor and that of his country.

VICTORY OR DEATH.

"William Barrett Travis, Lt. Col. comdt.

"P. S.—The Lord is on our side. When the enemy appeared in sight we had not three bushels of corn. We have since found in deserted houses eighty to ninety bushels and got into the walls twenty or thirty head of beeves."

125

THE MORMON BATTALION

James Ferguson

After the mob murder of their prophet Joseph Smith, the Mormons began their great westward trek seeking a Zion where they could practice their religion safe from American persecution. When the Mexican War began, Mormon men of all ages volunteered for a battalion and contributed their pay to their church. Sergeant Major James Ferguson, a veteran of this little-known incident, described it in a lecture in England in 1855.

"We were mustered into service on the 16th of July, 1846. A few hurried preparations, and the gray haired old men and striplings marched off merrily as our commander ordered the music to play a hasty farewell to 'the friends we left behind us.'

"Deprived of the rights granted to other volunteers, of choosing our own officers, Captain Allen, of the regular dragoons, was commissioned by the President of the United States to command us. But he was a gallant and brave officer. The rigid discipline and rough service of the army had failed to smother the better impulses of his generous heart. He was ever ready to befriend us, and but for his stern and willing interference, we would have been compelled to submit to, or avenge, various and repeated insults as we passed down the frontiers of Missouri to our place of outfit, Fort Leavenworth.

"But our bright hopes in him had an end here. Scarcely had we resumed our march, when the sad news of his death overtook us. A gloom overspread our whole camp, for there was not a heart but loved him.

"At Council Grove, we were halted to deliberate how to proceed. The command of the Battalion was here given to Lieutenant Smith, of the First Dragoons. Letters were despatched to President Polk, praying for the privilege due to us, of electing our commander. And now commenced a series of the most trying cruelties. Our commander was not of himself cruel and wicked, but he was weak, and became, to a great extent, the creature of Doctor Sanderson, a rotten-hearted quack, that was imposed upon us as our surgeon. The hospital wagons, designed for our use by Colonel Allen, were left behind. These abuses continued and increased until, when we mustered at Santa Fe, and on the Rio Grande, one hundred and fifty of the Battalion were pronounced unable to continue the march to California. These were ordered back to winter quarters at the Pueblo near Taos, where, in the midst of much suffering and exposure, their term of enlistment nearly expired. Some of them died there; and among the number, young Richards, to whom I have before referred, and Blanchard, an only son of aged depending parents.

"On our arrival at Santa Fe, instead of the favorable answer we had a right to expect from the government, we found Captain Cooke appointed to take command—an officer also of the First Dragoons, famous, in his own corps, for the tyrannical strictness of his discipline. Not a murmur was heard at this fresh indignity.

"With a sorry outfit of jaded mules, famished beeves, and scabby sheep, we resumed our march. While yet in the settlements of New Mexico, our rations were reduced a quarter; and for our comfort, we learned that for a march of a hundred days, over an undiscovered country, we had fifty days' scanty rations.

"Leaving the Rio Grande, about the southern boundary of New Mexico, without a guide who knew the country before us, we turned in a westerly course. We threaded our way through the Sierra del Madre, cutting a road through the "Pass of the Guadaloupe," alternately pulling our ponderous wagons up the sandy hills, and lifting them down the rocky descents. The various incidents of our travels, each day presenting something new, are materials for a long history. I can only glance hastily at some scenes as I pass along.

"Descending the Sierra del Madre, as we came in sight of the valley of the San Pedro, the vast prospect before us made us for a moment forget our fatigues and sufferings. Fresh hope seemed to enliven every heart. It seemed like a new world ready for population. Parched, and fainting with thirst, the waters of the river were before us, and the shade trees on its banks.

"While marching down this river, a scene occurred, which, while it afforded amusement to some and suffering to others, manifested the kind watch-care of our Heavenly Father. Our beeves had dwindled down to a few sickly skeletons. Our camp was threatened with scurvy, and many attacked with diarrhœa; and there seemed no hope for us. Surprised, and some of them wounded by our hunters, a herd of wild cattle made their appearance on all sides of us. Some, more furious than the rest, made a dash at our train. One pitched a poor fellow into the air, severely wounding him. Another tossed a mule on its horns, and tore his entrails, while another lifted a wagon out of its track.

"The troops of four 'Presidios,' having learned of our approach, had assembled at Tucson to interrupt our march. Heedless of the threats of the Mexican commandante, we advanced, and, as the troops retreated with their artillery, we marched through their walled town.

"A desert of seventy miles brought us to the Gila. We were welcomed by the rude hospitality of the Pimas. An old chief, at the head of his warriors, squaws, and little ones met us in the path, and presenting his cakes of sweet cornmeal, invoked upon us the protection of the Great Spirit as we passed on.

"On the 10th of January, 1847, we crossed the Colorado. An unsuccessful attempt to raft our provisions down the Gila had deprived us of a great part of them, although we were already reduced to quarter rations. Without a chance for rest, we entered upon the 'Tierra Calienta,' the Big Desert of the Colorado. Ninety miles without water, save in the deep wells we dug but had no time to drink from, brought us to the end of our deserts. Those alone who endured them can conceive the sufferings experienced on this desert. It was well named the Hot Land. In vain was our rear guard ordered to prevent the men from lagging behind; the stoutest staggered, and one after another fell fainting. They would revive, advance, and fall again; and many, when at last water and grass were found, fell down exhausted, unable to reach the camp. The clear stream appeared to laugh at them in mockery, and there they lay gasping till some feeling messmate returned with the replenished canteen.

"A few days brought us to the rancho of the American Warner. Unlike the hospitable Pimas, he hid his bread and drove his cattle into the mountains. Here we learned of the retreat of the Californians from Los Angeles. Without a pause for rest, we changed our course to meet them, but they concealed themselves till we had passed.

"Thus, despite of every attempt to bring us to an engagement, we reached our destination at San Diego, on the 31st of January, fulfilling the prediction of our President, that we should not fight a battle. God fought our battles for us, and our victories were not bought with blood. Garrison duty, drills, and entrenching the camp at Los Angeles, made up the balance of our service."

126

"WE HAVE COME AMONGST YOU"

Stephen Watts Kearny

In 1846, U.S. forces under General Stephen Watts Kearny occupied New Mexico. The General collected Santa Feans in the plaza and delivered the following proclamation—a beautiful summation of the national ideals. It should be sadly noted that before long U.S. troops were slaughtering Taos Indians by firing a cannon point blank into the church at their pueblo, and Navajo children were being auctioned into slavery (illegal in Mexico) at about $70 a head in the Santa Fe market.

"New Mexicans: We have come amongst you to take possession of New Mexico, which we do in the name of the government of the United States. We have come with peaceable intentions and kind feelings toward you all. We come as friends, to better your condition and make you a part of the republic of the United States. We mean not to murder you or rob you of your property. Your families shall be free from molestation; your women secure from violence. My soldiers shall take nothing from you but what they pay for. In taking possession of New Mexico, we do not mean to take away from you your religion. Religion and government have no connection in our country. There, all religions are equal; one has no preference over the other; the Catholic and the Protestant are esteemed alike. Every man has a right to serve God according to his heart. When a man dies he must render to God an account of his acts here on earth, whether they be good or bad. In our government, all men are equal. We esteem the most peaceable man the best man. I advise you to attend to your domestic pursuits, cultivate industry, be peaceable and obedient to the laws. Do not resort to violent means to correct abuses. I do hereby proclaim that, being in possession of Santa Fé, I am therefore virtually in possession of all New Mexico. Armîjo is no longer your governor. His power is departed; but he will return and be as one of you. When he shall return you are not to molest him. You are no longer Mexican subjects; you are now American citizens, subject only to the laws of the United States. A change of government has taken place in New Mexico and you no longer owe allegiance to the Mexican government. I do hereby proclaim my intention to establish in this Department a civil government on a republican basis, similar to those of our own states. It is my intention, also, to continue in office those by whom you have been governed, except the governor, and such other persons as I shall appoint to office by virtue of the authority vested in me. I am your governor—henceforth look to me for protection."

127

PADDY GRAYDON'S CIVIL WAR

During the Civil War, Confederate troops from Texas invaded New Mexico in 1861 and captured Albuquerque and Santa Fe and then ran into a strong Union force at Glorieta. The battle was considered a draw, but the rebels' supplies were exhausted and they withdrew. Paddy Graydon was one of the more colorful of the Union troopers and this exploit was recorded in Sibley's New Mexico Campaign.

Long a resident of New Mexico, Captain James "Paddy" Graydon was probably the most colorful figure of [Union general] Canby's command next to "Kit" Carson. Before the Federal troops evacuated Arizona, he had operated a saloon at Fort Buchanan. Later he recruited a company of Unionists who had been dispossessed and driven north by Southern sympathizers. To them, perhaps more than to the others, the present war was a personal matter. Graydon's Independent Spy Company served the four-fold purpose of spy, scout, police, and forager.

With Canby's permission [the night before the battle of Valverde], Graydon packed a dozen twenty-four-pounder howitzer shells in two wooden boxes. After lashing these on the backs of two old mules, he and three or four of his men crossed the river under cover of darkness and headed toward the Confederate camp. When within 150 yards of the enemy line, they lighted the fuses, drove the mules forward, and began a hasty retreat. On looking back, Graydon's party was horrified to see that the mules, instead of going toward the enemy, were following them! The shells soon exploded, bringing the Confederate camp quickly to arms. Graydon and his men were unharmed, and made their way back to Fort Craig, needless to say, without the mules.

128

CUSTER'S LAST
LETTER HOME

George Armstrong Custer

*Like the late General George S. Patton, General George Armstrong Custer was
one of those war lovers who delight in battle. While General Patton gloried in
combat from the comfort and safety of the rear, General Custer was as reckless
with his own life as he was with his men's. He wrote the following letter to his
wife on June 25, 1876. Four days later, Sioux warriors defending their homes
and families eliminated him and the Seventh Cavalry.*

Mouth of Rosebud, June 21, 1876. . . . Look on my map and you will find
our present location on the Yellowstone, about midway between Tongue
River and the Big Horn.

The scouting-party has returned. They saw the trail and deserted
camp of a village of three hundred and eighty (380) lodges. The trail was
about one week old. The scouts reported that they could have overtaken
the village in one day and a half. I am now going to take up the trail where
the scouting-party turned back. I fear their failure to follow up the Indians
has imperilled our plans by giving the village an intimation of our presence.
Think of the valuable time lost! But I feel hopeful of accomplishing great
results. I will move directly up the valley of the Rosebud. General Gibbon's
command and General Terry, with steamer, will proceed up the Big Horn
as far as the boat can go. . . . I like campaigning with pack-mules much

better than with wagons, leaving out the question of luxuries. We take no tents, and desire none.

I now have some Crow scouts with me, as they are familiar with the country. They are magnificent-looking men, so much handsomer and more Indian-like than any we have ever seen, and so jolly and sportive; nothing of the gloomy, silent red-man about them. They have formally given themselves to me, after the usual talk. In their speech they said they had heard that I never abandoned a trail; that when my food gave out I ate mule. That was the kind of a man they wanted to fight under; they were willing to eat mule too.

I am going to send six Ree scouts to Powder River with the mail; from there it will go with other scouts to Fort Buford. . . .

June 22d—11 A.M. . . . I have but a few moments to write, as we move at twelve, and I have my hands full of preparations for the scout. . . . Do not be anxious about me. You would be surprised to know how closely I obey your instructions about keeping with the column. I hope to have a good report to send you by the next mail. . . . A success will start us all towards Lincoln. . . .

I send you an extract from General Terry's official order, knowing how keenly you appreciate words of commendation and confidence, such as the following: "It is of course impossible to give you any definite instructions in regard to this movement; and were it not impossible to do so, the Department Commander places too much confidence in your zeal, energy, and ability to wish to impose upon you precise orders, which might hamper your action when nearly in contact with the enemy."

129

MRS. CUSTER
HEARS THE NEWS

Elizabeth Custer

In her book, Boots and Saddles, *published in 1885, the General's widow recalled the day the steamboat arrived with the wounded and the news.*

A picture of one day of our life in those disconsolate times is fixed indelibly in my memory.

On Sunday afternoon, the 25th of June, our little group of saddened women, borne down with one common weight of anxiety, sought solace in gathering together in our house. We tried to find some slight surcease from trouble in the old hymns: some of them dated back to our childhood's days, when our mothers rocked us to sleep to their soothing strains. I remember the grief with which one fair young wife threw herself on the carpet and pillowed her head in the lap of a tender friend. Another sat dejected at the piano, and struck soft chords that melted into the notes of the voices. All were absorbed in the same thoughts, and their eyes were filled with far-away visions and longings. Indescribable yearning for the absent, and untold terror for their safety, engrossed each heart. The words of the hymn,

> *"E'en though a cross it be,*
> *Nearer, my God, to Thee,"*

came forth with almost a sob from every throat.

At that very hour the fears that our tortured minds had portrayed in imagination were realities, and the souls of those we thought upon were ascending to meet their Maker.

On the 5th of July—for it took that time for the news to come—the sun rose on a beautiful world, but with its earliest beams came the first knell of disaster. A steamer came down the river bearing the wounded from the battle of the Little Big Horn, of Sunday, June 25th. This battle wrecked the lives of twenty-six women at Fort Lincoln, and orphaned children of officers and soldiers joined their cry to that of their bereaved mothers.

From that time the life went out of the hearts of the "women who weep," and God asked them to walk on alone and in the shadow.

Part Fourteen

◆

THE WESTERN WAY WITH WORDS

The West spiced the English language with its own regional flavor—as all regions do—adopting Spanish nouns such as mesa, butte, *and* arroyo *for terrain features and mixing in the working vocabulary of the cattle industry. But there's no reason to argue that Western rhetoric was any better or any worse than any other region's. However, the circumstances that provoked it were often unusual.*

130

"JOSÉ MARIA MARTÍN! STAND UP!"

Kirby Benedict (1811–1871) was a federal judge at Taos, New Mexico, in the 1860s when he issued the following verdict. As with the Alferd E. Packer case (see the following selection) the judge's blood-thirst may have been thwarted. Popular belief has it that Martín broke jail and vanished. Alas, Howard Bryan, longtime local colorist for the Albuquerque Tribune, *whom I rate the ultimate authority on such matters, assures me that Martín was actually executed.*

When the time for sentence had arrived the prisoner was brought before the judge, who addressed him as follows:

"José Maria Martin, stand up! José Maria Martin, you have been indicted, tried and convicted by a jury of your countrymen of the crime of murder, and the court is now about to pass upon you the dread sentence of the law. As a usual thing, José Maria Martin, it is a painful duty for the judge of a court of justice to pronounce upon a human being the sentence of death. There is something horrible about it, and the mind of the court naturally revolts from the performance of such a duty. Happily, however, your case is relieved of all such unpleasant features and the Court takes positive delight in sentencing you to death!

"You are a young man, José Maria Martin; apparently of good physical condition and robust health. Ordinarily you might have looked forward to

461

many years of life, and the Court has no doubt you have, and have expected to die at a ripe old age; but you are about to be cut off in consequence of your own act. José Maria Martin, it is now the spring-time, in a little while the grass will be springing up green in these beautiful valleys, and on these broad mesas and mountain sides flowers will be blooming; birds will be singing their sweet carols, and nature will be putting on her most gorgeous and her most attractive robes, and life will be pleasant and men will want to stay, but none of this for you, José Maria Martin; the flowers will not bloom for you, José Maria Martin; the birds will not carol for you, José Maria Martin; when these things come to gladden the senses of men, you will be occupying a space about six by two beneath the sod, and the green grass and those beautiful flowers will be growing above your lowly head.

"The sentence of the Court is that you be taken from this place to the county jail; that you be there kept safely and securely confined, in the custody of the sheriff until the day appointed for your execution. (Be very careful, Mr. Sheriff, that he have no opportunity to escape and that you have him at the appointed place at the appointed time.) That you be so kept, José Maria Martin, until—(Mr. Clerk, on what day of the month does Friday, about two weeks from this time come? March twenty-second, your Honor). Very well,—until Friday, the twenty second day of March, when you will be taken by the sheriff from your place of confinement to some safe and convenient spot within the county (that is in your discretion, Mr. Sheriff, you are only confined to the limits of this county), and that you be there hanged by the neck until you are dead, and the Court was about to add, José Maria Martin, 'May God have mercy on your soul,' but the Court will not assume the responsibility of asking an Allwise Providence to do that which a jury of your peers has refused to do. The Lord could not have mercy on your soul! However, if you affect any religious belief, or are connected with any religious organization, it might be well for you to send for your priest or your minister and get from him,—well,—such consolation as you can; but the Court advises you to place no reliance upon anything of that kind! Mr. Sheriff, remove the prisoner."

131

"STAND UP, YE SON-OF-A-BITCH"

Walker Dixon Grisso

*The eatery at the University of Colorado student union is called the Alferd E.
Packer Memorial Dining Room, making it the only diner known to be named
for a cannibal who misspelled his own name. Apparently the party of gold
prospectors Packer had guided into the mountains in 1875 was trapped by a
snow storm and ran out of food. Seven years later Packer was accused of
murdering his charges and eating them. He was convicted, got a new trial on
a technicality, and was again convicted and sentenced by Judge M. B. Gerry,
who seems to have been a Democrat. Packer was subsequently pardoned and
died in Denver in 1906. The following account is by Walker Dixon Grisso.
(Needless to say, the Dolan short version is the one most beloved by Westerners.)*

Judge M. B. Gerry (1843–1912), born in Florida and educated in Florida
and Georgia, studied and was admitted to the Bar of Georgia in 1870. In
1873 he opened a law office in Denver, Colorado. In 1882, he was elected
Judge of the large Seventh Judicial District, which included Hinsdale
County.

In 1883 at Lake City, the county seat of Hinsdale County, Alfred
Packer was tried for murder. He had guided a group of five persons into
the San Juan Mountains in the winter and had returned as the only
survivor. The evidence was clear that cannibalism as well as murder was
present.

A barfly, James Dolan, was a witness for the prosecution and when Judge Gerry sentenced Packer, he rushed to his favorite bar and reported the sentence in language substantially as follows:

"Stand-up, ye son-of-a-bitch and receive your sentence. You voracious, man-eating son-of-a-bitch, there were only six Democrats in Hinsdale County and you et five of them. I'm going to hang you on Friday and this should teach you a lesson not to reduce the Democratic population of this state."

Packer was not hung, for about the turn of the century he was pardoned, his champion being the newspaper *The Denver Post.*
The sentence in part is here repeated:

"In 1874 you, in company with five companions, passed through this beautiful mountain valley where stands the town of Lake City. At that time the hand of man had not marred the beauties of nature. The picture was fresh from the hand of the Great Artist who created it. You and your companions camped at the base of a grand old mountain, in sight of the place you now stand, on the banks of a stream as pure and beautiful as ever traced by the finger of God upon the bosom of earth. Your very surrounding was calculated to impress upon your heart and nature the omnipotence of Deity and the helplessness of your own feeble life. In this goodly favored spot you conceived your murderous designs.

"You and your victims had had a weary march, and when *the shadows of the mountains* fell upon your little party and night drew her sable curtain around you, your unsuspecting victims lay down on the ground and were soon lost in the sleep of the weary; and when thus sweetly unconscious of danger from any quarter, and particularly from you, their trusted companion, you cruelly and brutally slew them all. Whether your murderous hand was guided by the misty light of the moon, or the flickering blaze of the camp fire, you only can tell. No eye saw the bloody deed performed; no ear, save your own, caught the groans of your dying victims. You then and there robbed the living of life, and then robbed the dead of the reward of honest toil which they had accumulated; at least so say the jury.

". . . Be not deceived. God is not mocked, for whatsoever a man soweth, that shall he also reap. You, Alfred Packer, sowed the wind; you must now reap the whirlwind. Society cannot forgive you for the crime you have committed; it enforces the Old Mosaic law of a life for a life, and your life must be taken as the penalty of your crime. I am but the instrument of society to impose the punishment which the law provides. While society cannot forgive, it will forget. As the days come and go and the years of your pilgrimage roll by, the memory of you and your crimes will fade from the minds of men.

"With God it is different. He will not forget, but will forgive. He pardoned the thief on the Cross. He is the same God today as then—a God of love and of mercy, of long-suffering and kind forbearance; a God who tempers the wind to the shorn lamb, and promises rest to all the weary and heartbroken children of men; and it is to this God I commend you.

"Close your ears to the blandishments of hope. Listen not to its fluttering promises of life. But prepare to meet the spirits of thy murdered victims. Prepare for the dread certainty of death. Prepare to meet thy God; prepare to meet that aged father and mother of whom you have spoken and who still love you as their dear boy . . ."

132

WHY WILDERNESS?

Ed Abbey

His Desert Solitaire, a Season in the Wilderness, made the late Ed Abbey the guru of activist conservationists and also made him popular with those who enjoy clean prose, free of clichés and romance. He spoke for a myriad of Westerners who love the land and can tolerate people only in very small numbers. In this selection from his classic book he defines his concept of wilderness.

Wilderness. The word itself is music.

Wilderness, wilderness. . . . We scarcely know what we mean by the term, though the sound of it draws all whose nerves and emotions have not yet been irreparably stunned, deadened, numbed by the caterwauling of commerce, the sweating scramble for profit and domination.

Why such allure in the very word? What does it really mean? Can wilderness be defined in the words of government officialdom as simply "A minimum of not less than 5000 contiguous acres of roadless area"? This much may be essential in attempting a definition but it is not sufficient; something more is involved.

Suppose we say that wilderness invokes nostalgia, a justified not merely sentimental nostalgia for the lost America our forefathers knew. The word suggests the past and the unknown, the womb of earth from which we all emerged. It means something lost and something still present, something remote and at the same time intimate, something buried in our blood and nerves, something beyond us and without limit. Romance—but not to be dismissed on that account. The romantic view, while not the whole of truth, is a necessary part of the whole truth.

But the love of wilderness is more than a hunger for what is always beyond reach; it is also an expression of loyalty to the earth, the earth which bore us and sustains us, the only home we shall ever know, the only paradise we ever need—if only we had the eyes to see. Original sin, the true original sin, is the blind destruction for the sake of greed of this natural paradise which lies all around us—if only we were worthy of it.

Now when I write of paradise I mean *Paradise,* not the banal Heaven of the saints. When I write "paradise" I mean not only apple trees and golden women but also scorpions and tarantulas and flies, rattlesnakes and Gila monsters, sandstorms, volcanos and earthquakes, bacteria and bear, cactus, yucca, bladderweed, ocotillo and mesquite, flash floods and quicksand, and yes—disease and death and the rotting of the flesh.

Paradise is not a garden of bliss and changeless perfection where the lions lie down like lambs (what would they eat?) and the angels and cherubim and seraphim rotate in endless idiotic circles, like clockwork, about an equally inane and ludicrous—however roseate—Unmoved Mover. (Play safe; worship only in clockwise direction; let's all have fun together.) That particular painted fantasy of a realm beyond time and space which Aristotle and the Church Fathers tried to palm off on us has met, in modern times, only neglect and indifference, passing on into the oblivion it so richly deserved, while the Paradise of which I write and wish to praise is with us yet, the here and now, the actual, tangible, dogmatically real earth on which we stand.

Some people who think of themselves as hard-headed realists would tell us that the cult of the wild is possible only in an atmosphere of comfort and safety and was therefore unknown to the pioneers who subdued half a continent with their guns and plows and barbed wire. Is this true? Consider the sentiments of Charles Marion Russell, the cowboy artist, as quoted in John Hutchens' *One Man's Montana:*

"I have been called a pioneer. In my book a pioneer is a man who comes to virgin country, traps off all the fur, kills off all the wild meat, cuts down all the trees, grazes off all the grass, plows the roots up and strings ten million miles of wire. A pioneer destroys things and calls it civilization."

Others who endured hardships and privations no less severe than those of the frontiersmen were John Muir, H. D. Thoreau, John James Audubon and the painter George Catlin, all of whom wandered on foot over much of our country and found in it something more than merely raw material for pecuniary exploitation.

A sixth example and my favorite is, of course, Major J. Wesley Powell, one-armed veteran of the Civil War, sitting in a chair lashed to the deck of the small wooden boat with which he led his brave party into the unknown canyons of the Green, Grand and Colorado rivers. From the railroad town of Green River, Wyoming, to the mouth of the Grand Canyon in what is now Lake Mead, Powell's first journey took three months. Within that time he and his men withstood a variety of unpleasant experiences, including the loss of a boat, the hard toil of lowering their boats by rope down the worst of the rapids, moldy flour and shortages of meat, extremes of heat and cold, illness, and the constant fear of the unknown, the uncertainty of success, the ever-present possibility that around the next bend of the canyon they might encounter hazards worse than any they had so far overcome. This psychological pressure eventually proved too much for three of Powell's men; near the end of the voyage these three left the expedition and tried to make their way overland back to civilization—and were all killed by Indians. Powell knew the inner gorge of the Grand Canyon as a terrible and gloomy underworld, scene of much physical and mental suffering for himself and his men, but despite this and despite all that had happened in his explorations, he would write of the canyon as a whole in panegyric accent:

"The glories and the beauties of form, color and sound unite in the Grand Canyon—forms unrivaled even by the mountains, colors that vie with sunsets, and sounds that span the diapason from tempest to tinkling raindrop, from cataract to bubbling fountain. . . .

"You cannot see the Grand Canyon in one view, as if it were a changeless spectacle from which a curtain might be lifted, but to see it you have to toil from month to month through its labyrinths. It is a region more difficult to traverse than the Alps or the Himalayas, but if strength and courage are sufficient for the task, by a year's toil a concept of sublimity can be obtained never again to be equaled on the hither side of Paradise."

No, wilderness is not a luxury but a necessity of the human spirit, and as vital to our lives as water and good bread. A civilization which destroys what little remains of the wild, the spare, the original, is cutting itself off from its origins and betraying the principle of civilization itself.

If industrial man continues to multiply his numbers and expand his operations he will succeed in his apparent intention, to seal himself off from the natural and isolate himself within a synthetic prison of his own making. He will make himself an exile from the earth and then will know at last, if he is still capable of feeling anything, the pain and agony of final loss.

He will understand what the captive Zia Indians meant when they made a song out of their sickness for home:

> My home over there,
> Now I remember it;
> And when I see that mountain far away,
> Why then I weep,
> Why then I weep,
> Remembering my home.

133

"THE DIRTY NINCOMPOOP WHO EDITS THAT JOURNAL"

Frontier newspaper editors raised vituperation to a fine art—especially when lambasting one another. The following examples are from the Weekly Arizona Miner, *edited by John Marion at Prescott, and the* Arizona Sentinel, *edited by Judge William J. Berry at Yuma. The fact that the two men were old friends did not moderate the language.*

Having found a fighting editor to defend the *Sentinel* and its editor, Judge Berry returns to his long-standing feud with Marion of the *Arizona Miner*. Marion has questioned Berry's right to the title of judge, while conceding that he is a judge of whiskey. To this, Berry retorts.

In the daily issue of [The Arizona "Miner"] this most scurrilous sheet of October 27th, we find an article in reference to ourself, which is altogether characteristic of the dirty nincompoop who edits that journal.

We shall not attempt to reply scriatim to the charges brought against us in said article, but will simply say that it is a batch of infernal falsehoods from beinning to end. The infernal wretch who edits the *Miner* and who wrote that article, well knows, as every man in Arizona knows, who ever saw him, that

470

he is nothing if not a black-guard. He accuses us of being a gunsmith. We are proud of that, as many a man in Arizona knows that we are a good one. At the same time we are a better editor and a better and more respectable man than he is which fact is also well known. He charges us with demanding high prices for our gunsmith work. To that we have now to say, that we never got as much as our work was worth, and lost fifteen hundred dollars by trusting certain infernal scoundrels in Prescott and vicinity.

The miserable liar also says that he let us write a communication for the *Miner*, years ago. Why the miserable cuss used to beg us to write for his dirty abortion, and since we quit writing for it, many Arizonans say that the *Miner* is not worth a d—n, and that is our opinion too, though we never expressed it publicly before. Marion says we used to reside "up in *Osegon!*" Where is Osegon? (*sic*) We would like to know . . .

In regard to our being a "judge of whiskey," we will simply say that no man ever saw Wm. J. Berry laid out under its influence; while we had the extreme mortification of seeing the editor of the *Miner*, in a party given by Col. Baker in Prescott, laid out in the refreshment room, dead drunk, with candles placed at his head and his feet, and a regular "wake" held over him.

It was then for the first time that we discovered Darwin's connecting link. As he lay, with his drunken slobber issuing from his immense mouth which extends from ear to ear, and his ears reaching up so high, everyone present was forcibly impressed with the fact that there was a connecting link between the catfish and the jackass. What we have here faintly described is the truth, to attest which there are plenty of living witnesses. Now dry up, or we will come out with some more reminiscences.

(*Arizona Sentinel* of Nov. 7, 1874)

When two editors have such vivid personalities, each wants the last word. Since there is no pressing business at the time, a good fight adds sparkle to an infrequent moment of calm in the Territory. Marion then replies to Berry's latest editorial with:

We had intended to let the mammoth ape whose name appears as editor of the Yuma *Sentinel* severely alone, until a day or two ago when a citizen of Prescott requested us to inform our readers that Berry uttered a gratuitous falsehood when he stated . . . that "he lost $1,500 by trusting certain infernal scoundrels in Prescott and vicinity."

This being a reasonable and legitimate request, we now assert that Berry lied when he said so, and that it would take more than $1,500 to pay for the whiskey which Berry "bumed" during his long sojourn in Prescott, not to speak of that which he guzzled in our sister county of Mohave, previous to the day upon which he found himself debarred from the privilege of swallowing whiskey in Cerbat.

Again, we have been asked our reasons for not giving the lie to certain assertions of his, regarding ourself. Well, one reason is: Berry is a natural and artificial liar, whom nobody was ever known to believe. Then, he did tell one truth about us, i.e., that drink once got the better of us . . . We were drunk that night, and have never yet attempted to deny it. But, Berry drank ten times to our once, and the only reason he did not fall down and crawl on all fours like the beast that he is, was that there was not sufficient liquor in the house to fill his hogshead. Berry says no one ever saw him get drunk. When he lived in Prescott his first great care was to fill himself with whiskey, after which it was his custom to walk like the swine that he is, on all fours, to his den.

He cannot have forgotten his visit to Lynx Creek, in 1864, when he rolled over a pine log dead drunk, and served a useful purpose for a jacose man. Yes, Judge, we own up to that little drunk of ours; but, unlike you, we were not pointed out and derided as a regular whiskey bloat; nor did any person ever attempt to use us for a water-closet, as you were used that day on Lynx Creek.

As to your being a better editor than the writer of this, it is for the public to judge; not for you to assert, although you asserted it.

You have called us a blackguard, regardless of the old story about the kettle.

Then you have accused us of toadying to Gen. Crook; you, who have toadied and bent your knees to every placeholder, capitalist and bar-keeper in this section of Arizona; you, who made an ass of yourself by firing an anvil salute in honor of Gen. Stoneman, who, you will recollect, never acknowledged the "honor done him." And you take up the cudgels for thieving

Indian agents and, by so doing, go back on your record, made when you used to write and speak against the "Indian Ring Robbers and Murderers."

Ah, Judge, you have had many masters; have been everything (except an independent man), by turns and nothing long. Had you changed your shirts as often as you have changed masters, there would be one sand-bar less in the Colorado river, and we would not know that you are in Yuma when, according to your published statement, you should be in San Francisco.

Hoping that these few lines will find you drunk and obedient to your masters, as usual, we say, in your own "classic" language, "uncork and be d—d."

(*Arizona Miner* of Jan. 5, 1875)

134

"TO THE WORLD!!"

James W. Nesmith

Troubled by mudslinging in modern politics? Note the following handbill distributed on election day in an 1847 campaign in Oregon. Thornton won.

TO THE WORLD!!
J. QUINN THORNTON,

Having resorted to low, cowardly and dishonorable means, for the purpose of injuring my character and standing, and having refused honorable satisfaction, which I have demanded; I avail myself of this opportunity of publishing him to the world as a reclaimless liar, an infamous scoundrel, a blackhearted villain, an arrant coward, a worthless vagabond and an imported miscreant, a disgrace to the profession and a dishonor to his country.

James W. Nesmith.

Oregon City, June, 7, 1847

135

"I ASK: WHAT IS LIFE?"

Herman W. Knickerbocker

Riley Grannan was a mining country gambler who operated a saloon and variety theater in Rawhide, Nevada, and whose death in 1908 provoked the following eulogy. An itinerant minister, actor, and prospector named Herman W. Knickerbocker delivered it and a reporter for a California newspaper wrote it down for his column.

"I feel, that it is incumbent upon me to state that in standing here I occupy no ministerial or prelative position. I am simply a prospector. I make no claims whatever to moral merit or to religion, except the religion of humanity, the brotherhood of man. I stand among you today simply as a man among men, feeling that I can shake hands and say 'brother' to the vilest man or woman that ever lived. If there should come to you anything of moral admonition through what I say, it comes not from any sense of moral superiority, but from the depths of my experience.

"Riley Grannan was born in Paris, Kentucky, about forty years ago. I suppose he dreamed all the dreams of boyhood. They blossomed into phenomenal success along financial lines at times during his life. I am told that from the position of a bell boy in a hotel, he rose rapidly to be a celebrity of worldwide fame. He was one of the greatest plungers, probably, that the continent has ever produced.

"He died the day before yesterday in Rawhide.

"This is a very brief statement. You have the birth and the period of the grave. Who can fill the interim? Who can speak of his hopes and fears? Who can solve the mystery of his quiet hours that only he himself knew? I cannot.

"He was born in the sunny southland—in Kentucky. He died in Rawhide.

"There is the beginning and the end. I wonder if we can see in this picture what Ingersoll said at the grave of his brother? 'Whether it be near the shore, or in mid-ocean or among the breakers, at last a wreck must mark the end of one and all.'

"He was born in the sunny southland where brooks and rivers run musically through the luxuriant land; where the magnolia grandiflora, like white stars, glow in a firmament of green; where crystal lakes dot the greensward and the softest summer breezes dimple the wave lips into kisses for the lilies on the shore; where the air is resonant with the warbled melody of a thousand sweet-voiced birds and redolent of the perfume of many flowers. This was the beginning. He died in Rawhide, where in winter the shoulders of the mountains are wrapped in garments of ice, and in summer the blistering rays of the sun beat down upon the skeleton ribs of the desert. Is this a picture of universal human life?

"Sometimes, when I consider the circumstances of human life, a curse rises to my lips and, if you will allow me, I will say here that I speak from an individual point of view. I cannot express other than my own views. If I run counter to yours, at least give me credit for a desire to be honest.

"When I see the ambitions of man defeated; when I see him struggle with mind and body in the only legitimate prayer he can make to accomplish some end; when I see his aim and purpose frustrated by a fortuitous combination of circumstances over which he has no control; when I see the outstretched hand, just about to grasp the flag of victory, take instead the emblem of defeat, I ask, what is life? What is life? Dreams, awakening, and death; 'a pendulum 'twixt a smile and a tear;' 'a momentary halt within the waste, and then the nothing we set out from;' 'a walking shadow, a poor player that struts and frets his hour upon the stage and then is heard no more;' 'a tale told by an idiot; full of sound and fury, signifying nothing;' a child blown bubble that but reflects the light and shadow of its environment and is gone; a mockery, a sham, a lie, a fool's vision; its happiness but Dead Sea apples, its pain the crunching of a tyrant's heel. I feel as Omar did when he wrote:

" *'We are no other than a moving row*
Of magic shadow shapes that come and go

Round with the sun illumed lantern held
In midnight by the Master of the show;
But helpless pieces of the game He plays
Upon this checkerboard of nights and days,
Hither and thither moves, and checks and slays,
And one by one back in the closet lays.
The ball no question makes of ayes and noes,
But here or there as strikes the player goes;
And He that tossed you down into the field,
He knows about it all—He knows—He knows!'

"But I don't. This is my mood.

"Not so with Riley Grannan. If I have gauged his character correctly, he accepted the circumstances surrounding him as the mystic officials to whom the universe had delegated its whole office. He seemed to accept both defeat and victory with equanimity. He was a man whose exterior was as placid and gentle as I have ever seen, and yet when we look back over his meteoric past we can readily understand, if this statement be true, that he was absolutely invincible in spirit. If you will allow me, I will use a phrase most of you are acquainted with. He was a 'dead game sport.' I say it not irreverently, but fill the phrase as full of practical human philosophy as it will hold; and I believe that when you can say one is a 'dead game sport' you have reached the climax of human philosophy.

"I believe that Riley Grannan's life fully exemplified the philosophy of these verses:

" *'It's easy enough to be happy*
When life flows along like a song;
But the man worth while
Is the man who will smile
When everything goes dead wrong.'

" *'For the test of the heart is trouble,*
And it always comes with the years,
And the smile that is worth
The homage of earth
Is the smile that shines through tears.'

"I know that there are those who will condemn him. There are those who believe today that he is reaping the reward of a misspent life.

"There are those who are dominated by medieval creeds. To those I have no word to say in regard to him. They are ruled by the skeleton hand of the past, and fail to see the moral beauty of a character lived outside their puritanical ideas. His goodness was not of the type that reached its highest manifestations in any ceremonial piety. His goodness, I say, was not of that type, but of the type that finds expression in the hand clasp; the type that finds expression in a word of cheer to a discouraged brother, the type that finds expression in quiet deeds of charity; the type that finds expression in friendship—the sweetest flower that blooms along the dusty highway of life; the type that finds expression in manhood.

"He lived in the world of sport. I do not mince my words. I am telling what I believe to be true. In the world of sport—hilarity sometimes, and maybe worse. He left the impress of his character on the world and through the medium of his financial power he was able with his money to brighten the lives of its inhabitants. He wasted it, so the world says. But did it ever occur to you that the most sinful men and women who live in the world are still men and women? Did it ever occur to you that the men and women who inhabit the night world are still men and women? A little happiness brought into their lives means as much to them as happiness brought into the lives of the straight and good. If you can take one ray of sunlight into their night life and thereby bring them one single hour of happiness, I believe you are a benefactor.

"Riley Grannan might have 'wasted' some of his money in this way.

"Did you ever stop to think how God does not put all his sunbeams into corn, potatoes and flour? Did you ever notice the prodigality with which he scatters these sunbeams over the universe?

"Contemplate: God flings the Auroral beauties around the cold shoulders of the North; hangs the quivering picture of the mirage above the palpitating heart of the desert; scatters the sunbeams like gold upon the bosoms of myriad lakes that gem the verdant robe of nature; spangles the canopy of night with star-jewels and silvers the world with the reflected beams from Cynthia's mellow face; hangs the gorgeous crimson current of the Occident across the sleeping room of the sun; wakes the coy maid of dawn to step timidly from her boudoir of darkness to climb the steps of the Orient and fling wide open the gates of the morning. Then tripping over the landscape, kissing the flowers in her flight, she wakes the birds to herald with their music the coming of her King, who floods the world with refulgent gold. Wasted sunbeams, these? I say to you that the man who by the use of his money or power is able to smooth one wrinkle from the brow of care, is able to change one moan or sob into a song, is able to wipe away one tear and in its place put a jewel of joy—this man is a public benefactor. I believe that some of Riley Grannan's money was 'wasted' in this way.

* * *

"We stand at last in the presence of the Great Mystery. I know nothing about it, nor do you. We may have our hopes, but no knowledge. I do not know whether there be a future life or not. I do not say there is not. I simply say I do not know. I have watched the wicket gate close behind many and many a pilgrim. No word has come back to me. The gate is closed. Across the chasm is the gloomy cloud of death. I say I do not know. And if you will allow this expression, I do not know whether it is best that my dust or his at last should go to food the roots of the grasses, the sagebrush or the flowers, to be blown in protean forms by the low of the persistence of personal identity beyond what we call death. If this be all, 'after life's fitful fever, he sleeps well . . . nothing can harm him further.' God knows what is best.

"This may be infidelity; but if it is, I should like to know what faith means. I came into this universe without my volition—came and found a loving mother's arms to receive me. I had nothing to do with the preparation for my reception here. I have no power to change the environment of the future; but the same power which prepared the loving arms of a mother to receive me here will make proper reception for me there.

"God knows better than I what is good for me, and I leave it with God.

"If I had the power today by the simple turning of my hand to endow myself with personal immortality, in my finite ignorance I would refuse to turn my hand. God knows best. It may be that there is a future life. I know that sometimes I get very tired of this life. Hedged and cribbed, caged like a bird caught from the wilds that in its mad desire for freedom beats its wings against the bars only to fall back in defeat upon the floor, I long for death, if it will but break the bars that hold me captive.

"I was snowbound in the mountains once for three days. On account of the snow we had to remain immediately alongside the train. After three days of this, when our food had been exhausted, the whistle blew that meant the starting of the train out into the world again. It may be that death is but the signal whistle that marks the movement of the train out into the broader and freer stretches of spiritual being. As we stand in the presence of death we have no knowledge, but always, no matter how dark the gloomy clouds hang before me, there gleams the star of hope. Let us hope, then, that it may be the morning star of eternal day.

"It is dawning somewhere all the time. Did you ever pause to think that this old world of ours is constantly swinging into the dawn? Down the grooves of time, flung by the hand of God, with every revolution it is dawning somewhere all the time. Let this be an illustration of our hope.

Let us believe, then that in the development of its destiny, it is constantly swinging nearer and nearer to the sun.

"And now the time has come to say good-by. The word farewell is the saddest in our language. And yet there are sentiments sometimes that refuse to be confined in that world. I will say: Good-by, old man! We will try to exemplify the spirit manifested in your life in bearing the grief at our parting. Words fail me here. Let these flowers, Riley, with their petaled lips and perfumed breath, speak in beauty and fragrance the sentiments that are too tender for words. Good-by!"

Part Fifteen

◆

FICTION

It is said by defenders of fiction that it tells the truth while nonfiction merely reports the facts. The selections that follow were selected for that quality. The authors were writing about the people and landscapes they knew from personal experience.

136

THE RULES OF THE GAME

Charles Lummis

In this 1904 letter, veteran author and photographer Charles Lummis advises beginning novelist Mary Austin of some of the rules of writing about the Spanish West after the publication of her classic Land of Little Rain. *Lummis, a man of monumental ego, is still honored for his remarkable photographs of Southwestern Indian cultures, but Mary Austin could write rings around him. The letter is among those collected in* Literary America, *edited by T.M. Pearce.*

Los Angeles, Cal.
Nov. 24th, 1904
Out West
A Magazine of the Old Pacific and the New
EDITOR'S OFFICE

Dear Mrs. Austin:

I am just starting east but must answer, even if briefly, your friendly letter. If you are "not in the least ashamed of your ignorance of Spanish derivations" then you ought to be. You are more than right in assuming that there are lots of things about which I am equally ignorant. But you have brains enough, and enough intellect, to understand the difference. I don't try to write about the things I am

ignorant of. If you want to take a historic period, or a
geographic setting, to make fame or money, for you—or
even, let us say, in the very extreme of liberality, to fulfil
your mission toward rounding out literature—you are
entitled to give them a fair bargain. It is your business to
treat them with the respect that you would like to have for
your own work. If you ignorantly and carelessly mutilate
them, then by all justice your work ought to be laughed at.
Fair exchange is no robbery; but to feather your nest with
stolen plumage is worse than robbery.

I never have, and I never shall have, "scorn" for
modest ignorance. My whole life long, many of my trusted
friends have been ignorant people. My whole life long I
have been kind to ignorant work. But that was modest
ignorance. You know perfectly well that in the easily
satisfied East you are assumed to know as much about
California as you certainly do know about expressing
yourself; and no one has a higher estimate of this your great
gift. This, in itself, puts you under a moral obligation not to
swindle your readers; not to fill them up with any more
ignorance, which is already so predominant there and here.

You will never, my dear child, find anything "more
important to your stunt in the world's work" than knowing
what you are talking about. When you use Spanish names,
it is your business as a decent woman, and as a writer, to
have them right. What would you think of yourself if, as a
Californian, writing of California, you described seasons as
they are in New England? What would you think of yourself
if you made your stage-setting in Inyo county and described
the landscape such as the people of the north-east of Maine
are familiar with, and as no one ever saw in California?
Now you happen to know about these things, and therefore
realize the iniquity it would be to misrepresent them. It is an
equal iniquity—and I mean that word—to misrepresent
other things just as characteristic, just as easy to learn and
just as necessary to the picture.

Don't fill yourself with that Chautauqua idiocy about
leaving it to the dreadful scientists to know anything. It
won't hurt you any more than it hurts other people to be
right. There is a great deal to learn in this world, and most
of it is expensive education. Where in some case a person

who happens to have learned is willing to give you your examination paper for nothing, do not look on it with sneerness.

There is no such word as Relles; there never was; there never will be. If illiterate persons care to corrupt their own language, that is no reason why you should, with your larger gift and therefore your greater responsibility. You could call a heroine Mazen and explain that it meant "amazing grace"—for this would not add to the fund of ignorance. You can spell your own name as you like, for that is an American privilege. But you have not any business to write my name Loomis nor to write Callafunnier as the name of this state, nor to do any other high handed treason against the things which should be a comfort and a glory to you, and which you have no right to make cripples of for your own advantage.

I don't think I wrote you with any rage. God knows what I dictated—my stenographer doesn't, no more do I. I am not writing to you with any rage now. But I have softly whispered to you several times vague hints as to—not what I think but what every scholar knows about certain facts. You are not yet convinced; therefore I am going to see if I cannot make the matter plain.

Now, my dear child, your letter does not "seem unappreciative," nor do I wish mine to be. If you were not worth while, you may be sure I would not waste the time I cannot give my work, to you. I do not even wish to "make you uncomfortable"—except when it is temporarily necessary in order to set you right. For I do want you to be right. You have a right to be. We have a right to have you.

I am starting east directly to lecture to the eastern affiliated societies of the Archaeological Institute of America. I wish you would send your proofs to Mrs. Lummis, and I will instruct her to forward them to me wherever she can reach me at that time, and I will read them just as soon as they reach me.

With kindest regards and remembrances from all of us, Always Your Friend *Chas. F. Lummis*

THE OUTCASTS OF POKER FLAT

Bret Harte

Bret Harte (1836–1892) came to California as a teenager during the peak of the gold rush and based his short stories on local color and people he actually knew. They made him the first Western writer to win international fame. "Outcasts" typically reflects the Western attitude of Harte's time.

As Mr. John Oakhurst, gambler, stepped into the main street of Poker Flat on the morning of the 23d of November, 1850, he was conscious of a change in its moral atmosphere since the preceding night. Two or three men, conversing earnestly together, ceased as he approached, and exchanged significant glances. There was a Sabbath lull in the air, which, in a settlement unused to Sabbath influences, looked ominous.

Mr. Oakhurst's calm, handsome face betrayed small concern in these indications. Whether he was conscious of any predisposing cause was another question. "I reckon they're after somebody," he reflected; "likely it's me." He returned to his pocket the handkerchief with which he had been whipping away the red dust of Poker Flat from his neat boots, and quietly discharged his mind of any further conjecture.

In point of fact, Poker Flat was "after somebody." It had lately suffered the loss of several thousand dollars, two valuable horses, and a prominent citizen. It was experiencing a spasm of virtuous reaction, quite as lawless and ungovernable as any of the acts that had provoked it. A secret committee had determined to rid the town of all improper persons. This was done permanently in regard of two men who were then hanging from the boughs of a sycamore in the gulch, and temporarily in the banishment of certain other objectionable characters. I regret to say that some of these were ladies. It is but due to the sex, however, to state that their impropriety was professional, and it was only in such easily established standards of evil that Poker Flat ventured to sit in judgment.

Mr. Oakhurst was right in supposing that he was included in this category. A few of the committee had urged hanging him as a possible example and a sure method of reimbursing themselves from his pockets of the sums he had won from them. "It's agin justice," said Jim Wheeler, "to let this yer young man from Roaring Camp—an entire stranger—carry away our money." But a crude sentiment of equity residing in the breasts of those who had been fortunate enough to win from Mr. Oakhurst overruled this narrower local prejudice.

Mr. Oakhurst received his sentence with philosophic calmness, none the less coolly that he was aware of the hesitation of his judges. He was too much of a gambler not to accept fate. With him life was at best an uncertain game, and he recognized the usual percentage in favor of the dealer.

A body of armed men accompanied the deported wickedness of Poker Flat to the outskirts of the settlement. Besides Mr. Oakhurst, who was known to be a coolly desperate man, and for whose intimidation the armed escort was intended, the expatriated party consisted of a young woman familiarly known as "The Duchess;" another who had won the title of "Mother Shipton;" and "Uncle Billy," a suspected sluice-robber and con-firmed drunkard. The cavalcade provoked no comments from the specta-tors, nor was any word uttered by the escort. Only when the gulch which marked the uttermost limit of Poker Flat was reached, the leader spoke briefly and to the point. The exiles were forbidden to return at the peril of their lives.

As the escort disappeared, their pent-up feelings found vent in a few hysterical tears from the Duchess, some bad language from Mother Ship-ton, and a Parthian volley of expletives from Uncle Billy. The philosophic Oakhurst alone remained silent. He listened calmly to Mother Shipton's desire to cut somebody's heart out, to the repeated statements of the Duchess that she would die in the road, and to the alarming oaths that seemed to be bumped out of Uncle Billy as he rode forward. With the easy good humor characteristic of his class, he insisted upon exchanging his own riding-horse, "Five-Spot," for the sorry mule which the Duchess rode. But even this act did not draw the party into any closer sympathy. The young woman readjusted her somewhat draggled plumes with a feeble, faded coquetry; Mother Shipton eyed the possessor of "Five-Spot" with malevolence, and Uncle Billy included the whole party in one sweeping anathema.

The road to Sandy Bar—a camp that, not having as yet experienced the regenerating influences of Poker Flat, consequently seemed to offer some invitation to the emigrants—lay over a steep mountain range. It was distant a day's severe travel. In that advanced season the party soon passed out of the moist, temperate regions of the foothills into the dry, cold, bracing air of the Sierras. The trail was narrow and difficult. At noon the Duchess, rolling out of her saddle upon the ground, declared her intention of going no farther, and the party halted.

The spot was singularly wild and impressive. A wooded amphitheatre, surrounded on three sides by precipitous cliffs of naked granite, sloped gently toward the crest of another precipice that overlooked the valley. It was, undoubtedly, the most suitable spot for a camp, had camping been advisable. But Mr. Oakhurst knew that scarcely half the journey to Sandy Bar was accomplished, and the party were not equipped or provisioned for delay. This fact he pointed out to his companions curtly, with a philosophic commentary on the folly of "throwing up their hand before the game was played out." But they were furnished with liquor, which in this emergency stood them in place of food, fuel, rest, and prescience. In spite of his remonstrances, it was not long before they were more or less under its influence. Uncle Billy passed rapidly from a bellicose state into one of stupor, the Duchess became maudlin, and Mother Shipton snored. Mr. Oakhurst alone remained erect, leaning against a rock, calmly surveying them.

Mr. Oakhurst did not drink. It interfered with a profession which required coolness, impassiveness, and presence of mind, and, in his own language, he "could n't afford it." As he gazed at his recumbent fellow exiles, the loneliness begotten of his pariah trade, his habits of life, his very vices, for the first time seriously oppressed him. He bestirred himself in dusting his black clothes, washing his hands and face, and other acts characteristic of his studiously neat habits, and for a moment forgot his annoyance. The thought of deserting his weaker and more pitiable companions never perhaps occurred to him. Yet he could not help feeling the want of that excitement which, singularly enough, was most conducive to that calm equanimity for which he was notorious. He looked at the gloomy walls that rose a thousand feet sheer above the circling pines around him, at the sky ominously clouded, at the valley below, already deepening into shadow; and, doing so, suddenly he heard his own name called.

A horseman slowly ascended the trail. In the fresh, open face of the newcomer Mr. Oakhurst recognized Tom Simson, otherwise known as "The Innocent," of Sandy Bar. He had met him some months before over a "little game," and had, with perfect equanimity, won the entire fortune—amounting to some forty dollars—of that guileless youth. After the game was finished, Mr. Oakhurst drew the youthful speculator behind the door and thus addressed him: "Tommy, you're a good little man, but you can't gamble worth a cent. Don't try it over again." He then handed him his money back, pushed him gently from the room, and so made a devoted slave of Tom Simson.

There was a remembrance of this in his boyish and enthusiastic greeting of Mr. Oakhurst. He had started, he said, to go to Poker Flat to seek his fortune. "Alone?" No, not exactly alone; in fact (a giggle), he had run away with Piney Woods. Didn't Mr. Oakhurst remember Piney? She that used to wait on the table at the Temperance House? They had been engaged a long time, but old Jake Woods had objected, and so they had run away, and were going to Poker Flat to be married, and here they were. And they were tired out, and how lucky it was they had found a place to camp, and company. All this the Innocent delivered rapidly, while Piney, a stout, comely damsel of fifteen, emerged from behind the pine-tree, where she had been blushing unseen, and rode to the side of her lover.

Mr. Oakhurst seldom troubled himself with sentiment, still less with propriety; but he had a vague idea that the situation was not fortunate. He retained, however, his presence of mind sufficiently to kick Uncle Billy, who was about to say something, and Uncle Billy was sober enough to recognize in Mr. Oakhurst's kick a superior power that would not bear trifling. He then endeavored to dissuade Tom Simson from delaying further, but in vain. He even pointed out the fact that there was no provision, nor means of making a camp. But, unluckily, the Innocent met this objection by assuring the party that he was provided with an extra mule loaded with provisions, and by the discovery of a rude attempt at a log house near the trail. "Piney can stay with Mrs. Oakhurst," said the Innocent, pointing to the Duchess, "and I can shift for myself."

Nothing but Mr. Oakhurst's admonishing foot saved Uncle Billy from bursting into a roar of laughter. As it was, he felt compelled to retire up the cañon until he could recover his gravity. There he confided the joke to the tall pine-trees, with many slaps of his leg, contortions of his face, and the usual profanity. But when he returned to the party, he found them seated by a fire—for the air had grown strangely chill and the sky over-cast—in apparently amicable conversation. Piney was actually talking in an impulsive girlish fashion to the Duchess, who was listening with an interest and animation she had not shown for many days. The Innocent was holding forth, apparently with equal effect, to Mr. Oakhurst and Mother Shipton, who was actually relaxing into amiability. "Is this yer a d—d picnic?" said Uncle Billy, with inward scorn, as he surveyed the sylvan group, the glancing firelight, and the tethered animals in the foreground. Suddenly an idea mingled with the alcoholic fumes that disturbed his brain. It was apparently of a jocular nature, for he felt impelled to slap his leg again and cram his fist into his mouth.

As the shadows crept slowly up the mountain, a slight breeze rocked the tops of the pine-trees and moaned through their long and gloomy aisles. The ruined cabin, patched and covered with pine boughs, was set apart for the ladies. As the lovers parted, they unaffectedly exchanged a kiss, so honest and sincere that it might have been heard above the swaying pines. The frail Duchess and the malevolent Mother Shipton were proba-bly too stunned to remark upon this last evidence of simplicity, and so turned without a word to the hut. The fire was replenished, the men lay down before the door, and in a few minutes were asleep.

Mr. Oakhurst was a light sleeper. Toward morning he awoke be-numbed and cold. As he stirred the dying fire, the wind, which was now blowing strongly, brought to his cheek that which caused the blood to leave it,—snow!

He started to his feet with the intention of awakening the sleepers, for there was no time to lose. But turning to where Uncle Billy had been lying, he found him gone. A suspicion leaped to his brain, and a curse to his lips. He ran to the spot where the mules had been tethered—they were no longer there. The tracks were already rapidly disappearing in the snow.

The momentary excitement brought Mr. Oakhurst back to the fire with his usual calm. He did not waken the sleepers. The Innocent slum-bered peacefully, with a smile on his good-humored, freckled face; the virgin Piney slept beside her frailer sisters as sweetly as though attended by celestial guardians; and Mr. Oakhurst, drawing his blanket over his shoulders, stroked his mustaches and waited for the dawn. It came slowly in a whirling mist of snowflakes that dazzled and confused the eye. What could be seen of the landscape appeared magically changed. He looked over the valley, and summed up the present and future in two words, "Snowed in!"

A careful inventory of the provisions, which, fortunately for the party, had been stored within the hut, and so escaped the felonious fingers of Uncle Billy, disclosed the fact that with care and prudence they might last ten days longer. "That is," said Mr. Oakhurst *sotto voce* to the Innocent, "if you're willing to board us. If you ain't—and perhaps you'd better not—you can wait till Uncle Billy gets back with provisions." For some occult reason, Mr. Oakhurst could not bring himself to disclose Uncle Billy's rascality, and so offered the hypothesis that he had wandered from the camp and had accidentally stampeded the animals. He dropped a warning to the Duchess and Mother Shipton, who of course knew the facts of their associate's defection. "They'll find out the truth about us *all* when they find out anything," he added significantly, "and there's no good frightening them now."

Tom Simson not only put all his worldly store at the disposal of Mr. Oakhurst, but seemed to enjoy the prospect of their enforced seclusion. "We'll have a good camp for a week, and then the snow'll melt, and we'll all go back together." The cheerful gayety of the young man and Mr. Oakhurst's calm infected the others. The Innocent, with the aid of pine boughs, extemporized a thatch for the roofless cabin, and the Duchess directed Piney in the rearrangement of the interior with a taste and tact that opened the blue eyes of that provincial maiden to their fullest extent. "I reckon now you're used to fine things at Poker Flat," said Piney. The Duchess turned away sharply to conceal something that reddened her cheeks through their professional tint, and Mother Shipton requested Piney not to "chatter." But when Mr. Oakhurst returned from a weary search for the trail, he heard the sound of happy laughter echoed from the rocks. He stopped in some alarm, and his thoughts first naturally reverted to the whiskey, which he had prudently cachéd. "And yet it don't somehow sound like whiskey," said the gambler. It was not until he caught sight of the blazing fire through the still blinding storm, and the group around it, that he settled to the conviction that it was "square fun."

Whether Mr. Oakhurst had cachéd his cards with the whiskey as something debarred the free access of the community, I cannot say. It was certain that, in Mother Shipton's words, he "did n't say 'cards' once" during that evening. Haply the time was beguiled by an accordion, produced somewhat ostentatiously by Tom Simson from his pack. Notwithstanding some difficulties attending the manipulation of this instrument, Piney Woods managed to pluck several reluctant melodies from its keys, to an accompaniment by the Innocent on a pair of bone castanets. But the crowning festivity of the evening was reached in a rude camp-meeting hymn, which the lovers, joining hands, sang with great earnestness and vociferation. I fear that a certain defiant tone and Covenanter's swing to its chorus, rather than any devotional quality, caused it speedily to infect the others, who at last joined in the refrain:—

> *"I'm proud to live in the service of the Lord,*
> *And I'm bound to die in His army."*

The pines rocked, the storm eddied and whirled above the miserable group, and the flames of their altar leaped heavenward, as if in token of the vow.

At midnight the storm abated, the rolling clouds parted, and the stars glittered keenly above the sleeping camp. Mr. Oakhurst, whose professional habits had enabled him to live on the smallest possible amount of sleep, in dividing the watch with Tom Simson somehow managed to take upon himself the greater part of that duty. He excused himself to the Innocent by saying that he had "often been a week without sleep." "Doing what?" asked Tom. "Poker!" replied Oakhurst sententiously. "When a man gets a streak of luck,—nigger-luck,—he don't get tired. The luck gives in first. Luck," continued the gambler reflectively, "is a mighty queer thing. All you know about it for certain is that it's bound to change. And it's finding out when it's going to change that makes you. We've had a streak of bad luck since we left Poker Flat,—you come along, and slap you get into it, too. If you can hold your cards right along you're all right. For," added the gambler, with cheerful irrelevance—

> *" 'I'm proud to live in the service of the Lord,*
> *And I'm bound to die in His army.' "*

The third day came, and the sun, looking through the white-curtained valley, saw the outcasts divide their slowly decreasing store of provisions for the morning meal. It was one of the peculiarities of that mountain climate that its rays diffused a kindly warmth over the wintry landscape, as if in regretful commiseration of the past. But it revealed drift on drift of snow piled high around the hut,—a hopeless, uncharted, trackless sea of white lying below the rocky shores to which the castaways still clung. Through the marvelously clear air the smoke of the pastoral village of Poker Flat rose miles away. Mother Shipton saw it, and from a remote pinnacle of her rocky fastness hurled in that direction a final malediction. It was her last vituperative attempt, and perhaps for that reason was invested with a certain degree of sublimity. It did her good, she privately informed the Duchess. "Just you go out there and cuss, and see." She then set herself to the task of amusing "the child," as she and the Duchess were pleased to call Piney. Piney was no chicken, but it was a soothing and original theory of the pair thus to account for the fact that she did n't swear and was n't improper.

When night crept up again through the gorges, the reedy notes of the accordian rose and fell in fitful spasms and long-drawn gasps by the flickering campfire. But music failed to fill entirely the aching void left by insufficient food, and a new diversion was proposed by Piney,—story-telling. Neither Mr. Oakhurst nor his female companions caring to relate their personal experiences, this plan would have failed too, but for the Innocent. Some months before he had chanced upon a stray copy of Mr. Pope's ingenious translation of the Iliad. He now proposed to narrate the principal incidents of that poem—having thoroughly mastered the argument and fairly forgotten the words—in the current vernacular of Sandy Bar. And so for the rest of that night the Homeric demigods again walked the earth. Trojan bully and wily Greek wrestled in the winds, and the great pines in the cañon seemed to bow to the wrath of the son of Peleus. Mr. Oakhurst listened with quiet satisfaction. Most especially was he interested in the fate of "Ash-heels," as the Innocent persisted in denominating the "swift-footed Achilles."

So, with small food and much of Homer and the accordion, a week passed over the heads of the outcasts. The sun again forsook them, and again from leaden skies the snowflakes were sifted over the land. Day by day closer around them drew the snowy circle, until at last they looked from their prison over drifted walls of dazzling white, that towered twenty feet above their heads. It became more and more difficult to replenish their fires, even from the fallen trees beside them, now half hidden in the drifts. And yet no one complained. The lovers turned from the dreary prospect and looked into each other's eyes, and were happy. Mr. Oakhurst settled himself coolly to the losing game before him. The Duchess, more cheerful than she had been, assumed the care of Piney. Only Mother Shipton— once the strongest of the party—seemed to sicken and fade. At midnight on the tenth day she called Oakhurst to her side. "I'm going," she said, in a voice of querulous weakness, "but don't say anything about it. Don't waken the kids. Take the bundle from under my head, and open it." Mr. Oakhurst did so. It contained Mother Shipton's rations for the last week, untouched. "Give 'em to the child," she said, pointing to the sleeping Piney. "You've starved yourself," said the gambler. "That's what they call it," said the woman querulously, as she lay down again, and, turning her face to the wall, passed quietly away.

The accordian and the bones were put aside that day, and Homer was forgotten. When the body of Mother Shipton had been committed to the snow, Mr. Oakhurst took the Innocent aside, and showed him a pair of snowshoes, which he had fashioned from the old pack-saddle. "There's one chance in a hundred to save her yet," he said, pointing to Piney; "but it's there," he added, pointing toward Poker Flat. "If you can reach there in two days she's safe." "And you?" asked Tom Simson. "I'll stay here," was the curt reply.

The lovers parted with a long embrace. "You are not going, too?" said the Duchess, as she saw Mr. Oakhurst apparently waiting to accompany him. "As far as the cañon," he replied. He turned suddenly and kissed the Duchess, leaving her pallid face aflame, and her trembling limbs rigid with amazement.

Night came, but not Mr. Oakhurst. It brought the storm again and the whirling snow. Then the Duchess, feeding the fire, found that some one had quietly piled beside the hut enough fuel to last a few days longer. The tears rose to her eyes, but she hid them from Piney.

The women slept but little. In the morning, looking into each other's faces, they read their fate. Neither spoke, but Piney, accepting the position of the stronger, drew near and placed her arm around the Duchess's waist. They kept this attitude for the rest of the day. That night the storm reached its greatest fury, and, rending asunder the protecting vines, invaded the very hut.

Toward morning they found themselves unable to feed the fire, which gradually died away. As the embers slowly blackened, the Duchess crept closer to Piney, and broke the silence of many hours: "Piney, can you pray?" "No, dear," said Piney simply. The Duchess, without knowing exactly why, felt relieved, and, putting her head upon Piney's shoulder, spoke no more. And so reclining, the younger and purer pillowing the head of her soiled sister upon her virgin breast, they fell asleep.

The wind lulled as if it feared to waken them. Feathery drifts of snow, shaken from the long pine boughs, flew like white winged birds, and settled about them as they slept. The moon through the rifted clouds looked down upon what had been the camp. But all human stain, all trace of earthly travail, was hidden beneath the spotless mantle mercifully flung from above.

They slept all that day and the next, nor did they waken when voices and footsteps broke the silence of the camp. And when pitying fingers brushed the snow from their wan faces, you could scarcely have told from the equal peace that dwelt upon them which was she that had sinned. Even the law of Poker Flat recognized this, and turned away, leaving them still locked in each other's arms.

But at the head of the gulch, on one of the largest pinetrees, they found the deuce of clubs pinned to the bark with a bowie-knife. It bore the following, written in pencil in a firm hand:—

†

BENEATH THIS TREE

LIES THE BODY

OF

JOHN OAKHURST,

WHO STRUCK A STREAK OF BAD LUCK

ON THE 23D OF NOVEMBER 1850,

AND

HANDED IN HIS CHECKS

ON THE 7TH DECEMBER, 1850.

⊥

And pulseless and cold, with a Derringer by his side and a bullet in his heart, though still calm as in life, beneath the snow lay he who was at once the strongest and yet the weakest of the outcasts of Poker Flat.

138

THE BRIDE COMES
TO YELLOW SKY

Stephen Crane

Stephen Crane (1870–1900) is best known for The Red Badge of Courage, *a powerful and evocative novel of the battle in the Civil War—which Crane never experienced. An Easterner, he wrote this classic Western short story after a brief visit to West Texas.*

The great Pullman was whirling onward with such dignity of motion that a glance from the window seemed simply to prove that the plains of Texas were pouring eastward. Vast flats of green grass, dull-hued spaces of mesquit and cactus, little groups of frame houses, woods of light and tender trees, all were sweeping into the east, sweeping over the horizon, a precipice.

A newly married pair had boarded this coach at San Antonio. The man's face was reddened from many days in the wind and sun, and a direct result of his new black clothes was that his brick-coloured hands were constantly performing in a most conscious fashion. From time to time he looked down respectfully at his attire. He sat with a hand on each knee, like a man waiting in a barber's shop. The glances he devoted to other passengers were furtive and shy.

The bride was not pretty, nor was she very young. She wore a dress of blue cashmere, with small reservations of velvet here and there, and with steel buttons abounding. She continually twisted her head to regard her puff sleeves, very stiff, straight, and high. They embarrassed her. It was quite apparent that she had cooked, and that she expected to cook, dutifully. The blushes caused by the careless scrutiny of some passengers as she had entered the car were strange to see upon this plain, under-class countenance, which was drawn in placid, almost emotionless lines.

They were evidently very happy. "Ever been in a parlour-car before?" he asked, smiling with delight.

"No," she answered; "I never was. It's fine, ain't it?"

"Great! And then after a while we'll go forward to the diner, and get a big lay-out. Finest meal in the world. Charge a dollar."

"Oh, do they?" cried the bride. "Charge a dollar? Why, that's too much—for us—ain't it, Jack?"

"Not this trip, anyhow," he answered bravely. "We're going to go the whole thing."

Later he explained to her about the trains. "You see, it's a thousand miles from one end of Texas to the other; and this train runs right across it, and never stops but four times." He had the pride of an owner. He pointed out to her the dazzling fittings of the coach; and in truth her eyes opened wider as she contemplated the sea-green figured velvet, the shining brass, silver, and glass, the wood that gleamed as darkly brilliant as the surface of a pool of oil. At one end a bronze figure sturdily held a support for a separated chamber, and at convenient places on the ceiling were frescos in olive and silver.

To the minds of the pair, their surroundings reflected the glory of their marriage that morning in San Antonio; this was the environment of their new estate; and the man's face in particular beamed with an elation that made him appear ridiculous to the negro porter. This individual at times surveyed them from afar with an amused and superior grin. On other occasions he bullied them with skill in ways that did not make it exactly plain to them that they were being bullied. He subtly used all the manners of the most unconquerable kind of snobbery. He oppressed them; but of this oppression they had small knowledge, and they speedily forgot that infrequently a number of travellers covered them with stares of derisive enjoyment. Historically there was supposed to be something infinitely humorous in their situation.

"We are due in Yellow Sky at 3:42," he said, looking tenderly into her eyes.

"Oh, are we?" she said, as if she had not been aware of it. To evince surprise at her husband's statement was part of her wifely amiability. She took from a pocket a little silver watch; and as she held it before her, and stared at it with a frown of attention, the new husband's face shone.

"I bought it in San Anton' from a friend of mine," he told her gleefully.

"It's seventeen minutes past twelve," she said, looking up at him with a kind of shy and clumsy coquetry. A passenger, noting this play, grew excessively sardonic, and winked at himself in one of the numerous mirrors.

At last they went to the dining-car. Two rows of negro waiters, in glowing white suits, surveyed their entrance with the interest, and also the equanimity, of men who had been forewarned. The pair fell to the lot of a waiter who happened to feel pleasure in steering them through their meal. He viewed them with the manner of a fatherly pilot, his countenance radiant with benevolence. The patronage, entwined with the ordinary deference, was not plain to them. And yet, as they returned to their coach, they showed in their faces a sense of escape.

To the left, miles down a long purple slope, was a little ribbon of mist where moved the keening Rio Grande. The train was approaching it at an angle, and the apex was Yellow Sky. Presently it was apparent that, as the distance from Yellow Sky grew shorter, the husband became commensurately restless. His brick-red hands were more insistent in their prominence. Occasionally he was even rather absent-minded and far-away when the bride leaned forward and addressed him.

As a matter of truth, Jack Potter was beginning to find the shadow of a deed weigh upon him like a leaden slab. He, the town marshal of Yellow Sky, a man known, liked, and feared in his corner, a prominent person, had gone to San Antonio to meet a girl he believed he loved, and there, after the usual prayers, had actually induced her to marry him, without consulting Yellow Sky for any part of the transaction. He was now bringing his bride before an innocent and unsuspecting community.

Of course people in Yellow Sky married as it pleased them, in accordance with a general custom; but such was Potter's thought of his duty to his friends, or of their idea of his duty, or of an unspoken form which does not control men in these matters, that he felt he was heinous. He had committed an extraordinary crime. Face to face with this girl in San Antonio, and spurred by his sharp impulse, he had gone headlong over all the social hedges. At San Antonio he was like a man hidden in the dark. A knife to sever any friendly duty, any form, was easy to his hand in that remote city. But the hour of Yellow Sky—the hour of daylight—was approaching.

He knew full well that his marriage was an important thing to his town. It could only be exceeded by the burning of the new hotel. His friends could not forgive him. Frequently he had reflected on the advisability of telling them by telegraph, but a new cowardice had been upon him. He feared to do it. And now the train was hurrying him toward a scene of amazement, glee, and reproach. He glanced out of the window at the line of haze swinging slowly in toward the train.

Yellow Sky had a kind of brass band, which played painfully, to the delight of the populace. He laughed without heart as he thought of it. If the citizens could dream of his prospective arrival with his bride, they would parade the band at the station and escort them, amid cheers and laughing congratulations, to his adobe home.

He resolved that he would use all the devices of speed and plainscraft in making the journey from the station to his house. Once within that safe citadel, he could issue some sort of vocal bulletin, and then not go among the citizens until they had time to wear off a little of their enthusiasm.

The bride looked anxiously at him. "What's worrying you, Jack?"

He laughed again. "I'm not worrying, girl; I'm only thinking of Yellow Sky."

She flushed in comprehension.

A sense of mutual guilt invaded their minds and developed a finer tenderness. They looked at each other with eyes softly aglow. But Potter often laughed the same nervous laugh; the flush upon the bride's face seemed quite permanent.

The traitor to the feelings of Yellow Sky narrowly watched the speeding landscape. "We're nearly there," he said.

Presently the porter came and announced the proximity of Potter's home. He held a brush in his hand, and, with all his airy superiority gone, he brushed Potter's new clothes as the latter slowly turned this way and that way. Potter fumbled out a coin and gave it to the porter, as he had seen others do. It was a heavy and muscle-bound business, as that of a man shoeing his first horse.

The porter took their bag, and as the train began to slow they moved forward to the hooded platform of the car. Presently the two engines and their long string of coaches rushed into the station of Yellow Sky.

"They have to take water here," said Potter, from a constricted throat and in mournful cadence, as one announcing death. Before the train stopped his eye had swept the length of the platform, and he was glad and astonished to see there was none upon it but the station-agent, who, with a slightly hurried and anxious air, was walking toward the water-tanks. When the train had halted, the porter alighted first, and placed in position a little temporary step.

"Come on, girl," said Potter, hoarsely. As he helped her down they each laughed on a false note. He took the bag from the negro, and bade his wife cling to his arm. As they slunk rapidly away, his hang-dog glance perceived that they were unloading the two trunks, and also that the station-agent, far ahead near the baggage-car, had turned and was running toward him, making gestures. He laughed, and groaned as he laughed, when he noted the first effect of his marital bliss upon Yellow Sky. He gripped his wife's arm firmly to his side, and they fled. Behind them the porter stood, chuckling fatuously.

I I

The California express on the Southern Railway was due at Yellow Sky in twenty-one minutes. There were six men at the bar of the Weary Gentleman saloon. One was a drummer who talked a great deal and rapidly; three were Texans who did not care to talk at that time; and two were Mexican sheep-herders, who did not talk as a general practice in the Weary Gentleman saloon. The barkeeper's dog lay on the board walk that crossed in front of the door. His head was on his paws, and he glanced drowsily here and there with the constant vigilance of a dog that is kicked on occasion. Across the sandy street were some vivid green grass-plots, so wonderful in appearance, amid the sands that burned near them in a blazing sun, that they caused a doubt in the mind. They exactly resembled the grass mats used to represent lawns on the stage. At the cooler end of the railway station, a man without a coat sat in a tilted chair and smoked his pipe. The freshcut bank of the Rio Grande circled near the town, and there could be seen beyond it a great plum-coloured plain of mesquit.

Save for the busy drummer and his companions in the saloon, Yellow Sky was dozing. The new-comer leaned gracefully upon the bar, and recited many tales with the confidence of a bard who has come upon a new field.

"—and at the moment that the old man fell downstairs with the bureau in his arms, the old woman was coming up with two scuttles of coal, and of course—"

The drummer's tale was interrupted by a young man who suddenly appeared in the open door. He cried: "Scratchy Wilson's drunk, and has turned loose with both hands." The two Mexicans at once set down their glasses and faded out of the rear entrance of the saloon.

The drummer, innocent and jocular, answered: "All right, old man. S'pose he has? Come in and have a drink, anyhow."

But the information had made such an obvious cleft in every skull in the room that the drummer was obliged to see its importance. All had become instantly solemn. "Say," said he, mystified, "what is this?" His three companions made the introductory gesture of eloquent speech; but the young man at the door forestalled them.

"It means, my friend," he answered, as he came into the saloon, "that for the next two hours this town won't be a health resort."

The barkeeper went to the door, and locked and barred it; reaching out of the window, he pulled in heavy wooden shutters, and barred them. Immediately a solemn, chapel-like gloom was upon the place. The drummer was looking from one to another.

"But say," he cried, "what is this, anyhow? You don't mean there is going to be a gun-fight?"

"Don't know whether there'll be a fight or not," answered one man, grimly; "but there'll be some shootin'—some good shootin'."

The young man who had warned them waved his hand. "Oh, there'll be a fight fast enough, if any one wants it. Anybody can get a fight out there in the street. There's a fight just waiting."

The drummer seemed to be swayed between the interest of a foreigner and a perception of personal danger.

"What did you say his name was?" he asked.

"Scratchy Wilson," they answered in chorus.

"And he will kill anybody? What are you going to do? Does this happen often? Does he rampage around like this once a week or so? Can he break in that door?"

"No; he can't break down that door," replied the barkeeper. "He's tried it three times. But when he comes you'd better lay down on the floor, stranger. He's dead sure to shoot at it, and a bullet may come through."

Thereafter the drummer kept a strict eye upon the door. The time had not yet been called for him to hug the floor, but, as a minor precaution, he sidled near to the wall. "Will he kill anybody?" he said again.

The men laughed low and scornfully at the question.

"He's out to shoot, and he's out for trouble. Don't see any good in experimentin' with him."

"But what do you do in a case like this? What do you do?"

A man responded: "Why, he and Jack Potter—"

"But," in chorus the other men interrupted, "Jack Potter's in San Anton'."

"Well, who is he? What's he got to do with it?"

"Oh, he's the town marshal. He goes out and fights Scratchy when he gets on one of these tears."

"Wow!" said the drummer, mopping his brow. "Nice job he's got."

The voices had toned away to mere whisperings. The drummer

wished to ask further questions, which were born of an increasing anxiety and bewilderment; but when he attempted them, the men merely looked at him in irritation and motioned him to remain silent. A tense waiting hush was upon them. In the deep shadows of the room their eyes shone as they listened for sounds from the street. One man made three gestures at the barkeeper; and the latter, moving like a ghost, handed him a glass and a bottle. The man poured a full glass of whisky, and set down the bottle noiselessly. He gulped the whisky in a swallow, and turned again toward the door in immovable silence. The drummer saw that the barkeeper, without a sound, had taken a Winchester from beneath the bar. Later, he saw this individual beckoning to him, so he tiptoed across the room.

"You better come with me back of the bar."

"No, thanks," said the drummer, perspiring; "I'd rather be where I can make a break for the back door."

Whereupon the man of bottles made a kindly but peremptory gesture. The drummer obeyed it, and, finding himself seated on a box with his head below the level of the bar, balm was laid upon his soul at sight of various zinc and copper fittings that bore a resemblance to armour-plate. The barkeeper took a seat comfortably upon an adjacent box.

"You see," he whispered, "this here Scratchy Wilson is a wonder with a gun—a perfect wonder; and when he goes on the wartrail, we hunt our holes—naturally. He's about the last one of the old gang that used to hang out along the river here. He's a terror when he's drunk. When he's sober he's all right—kind of simple—wouldn't hurt a fly—nicest fellow in town. But when he's drunk—whoo!"

There were periods of stillness. "I wish Jack Potter was back from San Anton'," said the barkeeper. "He shot Wilson up once—in the leg—and he would sail in and pull out the kinks in this thing."

Presently they heard from a distance the sound of a shot, followed by three wild yowls. It instantly removed a bond from the men in the darkened saloon. There was a shuffling of feet. They looked at each other. "Here he comes," they said.

I I I

A man in a maroon-coloured flannel shirt, which had been purchased for purposes of decoration, and made principally by some Jewish women on the East Side of New York, rounded a corner and walked into the middle of the main street of Yellow Sky. In either hand the man held a long, heavy, blue-black revolver. Often he yelled, and these cries rang through a semblance of a deserted village, shrilly flying over the roofs in a volume that seemed to have no relation to the ordinary vocal strength of a man. It was as if the surrounding stillness formed the arch of a tomb over him. These cries of ferocious challenge rang against walls of silence. And his boots had red tops with gilded imprints, of the kind beloved in winter by little sledding boys on the hillsides of New England.

The man's face flamed in a rage begot of whisky. His eyes, rolling, and yet keen for ambush, hunted the still doorways and windows. He walked with the creeping movement of the midnight cat. As it occurred to him, he roared menacing information. The long revolvers in his hands were as easy as straws; they were moved with an electric swiftness. The little fingers of each hand played sometimes in a musician's way. Plain from the low collar of the shirt, the cords of his neck straightened and sank, straightened and sank, as passion moved him. The only sounds were his terrible invitations. The calm adobes preserved their demeanour at the passing of this small thing in the middle of the street.

There was no offer of fight—no offer of fight. The man called to the sky. There were no attractions. He bellowed and fumed and swayed his revolvers here and everywhere.

The dog of the barkeeper of the Weary Gentleman saloon had not appreciated the advance of events. He yet lay dozing in front of his master's door. At sight of the dog, the man paused and raised his revolver humorously. At sight of the man, the dog sprang up and walked diagonally away, with a sullen head, and growling. The man yelled, and the dog broke into a gallop. As it was about to enter an alley, there was a loud noise, a whistling, and something spat the ground directly before it. The dog screamed, and, wheeling in terror, galloped headlong in a new direction. Again there was a noise, a whistling, and sand was kicked viciously before it. Fear-stricken, the dog turned and flurried like an animal in a pen. The man stood laughing, his weapons at his hips.

Ultimately the man was attracted by the closed door of the Weary Gentleman saloon. He went to it and, hammering with a revolver, demanded drink.

The door remaining imperturbable, he picked a bit of paper from the walk, and nailed it to the framework with a knife. He then turned his back contemptuously upon this popular resort and, walking to the opposite side of the street and spinning there on his heel quickly and lithely, fired at the bit of paper. He missed it by a half-inch. He swore at himself, and went away. Later he comfortably fusilladed the windows of his most intimate friend. The man was playing with this town; it was a toy for him.

But still there was no offer of fight. The name of Jack Potter, his

ancient antagonist, entered his mind, and he concluded that it would be
a glad thing if he should go to Potter's house, and by bombardment induce
him to come out and fight. He moved in the direction of his desire,
chanting Apache scalp-music.

When he arrived at it, Potter's house presented the same still front
as had the other adobes. Taking up a strategic position, the man howled
a challenge. But this house regarded him as might a great stone god. It gave
no sign. After a decent wait, the man howled further challenges, mingling
with them wonderful epithets.

Presently there came the spectacle of a man churning himself into
deepest rage over the immobility of a house. He fumed at it as the winter
wind attacks a prairie cabin in the North. To the distance there should
have gone the sound of a tumult like the fighting of two hundred Mexicans.
As necessity bade him, he paused for breath or to reload his revolvers.

I V

Potter and his bride walked sheepishly and with speed. Sometimes they
laughed together shamefacedly and low.

"Next corner, dear," he said finally.

They put forth the efforts of a pair walking bowed against a strong
wind. Potter was about to raise a finger to point the first appearance of the
new home when, as they circled the corner, they came face to face with
a man in a maroon-coloured shirt, who was feverishly pushing cartridges
into a large revolver. Upon the instant the man dropped his revolver to
the ground and, like lightning, whipped another from its holster. The
second weapon was aimed at the bridegroom's chest.

There was a silence. Potter's mouth seemed to be merely a grave for
his tongue. He exhibited an instinct to at once loosen his arm from the
woman's grip, and he dropped the bag to the sand. As for the bride, her
face had gone as yellow as old cloth. She was a slave to hideous rites, gazing
at the apparitional snake.

The two men faced each other at a distance of three paces. He of the
revolver smiled with a new and quiet ferocity.

"Tried to sneak up on me," he said. "Tried to sneak up on me!" His
eyes grew more baleful. As Potter made a slight movement, the man thrust
his revolver venomously forward. "No; don't you do it, Jack Potter. Don't
you move a finger toward a gun just yet. Don't you move an eyelash. The
time has come for me to settle with you, and I'm goin' to do it my own
way, and loaf along with no interferin'. So if you don't want a gun bent
on you, just mind what I tell you."

Potter looked at his enemy. "I ain't got a gun on me, Scratchy," he said. "Honest, I ain't." He was stiffening and steadying, but yet somewhere at the back of his mind a vision of the Pullman floated: the sea-green figured velvet, the shining brass, silver, and glass, the wood that gleamed as darkly brilliant as the surface of a pool of oil—all the glory of the marriage, the environment of the new estate. "You know I fight when it comes to fighting, Scratchy Wilson; but I ain't got a gun on me. You'll have to do all the shootin' yourself."

His enemy's face went livid. He stepped forward and lashed his weapon to and fro before Potter's chest. "Don't you tell me you ain't got no gun on you, you whelp. Don't tell me no lie like that. There ain't a man in Texas ever seen you without no gun. Don't take me for no kid." His eyes blazed with light, and his throat worked like a pump.

"I ain't takin' you for no kid," answered Potter. His heels had not moved an inch backward. "I'm takin' you for a damn fool. I tell you I ain't got a gun, and I ain't. If you're goin' to shoot me up, you better begin now; you'll never get a chance like this again."

So much enforced reasoning had told on Wilson's rage; he was calmer. "If you ain't got a gun, why ain't you got a gun?" he sneered. "Been to Sunday-school?"

"I ain't got a gun because I've just come from San Anton' with my wife. I'm married," said Potter. "And if I'd thought there was going to be any galoots like you prowling around when I brought my wife home, I'd had a gun, and don't you forget it."

"Married!" said Scratchy, not at all comprehending.

"Yes, married. I'm married," said Potter, distinctly.

"Married?" said Scratchy. Seemingly for the first time he saw the drooping, drowning woman at the other man's side. "No!" he said. He was like a creature allowed a glimpse of another world. He moved a pace backward, and his arm, with the revolver, dropped to his side. "Is this the lady?" he asked.

"Yes; this is the lady," answered Potter.

There was another period of silence.

"Well," said Wilson at last, slowly, "I s'pose it's all off now."

"It's all off if you say so, Scratchy. You know I didn't make the trouble." Potter lifted his valise.

"Well, I 'low it's off, Jack," said Wilson. He was looking at the ground. "Married!" He was not a student of chivalry; it was merely that in the presence of this foreign condition he was a simple child of the earlier plains. He picked up his starboard revolver, and, placing both weapons in their holsters, he went away. His feet made funnel-shaped tracks in the heavy sand.

139

CABIN FEVER

Dorothy Scarborough

In The Wind, which many consider the most powerful "Texas novel" ever written, Dorothy Scarborough gave readers such a true look at the inhospitality of the high plains that West Texas towns tried to suppress the book. Here she shows us the bane of women settlers in lonely country—cabin fever.

The wind was the cause of it all. The sand, too, had a share in it, and human beings were involved, but the wind was the primal force, and but for it the whole series of events would not have happened. It took place in West Texas, years and years ago, before the great ranges had begun to be cut up into farms and ploughed and planted to crops, when there was nothing to break the sweep of the wind across the treeless prairies, when the sand blew in blinding fury across the plains, or lay in mocking waves that never broke on any howsoever-distant beach, or piled in mounds that fickle gusts removed almost as soon as they were erected—when for endless miles there seemed nothing but wind and sand and empty, far off sky.

But perhaps you do not understand the winds of West Texas. And even if you knew them as they are now, that would mean little, for today they are not as they used to be. Civilization has changed them, has tamed them, as the *vacqueros* and the cowboys changed and gentled the wild horses that roamed the prairies long ago. Civilization has taken from them something of their fiery, elemental force, has humbled their spirit. Man, by building houses here and there upon the plains, by stretching fences, by planting trees, has broken the sweep of the wind—by ploughing the land into farms where green things grow has lessened its power to hurl the sand in fury across the wide and empty plains. Man has encroached on the domain of the winds, and gradually, very gradually, is conquering them.

But long ago it was different. The winds were wild and free, and they were more powerful than human beings.

Among the wild horses of the plains there would be now and then one fleet and strong and cunning, that could never be trapped by man, that had never felt the control of bridle, the sting of spur—a stallion that raced over the prairies at will, uncaptured and uncapturable; one with supernatural force and speed, so that no pursuer could ever come up with him; so cunning that no device could ever snare him—a being of diabolic wisdom. One could hear his wild neighing in the night, as he sped over the plains. One could fancy he saw his mane flying back, his hoofs striking fire even from the yielding sand, a satanic horse, for whom no man would ever be the match. Some thought him a ghost horse, imperishable. But now his shrill neighing is heard no more on the prairies by night, for man has driven him out. He has fled to other prairies, vast and fenceless, where man has not intruded, and now one knows him only in legend.

So the norther was a wild stallion that raced over the plains, mighty in power, cruel in spirit, more to be feared than man. One could hear his terrible neighings in the night, and fancy one saw him sweeping over the plains with his imperious mane flying backward and his fiery hoofs ready to trample one down.

In the old days, the winds were the enemies of women. Did they hate them because they saw in them the symbols of that civilization which might gradually lessen their own power? Because it was for women that men would build houses as once they made dugouts?—would increase their herds, would turn the unfenced pastures into farms, furrowing the land that had never known touch of plough since time began?—stealing the sand from the winds?

The winds were cruel to women that came under their tyranny. They were at them ceaselessly, buffeting them with icy blasts in winter, burning them with hot breath in summer, parching their skins and roughening their hair, and trying to wear down their nerves by attrition, and drive them away.

And the sand was the weapon of the winds. It stung the face like bits of glass, it blinded the eyes; it seeped into the houses through closed windows and doors and through every crack and crevice, so that it might make the beds harsh to lie on, might make the food gritty to taste, the air stifling to breathe. It piled in drifts against any fence or obstruction, as deep as snow after a northern blizzard.

How could a frail, sensitive woman fight the wind? How oppose a wild, shouting voice that never let her know the peace of silence?—a resistless force that was at her all the day, a naked, unbodied wind—like a ghost more terrible because invisible—that wailed to her across waste places in the night, calling to her like a demon lover? . . .

The hands that lay loosely in her lap were trembling. "But what is the trouble with the country—that you tell me to go back?"

"It's all right for them that like it. Some do—mostly men, though. It's hard on the women. Folks say the West is good enough for a man or a dog, but no place for a woman or a cat."

"But why, why?"

"The wind is the worst thing."

She drew a relieved sigh. "Oh, wind? That's nothing to be afraid of."

He went on as though she had not spoken. "It's ruination to a woman's looks and nerves pretty often. It dries up her skin till it gets brown and tough as leather. It near 'bout puts her eyes out with the sand it blows in 'em all day. It gets on her nerves with its constant blowing—makes her irritable and jumpy."

She gave a light, casual gesture with one hand. "It blows everywhere, I reckon, even in Virginia. Sometimes in winter we have regular storms of wind and rain. But we don't think anything of them." . . .

When she gazed in the mirror now, she was startled. Instead of the laughing girlish beauty that had once been hers, a creature almost unrecognizable stared back at her, a woman worn and faded, with tragic eyes. Her yellow hair, bleached by the sun and made brittle by the dry winds, had lost its soft waves, and instead of rippling back from the forehead girlishly, was strained back like that of an old woman. Her skin was sunburned and rough, her cheeks were sunken and sallow, and her eyes, no longer blue as periwinkles in an old-fashioned garden, were inflamed from the wind and sand, drawn in from constant shrinking from the glare, and faded from weeping.

And still the wind blew. The wind had robbed her of her beauty, her youth, her hope, she muttered to herself. Would it some time take away her reason or her life? It shrilled round the house by night as by day—or was it the wind that she heard as she lay awake to listen to the shrill, incessant, relentless sound—the wind or the keening coyotes? . . .

140

HONEY IN
THE HORN

H. L. Davis

H. L. Davis (1896–1960) set out to deromanticize the West in Honey in the
Horn. *It won the Harper Prize in 1935 and the Pulitzer Prize for fiction in 1936.
The opening scene follows.*

There waas a run-down old tollbridge station in the Shoestring Valley of
Southern Oregon where Uncle Preston Shiveley had lived for fifty years,
outlasting a wife, two sons, several plagues of grasshoppers, wheat-rust and
caterpillars, a couple or three invasions of land-hunting settlers and real-
estate speculators, and everybody else except the scattering of old pioneers
who had cockleburred themselves onto the country at about the same time
he did. The station, having been built in the stampeding days when people
believed they were due for great swarms of settlement and travel around
them, had a great many more rooms and a whole lot more space than there
was any use for; and so had the country behind it. Outside the back fence
where the dishcloths were hung to bleach and the green sheep-pelts to cure
when there was sun was a ten-mile stretch of creek-meadow with wild
vetch and redtop and velvet-grass reaching clear to the black-green fir
timber of the mountains where huckleberries grew and sheep pastured in
summer and young men sometimes hid to keep from being jailed.
   The creek-meadow in season was full of flowers—wild daisies, lamb-

tongues, cat-ears, big patches of camas lilies as blue as the ocean with a cloud shadowing it, and big stands of wild iris and wild lilac and buttercups and St. John's wort. It was well-watered—too blamed well in the muddy season—and around the springs were thickets of whistle-willow and wild crabapple; and there were long swales of alder and sweetbrier and wild blackberry clumped out so rank and heavy that, in all the years the valley had been settled, nobody had ever explored them all. When the natural feed in the mountains snowed under late in the year, deer used to come down and graze the swales and swipe salt from the domestic stock; and blue grouse and topknot-quail boarded in all the brush-piles and thorn-heaps by the hundreds all the year round.

It was a master locality for stock-raising, as all good game countries are. Why the old settlers had run stock on it for so many years without getting more out of it than enough to live on would have stumped even a government bulletin to explain. They did get a good living regularly, even in times when stock-raisers elsewhere were wearing patched clothes, shooting home-reloaded cartridges, and making biscuits out of hand-pounded wheat. But in the years when those same localities were banking and blowing in great hunks of money on hardwood-floored houses and coming-out parties for the youngsters and store-bought groceries and candidacies for the Legislature for the voting males, the old people up Shoestring went right on living at their ordinary clip, neither able to put on any extra dog in the good times nor obliged to lank down and live frugal in the bad ones.

None of the Shoestring settlers had much of a turn for practical business, probably because living came so easy that they had never needed to develop one. What they had developed, probably unconsciously and certainly without having a speck more use for it, was a mutual oppositeness of characters; and it had changed them from a rather ordinarily-marked pack of restless young Western emigrants with nothing about any of them except youth and land-fever, to an assortment of set-charactered old bucks as distinct from one another in tastes, tempers, habits, and inclinations as the separate suits of a deck of cards.

Not that there was anything especially out of line about that. There used to be plenty of communities where old residenters, merely by having looked at one another for years on end, had become as different as hen, weasel, and buzzard. But the fact that the thing was common didn't make it explain any faster, and the Shoestring settlement's case was harder because the men's characters were so entirely different and all their histories so precisely alike. They had all started even, as adventurous young men in an emigrant-train; they had gone through the same experiences getting to Oregon, had spread down to live in the same country, had done the same work, and had collogued with the same set of neighbors over the same line-up of news and business all their lives long. It looked as if they had treated the human range of superficial feelings to the same process of allotment that they had used on the valley itself, whacking it off into homestead enclosures so each man could squat on a patch of his own where the others would be sure not to elbow him.

They had, of course, done no such fool thing. It was more likely merely something that had happened to them. Whatever it was, they had all come in for it, and it made both monotony and complications of character among them impossible. As far as personality went, they were each one thing, straight up and down and the same color all the way through. Grandpa Cutlack, who lived on Boone Creek nearest the mouth of the valley, ran entirely to religion, held family prayer with a club handy to keep the youngsters from playing hooky on the services, and read his Scriptures with dogged confidence that he would one day find out from them when the world was going to end. He was a short, black-eyed man with bow-legs and an awful memory for smutty expressions, which were continually slipping into his conversation in spite of him, and even into his prayers.

Next up the valley beyond him lived Phineas Cowan, whose inclinations, in spite of his advanced age, were lustful and lickerous. He had begotten half-breed children enough to start a good-sized town, kept squaws distributed around the country so that he could ride for two weeks without doubling his tracks a single mile or sleeping alone a single night, and was still willing to tie into any fresh one who failed to outrun him. Then came Orlando Geary, a tremendous man with a pot belly, a dull marbly eye, and a bald head so thick that getting the simplest scrap of information through it required the patience of a horse-breaker. Not having imagination enough to be afraid of anything, he was always retained to make arrests, serve legal papers, and sit up at night with dead people. He was also one of the several dozen early-day men about whom it was told that he had gone out single-handed after a bunch of horse-thieving Indians, and that he not only brought back all the horses, but also the Indian chief's liver, which he ate raw as a sort of caution to the surviving redskins not to do that again.

Beyond his place was a strip of open country, and then came a clearing which belonged to Pappy Howell, who promoted horseraces and gambled on them. Next to that was a deserted two-story ranchhouse where Deaf Fegles had killed himself in a drunk by jumping out of an upstairs window to get away from some imaginary snakes; and next to that a measly two-room cabin with a pole-and-puncheon roof which was Joel Hardcastle's. His passion was thrift, and he was so close and careful about saving money that he had never got round to making himself any. His was the last place up the valley except the toll-bridge station on Little River that was Uncle Preston Shiveley's.

The station was not of Uncle Preston's founding or construction. He was the scholar of the community, with a great swad of intellectual interests like writing and inventing and experimenting with plants and minerals and historical research, and no concern whatever about anything so low as charging a wayfarer a round dollar to cross a river on a home-made bridge. But he had taken the station over ready-built by marrying the original proprietor's daughter, and he ran it, even when it interfered with his more serious work, as a sort of tribute to her memory. On it, by way of reminding posterity that he skirmished that ground too, he had planted an apple-orchard, built up a band of coarse-wooled sheep, and raised a couple of bad-acting sons who got drunk, fought and trained around with thieving half-breeds until, to keep from being distracted from his studies by the neighborhood rows they got into, he called in Orlando Geary and had them formally kicked off his property for good.

None of Uncle Preston's studies had ever brought him in the worth of a mule's heel full of hay, but he was death on anything that distracted him from them. He had been known, while trying to write up a pamphlet on his pioneer memories, to sit watching a coyote chase three valuable lambs right up to the barnyard fence without lifting pen from paper until the women disturbed him by yelling for somebody to do something quick. Then he got up and killed the coyote with a shotgun; and, to make it strictly fair all the way round, he also killed the three lambs for having got themselves where a coyote could bushwhack them, and for bringing their troubles in to bother him with. He was a short man with long arms and tremendous shoulders and an alert glary eye like a fighting horse, and he was full of tall principles of justice about human rights and the sacredness of privacy. Horning in on a man's time, he argued, was stealing, and ought to be punished as such; and when his two sons got drunk and decided to come back on him after he had evicted them, he got permission from the district court to buckshot the pair of them the minute they set foot on his premises. They stayed away from him after that, a matter of ten years, until one of them killed the other in a fight and took to the brush with a reward up for his scalp with or without the ears attached. Uncle Preston buried the dead son, closed up their house and hauled off their furniture and effects, and gave the Indian woman they had been living with twenty dollars to go home. Then he went back to writing a history of the early statutes of Oregon, and he was still at it in the fall when a fierce flood of early rain drowned the country, hoisted the river clear up to the toll-bridge deck-planks, and caught all his sheep to hellangone in the mountains with only about a nine-to-eleven chance of getting out.

Even to a country accustomed to rain, that was a storm worth gawking at. It cracked shingles in the roof, loaded the full-fruited old apple-trees until they threatened to split apart, and beat the roads under water belly-deep to a horse. Ten-foot walls of spray went marching back and forth across the hay-meadow as if they owned it, flocks of wild ducks came squalling down to roost in the open pasture till the air cleared, and the river boiled yellow foam over the toll bridge and stumps, fence rails, pieces of old houses, and carcasses of drowned calves and horses against it. Uncle Preston sat locked in an old upstairs storeroom writing his history, and, about dark, the young housekeeping girl got tired of being scared all by herself and climbed the stairs to tell him how much of his property he had better get ready to see the last of. The sheep hadn't been heard from and were probably stuck up in the mountains to die; the toll bridge had slipped downstream two feet and promised more; a couple of apple-trees had split at the forks; the house itself was not exactly as safe as the ark, because one of the trees was liable to fall on it and cave in the roof.

"If it caves in we'll move to the barn," said Uncle Preston through the door. "If it don't, I'll finish this chapter here. Did I hear a wagon on the road toward Round Mountain awhile back?"

She said the roads were so bad no wagon could be out in them. Then a tree cracked horribly and scared her downstairs; and he went back to his writing. His chapter was about the first violation of the state statute against polygamy. The transgressor had been, not a Mormon, as one might have supposed, but an Indian in the Kettle River country who was suspected of murdering a white packer. There was no proof against him, but somebody discovered that he had six wives, so they arrested him for that, and, camping overnight on the way in with him, burned him with a red-hot ramrod till he got up and ran. Since that was legally an attempt to escape, they shot him, which was what he had coming in the first place. It proved that the old days had enforced justice strictly in spite of their roughness and offhandedness, and Uncle Preston hauled his books together and wrote fiercely to get done before the apple-tree fell in on the roof. It let out a crack like an explosion and came down somewhere with a thump that jolted the whole house, and the housekeeping girl climbed the stairs again.

"It fell," she said, breathing short. "It smashed through the granary. And they're burning the signal fire down on Round Mountain. A mile high, it looks like. But they've changed it and I can't tell what it means."

"You can, but you want an excuse to tell me about it," said Uncle Preston. Everybody in the country had been warned that a fire on Round Mountain would mean Wade Shiveley's tracks had been picked up and that the people in Shoestring were to look out for him. Everybody had expected that he would head back into the valley sometime because it was country he was most familiar with. It was almost a relief to know that it had happened at last. "He won't come here," said Uncle Preston. "If he does, I'll shoot him, and he knows it. You know it bothers me to hear about him when I'm writin', so what do you come hintin' around about him for?"

"There was to be only one fire if he came this way," said the girl, leaning aginst the door. The hallway was dark, with a lonesome smell of bitterish willow-bark that the rain had crushed outside. "There's two fires, right alongside of one another. I can't tell what they mean. And the sheep aren't in yet. I tried to send the Indian boy out to look for them, but he wouldn't go. He sassed me."

Uncle Preston said to let the sheep go to hell and let the Indian boy alone. In the old days, two fires on Round Mountain had meant that some lost youngster had been found and that all the searching-parties could knock off looking for him and come in. But no youngsters got lost any more—none, at least, that anybody wanted to find again—so what it probably meant was that Wade Shiveley had done something else. Not but what it seemed wasteful to light fires over an ordinary course-of-nature episode like that. If people held an illumination every time his son cut another notch in his hell-stick, the country's supply of standing timber would be used up before the lumber companies got round to stealing it. "Whatever he's been up to, he won't bother us," said Uncle Preston. "You can go on back—" He stopped, and the front legs of his chair hit the floor with a thump. Two horses were wading the wet leaves under the dripping apple-trees. "Go and see who that is. If it's him, shine a lamp through the back door so I can git a sight on him when he lights down. Damn his soul, I told him I'd shoot him if he come botherin' me at work!"

She came back and reported with her voice panicky; but it was only two herders from the sheep, after all. What jumped her was that the sheep were down at the edge of the timber, drowning, and the two men had given up and come in to find out about the fires on Round Mountain. The third herder, a drip-nosed youth whom Uncle Preston had inherited from his sons' abandoned household, was staying with them through ignorance and contrariness, but it was no use sending anybody to help him. When sheep decided to go down, they stayed down, and any effort to reason them out of it would be simply elbow-grease gone to hell.

Uncle Preston took it as if dropping four thousand dollars' worth of mutton down a mudhole was an everyday operation. "Well, we won't have 'em to winter," he said. "Go get supper and let me finish this chapter before some goddamned thing does happen. You men didn't hear a wagon on the road half an hour ago, did you?"

141

"IT MUST
BE SOMETHING
EXCITING"

Wallace Stegner

In 1972 Wallace Stegner won the Pulitzer Prize for Angle of Repose. While the book is a novel, the following section closely parallels part of the life of Mary Hallock Foote, one of the West's most neglected early novelists. In this segment the young bride reaches Leadville, Colorado, at the first moments of its famous boom. While the style is finest Stegner, many of the facts came from Foote's letters.

Leadville made its appearance as a long gulch (Evans) littered with wreckage, shacks, and mine tailings. It was rutted deep by ore wagons, scalped of its timber. The smoke of smelters and charcoal kilns smudged a sky that all down the pass had been a dark, serene blue. They passed a string of corrals, then a repair yard where the bodily parts of a hundred wagons were strewn. People appeared and thickened—walkers, riders, drivers of buggies and wagons. A log cabin wore a simple sign, SALOON: it looked to be a half mile from anywhere. Farther down, a shack had scrawled in charcoal above its door "No chickens no eggs no keep folks dam." The shacks grew thicker, the road became the parody of a street. A false-fronted shack said ASSAY OFFICE.

Ahead, something seemed to be happening. People were hurrying, others stood in doorways looking toward the center of town. A young man with a flapping vest and a face pink with high-altitude exertion passed them, running hard. Still aggrieved with each other, Susan and Oliver had been traveling without much talk, but when she heard shouting up ahead Susan could not help saying, "What is it? Is it always like this?"

"Not necessarily." He stood up to look, he shrugged and sat down. The crowd sound ahead stopped as if hands had choked it off. Now Susan stood up. She could see a dense crowd from sidewalk to sidewalk in a street between false fronts, and men coming in from every direction. "What on earth! It must be something exciting."

She was jolted back into the seat, and Oliver stood up; they popped up and popped down like counterweighted jumping jacks. She heard him grunt, a hard inarticulate sound, and abruptly he cracked the whip on the haunch of their new horse, as dragging and wheezing almost as the one they had left behind, and swung the team left up a wallowed side hill between shacks.

"My goodness," Susan said. "Is this the road to our place?"

"One way."

"Could you see what was happening down there?"

"Some kind of ruckus. Nothing you need to see."

"You protect me too much," she said, disappointed and rebellious.

"No I don't."

"We agreed it was a mistake for me to stay so far out of things at New Almaden."

"This isn't New Almaden."

They bumped up the stumpy hillside. Down to the right she could see packed roofs, and beyond them smelter smokes. All across the West were the peaks she knew were the Sawatch Range. The crowd was out of sight, but she could hear it, a loud continuous uproar, then a stillness, then a harsh, startling outcry. "*Something* is certainly going on," she said.

Oliver, with his head dropped, watched the laboring sick horse. She thought his face was stern and unloving, and she hated it that they should arrive at their new home in that spirit. Then he pointed with his whip. "There's your house."

She forgot the excitement down below, she forgot the misunderstanding that had kept them silent down the gulch. There it sat, the second house she would try to make into a Western home: a squat cabin of unpeeled logs with a pigtail of smoke from its stovepipe. "Looks as if Frank's made you a fire," Oliver said. "You'll learn to appreciate that boy."

"Frank, that's your assistant?"

"General Sargent's third son, come out West to be an engineer."

"Just like you."

"Just like me."

Her quick, upward, smiling look asked or gave forgiveness for what had been between them. "Is he going to be as good as you?"

"That's a hard standard to hold him to."

They laughed. It was better already. At the ditch bank she took his hand and teetered prettily before jumping down. The ditch was like no ditch she had ever imagined. This was a clear as water in a glass, and it shot past as if chased. When she stooped impulsively to drag her hand in it it numbed her fingers.

Two planks crossed it for a bridge. Oliver tied the team to a stump and led her across as if it were as dangerous as a high wire. At the door he stood a moment, frowning, listening to the crowd noise from below, and then with an odd, angry shrug he yanked the buckskin latchstring. "Maybe we should begin with the right omens," he said, and gravely lifted her across the sill and set her down. "In case you think you've come down in the world, let me tell you there's nothing grander in Leadville."

It was one room, perhaps fifteen by twenty-five feet. Two windows, curtainless. Five chairs, one broken, one a rocker. A Franklin stove with a fallen, ashy fire smoking in it. Two canvas cots made up with gray blankets. A table that had been knocked together out of three wide boards and two sawhorses.

"Don't look around for the kitchen or bedroom," Oliver said.

Perhaps she had been remembering the New Almaden cottage, so much better than her expectations, and so had built up expectations of this cabin that it could not support. It took an effort to conceal her disappointment. Yet as she looked around she had to admit that a log house *was* picturesque, and a house with a welcoming fire on its hearth was touching. She summoned back for her inner eye the image of the peaks rimming the world outside. "It's charming. I can hang curtains around the cots. We'll be snug. How will we cook?"

"Breakfast on the Franklin, dinner out of a sardine can, supper at the Clarendon. I'm afraid I won't be here for dinner much."

"I'm sure you'll be welcome when you can come," she said. "But I'll be busy—you'll have to keep out of my way. I brought some blocks for a novel of Louisa Alcott's."

He said seriously, "Maybe you'll want to stay at the hotel."

She pulled off her hat, she made herself at home. Feeling better all the time, she went around examining the cabin. She rocked the table—the sawhorses wobbled. She bent and tried one of the cots, and looking up to find him gravely watching her, she smiled at him with a great rush of affection and said, "I think it will do very nicely here."

"You could have a lonesome summer."

"I'll manage, I'm sure." He looked so solemn, responsible, and concerned that she skipped up to him and hugged his arm.

"It's only women we're short of. Plenty of perfectly presentable men. Plenty of other kinds too. Plenty visitors likewise. I think Conrad and Janin are coming through. Every mining man has to see Leadville once."

The thought of Oliver's elegant brother-in-law in that cabin started her giggling. "Can you imagine entertaining Conrad here? Cooking him a steak on the Franklin? Walking around that table with a bottle of wine in a napkin?"

"Do him good. He's got effete."

"Anyway, by the time he comes we'll be fixed up. Can I buy some calico for curtains?"

"I'll take you to Daniel and Fisher's tomorrow."

Just then she looked out the window and saw a man running hard up the ditch bank. Below the standing team he jumped the ditch, and his corduroy coattails flew out behind. "Someone's coming in a terrible hurry," she said, and turned in time to see the doorway filled by a very tall young man, panting, ablaze with some news.

"Frank," Oliver said, "you're just in time to meet Mrs. Ward, our civilizing influence."

She thought she had never seen a face more alive. His brown eyes snapped and glowed, he was hot from running, the smile that he produced for her, swallowing both his panting and his news, showed a mouthful of absolutely perfect teeth. "Ah, welcome to Leadville!" he said. "What kind of trip did you have? How'd you like Mosquito Pass?"

"Not as well as I like it here," Susan said. "It must have been you who had a fire going for us. That made it nice and homey to arrive."

"I hunted around for flowers," Frank said. "I wanted to put our best foot forward, but I couldn't find any feet. Nothing's out yet. I was going to be here to greet you, too, but they started . . . You almost ran into something, you know that? Did you come through town?"

She saw, or half saw, a look from Oliver that checked him. She said, "We heard a lot of shouting. What was it?"

"A town like this is full of drunks," Oliver said.

"No!" Susan said, and she may have stamped her foot. "You shan't protect me from everything! Tell us, Mr. Sargent."

"Oh, it was . . . nothing much. Little . . . business."

He looked, breathing hard still, at Oliver. Oliver looked expressionlessly back, and then moved his shoulders as if giving up.

"Tell us," she said.

He looked at Oliver one last time for confirmation or authority. "They, ah, just hanged a couple of men. Out in front of the jail."

She heard him with a surprising absence of surprise. It was more or less the sort of thing she had learned to expect in mining camps from reading Bret Harte and *Leslie's Illustrated Newspaper*. Examining herself for horror or disgust, she found only a sort of satisfaction that now she had really joined Oliver where he lived his life, some corroboration of her notions of what the wife of a mining engineer might have to expect. "Who?" she said. "What for?"

Sargent spoke directly to Oliver. "One was Jeff Oates."

Oliver took the word without expression, thought a few seconds, flattened his mouth under the mustache, lifted his blue steady eyes to hers. "Our claim-jumping neighbor. He was a little crazy, like a dog that can't stand to see another dog with a bone. It didn't call for hanging."

"If you ask me," Sargent said, "he got just what he deserved. You can't simply go around . . ."

"Who was the other one?" Oliver said.

"A road agent that shot up the stage on the grade yesterday. They had him before he got to English George's."

"And he's dead before another sundown."

"It had to happen," Frank said earnestly. "There had to be an object lesson or two. If it isn't stopped it gets worse and worse."

But Susan was looking at her husband. "You knew it, didn't you? You saw what was happening. That's why we turned up the side hill."

"It didn't look good. I couldn't tell what it was." Wry-mouthed and squinting, he held her eye. "It's not the pattern. So far as I know, it's never happened before in Leadville. If it had, I wouldn't have let you come. This fireeater here thinks it ought to be repeated, but he's wrong. If it is, I won't let you stay. So you cool down, Frank, you hear? The longer we have vigilante law, the longer it will be before we get real law."

"I suppose," Susan said, confused. Frank took the rebuke with an exaggerated cringing gesture, protecting his head with his arms as if blows were falling on him.

Oliver said, "At least now you know why that stage driver was coming hell for leather down the pass and would have run over us if we hadn't got out of his way. You know why I wouldn't stop for the boys in the bogged-down ore wagon. The way for you to live in this place is to stay out of it."

142

McTEAGUE

Frank Norris

Some students of literature argue that Frank Norris's 1899 tale of a San Francisco dentist is the ultimate American novel. Two excerpts follow.

It was Sunday, and according to his custom on that day, McTeague took his dinner at two in the afternoon at the car conductors' coffee joint on Polk Street. He had a thick, gray soup; heavy, underdone meat, very hot, on a cold plate; two kinds of vegetables; and a sort of suet pudding, full of strong butter and sugar. On his way back to his office, one block above, he stopped at Joe Frenna's saloon and bought a pitcher of steam beer. It was his habit to leave the pitcher there on his way to dinner.

Once in his office, or as he called it on his signboard, Dental Parlors, he took off his coat and shoes, unbuttoned his vest, and having crammed his little stove full of coke, lay back in his operating chair at the bay window, reading the paper, drinking his beer, and smoking his huge porcelain pipe while his food digested; crop full, stupid, and warm. By and by, gorged with steam beer and overcome by the heat of the room, the cheap tobacco, and the effects of his heavy meal, he dropped off to sleep. Late in the afternoon his canary bird, in its gilt cage just over his head, began to sing. He woke slowly, finished the rest of his beer—very flat and stale by this time—and taking down his concertina from the bookcase, where on weekdays it kept the company of seven volumes of *Allen's Practical Dentist,* played upon it some half dozen very mournful airs.

McTeague looked forward to these Sunday afternoons as a period of relaxation and enjoyment. He invariably spent them in the same fashion. These were his only pleasures—to eat, to smoke, to sleep, and to play upon his concertina.

The six lugubrious airs that he knew always carried him back to the time when he was a car boy at the Big Dipper Mine in Placer County, ten years before. He remembered the years he had spent there trundling the heavy cars of ore in and out of the tunnel under the direction of his father. For thirteen days of each fortnight his father was a steady, hard-working shift boss of the mine. Every other Sunday he became an irresponsible animal, a beast, a brute, crazy with alcohol.

McTeague remembered his mother, too, who, with the help of the Chinaman, cooked for forty miners. She was an overworked drudge, fiery and energetic for all that, filled with the one idea of having her son rise in life and enter a profession. The chance had come at last when the father died, corroded with alcohol, collapsing in a few hours. Two or three years later a traveling dentist visited the mine and put up his tent near the bunkhouse. He was more or less of a charlatan, but he fired Mrs. McTeague's ambition, and young McTeague went away with him to learn his profession. He had learned it after a fashion, mostly by watching the charlatan operate. He had read many of the necessary books, but he was too hopelessly stupid to get much benefit from them.

Then one day at San Francisco had come the news of his mother's death; she had left him some money—not much, but enough to set him up in business; so he had cut loose from the charlatan and had opened his Dental Parlors on Polk Street, an accommodation street of small shops in the residence quarter of the town. Here he had slowly collected a clientele of butcher boys, shopgirls, drug clerks, and car conductors. He made but few acquaintances. Polk Street called him the Doctor and spoke of his enormous strength. For McTeague was a young giant, carrying his huge shock of blond hair six feet three inches from the ground; moving his immense limbs, heavy with ropes of muscle, slowly, ponderously. His hands were enormous, red, and covered with a fell of stiff, yellow hair; they were hard as wooden mallets, strong as vises, the hands of the old-time car boy. Often he dispensed with forceps and extracted a refractory tooth with his thumb and finger. His head was square-cut, angular; the jaw salient, like that of the carnivora.

McTeague's mind was as his body, heavy, slow to act, sluggish. Yet there was nothing vicious about the man. Altogether he suggested the draft horse, immensely strong, stupid, docile, obedient.

When he opened his Dental Parlors, he felt that his life was a success, that he could hope for nothing better. In spite of the name, there was but one room. It was a corner room on the second floor over the branch post office, and faced the street. McTeague made it do for a bedroom as well, sleeping on the big bed-lounge against the wall opposite the window. There was a washstand behind the screen in the corner where he manufactured his molds. In the round bay window were his operating chair, his dental engine, and the movable rack on which he laid out his instruments. Three chairs, a bargain at the secondhand store, ranged themselves against the wall with military precision underneath a steel engraving of the court of Lorenzo de' Medici, which he had bought because there were a great many figures in it for the money. Over the bed-lounge hung a rifle manufacturer's advertisement calendar which he never used. The other ornaments were a small marble-topped center table covered with back numbers of *The American System of Dentistry,* a stone pug dog sitting before the little stove, and a thermometer. A stand of shelves occupied one corner, filled with the seven volumes of *Allen's Practical Dentist.* On the top shelf McTeague kept his concertina and a bag of birdseed for the canary. The whole place exhaled a mingled odor of bedding, creosote, and ether.

But for one thing, McTeague would have been perfectly contented. Just outside his window was his signboard —a modest affair—that read: "Doctor McTeague. Dental Parlors. Gas Given"; but that was all. It was his ambition, his dream, to have projecting from that corner window a huge gilded tooth, a molar with enormous prongs, something gorgeous and attractive. He would have it someday, on that he was resolved; but as yet such a thing was far beyond his means. . . .

[END OF NOVEL, IN DEATH VALLEY]

Marcus ran on, firing as he ran. The mule, one foreleg trailing, scrambled along, squealing and snorting. Marcus fired his last shot. The mule pitched forward upon his head, then rolling sideways, fell upon the canteen, bursting it open and spilling its entire contents into the sand.

Marcus and McTeague ran up, and Marcus snatched the battered canteen from under the reeking, bloody hide. There was no water left. Marcus flung the canteen from him and stood up, facing McTeague. There was a pause.

"We're dead men," said Marcus.

McTeague looked from him out over the desert. Chaotic desolation stretched from them on either hand, flaming and glaring with the afternoon heat. There was the brazen sky and the leagues upon leagues of alkali, leper white. There was nothing more. They were in the heart of Death Valley.

"Not a drop of water," muttered McTeague; "not a drop of water."

"We can drink the mule's blood," said Marcus. "It's been done before. But—but"—he looked down at the quivering, gory body—"but I ain't thirsty enough for that yet."

"Where's the nearest water?"

"Well, it's about a hundred miles or more back of us in the Panamint hills," returned Marcus doggedly. "We'd be crazy long before we reached it. I tell you, we're done for, by damn, we're done for. We ain't ever going to get outa here."

"Done for?" murmured the other, looking about stupidly. "Done for, that's the word. Done for? Yes, I guess we're done for."

"What are we going to do *now?*" exclaimed Marcus sharply after a while.

"Well, let's—let's be moving along—somewhere."

"*Where,* I'd like to know? What's the good of moving on?"

There was a silence.

"What's the good of stopping here?"

"Lord, it's hot," said the dentist finally, wiping his forehead with the back of his hand. Marcus ground his teeth.

"Done for," he muttered; "done for."

"I never *was* so thirsty," continued McTeague. "I'm that dry I can hear my tongue rubbing against the roof of my mouth."

"Well, we can't stop here," said Marcus finally; "we got to go somewhere. We'll try and get back, but it ain't no manner of use. Anything we want to take along with us from the mule? We can—"

Suddenly he paused. In an instant the eyes of the two doomed men had met as the same thought simultaneously rose in their minds. The canvas sack with its five thousand dollars was still tied to the horn of the saddle.

Marcus had emptied his revolver at the mule, and though he still wore his cartridge belt, he was for the moment as unarmed as McTeague.

"I guess," began McTeague coming forward a step, "I guess, even if we are done for, I'll take—some of my truck along."

"Hold on," exclaimed Marcus with rising aggressiveness. "Let's talk about that. I ain't so sure about who that—who that money belongs to."

"Well, I *am,* you see," growled the dentist.

The old enmity between the two men, their ancient hate, was flaming up again.

"Don't try an' load that gun either," cried McTeague, fixing Marcus with his little eyes.

"Then don't lay your finger on that sack," shouted the other. "You're my prisoner, do you understand? You'll do as I say." Marcus had drawn the handcuffs from his pocket and stood ready with his revolver held as a club. "You soldiered me out of that money once and played me for a sucker, an' it's *my* turn now. Don't you lay your finger on that sack."

Marcus barred McTeague's way, white with passion. McTeague did not answer. His eyes drew to two fine, twinkling points, and his enormous hands knotted themselves into fists, hard as wooden mallets. He moved a step nearer to Marcus, then another.

Suddenly the men grappled, and in another instant were rolling and struggling upon the hot, white ground. McTeague thrust Marcus backward until he tripped and fell over the body of the dead mule. The little bird cage broke from the saddle with the violence of their fall and rolled out upon the ground, the flour bags slipping from it. McTeague tore the revolver from Marcus's grip and struck out with it blindly. Clouds of alkali dust, fine and pungent, enveloped the two fighting men, all but strangling them.

McTeague did not know how he killed his enemy, but all at once Marcus grew still beneath his blows. Then there was a sudden last return of energy. McTeague's right wrist was caught; something clicked upon it; then the struggling body fell limp and motionless with a long breath.

As McTeague rose to his feet, he felt a pull at his right wrist; something held it fast. Looking down, he saw that Marcus in that last struggle had found strength to handcuff their wrists together. Marcus was dead now; McTeague was locked to the body. All about him, vast, interminable, stretched the measureless leagues of Death Valley.

527